AMERICAN PHILANTHROPY

in the

NEAR EAST

AMERICAN PHILANTHROPY

in the

NEAR EAST

1820-1960

by Robert L. Daniel

OHIO UNIVERSITY PRESS

Athens

CREDITS: Maps on pages 9, 26–7 and 257
"Europe and the Near East"
© 1943 by the National Geographic
Society, Washington, D. C.

To Barbara

TABLE OF CONTENTS

Abbreviations

For the sake of brevity, the following abbreviations have been employed.

ABC	American Board of Commissioners [for Foreign Missions]
ABCFM	American Board of Commissioners for Foreign Missions
ACASR	American Committee for Armenian and Syrian Relief
ACG	American College for Girls
AUB	American University of Beirut
AUB and IC	American University of Beirut and International College
BFMPC	Board of Foreign Missions, Presbyterian Church, U.S.A.
CWC	Constantinople Woman's College
DAB	Dictionary of American Biography
ETM	European Turkey Mission
FO	(British) Foreign Office
NECA	Near East College Association
NEF	Near East Foundation
NER	Near East Relief
PML	Presbyterian Mission Library
RC	Robert College
RC and ACG	Robert College and American College for Girls
SDDF	State Department Decimal Files
SDNF	State Department Numerical Files
SPC	Syrian Protestant College
UCBWM	United Church Board for World Ministries
WTM	Western Turkey Mission

PREFACE

ONE OF the first overseas areas in which Americans deliberately sought to change native mores, customs, and technology was the Near East. Philhellenes, moved by the romantic passions of the moment, alternated bearing arms in the cause of Greek independence with dispensing alms and, in the person of Samuel Gridley Howe, sought ways of making the impoverished refugees self-supporting. But the crisis over, the philhellenes retired from the scene to pursue other interests. Missionaries who went to Syria, Turkey, and Persia in the early nineteenth century armed only with the Bible carried also Western ideas of education and science. Driven by a compelling sense of Christian duty, turning the cheek to indifference and hostility, taking isolation and deprivation in stride, they persisted in founding schools, mission presses, and hospitals. In the 1860's Cyrus Hamlin and Daniel Bliss, resigning their missionary posts, established the first American colleges abroad, Robert College at Constantinople and the Syrian Protestant College at Beirut. During the distress of World War I, American missionaries abroad, supported by sponsors at home, organized the Near East Relief, a hundred-million-dollar enterprise ministering to tens of thousands of "starving Armenians." In the late 1920's, a generation before President Truman enunciated his Point Four concept, American philanthropists organized the Near East Foundation, the first group to make technical assistance its primary goal. Thus early nineteenth-century philanthropy, initiated as an auxiliary to missionary endeavors, evolved into complex programs designed to induce broad changes in the technology and culture of Near Eastern societies while training native leaders who could continue the work on their own.

Caught up in their day-to-day affairs, these American philanthropists, particularly in the nineteenth century, made little effort to define philanthropy, leaving the historian to infer their concept from their activities. In its simplest form the philanthropic impulse expressed itself in meliorating

ix

the condition of victims of war, persecution, and famine. But the Americans also began to promote changes in the ordinary structure of Near Eastern institutions and in the mores, customs, and technology of the people. Initially the missionaries opened schools and published teaching materials as a means of making contact with natives, but they came shortly to support these programs as ends in themselves. To distinguish between the work carried on as an integral part of the missionary effort and the activities supported for humanitarian reasons is impossible. Motives were often mixed. Although endeavors to introduce American forms of religious worship and instruction do not seem to be a proper part of this account, the efforts to direct schools, provide teaching materials, and improve health are decidedly pertinent. For over forty years, 1820–1863, a missionary society was the only organization operating sustained programs in the Near East; and it is abundantly clear that it was out of these programs, mixed as motives sometimes were, that secularly supported and directed educational, medical, agricultural and technical assistance, and rural community development projects evolved.

This study focuses on the evolution of private philanthropy in the Near East, through the activities of a series of related organizations. Particular emphasis is laid on the formulation of goals and methods by the philanthropists and on the manner in which their ventures were furthered or hindered by problems of organization, raising funds, and recruiting personnel as sponsorship of philanthropy shifted from church societies to secular organizations.

The impact of American philanthropy has been noted wherever possible as Americans, including those most sensitive to the reactions of the area's peoples, recorded it. The assessment of impact of the American activities on the native culture, while of great importance, is most elusive. The material impact—the food, clothing, and funds—can be documented with a degree of precision. So can the introduction of new institutions—schools, presses, and dispensaries. The intellectual impact is less easy to evaluate. In the case of the Near East Foundation, which concentrated on numerous, concrete, well-defined innovations, the impact can be assessed directly: the suggested innovation was adopted or it was rejected. One may even appraise the degree of importance of these innovations. But in the case of the colleges, the problem becomes complex. It is one thing to establish that the colleges aspired to instill a particular view of "character," social attitudes, or Western ideas; it is quite another to measure the degree to which the students' outlook or behavior was transformed as a result. The contribution of American activities to the development of native nationalism and of pro- or anti-Western and pro- or anti-American attitudes is still more difficult to evaluate. Here and there one can identify tentative links, but to measure the American impact requires assessing it in relation to the interaction of

European and indigenous forces pressing toward similar goals. Such an assessment is beyond the scope of this study. The emphasis here is on what Americans did, and how, and often why, and what they thought about their activities—the *res gestae* of American philanthropy.

The significance of American philanthropy in the Near East lies in the scale of the activities and in the pioneer character of many of the projects: the elementary school, education for girls, American-Arabic movable type, the overseas college, Western medical instruction, the agricultural school, and agricultural technical assistance. While romantic philhellenism proved unable to sustain support of overseas philanthropy, the missionary movement could and did. Before World War I, over a thousand American philanthropists had served in the Near East, far and away a larger number of such persons than any other country had sent into the region. As a field of work, the Near East drew as much attention as either India or China, the other major centers of American philanthropy abroad.

Of central importance is the organic relationship between the major sponsoring organizations: the missionary boards, the independent colleges, the Near East Relief, and the Near East Foundation. Because of this relationship, the philanthropic programs enjoyed a high degree of continuity and stability. The mission schools provided many of the students and faculty of the independent colleges. Near East Relief was a combined effort of all groups with philanthropic interests in the region. And Near East Foundation took over the unfinished affairs of Near East Relief. From 1820 to 1960 these organizations widened the variety of activities undertaken in the Near East and broadened the base of support at home. In short, this is a study of the principal philanthropic enterprises in a major theater of American overseas philanthropy.

Because of this focus, I have not treated the activities of every American group that at any time undertook work in the Near East. In particular, I have not dealt with American efforts among the Jews. The American groups operating in the Near East before World War I had few and unimportant connections with the indigenous Jewish population. The small American-Jewish communities established in the Holy Land in the nineteenth century were self-contained and without impact on the main currents of overseas philanthropy. The migration of thousands of European Jews to the Holy Land after World War I generated animosities between Arab and Jew that the American organizations operating in the area could not bridge. Separate organizations have served Arab and Jew. The large work conducted by American-Jewish organizations among the ever-growing Jewish community in Palestine after World War I and in Israel since 1948 is of major importance, but these organizations had no impact on the evolution of philanthropic practice discussed here and so lie outside the theme of this study. For analogous reasons I have not dealt with the recent efforts of American oil firms operating in Saudi Arabia to introduce elements of Western culture among their native employees. I do not mean to imply that their activities—a mixture of welfare capitalism, paternalism, and open-handed philanthropy—are inconsequential, only that they constitute a new story.

Nor have I treated American activities in Egypt, though by some standards Africa north of the Sahara from Suez west to Morocco is considered a part of the Near East. The Presbyterian mission schools in Egypt, the college at Assiut, and the American University of Cairo have an importance of their own. But as these activities began later than similar work in Turkey, Syria, and Lebanon, the experiences in Egypt made no contribution to the development of the principles or practices of philanthropy that form the heart of this study. Nor was there any administrative connection between American activities in Egypt and those discussed here. On the other hand, because significant experiences of the missionaries, Near East Relief, and Near East Foundation occurred in the Balkans, I have discussed these developments.

This study concludes with 1960. Convenience, rather than any major event such as the Turkish revolution of that year, has guided the choice. Yet this date is not wholly arbitrary. The year 1960 marks an end to the postwar period in which the independent colleges and the Near East Foundation still constituted the main current of American philanthropy in the Near East and the start of a new era in which a host of grant-making and program-operating organizations became forces of comparable consequence, adding their thrust to that of the older organizations. Nevertheless, the reader must understand the approximate character of the terminal date. As nearly as possible, I have followed the established programs to some logical turning point in their internal development rather than slavishly carry each to midnight, December 31, 1960.

The magnitude of American philanthropy as measured in dollars must be treated with caution. Because of changes in price levels, the reader must keep in mind that whereas $400 sufficed to support a missionary philanthropist in the 1830's, twenty times that amount would not suffice today. While the mission boards reported the number of dollars expended in the Near East, the amounts allocated to philanthropic as opposed to evangelical work can only be estimated. At best one must accept the judgment of mission executives that approximately one-third of the total was expended on the educational work. Furthermore, in the twentieth century all of the operating organizations have been supported by funds from a variety of sources, some private, some public. The chief accounting problem here is that the foundations, corporations, and public agencies each issue independent reports of their respective contributions and expenditures. The separate figures are valid, but care must be exercised in adding the expendi tures of the grant-making organizations to those of the operating organizations.

Based primarily on the records, often fragmentary and scattered, of the various American organizations and their personnel, this study views the failures and the successes of the overseas projects through American eyes. No doubt the study would have gained an added dimension if the reactions of various native groups, private and public, could have been canvassed, but the problems of travel to scattered centers in Albania, Bulgaria, Greece, Syria, Lebanon, Turkey, and Iran as well as the multiplicity of languages employed in the Near East precluded this. On the other hand, reports from American and British consular and diplomatic personnel have provided contemporary, independent views of the work.

In the undertaking of this project I am indebted to Professor Merle Curti for initially pointing me toward a study of philanthropy abroad and for his continuing encouragement. The courtesies of the late Edward C. Miller of the Near East Foundation, Richard Quaintance of the Near East College Association, and Mary Walker of the United Church Board for World Ministries made the task of exploring organizational records a pleasant one. Special thanks are extended to the American Philosophical Society and to the Ohio University Research Fund for grants which permitted the examination of State Department records in the National Archives and the American Board Papers at the Houghton Library. A grant from the Baker Fund of Ohio University permitted me to utilize British materials in the Public Record Office, London. A final acknowledgment is due my wife, Barbara, who, by sharing at some points in the research, by criticizing the manuscript in its various stages of preparation, and by her encouragement, has contributed immeasurably to the completion of this work.

Athens, Ohio   RLD

CHAPTER

I

The Grecian Adventure

THE COMING of the Greek War of Independence in 1821 captured the imagination of Americans and simultaneously brought appeals for any assistance Americans might give. The response to these cries resulted in the first sustained American venture in overseas philanthropy. Although a pioneer undertaking, the experience foreshadowed the problems and directions American philanthropy took in the century and a half that followed. On the one hand the predicament of the Greeks reflected the calamity of war in which a civilian population was reduced to the direst of extremities, while on the other hand it illustrated the misery born of endemic poverty. Basic problems were encountered in organizing fund-raising agencies in America and relief-administering facilities abroad. The role of government in seeking political solutions and in sharing the financial burdens of relief was explored. While the number of Americans immediately involved in this venture was limited, their impact both on Greece and on American philanthropy was substantial.

· I ·

Early in the fall of 1821 the revolutionary Greek Senate appealed to the United States in the name of liberty and Christianity to "purge Greece from the barbarians, who for four hundred years have polluted the soil." [1]

[1] [Edward Everett], "Affairs of Greece," *North American Review*, XVII (October, 1823), 415–416.

The appeal was transmitted via two channels. One, through Albert Galla-tin, then in Paris, went to the American State Department as a request for government assistance; the other, conveyed by Adamantios Koraës, a widely known Greek scholar living in Paris, went to Edward Everett, editor of the *North American Review* and the foremost Greek scholar in the United States, as a request for private assistance.

Romantic misconceptions of the overseas scene played at least as large a role in the American response as realistic appraisals of the Greek position. Cultivated Americans were far better acquainted with the personalities and problems of Periclean Athens than with those of contemporary Greece. While the Athens of antiquity lived on vividly in memory, the city, like its most famous structure, the Parthenon, had suffered from the ravages of time, neglect, and war, becoming "no more than the shadow of its former self." [2] The diaries, journals, and letters of American travelers in Greece underscore the intensity of their identification with the Greece of antiquity. A fragmentary inscription or a broken column was enough to unloose a flood of allusions to ancient grandeur and a catalogue of events and personages associated with the hallowed object or place. Crusty American sailors felt obliged to spend their shore leaves in the eastern Mediterranean touring scenes of antiquity, and many a captain returned to the United States with artifacts to grace his home or to adorn a mu-seum. Even Edward Everett, from whom one might have expected a criti-cal and discerning view of Greece, found himself laughed at for his mis-conceptions of the language of modern Greece.[3]

News of the rebellion in Greece made Americans tingle with excitement. The Greeks, rousing themselves from centuries of subservience to the Turks, seemed to be reasserting the values and virtues of their heroic fore-fathers. Also, they were emulating the United States which only a half century before had freed itself from Great Britain. Inevitably many re-garded the struggle as "a war of the crescent against the cross." [4] It is not surprising that even backwoods Americans succumbed to the fever, tak-ing for their new settlements the place names of ancient Greece, half hop-ing thereby to acquire for themselves some of the glory of the original.[5]

The Greeks were fortunate in the American philhellenes, who were unusually well-placed and articulate; they also had access to the press.

[2] Henry A. S. Dearborn, *A Memoir on the Commerce and Navigation of the Black Sea and the Trade and Maritime Geography of Turkey and Egypt* (2 Vols., Boston: Wells & Lilly, 1819), II, 202.

[3] Stephen A. Larrabee, *Hellas Observed: The American Experience of Greece, 1775–1865* (New York: New York University Press, 1957) is a thorough report on the reactions of successive American visitors to Greece.

[4] [Everett], *North American Review*, XVII (1823), 420.

[5] Walter Agard, "Classics on the Midwest Frontier," in Walker D. Wyman and Clifton B. Kroeber, eds., *The Frontier in Perspective* (Madison: University of Wis-consin Press, 1957), 165 ff.

Among their leaders were Mathew Carey, book publisher and philanthropist of Philadelphia; William Cullen Bryant, the nation's foremost poet, recently turned editor of the New York *Evening Post;* Hezekiah Niles of *Niles' Weekly Register;* and Thomas Ritchie of the *Richmond Enquirer.* Businessmen like Nicholas Biddle and William Bayard were moved, as were such influential politicians as James Madison, James Monroe, John Q. Adams, Daniel Webster, and Henry Clay. Chief spokesman and organizer was Edward Everett. Philhellenes in Washington responded speedily to the appeal from Greece by requesting the Congress to appropriate two or three million dollars in "provisions and whatever may be necessary to the Greeks, as an easy and honorable mode of acknowledging the aid, bounty, and obligation received from France in like circumstances" during the American Revolution.[6]

At this point the philhellenes came face-to-face with the requirements of American merchants operating in the Near East, as well as some basic requirements of American foreign policy. Official American policy was modestly favorable to expanding trade opportunities in the Mediterranean, which in turn required the negotiation of a treaty of commerce with Ottoman Turkey. The topic had first been discussed in the 1780's as a means of offsetting the loss of the British West Indian trade; again during the Jefferson administration, while a naval war was fought against the Barbary powers, the efficacy of treating with the Turks was broached; finally, in the 1820's the successive administrations of Monroe, Adams, and Jackson sought to open the Black Sea trade and to promote the Smyrna trade. Interest in a treaty with the Sublime Porte, never, even in the 1820's, took precedence over other matters, but it did furnish a brake on American enthusiasm for the Greeks. In the mind of Henry Clay the opposition of merchants to the Greek cause grew out of a "wretched invoice of figs and opium." Hopeful of negotiating a commercial treaty with Turkey, John Quincy Adams, first as secretary of state then as president, was reluctant to alienate Turkish officials by lending official federal support or sanction to the relief of the Sultan's rebellious subjects.[7]

[6] Merle Curti, *American Philanthropy Abroad: A History* (New Brunswick: Rutgers University Press, 1963), 23. See also Myrtle A. Cline, *American Attitude Toward the Greek War of Independence 1821–1828* (Atlanta, 1930).

[7] Henry Clay, *The Works of Henry Clay,* Calvin Colton, ed. (10 Vols., New York: G. P. Putnam's Sons, 1904), I, 270; There is no adequate treatment in print of early diplomatic relations with Turkey. Walter L. Wright, Jr., "American Relations with Turkey to 1831," Ph.D. dissertation, Princeton, 1928, is thorough. Particularly relevant are Thomas Jefferson, *Papers,* Julian P. Boyd, ed. (Princeton: Princeton University Press, 1950–   ), VII, 261–271; Vergennes in 1786 advised that such a treaty would be expensive and unwise until there was "a prospect of settlement with the Algerines." Jefferson to Jay, May 23, 1786, in *ibid.,* IX, 567–68. For the diplomacy of the Barbary wars see Ray W. Irwin, *The Diplomatic Relations of the United States with the Barbary Powers, 1776–1816* (Chapel Hill: University of North Carolina Press, 1931). For the 1820's see Charles Francis Adams, ed., *Memoirs of John Quincy Adams* (12

An even more fundamental objection to official aid to the Greeks lay in the policy enunciated by President Washington and reiterated by his successors to avoid subordinating American foreign policy to the "inveterate hatred" or "passionate attachments" to foreign powers.[8] Jefferson, now an elder statesman, recognized the problem and outlined the American response. Writing to Adamantios Koraës, whom he had known in Paris, Jefferson explained that Americans might sympathize in a private capacity, but could not assent to official aid:

> No people sympathize more feelingly than ours with the sufferings of your countrymen; none offer more sincere and ardent prayers to heaven for their success. And nothing indeed but the fundamental principle of our government, never to entangle us with the broils of Europe, could restrain our generous youth from taking some part in this holy cause.[9]

In his Annual Message of 1822 President Monroe recognized the "exalted sentiments" that the mention of Greece evoked and acknowledged the "excitment and sympathy" that Americans felt toward the Greeks, but he declined to support American intervention in Greece.[10]

The "contagion of philhellenism" did not down easily. In 1823 Daniel Webster, supplied with data by Edward Everett and supported politically by both Henry Clay and John C. Calhoun, pronounced the struggle in Greece to be part of the greater contest between "absolute and regulated governments." Although he concluded that "our place is on the side of free institutions," Webster asked only that the administration send an agent to Europe to determine the exact state of affairs in Greece and to advise on the granting of diplomatic recognition.[11] To Webster's appeals were added resolutions of the legislatures of Maryland, South Carolina, and Kentucky, along with messages of warm sympathy for the Greeks from the governors of New York and Massachusetts. Seeking to rouse popular support for Webster's position, Edward Everett urged that Amer-

---

Vols., Philadelphia: J. B. Lippincott, 1874–77); and Daniel Webster, *Private Correspondence of Daniel Webster*, Fletcher Webster, ed. (2 Vols., Boston: Little, Brown & Co., 1857).

[8] George Washington, "Farewell Address," in James D. Richardson, ed., *A Compilation of the Messages and Papers of the Presidents, 1789–1897* (10 Vols., Washington: GPO, 1896–99), I, 221.

[9] Thomas Jefferson, *Writings of Thomas Jefferson*, H. A. Washington, ed. (9 Vols., Washington: Taylor & Maury, 1853), IX, 159.

[10] Richardson, *Messages and Papers of the Presidents*, II, 193.

[11] Daniel Webster, *Writings and Speeches of Daniel Webster* (National Edition; 18 Vols., Boston: Little, Brown & Co., 1903), V, 65–67 ff. Webster's resolution read: "Resolved, that provision ought to be made by law for defraying the expense incident to the appointment of an Agent or Commissioner to Greece, whenever the President shall deem it expedient to make such appointment." See also Edward Mead Earle, "Early American Policy Concerning Ottoman Minorities," *Political Science Quarterly*, XLII (1927), 337–367.

ican recognition of the Greek rebels would be an act "peculiarly in character." [12]

John Quincy Adams, the tough-minded secretary of state, closed the door, at least for the moment, on the possibility of political aid. The American people, he assured the Greek rebels, sympathize with "the cause of freedom and independence, wherever its standard is unfurled," although "while cheering with their best wishes the cause of the Greeks, the United States are forbidden, by the duties of their situation, from taking part in the war, to which their relation is that of neutrality." [13] Should the Greeks secure their independence, the United States would be among the first to welcome them to the society of nations. And in Congress, "the sentiment of the House" was also against "meddling with the subject." [14]

· II ·

If Everett and other philhellenes failed to secure official aid for the Greeks, they succeeded in awakening many of their fellow citizens. Spontaneously philhellenes in cities such as New York, Philadelphia, Albany, and New Haven called meetings. At Albany, for example, prominent citizens gathered at the capital to discuss means of aiding the Greeks. Committees appointed at this meeting addressed letters to distinguished men in Washington, to the governors of the several states, and to the magistrates of the chief cities. Although the New York *Commercial* reported that meetings to solicit aid for Greece were too numerous to record, Albany, Boston, New York, and Philadelphia were apparently the most active centers. Committees in each of these cities operated independently of one another and made no effort to coordinate their activities.

Money was raised by means of benefit performances, special sermons and collections in the churches, and silver collections at public debates. Sympathetic merchants donated a percentage of their profits for a given day, while laborers contributed a day's wage; ship owners offered space. Still other aid was made possible by charity balls and fairs. School children handed up their pennies, while college men at Yale, Columbia, Hamilton, Brown, Andover, and West Point collected dollars. The sums raised by these spontaneous, independently-directed campaigns reached a respectable $32,000 to $37,000, an amount almost as large as the Greek Committee

[12] [Everett], *North American Review*, XVII (1823), 413; Edward Mead Earle, "American Interest in the Greek Cause, 1821–1827," *American Historical Review*, XXXIII (Oct., 1927), 52.
[13] Adams to Andreas Luriottis, Aug. 18, 1823, quoted in *Niles' Weekly Register*, XXV (Jan. 10, 1824), 299.
[14] *Annals of Congress*, 17 Cong., 2 Sess., 457 ff.

in England had collected in the preceding eighteen months. In this first phase of private fund-raising, the Americans contented themselves with turning the funds over directly to the Greeks for buying military supplies.[15]

While many Americans sent their contributions to the Greek cause, a handful of Americans went abroad to give their personal services. Among them were George Jarvis, Jonathan P. Miller, and Samuel Gridley Howe. Jarvis, the most outstanding of the early American volunteers, American-born but German-educated, went to Greece in 1822, arriving friendless and ignorant of the language. Becoming a "complete Greek in dress, manners, and language," Jarvis, still in his mid-twenties, rose to the rank of lieutenant-general in the Greek forces. Howe, who met him later, regarded him as "almost the only foreigner who has uniformly conducted himself with prudence and correctness." [16] Having seen "more fighting and undergone more hardship than any foreigner," Jarvis died at Argos in August, 1828. One of his Greek compatriots expressed regret that "so brave a man" had been cut off by disease and had not fallen on the battle field.[17]

Jonathan Peckham Miller, a noncommissioned veteran of the War of 1812 and onetime student of law, went out in 1824 for the Boston Greek Committee. He departed with a reputation as a man with "an iron constitution, a cultivated mind, and a thorough knowledge of military tactics." Like Jarvis, whom he served, Miller adopted Greek garb. With his head shaved and dressed in the Greek *floccata* and petticoat trousers, with his pistols and dagger stuck in his belt, and a musket on his shoulder, he cut a most striking figure.[18]

In November, 1824, Samuel Gridley Howe, a recent medical graduate, spurning his sister's tears and his father's pleas, chose to go to Greece rather than practice medicine in Boston. Howe arrived at Nauplion in mid-January, 1825, meeting Miller and Jarvis. The fighting was momentarily at a lull, and internal bickerings among the Greeks were silenced. He lent his medical services to the Greek forces in the Morea and the Aegean islands. The youthful Howe found the experience romantic and exhilarating, tempered by a dash of homesickness. "It is now three months since I have slept on a bed," he reported to his family, "and I have passed weeks without taking off my clothes, day or night. As for a chair, table, looking-glass, knife and fork, or any such things, you might as well look for them

---

[15] Curti, *American Philanthropy Abroad*, 28 ff. See also, Earle, *American Historical Review*, XXXIII (1927), 50–51.

[16] Samuel Gridley Howe, *Letters and Journals of Samuel Gridley Howe*, Laura E. Richards, ed. (2 Vols., Boston: Dana Estes & Co., 1906–09), I, 29.

[17] Larrabee, *Hellas Observed*, 107.

[18] *Ibid.;* Jonathan P. Miller, *The Condition of Greece in 1827 and 1828* (New York: J. & J. Harper, 1828); Howe, *Letters and Journals*, I, 29.

in the moon as in a Greek hut in the country. . . . It is all the same when one gets used to it, and now I can squat down with the soldiers upon the ground, and dine on olives, figs, and bread, with as good an appetite as that with which I used to attack your roast beef and Indian pudding. Oh, roast beef and Indian pudding! When shall I see you again? When shall I again fall foul of the hot rolls and butter, and the toast and tea of America?" [19]

But as month followed month, the war lost its glamour. When the Turks decapitated and impaled their captives, the Greeks retaliated by slaughtering their prisoners. The Greek forces, in fact, were led by a variety of native chieftains and foreign adventurers with a minimum of co-ordination. Among the adventurers who did no credit to themselves and gave little aid to the Greek cause were two young men. Whitcomb, "a fickle-minded, harebrained boy" was without "one spark of generous or philanthropic feeling towards Greece," a mere glory-hunter. The other, William T. Washington, a onetime cadet at West Point, represented himself as a nephew of George Washington. [20] Even before Howe's arrival, the war against the Turk had become secondary to a civil war between rival bands of Greeks; armed bands of Klephts, brigands who mixed patriotism with thievishness, terrorized the countryside.

During the summer of 1825, the Greek cause reached its nadir. The Turks besieged Missolonghi (Mesolongion), and while the besieged Greeks held out for months, their fate was sealed when Ibrahim, son of the viceroy of Egypt, intervened on the side of the Turks. A keen strategist and a student of European warfare with well-drilled troops who fought with precision, Ibrahim succeeded in overrunning the town in the spring of 1826, putting the survivors to the sword. [21] Henry A. V. Post, one of the Americans in Greece, spoke the mind of many in declaring that the contest was "no heroic game of the sword and buckler; it was a vulgar, practical fight with lead and villanous [*sic*] saltpetre." [22]

As Howe grasped the reality of the struggle, he all but lost faith in the capacity of the Greeks to manage their affairs. "Nothing is done," he confided to his journal. "It is this insubordination, this absolute want of order or system, that is ruining Greece." The army he came to regard as incompetent; the soldiers, without honor, deserted at will and stole even from their leaders. [23] Yet he recognized that he was gaining invaluable experience as a surgeon, performing in a few months more operations than he might do in a lifetime at Boston. He dressed the wounded until exhausted, then

[19] Howe, *Letters and Journals*, I, 167.

[20] *Ibid.*, I, 42; Charles Oscar Paullin, *Commodore John Rodgers* (Cleveland: Arthur Clark, 1910), 357.

[21] Harold Schwartz, *Samuel Gridley Howe, Social Reformer, 1801–1876* (Cambridge: Harvard University Press, 1956), 13 ff., summarizes Howe's experiences.

[22] Henry A. V. Post, *A Visit to Greece and Constantinople in the Year 1827–8* (New York: Sleight and Robinson, 1830), 257.

[23] Howe, *Letters and Journals*, I, 121; Schwartz, *Samuel Gridley Howe*, 16.

throwing himself on the ground and resting a few moments, he would again resume his labors.[24]

Nor was Howe alone in taking a dim view of the Greeks. American naval officers, predisposed by the romance of antiquity to be pro-Greek, found the Greek of reality "not qualified for self-government"; the higher classes were "aristocratical and corrupt, the lower classes debased, deceitful, and cruel. . . ." The naval officers were further alienated by the piratical attacks of the Greeks upon American shipping as well as by their propensity to sell civilian prisoners into slavery.[25]

Because compassion for the misery of the Greek people outweighed contempt for the weaknesses of the Greek leaders, Howe, Miller, and Jarvis stayed on, but increasingly their concern was with ministering to distressed civilians. From December, 1825, to October, 1826, Howe operated a small hospital at Nauplion. Then in the fall of 1826 he returned to the Greek fleet as medical director. But meantime in America the groundwork was laid for a large-scale relief mission. A letter from the Greek leader Theodorus Kolokotrones to Lt. General Jarvis, relayed to the Philadelphia publisher Mathew Carey, sparked a revival of relief committees. Again separately organized committees in Philadelphia, New York, and Boston purchased cargoes of food and clothing. But this time the cargoes were placed in charge of a trusted representative who accompanied the goods to Greece and, in connection with one of the Americans already on the scene, undertook to distribute the goods. The *Tontine*, the first of eight relief ships to be dispatched in 1827, arrived at Poros on the Gulf of Aegina on May 19, bearing a cargo valued at $13,856. Four days later the *Chancellor*, sponsored by committees in New York City and Albany, arrived at Nauplion with goods valued at over $17,000. By fall three other ships—the *Levant*, the *Six Brothers*, and the *Statesman*—arrived. With the war against Turkey again in full swing and Greek soldiers badly in want, Greek officials were tempted to appropriate the supplies for the military. Officials seized the cargo of the *Tontine*, promising to dispose of it according to the instructions of the Committee. Instead, they sold it for their own benefit and at a "shameful" price, getting $2,500 for what had cost $12,000. Subsequently, Howe, Miller, and the others used all possible means, including the aid of American naval officers, to restrict the relief supplies to civilians.[26]

Quickly the Americans hit on a system for the distribution of supplies, permitting a half-dozen mainland towns as well as the offshore islands to share the goods. John Reade Stuyvesant, who arrived in Greece with the

---

[24] Howe, *Letters and Journals*, I, 26–27, 129.

[25] *National Journal* (Washington), Dec. 25, 1825, quoted in Larrabee, *Hellas Observed*, 80. See also Paullin, *Commodore John Rodgers*, 335–336 and Richardson, *Messages and Papers of the Presidents*, II, 308–309.

[26] Schwartz, *Howe*, 21 ff. Howe, *Letters and Journals*, I, 224.

THE BALKANS

0   100   200
Scale of Miles

Six Brothers in July, 1827, described the procedures. While Howe was dispensing relief in the more remote areas of the Morea, Stuyvesant teamed up with Jarvis, who for the moment combined his military role with that of philanthropist. Upon landing at Angistri "we sent around to collect the poor, and in the course of two hours they were seen coming in droves to the shore. The flour was given out under the direction of Mr. Jarvis, who had his soldiers to keep off the half-starved wretches, in portions of 15 pounds to each. The joy they expressed is indescribable. They retired from the beach, calling on God to bless us, and the Americans. I clothed all who were naked, as far as my means would admit." [27]

Howe's method varied somewhat. He preferred to visit the "huts and holes" of the poor, giving "orders" for flour to those whom he found in misery—that is "half-naked, without shoes, lying under a miserable hut made of the branches of trees . . . without food, except the grass and herbs they could pick up around the houses." [28] By this means he could funnel scarce supplies to the most deserving. "My object," he declared, "is not to give to all the poor, but to those poor who are in distress and have not the means to get their daily bread." [29] In the judgment of George Finlay, an English philhellene who was on the scene and who subsequently wrote the history of the Greek Revolution, American relief during the summer, fall, and winter of 1827 provided the critical margin which kept the Greeks going until the European intervention in the summer of 1827 and the destruction of the Turkish fleet at Navarino on October 20, 1827, assured ultimate victory to the Greeks.[30]

By mid-1827 Howe regained his perspective toward the Greeks. While fully cognizant of their individual shortcomings, he now concluded that they "*are not a bad people* in fact all things considered it is strange that they are so good!" [31] He also concluded that the Greeks needed more than a handout. Rather, they required permanent institutions to minister year-round. As a doctor, his mind turned to the founding of a hospital for "the gratuitous relief of the poor sick." [32] J. P. Miller and John D. Russ joined Howe in writing the Boston Committee that sponsored Russ: "We feel thoroughly persuaded that more good will be done, more misery relieved by this measure than by any distribution of triple the quantity of goods and provisions which we have appropriated to it." [33]

Howe promptly established a fifty-bed hospital at Poros. Placing it in

[27] Larrabee, *Hellas Observed*, 155.
[28] Howe, *Letters and Journals*, I, 229.
[29] *Ibid.*, 247.
[30] George Finlay, *History of the Greek Revolution* (2 Vols., Edinburgh: W. Blackwood & Sons, 1861), II, 159.
[31] Howe quoted in Schwartz, *Howe*, 24.
[32] Howe, *Letters and Journals*, I, 269.
[33] *Ibid.*

the charge of Russ, a graduate of the Yale Medical College, Howe returned to the United States to solicit additional funds. Russ, unacquainted with the Greek language, subsequently reviewed the decision: "Amidst a nation of robbers, and sharpers, without a friend to aid or assist me," it was "an act approaching madness." Essentially the hospital was a one-man project. Russ had to perform all the operations, prepare the medicines, purchase the supplies, and supervise the facility. "The halls would not be cleaned, the beds shifted or the comfort of the patients attended to unless I ordered it." Nor were his patients invariably pleasant to deal with. The women, he complained, were immodest and the men the "greatest poltroons that ever disgraced civilized society." But in the course of nearly a year, Russ cared for more than nine hundred sick, aged, and infirm persons.[34]

Meantime in the United States the question of the role of government in providing overseas assistance was reopened, debated, and disposed of along much the same lines as in 1823. Early in 1827, Congressman Edward Livingston of Louisiana proposed a bill appropriating $50,000 "to clothe the naked, to feed the hungry, to comfort the despairing—to do that which a civilized enemy would himself do." The opposition, however, held that even non-military relief would make the United States a party to the war. The proposal was defeated decisively, thus assuring that whatever was done for the Greeks must be done with private funds.[35]

When Howe arrived home, he discovered that interest in Greece had again lagged, but that he personally was a celebrity. First, Howe reported to the New York Committee to solicit support for his hospital. The Committee agreed to give support and further spelled out its policy: It declined to take part in the controversy between the Greeks and Turks; provisions and clothing were not to be supplied to military personnel, but were exclusively for "women, children, and old men, the noncombatants of Greece"; finally, relief goods were to be distributed only through Americans sent abroad for that purpose.[36]

Next, Howe, capitalizing on his fame, spent the better part of a year writing and speaking about Greece. Hastily he put together *An Historical Sketch of the Greek Revolution*,[37] to acquaint Americans with the situation. In a speaking tour of the smaller towns of New England and the Hudson Valley he succeeded in rekindling interest in the Greeks. In the early months of 1828 the New York Committee alone raised $59,809.43, while the Boston Committee collected additional funds. These funds,

[34] Larrabee, *Hellas Observed*, 163–164.
[35] Curti, *American Philanthropy Abroad*, 30.
[36] Miller, *Condition of Greece*, 11–12.
[37] Samuel Gridley Howe, *An Historical Sketch of the Greek Revolution* (New York: White, Gallaher and White, 1828).

which brought the total contributions of 1827 and 1828 to $138,000, permitted the sending of the last two relief ships, the *Herald* and the *Suffolk*. On the latter ship Howe returned to Greece for a second tour of duty and his most imaginative work abroad.[38]

· III ·

Upon arriving in November, 1828, Howe turned first to dispensing relief. In order to assure that the scarce supplies would reach the most deserving, he again made the rounds of the homes in order to compile a list of the worthy poor. Where he was unable to operate in person, Howe had the head man of each area make a catalogue of the poor. These catalogues he perused carefully before releasing relief supplies, for he discovered that local people listed their friends and relatives down to the "thirty-ninth degree" and then added as many hundred common people as they thought would be received without suspicion. His general rule was to allow about one-fifth of the population as lacking the means of subsistence. His method was not foolproof, as Howe admitted to himself, for he noted instances where he had given warm clothes to women with children in arms, only to have some of them return clad again in rags. He hypothesized that they had sold the clothes and put on their rags again to excite pity and to get additional assistance. "I fear I am too often imposed upon in the same way . . . ," he noted in his journal. Even so, it would seem that his methods combined a generous impulse to assist with a conscientious determination to maximize the number of persons benefitted.[39]

Howe's greater interest was directed toward attacking the causes of distress, using charity as an instrument for basic reform. "Why, then," he asked himself, "should I give away these donations to be consumed in idleness, when by a proper use of them I can give employment to hundreds in some ways that keep them out of idleness and result in some permanent public good, making a road, draining a marsh, building a hospital, school or something of the kind?"[40] His first venture was to build a quay and improve the harbor at Aegina, an island southwest of Athens, where three hundred refugee families from Athens had gathered. Because of the destruction of the piers and the accumulation of mud and filth, the port had been reduced to a state resembling a swamp. "To remedy this and render the port at once commodious, salubrious and beautiful, requires only that a solid wall should be built around the border of the port a little way within the water, and then filled up behind with stones and

[38] Howe, *Letters and Journals*, I, 278 ff. *Niles' Weekly Register*, June 7, 1828.
[39] Howe, *Letters and Journals*, I, 321.
[40] *Ibid.*, 286.

earth; and after that is done the mud should be dredged from the port within the wall and the whole filling be covered with stones." [41]

Little time was lost in instituting the project. Work on the quay took nearly four months during the winter of 1828–29, providing support to seven hundred poor. Men did the heaviest work, but even women engaged in manual labor. However, whenever it rained, Howe discharged the women but gave them their rations as if they had worked. As the project neared completion in March, 1829, Howe took pride that he had succeeded in keeping these refugees "from idleness, yet not fed them like beggars." Most of all, he was pleased to have enriched the island by "a beautiful, commodious, and permanent quay. . . ." He departed with the gratitude of the natives and their cries of "Long live the Americans!" uppermost in his thoughts. [42]

While work progressed on the mole at Aegina, Howe undertook to assist some destitute farmers at Megara, on the mainland west of Athens. He proposed to lend them seed. The expectation of being able to produce food of their own in the future, he reasoned, would keep these people busy and content, while inducing them to find their own means of subsistence until harvest. To increase food production, Howe proposed to sell some relief supplies to buy Egyptian seed, which was regarded as superior. The recipients of this aid were obligated to pay in at harvest one-third of the yield, which would be used to support a Lancastrian school for their village. Thus, ideally, the terms of Howe's relief would make the recipients self-supporting and provide the means of initiating a continuing institution. Although the plan was largely self-executing, inevitably difficulties were encountered. In mid-February, 1829, as the first shoots came up, Greek troops, scavenging for food, picked the young beans for food and turned their horses into the grain fields to forage. Howe protested, but the Greek government was too impotent to restrain the soldiery, and so this plan miscarried. [43]

The largest and last of Howe's work-projects was at Hexamilion on the Corinth peninsula, where he proposed to resettle homeless men and women on farms. In mid-March, 1829, as work was being completed on the mole at Aegina, Howe went to Hexamilion to locate a site for his project. Having found one, he secured official permission twelve days later to go ahead with it. The terms of his grant from the government gave him the use of 10,000 stremmata (2,000 acres) for five years, tax free. Next, Howe made arrangements with the local authorities regarding the land and employed an Italian agriculturist to assist him. As a start Howe had twenty-six families, refugees from Athens, Chios and Kydoniai. To

[41] *Ibid.*, 306.
[42] *Ibid.*, 344.
[43] *Ibid.*, 316, 337.

provide them with shelter he employed two hundred local persons, all poor, to erect dwellings, one for each family. Building materials were found locally, stone and wood; the earth made a suitable mortar. He met the expense for collecting the materials and for assembling them by paying the laborers in foodstuffs from the relief supplies.

Meantime the colonists, under the direction of Howe's agriculturist, began to cultivate the soil. During April, oxen were purchased and tools were made—plows, rakes, hoes, shovels, and spades. Howe personally fashioned a wheelbarrow. While the Greeks had a rude plow, the other tools were entirely unknown to the Greek farmer. Each colonist was given as much land as he could till individually. Pending the first harvest, the colonists were supplied a ration of 1⅓ pounds of cornmeal per person per day. At harvest time one-half of the crop was to be paid to the manager of the colony to reimburse the initial costs, which had been a modest $20 per family. As Howe's plans were flexible, he envisaged the gradual expansion of the colony. The number of families did, in fact, increase to thirty-six by June and to fifty by the end of the year. Howe began to foresee a maximum of some two hundred within a decade.

In connection with the colony Howe founded a Lancastrian school. This system of education, then the rage in England and America, permitted the instruction of large numbers of pupils at a minimum cost by employing an experienced teacher to plan the curriculum and to teach the older students who, in turn, taught the younger ones. The school, conducted by a young Greek who had received training in Lancastrian methods in England, was Howe's "favourite resort." When discouraged or troubled, Howe, an imperious soul who did not take frustrations lightly and who at this time was ill with malaria, retreated to his school and "immediately all my disgust is gone, and all my hopes and anticipations are revived. . . ." [44]

Although the basic plans for the Hexamilion colony were realized, Howe's total plans were not. In his more expansive moments, he proposed to rebuild the port, planned a fifty-bed hospital to be financed from the profits from the loan of grain to the resettled farmers, and talked of digging a canal across the isthmus of Corinth. But these were not to be. Getting the first fifty families settled on the land, crops planted, shelter built, and a school under way, fully occupied him. He labored there day and night, in season and out, and was "governor, legislator, clerk, constable, and everything but patriarch." [45] And on the whole this role was satisfying. Years later, from the perspective of a life that would have busied several lesser men, Howe recalled the days at Hexamilion as the most rewarding of his life. But by the summer of 1830 peace had returned to

---

[44] *Ibid.*, 356, 347 ff.
[45] Howe to Horace Mann, quoted in *ibid.*, 366.

Greece, and the people were slowly putting their own affairs in order. Howe, recuperating from a siege of malaria, felt the need to go to a healthier climate, and he was anxious to be about other business.[46]

And what of this pioneer venture in overseas philanthropy? Measured in personal terms, there were thousands of Greeks who between 1824 and 1830 received food or clothing they would have gone without, had not Jarvis, Miller, Howe, and their associates given of themselves. Howe and Russ restored to health hundreds of Greeks, both civilians and military, when no other medical aid was at hand. Nor were the personal sacrifices of the American almoners taken for granted. Years later, Greeks whom Howe had befriended recognized him when he returned unannounced to scenes of earlier activity. As he rode through the village of Hexamilion, older people took note of the figure on horseback, exclaiming to one another: "This man looks like Howe!" Then, their judgments confirmed by others: "It must be Howe himself!" He was surrounded. Spontaneously a feast was arranged; old friends thronged about him, "eager to express their joy in seeing him." [47] Nor was this experience an isolated one. American travelers visiting in after-years reported numerous incidents in which Greeks spoke with affection of Howe, in particular, or of American aid generally. After one such encounter Edward Joy Morris, who became Lincoln's minister to Turkey, commented that at that moment he would not "have exchanged the name of an American for the proudest title on earth." [48]

This pioneer venture in overseas philanthropy was in response to a concrete situation that aroused the sympathy of romantic philhellenes. Efforts to secure government support were unavailing, leaving the burden to private individuals. The private sponsors, organized *ad hoc* city-by-city, successfully raised funds to meet specific crises, but they were unable to develop a continuing, central organization to coordinate either the fundraising at home or the administration of relief abroad. Effective administration of Greek relief resulted from the good sense and dedication of a handful of American volunteers in Greece, particularly Jonathan P. Miller and Samuel G. Howe. This was the first step in a long, distinguished career in philanthropy for Howe. The experience made him sensitive to the possibility of combining emergency relief with measures for permanent reform. But the *ad hoc* organization of the relief committees in America meant that the experience gained in Greece could not be transmitted easily to directors of subsequent relief missions, nor was there any means of carrying out Howe's plans. A century would pass before the

[46] *Ibid.*, 369.
[47] Larrabee, *Hellas Observed*, 253.
[48] Edward Joy Morris, *Notes of a Tour Through Turkey, Greece, Egypt, Arabia Petraea, to the Holy Land . . .* , (2 Vols., Philadelphia: Carey & Hart, 1842), I, 161–162. See also Earle, *American Historical Review*, XXXIII (1927), 57.

disaster relief workers pushed beyond the methods and goals tested in Greece in the 1820's.

Although the experience alerted Americans to the problems of others, making them less parochial in their concerns, it was left to American missionaries, just entering the eastern Mediterranean in the 1820's, to recognize the needs of the natives and to employ their organizational apparatus to direct sustained philanthropic activities.

II

Strivings in Malta and Syria, 1820-1861

WHILE THE GREEKS were taking the first tentative steps towards securing their independence, two youthful New Englanders, Levi Parsons and Pliny Fisk, set sail in November, 1819, on an adventure that initiated a second, far more significant line of philanthropy. Evangelization rather than philanthropy was foremost in their minds and in the minds of their sponsors. But circumstances led some thousand missionaries who followed Parsons and Fisk to the Near East in subsequent years to make major contributions to the theory and practice of philanthropy. As a result, the development of Syria and Lebanon was considerably affected. Despite rebuffs, disappointments, and false starts, a modest but solid beginning had been achieved by 1860.

• I •

The departure of Parsons and Fisk for the Near East reflected the great changes which were reshaping American Protestantism in the early nineteenth century. During the closing years of the eighteenth century, a general reaction against rationalism and deism occurred. Whereas on the American frontier the result was the noisy, uninhibited revival, on the East Coast there was a resurgence of evangelical Protestantism culminating in the founding of home and foreign mission societies. When the Congregational Church was divided by the emergence of a liberal, unitarian wing, an evangelical element, followers of Samuel Hopkins, organized the American Board of Commissioners for Foreign Missions. In this move they were supported by like-minded men in both the Presbyterian Church and the Reformed Church. Although these evangelicals placed great emphasis upon personal piety, their view of religion also stressed the concept of "disinterested benevolence." For the greater glory of God, the elect should engage in any service, however distasteful, that added to the sum total of human happiness. Imperative duty, not romance or adventure, impelled men to the ends of the earth to lift mankind to a higher plane of living. Park Street Church, Boston, which was virtually the parish church of the American Board, was also at the center of such domestic reform movements as the American Peace Society, the American Temperance Society, and the anti-slavery movement. Although Congregationalism and Presbyterianism were broad enough ideologically to support both missions and secular reforms, scarce funds and limited manpower raised questions about priorities. Both the missionaries abroad and the American Board at home had to develop a sense of how far secular philanthropy might be supported by a missionary society.[1]

Incorporated in 1812, the American Board had accumulated some experience by the time it commissioned Parsons and Fisk. Mission stations had been established in Bombay, Ceylon, and Hawaii as well as among the Cherokee, Choctaw, and Arkansas Indians of the United States. Experiences in India and among the American Indians convinced the American Board that the missionary must do more than expound the Bible. In keeping with Protestant tradition it insisted that the Christian convert must be able to read the scriptures for himself. In the absence of commercial publishers equipped to undertake the production of the Bible, Testaments, and tracts, the American Board quickly found itself operating mission presses. To promote literacy and to train native workers, the Board founded schools. By 1820 missionaries of the American Board were conducting a school for native children in India, while the Board established a boarding school at Cornwall, Connecticut, primarily for American Indians. Here heathen youth hopefully were trained to become "missionaries, physicians, surgeons, schoolmasters or interpreters; and to communicate to the heathen nations such knowledge in agriculture and the arts, as may prove the means of promoting Christianity and civilization." [2]

The American Board was still feeling its way when it commissioned

---

[1] Oliver Wendell Elsbree, *The Rise of the Missionary Spirit in America, 1790-1815* (Williamsport, Penna.; Williamsport Printing and Binding Co., 1928), 141, relates the American Board to the intellectual currents of the day. The book deserves to be more widely known.

[2] ABCFM, *First Ten Reports* (Boston, 1834), 307.

Parsons and Fisk. The establishment of a mission in the Holy Land was appealing to the Board, for it meant taking the Gospel back to the land whence it came. From the limited knowledge the Board had of the area, the whole population appeared to be in "a state of deplorable ignorance and degradation, destitute of the means of divine knowledge and bewildered with vain imaginations and strong delusions." [3] English evangelicals, with whom the Board felt a close affinity, also encouraged the Americans to begin work in the Holy Land. Indeed, the Board was in communication with William Jowett, who went to Malta for the Church Missionary Society. More importantly, Charles Williamson, Chaplain of the English Consulate in Smyrna, urged the American Board to send missionaries and an evangelical press to the Near East. Although the Board instructed Parsons and Fisk to go to Jerusalem, it also directed them to contact Jowett at Malta and to establish friendly relations with Williamson at Smyrna. [4]

Levi Parsons, moody and introspective, and Pliny Fisk, intense and pious, were perhaps as well-equipped to undertake this commission as any pair of newly ordained clergymen. Both were born in 1792 in the hill country of northwestern Massachusetts; they had been classmates at Middlebury College and again at Andover Seminary. Departing from Boston late in 1819, they reached Smyrna (now Izmir) in mid-January, 1820. For months they struggled with languages. Fisk, an indifferent scholar, was especially distressed by written Arabic with its "thirteen conjugations, and twenty ways of forming the plural, and thirty-three ways of forming the infinitive; with its consonants without vowels, and its unnumbered dialects." [5] Once initiated in Greek and Arabic, the two men began to tour the area of the historic "Seven Churches of Asia." To hasten the survey, Fisk returned to Smyrna, while Parsons made his way to Jerusalem, intending to establish a permanent mission there. [6] Shortly after his arrival, however, the Greek War for Independence began, and Parsons, who carried letters of introduction to the Greeks of Jerusalem, soon found his position untenable. He made his way slowly back to Smyrna, his health seriously undermined by disease. Partly for reasons of health and partly to return to Palestine from the south, Parsons, in the company of

[3] *Ibid.*, 230–231.

[4] The interactions of the American and English evangelicals is detailed in A. L. Tibawi, *American Interests in Syria, 1800–1901: A Study of Educational, Literary and Religious Work* (Oxford: Clarendon Press, 1966), 3–12. See also, ABCFM, *First Ten Reports*, 231, 278.

[5] Levi Parsons, *Memoir of Rev. Levi Parsons*, compiled by Daniel O. Morton (Poultney, Vt.: Smith & Shute, 1824), 273 ff.; Pliny Fisk, *Memoir of the Rev. Pliny Fisk*, Alvan Bond, ed. (Boston: Crocker & Brewster, 1828), 112 ff. The Fisk *Memoir* is more informative.

[6] Levi Parsons has sometimes been described as "the first Protestant missionary who ever entered" Jerusalem. James Connor of the Church Missionary Society, Christian Burckhardt of the British and Foreign Bible Society, and Melchoir Tschoudy of the London Jews Society preceded him. Tibawi, *American Interests in Syria*, 20.

Fisk, went to Alexandria, Egypt, where he died in February, 1822. After recruiting two new companions, Jonas King and Joseph Wolff, Fisk completed the survey of Syria.

In the 1820's this region, which knew Western culture chiefly through the medium of Egypt, was a backwater of the Ottoman Empire. A variety of peoples, divided both ethnically and religiously, inhabited Lebanon and Syria: Turks and Arabs, Druzes, Greek Orthodox, and Maronites. In the back country adjoining the Arabian desert and the mountainous areas of Iraq were nomadic Bedouins and Kurds. Beirut was a provincial village of 7,000 to 8,000 inhabitants. Its long, rocky roadstead made the port suitable only for coastal vessels and minimized direct contacts with the West. Syria was so lacking in the amenities that naval personnel regarded assignment to the Levant as "little less than a grievance." [7] While the walled city was "small and not particularly attractive or repulsive," the environs beyond the walls presented "an enchanting prospect" of an uninterrupted succession of gardens. The profusion of lilac, pomegranate, fig, and cactus in the bright sun was striking, and the foliage provided welcomed shade. Back of the city was "the goodly mountain," Mount Lebanon, whose snowy ridges and the villages occupying its declivities added interest to its ever-varying appearance. [8]

Very different was Smyrna, the chief port of Turkey, and the point through which Syria then had contact with the outside world. Lying on the west coast of Asia Minor at the far end of a deep gulf, Smyrna's harbor was commodious and its anchorage excellent. Viewed from the water on a calm, bright day, the city presented "one of the most transcendently beautiful prospects in the world. . . ." [9] To some Western visitors the mixed population of Turks, Greeks, Armenians, and Jews numbering some 130,000 or even 150,000, each occupying a separate quarter of the city and each with a characteristic dress, was excitingly romantic. To others the houses, few of them less than three stories, the upper floors jutting over dank, narrow streets, created an impression less favorable. Here congregated individuals from all over the world, drawn to the trad-

[7] David Porter to Edward Livingston, Jan. 12, 1832, in Despatches, Turkey, II. General Records of the Dept. of State, Rec. Group 59, National Archives, Washington, D.C. William R. Polk, *The Opening of South Lebanon, 1788–1840: A Study of the Impact of the West on the Middle East* (Cambridge: Harvard University Press, 1965) discusses the role of Egypt in opening Lebanon to Western culture.

[8] Henry A. S. Dearborn, *A Memoir on the Commerce and Navigation of the Black Sea and the Trade and Maritime Geography of Turkey and Egypt* (2 Vols., Boston: Wells & Lilly, 1819), II, 155 ff. and Edward W. Hooker, ed., *Memoir of Mrs. Sarah Lanman Smith* (Boston: Perkins & Marvin, 1839), 179, 191, contain eyewitness reactions of Americans.

[9] Samuel Woodruff, *Journal of A Tour to Malta, Greece, Asia Minor, Carthage, Algiers, Port Mahon, and Spain in 1828* (Hartford: Cooke & Co., 1831), 153. Henry A. V. Post, *A Visit to Greece and Constantinople in the Years 1827-8* (New York: Sleight and Robinson, 1830), 279.

ing houses of the Franks (as all Christians were termed). Among these were a small handful of resident American merchants. George and Thomas Perkins, originally of Boston, had long been residents of the city when Parsons and Fisk arrived. More important were Joseph Langdon of Boston, whose home was a rendezvous for Americans visiting Smyrna in the 1820's, and David Offley, who more than anyone else was responsible for the growth of the Smyrna trade and who long served as the American consular agent. As a port easily accessible to American ships, Smyrna became a mission station in 1820.[10]

A third base of operations was the island of Malta. Located south of Sicily in the central Mediterranean, it could serve mission stations in Italy, Greece, the Aegean islands, Anatolia, or Syria with almost equal ease. But its major attraction was the British flag that flew over it, promising a sanctuary not to be found in the Papal States, the war-wracked Morea, or the lands of the Sultan. Like Smyrna, Malta was an important trade center and port of call. It was congenial because of a sizable English community, although most of the English were military or naval personnel. The Maltese, a Semitic people, impressed one missionary wife as "poor, ignorant degraded beings, such as you never beheld. Some of the most miserable of our [American] Indians will give you some idea of them." [11]

The explorations of Parsons and Fisk convinced the American Board that a direct effort to evangelize Moslems was impossible. Furthermore, the Board was appalled at the state of the several Christian churches of the Levant. Their use of charms, relics, and miraculous pictures as well as the superstitious and "idolatrous rites and worship in an unknown tongue, manipulated by an ignorant, degraded selfish priesthood" seemed to require reformation before Christianity could ever appear attractive to the Moslem, Jewish, and pagan population.[12] Consequently, the Americans resolved to work with the native Christians, hoping to spur reform within the local churches. This tactic brought only limited success, for Parsons and Fisk offended the Greek and Maronite clergy with the tracts they distributed. Polemical replies by Fisk and others served only to stiffen Maronite opposition to anything the Americans might attempt.

---

[10] Parsons, *Memoir*, 273, 297; Fisk, *Memoir*, 112–113. Daniel H. Temple, *Life and Letters of Rev. Daniel Temple* (Boston: Congregational Board of Publications, 1855), 103. Sketches of David Offley and Thomas Handasyd Perkins appear in the *Dictionary of American Biography* (21 Vols., New York: Charles Scribner's Sons, 1928–37).

[11] Hooker, *Memoir of Sarah Lanman Smith*, 158. Mrs. Smith had worked among the Indians of New York State before going abroad.

[12] Quoted in N. G. Clark, "The Gospel in the Ottoman Empire," ABCFM, *Annual Report, 1878*, xix. Also ABCFM, *First Ten Reports*, 230–231.

· II ·

As the avowed purpose of the American Board was to spread the pure Gospel by word and print, its philanthropic activities developed as much by drift as by design. In 1822, to facilitate the dissemination of the Gospel and to provide auxiliary materials as needed, the American Board established a mission press at Malta under the supervision of the Reverend Daniel Temple. Temple, educated at Dartmouth and Andover Seminary, embarked for Malta with his bride of a few days; it was the start of a career as translator, editor, and publisher. The next six years brought a mixture of achievement and tragedy to this gloomy New Englander. Initially, Temple studied Italian that he might better superintend the editing and publication of works destined for Italy. But the religious climate of Catholic Italy, intensified by the political reaction of post-Napoleonic Europe, proved increasingly hostile to the circulation of Protestant tracts and literature. The press, also equipped with fonts of Greek type, produced materials in that language. The work was hindered by painful embarrassments. Temple's limited command of Greek made him unduly dependent upon native translators. In Homan Hallock, who arrived late in 1826, Temple acquired a youthful colleague, a printer, but the two men did not work together smoothly. Yet, by 1828 Temple had published over forty works in Italian and more than sixty in modern Greek. Personal tragedy, the loss within a few weeks of his wife and two children by consumption, sent the grief-stricken man back to the United States temporarily. Cryptically Temple commented: "Everything except wickedness, moves at a slow pace." [13]

Out of initial difficulties and discouragements came experience and growing competence. Furthermore, the difficulties encountered in making contact with religious leaders in Greece inclined the mission to pursue other opportunities that opened in the late 1820's. The new Greek nation was eager for schools; given the strong religious flavor that infused the spellers and readers then current in American schools, the mission found it quite proper and expedient to employ the Malta press to publish similar schoolbooks for the Greeks. During his visit to the United States in 1828–29, Temple procured a variety of "the most approved schoolbooks" to take back to Malta to be used as models. At the direction of the Prudential

[13] Temple to Anderson, Dec. 18, 1830, in ABC 16.9, Vol. 1. Also Temple, *Life and Letters*, *passim*. Prudential Committee to Temple, Jan. 1830, in ABC 8.1, Vol. 1, #2 in American Board Papers, Houghton Library, Cambridge, Mass. Malta was also the site of four other Protestant mission presses—the British and Foreign Bible Society, the London Missionary Society, the London Jews Society, and the Church Missionary Society. Cooperation between the presses was close.

Committee, the policy-making body of the American Board, he was instructed to make his books "fully accomplish their secular purpose," taking care to stress quality rather than quantity. Approximately half of the output of the Malta press in the early 1830's was devoted to the production of texts in spelling, geography, grammar, and literature. In some instances Temple chose to translate and edit such standard American texts as the geographies of Peter Parley (Samuel Griswold Goodrich) and William Channing Woodbridge; in other cases he produced works largely of his own authorship.[14]

Publishing for the Greeks continued to be marked by difficulties. Some were passing. The press needed special fonts of type in order to publish algebra and geometry texts. It required cuts for illustrative purposes, and, unable to produce its own maps, it had to locate suitable supplies in Europe. While delays ensued, such problems were resolved. More ominous were the reactions of Greek officials, who first criticized the quality of the American books then increasingly sought to monopolize for themselves the production of school materials. In fact, the Americans had plunged into the business with more goodwill than expertise. The first texts, printed during Temple's absence in America, had been inadequately edited. Greek authorities complained that "faults of style, foreign turns of expression, barbarisms and, in fine, solecisms swarm on almost every page and render the reading of the books unintelligible, fruitless and insupportable to the reader." Although discouraged by these criticisms, Temple had "no doubt" that many of the earliest publications "well deserve the severe language. . . ."[15] In many ways these objections cloaked a growing Greek nationalism which, increasingly self-conscious and exclusive, made it a point of honor that education and textbooks should be entirely controlled by the State. Finally, in 1836 the Greek government, now a monarchy, issued a decree essentially restricting to the royal press the publication of texts for the Greek schools. Unable to circulate its material in Italy and encountering growing difficulties with its publications in Greece, the press was divided; the Arabic branch moved to Beirut and the rest to Smyrna.[16]

---

[14] *Ibid.*, May 31, 1831 and Temple to Anderson, July 5, 1831, in ABC 16.9, Vol. 1.

[15] Temple to Anderson, Jan. 30, 1831, in *ibid*. E. Smith to Anderson, July 5, 1831, in *ibid*.

[16] Temple to Anderson, May 14, 1836, in ABC 16.9, Vol. 3, #35; Smith to Temple, Apr. 22, 1830, in ABC 16.9, Vol. 1, #64; Goodell to Temple and Smith, Oct. 16, 1832, in *ibid.*, #156; Temple to Anderson, Feb. 12, 1833, in *ibid*.

· III ·

While Daniel Temple nurtured the mission press at Malta, two colleagues, Isaac Bird and William Goodell, were busy establishing a mission station at Beirut. Their arrival in November, 1823, created a stir as half-naked Arab porters carried the families through the surf, the ladies clutching their "plain but ample skirts and simple bonnets." Fortunately, Peter Abbott, the British consul and the only Englishman in town, heard the commotion on the water front and came to meet them. He invited the Birds and Goodells to join his household until they located housing of their own, a real blessing, for Abbott had the only house in Beirut with glass windows, and winter was at hand.[17]

The first order of business was to study the languages of the area, to distribute religious tracts, and to make such contacts with the natives as were possible. In the course of several years Bird, a patient, studious, hardworking observer, became very proficient in the use of Arabic, the prevailing language of Lebanon and Syria. Goodell made a start on Arabic but transferred to Constantinople, making his mark there. The evangelical activities, especially the publication of controversial tracts attacking the practices of the local Maronite church and the conversion of a young Syrian of the Greek Orthodox faith, As'ad Shidyāq, brought the mission into sharp conflict with local authorities. The youth was imprisoned and died in chains, becoming celebrated in death as "The Martyr of Lebanon." [18] In 1824 the Porte, at the urging of Maronite and Greek Orthodox leaders, issued a decree forbidding the importation of Bibles into Syria, because they had caused the people "apprehension, disputation, and disturbance." [19] Anathemas and curses were directed at Christians who fraternized with the Americans. With their opportunities to engage in direct evangelical work virtually blocked, the missionaries turned to indirect methods—the operation of classes—in order to penetrate the linguistic, cultural, and religious barriers separating them from the local population.

Of the early educational work, much remains shrouded in obscurity. The first school was started in 1824, as soon as Bird and Goodell acquired a beginner's competence in Arabic. About this school there are few details, but inevitably instruction was elementary, the facilities makeshift, and the school term brief. Even this tentative start was disrupted in

---

[17] David H. Finnie, *Pioneers East: The Early American Experience in the Middle East* (Cambridge: Harvard University Press, 1967), 191; Charles T. Riggs, "Near East Missionary Biographies," typescript, Istanbul, July 9, 1953, in Archives, UCBWM, Boston, Mass.

[18] See *Missionary Herald*, xxiii (1827), 71–76, 97–101, 129–136, 169–177.

[19] Finnie, *Pioneers East*, 124.

March, 1826, when a dozen Greek ships anchored at Beirut and landed five hundred men to besiege the city. Although Turkish troops promptly arrived and the Greeks withdrew, restless Bedouins kept Beirut in disorder. William Goodell has left a graphic account of an attack that one armed group made on his home. "Some of their more resolute and reckless ones came, and, in their strong guttural manner, called upon me to 'Iftah el Bab' (open the door). I told them I should not 'Iftah hoo' (open it)." It took the Arabs a half hour to break through the door while Goodell was "reasoning with them" from a narrow window above. Once inside, the Arabs charged upstairs. Goodell safeguarded his wife by telling the intruders that her room was a harem and thus forbidden to true sons of the Prophet. This ploy succeeded. Subsequently, with the aid of Consul Abbott, Goodell lodged a strong complaint with the governor for this outrage. To "document" his claim an illustration drawn by a local artist to Goodell's specification was presented to the governor, who accepted it as conclusive proof of the crime. To make amends, the governor paid Goodell $300 for his losses.[20]

Opposition to the mission's activities continued. Despite determined efforts, work among the Jews and Greeks of Jerusalem got nowhere. Nor were the efforts to make contact with the Maronites of Beirut successful. The initial suspicion and hostility roused by Pliny Fisk and a companion, Jonas King, were the prelude to a series of thrusts and counterthrusts. After a Maronite bishop at Rome replied to King's exposé of Maronite errors and superstitions, Isaac Bird wrote a series of thirteen epistles, attacking the Maronite Church. Thus, the breach was widened and deepened so that persons who accepted the religious teachings of the Americans felt compelled to leave their native church. Yet the schools organized by the Americans were so attractive that some Maronite parents risked censure to let their children attend. Nor were the Maronite clergy all of one mind, so that the degree of opposition to American activities—both religious and educational—varied from week to week and from place to place. In 1827 the Syrian mission was directing thirteen schools with a total enrollment of six hundred pupils.[21]

This encouraging start was interrupted again as Beirut suffered the effects of the Greek War for Independence. The intervention of the Great Powers, and of England in particular, on behalf of the Greeks, forced the English consul, on whom the Americans depended for protection, to flee Beirut in 1828. Closing their schools, Bird and his fellow Americans took refuge at Malta until peace returned.

When the Syrian mission resumed its activities in 1830, Syria was espe-

[20] *Ibid.*, 192–193.

[21] ABCFM, *Annual Report*, 1826, 93; *ibid.*, 1827, 45–49; *ibid.*, 1828, 37, 44. Robert Carlton Delk, "The History and Influence of American Education in the Near East, 1823–1914," typescript, 1949, in Archives, UCBWM.

RUM.

● Lovech

BULGARIA

● Eske Zagra

● Philippopolis

● Drama

● Adrianople

T H R A C E

BLACK

Istanbul
(Constantinople)

Bosporus

Rodosto

Sea of
Marmara

Scutari

● Izmid

● Adabazar

Dardanelles

Brousa

Ankara
(Angora)

T   U

MYTILENE

● Afyon Karahısar

L Tuz

CHIOS

Izmir
(Smyrna)

● Konıa

A E G E A N   S E A

Adalia ●

TAURUS

M

RHODES

CRETE

⊛ Ni

CYPRUS

MEDITERRANEAN   SEA

TURKEY AND SYRIA

0   50   100   200
Scale of Miles

cially receptive to Western influences. Physical isolation from Turkey
had minimized the impact on Syria of the very modest reforms initiated
by Selim III (1789–1807) and Mahmud II (1808–39). However, the occupation of Syria from 1831 to 1840 by Mehemet Ali and his son, Ibrahim
Pasha, created an environment favorable to reform. One of the great men
of his age, Mehemet Ali had made himself master of a largely autonomous
Egypt in the first years of the nineteenth century. His intervention on
behalf of the Sultan during the Greek War had proved disastrous to his
fortunes. Casting about for a venture that would restore his luster and
replenish his dwindling treasury, he sent Ibrahim into Syria. The latter
met unalloyed success, taking Acre in May, 1832, and delivering the Sultan's forces a crushing defeat at Konia shortly thereafter. In 1833 Sultan
Mahmud II and the rebellious Mehemet came to terms by which Syria,
Adana, and Tarsus were placed under Ibrahim's authority. The immediate
effect of Ibrahim's rule, so far as the Americans were concerned, was to
weaken the political power of the Maronite Patriarch, thus opening up the
southern portions of Lebanon to missionary work. Ibrahim's regime in
other ways marked the beginning of the modern age for Syria. Taxes
were regularized; justice was administered more impartially; commerce
was promoted; foreigners were less subject to abuse; education was promoted and a higher degree of law and order was maintained. His rule
promised "toleration to all sects of whatever religion they may be," reported one of the missionaries. And Ibrahim, for a time a near-neighbor of
the Americans in Beirut, seemed personally attractive, "a large, jolly,
laughing, cunning man, with a very penetrating eye." [22]

Taking advantage of the new atmosphere, the Syrian mission was able
to put down roots and to contribute importantly to the social, cultural,
and economic changes that were stirring in Syria. The most immediate
American contribution was in the field of education. Progress was the
product of persistence and self-sacrifice on the part of dozens of nameless
individuals. At first even the desire for education had to be generated, for
all classes manifested "a distressing apathy." [23] Furthermore, the cultural
differences between the Syrian and the American made communication
difficult and promoted misunderstanding and suspicion. Accustomed to a
highly liturgical church, the Maronites could not understand the ascetic
forms of worship of the Americans. A native servant of one missionary
acknowledged to a friend that the Americans did "not lie, nor steal, nor
quarrel, nor do any such things; but poor creatures," said she, "they have

[22] Polk, *The Opening of South Lebanon*, Ch. 7; Sydney Nettleton Fisher, *The
Middle East: A History* (New York: Alfred A. Knopf, 1959), 282 ff.; Temple to
Anderson, Oct. 19, 1832, in ABC 16.9, Vol. 1 and Patrick Campbell to Lord Palmerston,
July 31, 1836, FO 78, Vol. 283, #25, Public Record Office, London. Hooker, *Memoir
of Sarah Lanman Smith*, 289.
[23] Quoted in Delk, "American Education in the Near East," 42.

no religion." [24] This lack of understanding carried over into all relations with the Americans. Even though the Americans made no effort to proselytize their students, native parents were easy prey to rumors that the mission would spirit their children out of the country. In face of such difficulties, a school system was fashioned.

In Beirut and many of the villages the Americans founded elementary schools. The role of the American was that of organizer, supervisor, and patron. Instruction was entrusted to native teachers. These schools, occupying rented quarters, were highly ephemeral. Terms were short, and the schools were frequently disbanded and reorganized. Little more than reading and beginning arithmetic were taught. Whether these first mission schools were superior to the native schools is doubtful. The Maronites, the Greek Orthodox, and the Arabs all operated schools that served their own communities. None had an adequate system. The number of schools was small; their quality was poor. The curriculum was limited; learning was by rote. Textbooks were scarce; teachers were deficient in training. The advantage of the Americans as educators lay in their sophistication and learning. Coming from a society that was under the spell of the idea of progress, they had an awareness of what might be and of how one might go about creating a new structure.

The first step toward the professionalization of the mission schools lay in the establishment of a school for girls. In 1833 two missionary wives gathered six or eight neighborhood girls in their parlors, meeting with them for an hour or two a day for instruction in sewing and reading. More time than this the women did not have, and besides the brief, irregular sessions were less likely to attract undue attention. Early in January, 1834, Sarah Smith, bride of Eli Smith, arrived. Within two weeks she was teaching in the "school," and within six months she assumed direction of it.[25]

The daughter of a prominent Norwich, Connecticut, family, Sarah Lanman Huntington Smith had spent several years as a missionary working among Indians in New England before she met and married Eli Smith in 1833. A bit of a patrician, she was at times dismayed at having her house invaded by curious native women, "asking questions and prying into a hundred things which did not concern them." To friends at home she confided her reservations: "If the people were cleanly in their habits, it would be more pleasant to have them about our persons. I often think of the Savior, surrounded as he was by a multitude of the lower classes. . . ." [26]

---

[24] Hooker, *Memoir of Sarah Lanman Smith*, 215.

[25] *Ibid.*, 381 ff.; ABCFM, *Annual Report*, 1827, 45; Henry Harris Jessup, *The Women of the Arabs, with a Chapter for Children*, Charles S. Robinson and Isaac Riley, eds. (New York: Dodd and Mead, 1873), 50–52.

[26] Quoted in Finnie, *Pioneers East*, 198.

But rather than turn her back, she determined to correct the faults she observed.

Mrs. Smith recognized that the problems of introducing education for girls were formidable. The ability to read and write was regarded as unfeminine in the Levant; for this reason it was a serious obstacle to marriage, which was "the principal object of the parent's heart." [27] In these circumstances Mrs. Smith concluded that education for girls must be placed on a solid, professional footing. With the courage of her convictions she broadened the curriculum to include spelling, geography, and arithmetic. Next, she urged Miss Rebecca Williams, a friend and an experienced teacher, to join her and share in operating the school. Miss Williams became the first of dozens of single women who undertook teaching assignments in mission schools of the Near East. Finally, Mrs. Smith, with help from the European community in the Levant and from friends in America, obtained funds with which to build a schoolhouse. A "substantial stone building," the first edifice ever built in the Turkish Empire for the education of women, was completed in the spring of 1835.[28]

The next year her health failed. Believing in the curative value of sea air, her husband took her on a sea voyage, but to no avail. The crew and passengers were disagreeable. "Horrid profanity was heard, instead of prayer and praise," and on the fifth night out the leaky, old coaster ran upon a reef on the coast of Cyprus.[29] Soaking wet and cold, the Smiths reached shore alive. Days passed before they were rescued by a Turkish lumber vessel which at last delivered them in Smyrna. Her condition worsened by the ordeal, Mrs. Smith died there on September 30, 1836. Her death, coinciding with the breaking of a depression in the United States that seriously reduced the income of the American Board, resulted in the closing of her school. But her work was not in vain, for it established a precedent and a memory that encouraged a second attempt.

From the start the missionary was surprisingly aware of the problems implicit in promoting cultural change. He recognized that he might promote an innovation, but if it were to take hold and become a vital part of the native way of life, then natives had to be trained to direct and nurture it. This principle applied no less to the secular work of the mission than to the religious program.[30] Despite its financial stringencies, the mission, recognizing the need for native assistants—evangelists, colporteurs, copyists, printers, editors, and teachers—moved to establish a secondary school.

In December, 1835, the Syrian mission opened at Beirut its first secondary school in the Near East. Problems relating to the level of the curricu-

---

[27] Hooker, *Memoir of Sarah Lanman Smith*, 316.
[28] *Ibid.*, 381 ff.
[29] Quoted in Finnie, *Pioneers East*, 200.
[30] As the more articulate debate on this subject occurred in Turkey, the subject will be more fully explored in Chapter III.

lum, the language of instruction, and finance were confronted and resolved for the moment. As the mission could afford only one school and as youth who might be attracted to a Protestant-operated institution were widely dispersed, necessarily it operated as a boarding school, a decision which committed the mission to detailed supervision of their young charges. The curriculum had to be sufficiently general that the youth might become either evangelists or teachers. Although the missionaries perpetually worried lest their native evangelists become too worldly, they were compelled to include a rather broad range of general courses in mathematics and the sciences in order to train potential teachers. As there were few natives competent to teach at the secondary level, Americans staffed the secondary schools. In turn, the absence of suitable texts in Arabic and the inexpertness of the Americans in that language led to a decision to offer instruction in English. The political stability that Ibrahim provided in Syria created a climate in which the school thrived. On the other hand, the depression in the United States restricted the funds available with which to hire lay teachers, enlarge the facilities, or improve the course of study.[31]

A significant feature of the American-sponsored schools was the emphasis on science in the curriculum. This interest of the missionary in modern science reflected the acceptance of modern science by New England clergymen as a useful tool in demonstrating the wondrous ways of God, as well as the breadth of their undergraduate training at colleges such as Williams, Amherst, Yale, and Middlebury. In 1842, members of the Syria mission organized a Scientific Society headed by Eli Smith, with Cornelius Van Dyck as treasurer. This interest carried over into the curriculum of both the high school and the seminary. The mission acquired a variety of equipment for laboratory demonstrations. These included an orrery, an electro-static generator, condensers, an air pump, microscopes, and stethoscope. Given the absence of an organized school system in Syria, the American effort was all the more important for introducing Western science to this part of the Arab world.[32]

However, the results of this first venture into secondary education proved disappointing to the mission. A retrospective analysis by the mission concluded that the students had been too young, eight to twelve years, to receive maximum benefit, while the intensive supervision of the boarding school had denationalized them, making it difficult for them to

[31] Mission personnel who developed great skill as linguists generally were assigned to editorial duties; the less expert taught school. In 1884 of seven missionaries in Syria, only two were fluent in Arabic. [Report], in ABC 16.8.1, Vol. 1, #19; "Report," Dec. 31, 1836, in *ibid.*, #48.

[32] Frederick Rudolph, *The American College and University: A History* (New York: Vintage Books, 1965), 226; E. Beadle to Prudential Committee, Apr. 14, 1842, in ABC 16.8.1, Vol. 1, #7; C. Van Dyck to Anderson, Oct. 5, 1847, in *ibid.*, Vol. 5.

fit easily into their own society. Finally, as Beirut ceased to be a provincial village, it seemed to be less and less desirable as a site for a school. How did one get the lads back to the villages after they had been to Beirut? Pending the solution of these problems, the mission, bowing nominally to the persistent financial stringencies of the day, disbanded the school in August, 1842.[33]

· IV ·

The activities of the mission press, the Arabic portion of which moved to Beirut from Malta in 1834, proved as significant as the educational work. The press was directed by Eli Smith. Preacher, explorer, linguist, translator, and printer, Smith was the outstanding figure of the Syrian Mission. Enlisting with the American Board, he was assigned in 1827 to Beirut to learn Arabic. Forced to leave with other Westerners in 1828, Smith made a tour of Greece in 1829, and in 1830–31, accompanied by Harrison Gray Otis Dwight, a fellow missionary, he undertook a 2,400-mile exploration of Asia Minor that carried the pair into the Caucasus and northwest Persia. Reports of both trips provided vital information with which to plan mission policy. Their book, *Missionary Researches in Armenia,* is a travel classic. After seeing to its publication in America, Smith married Sarah Lanman Huntington and returned in 1834 to Beirut, where he developed into an expert Arabic linguist.[34]

Smith's great achievement was the design of an Arabic-script type that was both esthetically pleasing and orthographically correct. His work consisted of collecting specimens of Arabic script as models for the new type. The work of months received a severe setback when he lost his samples in a shipwreck. After a year's delay he delivered a new set of models to the mission's master printer, Homan Hallock.

One of the first lay missionaries, Hallock was a forceful personality who was eccentric, sarcastic, and resentful of authority but also down-to-earth. By 1837 he had eleven years of experience as a printer of various European and Oriental languages. Completion of the Arabic type, though a mechanical task, required no less skill than the design of models, for it was necessary to incorporate the points and the body of the Arabic character on a single type block. With the Yankee's proverbial skill at innovation, Hallock designed a machine on pantographic principles that permitted him to transfer a reversed facsimile of Smith's models to the face of

[33] W. Thomson to Anderson, Apr. 28, 1838, in *ibid.,* Vol. 1, #5; "Report," Dec. 31, 1836, in *ibid.,* #48; "Seminary at Beirut," Apr. 16, 1844, in *ibid.,* #23.
[34] Eli Smith and H. G. O. Dwight, *Missionary Researches in Armenia: Including a Journey Through Asia Minor, and into Georgia and Persia* (2 Vols., London: George Wightman, 1834).

a steel punch in any size desired and in perfect proportion. After resolving the mechanical problems of joining points to the body of the type, he began the preparation of the requisite punches and matrices. Ultimately, on Hallock's urging, the American Board established a type foundry at Smyrna where he completed the casting of his first font of Arabic type in 1841.[35]

Hallock left the employ of the American Board in 1841. Returning to the United States, he continued the work he had begun at Smyrna, evolving seven sizes of Arabic type. This "American Arabic" typeface of Smith and Hallock won the approval of Arab scholars, becoming the standard. The Bernhard Tauchnitz foundry at Leipzig, the leading European publishing house working in Arabic, procured Hallock's matrices, while the mission foundry at Beirut subsequently supplied print shops from Morocco to the Philippines with the type. Hallock also designed a typeface for the Syriac script used by the Nestorians of northwest Persia. Throughout his professional career he produced punches and matrices and cast type in exotic languages for his former employer as well as for other mission and Bible societies in the United States and England.

This work in education and printing was but fairly started when in 1840 Syria was again convulsed by internal revolutions and an external war that further exposed the region to European influences. Ibrahim's rule had become increasingly oppressive within Syria, while his effort to monopolize Syrian trade was resented by the Great Powers. Taking advantage of a Maronite uprising directed against Ibrahim, the British in the fall of 1840 induced Russia, Prussia, and Austria to join in ousting Ibrahim. While the French, who sympathized with Mehemet Ali, were momentarily paralyzed by a domestic crisis, British and Austrian forces quickly forced Ibrahim's evacuation of Syria, returning the province to the Sultan's sovereignty.[36]

Thereafter, the European powers assumed responsibility for the general peace of the province. Stability proved elusive, for the British intervention had destroyed the power of Emir Bashir Shihab, who had managed to hold his position as the leading local ruler under successive governments from the time of Napoleon's Syrian campaign. An effort to govern Syria through a Turkish pasha satisfied no one and put the Maronites and Druzes at one another's throats. European pressure, largely under British initiative, resulted in a compromise by which the northern portions of Syria were administered by a Maronite pasha who tended to be pro-

[35] Hallock to Anderson, Apr. 30, 1834, Oct. 24, 1834, Jan. 14, 1836, and Jan. 1, 1837, in ABC 16.9, Vol. 3.

[36] E. Smith to Anderson, Jan. 6, 1843, in ABC 16.8.1, Vol. 160, gives a missionary assessment of these disorders.

French, while the southern part was governed by a Druze chieftain under British patronage. Though this arrangement was far from ideal, it functioned for a decade. Lebanon and Syria were now open to direct trade with western Europe.[37]

The political transformation initiated in 1840 had the effect of identifying the missionary enterprise of the Americans with the political interests of the British. English diplomats were not long in perceiving that France, as champion of the Sultan's Roman Catholic subjects, and Russia, as protector of the Greek Orthodox, had established pretexts for intervention in Turkey's affairs. Accordingly, Britain took her stand as an advocate of religious liberty for Turkey generally and as the special protector of the Sultan's Protestant subjects. Thus, it was in England's interest to nurture the American missionary effort as the leading Protestant group in the Near East. At almost the same instant Druze chieftains expressed an interest in both Protestantism and British protection, almost as though these were inseparable. In fact the Druze chieftains, uncertain of their position in the face of the close ties between the Maronites and French, were willing to embrace Protestantism and to patronize the American schools as bait to secure English protection. This tactic did not deceive the missionaries.[38] While the Americans at no point shaped their policies or programs in terms of British interests, there is no doubt that the American institutions were used by self-seeking natives and by the British when it was expedient.

In the troublesome days of the early 1840's the future of the whole mission enterprise—evangelistic as well as philanthropic—seemed dismal. Nine of the staff sent to Syria had died abroad; four others had returned home for reasons of health; and three more returned believing the prospects of success too slim to warrant their staying. In these circumstances the American Board inquired in 1842 whether the enterprise ought not be abandoned as a failure. Assuming a stoic pose, Eli Smith answered for the mission. The recent disorders had not brought harm to any American property or personnel, nor to native Protestants. More importantly, he reported, no one in Syria had thus far given thought to the desirability of quitting. Yet Smith had to admit before the turbulence ended that Syria was a land "where nothing seems stable, but bigotry and superstition." [39]

The depths of the disorders were reached in 1845 when Syria was plunged into a brief, bloody, civil war between the Maronites and Druzes. In this contest Maronite and Druze neighbors mingled their "private and personal injuries and insults" with public grievances. "At the fatal war-

---

[37] Polk, *The Opening of South Lebanon, 1788–1840, passim.*
[38] Smith to Anderson, Apr. 28, 1842, in ABC 16.8.1, Vol. 1, #151.
[39] ABCFM, *Annual Report,* 1843, n.p.; Smith to Anderson, Jan. 6, 1843, in ABC 16.8.1, Vol. 1, #160.

signal, every shepherd, farmer and mechanic, every shopkeeper, skeikh and Emeer" hurried to the fight with "a rickety gun on his shoulder, a pair of pistols thrust through his girdle, an old rusty sword or villainous looking kharger hanging by his side, and an ugly butcher knife in its sheathe, concealed in his bosom. With savage yells he bursts into his neighbor's house, blows out his brains, drives the cold dagger through his heart, cuts off his head with his long knife, and with his right hand red with gore, sets fire to the house, and consumes whatever his plundering cupidity has not carried off." Waged in such fashion, the war caused much injury and much property damage, perhaps as many as eight hundred houses being burned, but surprisingly few deaths.[40] In these disorders the mission station at Abeih, a village a few miles to the southeast of Beirut, became involved tangentially when Druze partisans invaded the station grounds, and barricading themselves in a partially finished building, sniped at Maronites. As the skirmish ended, the station doctor tended the wounded, while other personnel provided bread for the homeless. By prompt action the station summoned the British consul at Beirut to come with his dragoman and kavasses to conduct some six hundred refugees to safety at Beirut.[41]

The political changes in Syria were accompanied by a change in the character of the mission. Experience had made it apparent that the Maronite clergy were not prepared to reform their church along Protestant lines, while the Druzes, who were more accessible to the Americans, were inhibited by their Moslem background from becoming Christians in any significant numbers. Thus, those Maronites and Druzes who accepted the teachings of the Americans had no means of corporate worship except as the Americans provided for it. When developments in Constantinople among the Armenians led to the creation of an Evangelical Church, the Syrian Mission followed suit and organized a native church. Thereafter the mission employed its schools and the press as instruments to reach people not accessible to the evangelist and to preserve and nurture the infant Protestant community. Only in this manner could the latter ever become self-sustaining and self-propagating.[42]

In spite of the political turmoil in Syria the mission moved ahead. In June, 1843, it founded a secondary school at Abeih which endured. Its founder, Doctor Cornelius Van Dyck, first studied medicine with his father. Although he had no liberal arts training, Van Dyck had spent a year at the Jefferson Medical College. After going to Syria in 1840 he studied theology with his colleagues and was ordained in the field. His main inter-

---

[40] Thomson and DeForrest to Anderson, July 29, 1845, in *ibid.*, Vol. 3, #17.
[41] G. Whiting to Anderson, June 7, 1845, in *ibid.*, #14.
[42] G. B. Whiting and W. M. Thomson, "Report on Christian Policy of the Mission," Apr. 15, 1844, in *ibid.*, Vol. 1, #20.

ests were those of the scientist and scholar; accordingly, he spent little time or energy in preaching or in sectarian propaganda but devoted himself chiefly to teaching and to organizing the schools.[43]

The Academy, as it was called, accorded much attention to the Bible, which was used as a reader, but geography, trigonometry, logarithms, and physics were also taught in Arabic from textbooks in Arabic. Van Dyck's interests were too diverse to permit him to direct the school for more than a brief period, and the mundane administrative responsibilities devolved on Simeon Calhoun, under whose direction the school emphasized teacher-training. The teaching staff, consisting of two or three Americans, was adequate for a student population that numbered but twenty-four a decade after the school's founding. It was in this school that Daniel Bliss, a pioneer of collegiate education in Syria, got his first teaching experience.[44]

Nor was the mission press inactive. Equipped with the "American Arabic," it served the native population more effectively than ever before. Along with the schools, the press contributed importantly to a renaissance of Arabic literature. The spoken idiom of the rural and tribal Arabs through the centuries had diverged from the grammatical idiom of literate, urban Arabs, and when Arab power collapsed in the face of the Ottoman conquest, Arab society lost its means of preserving or adding to its literary heritage. The Arab world was isolated from the influences of the commercial, scientific, and technological revolutions that affected Western Europe from the fifteenth century on. By 1800 few Arabs had any awareness of their own literary heritage, and the language lacked the vocabulary necessary to discuss modern political and scientific thought.[45]

The political and commercial penetration of the Levant by England and France, starting in the 1840's, brought the Arab face-to-face with European systems of political and economic power. The role of the American schools and press in Syria was to initiate a revival of the Arabic language and an awareness of past Arabic achievements, which in time played into the hands of the slowly emerging leaders of Arab nationalism. Eli Smith and Cornelius Van Dyck, Arab scholars of high competence, were significant figures in making possible the Arab awakening. The latter mastered Arabic poetry, proverbs, history, and science and "had no peer among foreigners in his knowledge of the Arabic language and literature." [46] As Smith and Van Dyck revived the classical literature and its grammatical

---

[43] Lutfi M. Sa'di, "Al-Hakim Cornelius Van Alen Van Dyck (1815–1895)," *Isis,* XXVII (1937), 25.

[44] F. J. Bliss, ed., *The Reminiscences of Daniel Bliss* (New York: Fleming H. Revell, 1920), 111–112.

[45] George Antonius, *The Arab Awakening: The Story of the Arab National Movement* (Philadelphia: J. B. Lippincott, 1939).

[46] Henry Harris Jessup, *Fifty-three Years in Syria* (2 Vols., New York: Fleming H. Revell, 1910), I, 107.

idiom, the mission schools produced a growing audience for this literature, while the press provided the means for reaching those outside the schools.

The native collaborators of Smith and Van Dyck became prime movers in kindling the Arab literary renaissance. One of these, Nasif Yazeji, established a reputation as a scholar of Arabic literature and directed his appeal for purity of style to Arabs of all sects. Nearly all Arab writers of the next half century were influenced directly or indirectly by him. The other, Butrus al-Bustani, had somewhat broader interests. He was eager that Arabic prose, while remaining true to its past in grammar and idiom, be made capable of expressing "simply, precisely, and directly the concepts of modern thought." From his circle of family, friends, and pupils came the modern novel and drama in Arabic, as well as modern Arabic journalism. Bustani was equally devoted to acquainting the Arab world with the thought and science of modern Europe. As his own contribution he founded in 1863 his own National School (al-madrasa al-wataniyya) where the Arabic language and modern sciences were taught well. He founded a journal, often edited by his sons though published under his name, that set a high standard for other journalists to imitate and acquainted its readers with the problems of the day. His more enduring work consisted of an Arabic dictionary, *al Muhit*, and an Arabic encyclopedia, *Da'irat al-ma'arif*, which contained much material from Arabic literary and historical sources but also displayed evidence of original work.[47]

As an essayist Bustani urged the Near East to learn from Europe first of all the importance of national unity, a willingness of those who share a common area to cooperate for the common welfare. "Love of Country is an article of faith," he emphasized. Although Bustani never hinted at Arab separatism, his writings were addressed to his fellow Syrians, and he was, according to Albert Hourani, perhaps the first writer to talk with pride of his "Arab blood." Although these are the attitudes of nationalism, the Arab self-consciousness generated by Yazeji and Bustani did not result in an organized movement immediately. But the emphasis on a common language permitted later nationalists to employ it as a device for uniting Arabs of varying religious backgrounds. Furthermore, because Protestantism was devoid of any political program, after 1850 a disproportionate number of the enlightened Syrian Arab writers identified themselves with the Protestant community.[48]

This era of beginnings in Syria ended in 1860–61 as a variety of events altered the conditions under which mission work would or could be conducted in Syria. In 1857 the last of the pioneers of mission philanthropy,

---

[47] Albert Hourani, *Arabic Thought in the Liberal Age, 1798–1939* (London: Oxford University Press, 1962), 99–100.

[48] *Ibid.*, 100–103; see also, Antonius, *The Arab Awakening*, 45–49.

Eli Smith, died, and the conduct of the work passed to a younger generation. The coming of the Civil War in the United States seriously restricted American Board funds, forcing retrenchments in the mission program. In 1861 Sultan Abdul Medjid died and was succeeded by his ineffective brother Abdul Aziz (1861–76). But more fateful for Syria, a renewal of hostilities between Maronites and Druzes resulted in the establishment of an autonomous régime for Mount Lebanon that vested power in a Christian governor appointed by the Porte but in effect selected by the Powers.

At this point one may well ask: how did the missionaries view their role as philanthropists? In truth, much of the time they were reluctant philanthropists. As Men of God, their preference was for preaching the Gospel. They had been led, providentially as they thought, to the publication of secular books and the operation of schools as a means of gaining entrée to persons otherwise indifferent to them. Yet as soon as it became apparent that an independent evangelical church must be created, the Americans recognized that the native community required its own supporting institutions, of which a press and schools were most vital. As the funds available to the Americans were limited, the mission periodically fretted that so much of its time and money had to be devoted to non-evangelistic activities. Most of the mission personnel, after all, were professional clergymen by training, not printers or teachers. In a mission-wide debate on ends and means, the consensus was unmistakable that if they were excluded altogether from preaching, many would return to the United States. Furthermore, Cornelius Van Dyck, one of the few laymen who went abroad as a missionary, made two particularly telling points. First, men might "voluntarily exile themselves from the society of those they love, from civilization, refinement, Christian privileges and a host of other precious things" to preach the Gospel, even in the face of indifference or opposition but, "mere benevolence, philanthropy, a desire to do good in general, to elevate and enlighten" was inadequate motivation. Second, he thought it doubtful that funds could be raised for more than a season or two to teach the sciences or to dispel superstition. In short, the incidental philanthropy of the missionaries was all that American society was prepared to sustain.[49]

The methods and values of the missionaries in approaching their philanthropic efforts anticipated the practices of the professional philanthropist of the mid-twentieth century. The effort to change the values and practices of the Eastern churches, though not philanthropic, none the less provided the missionary with experience in deliberately introducing social and cultural changes. Thus initially they aspired not to create new

[49] C. Van Dyck, Sept. 29, 1855, in ABC 16.8.1, Vol. 4, #56; W. Bird to S. Pomroy, June 25, 1855, in *ibid.*, #283.

churches, but rather to reform the existing ones. But when they created a separate church, the Americans recognized that they must always appear "as strangers," and that the native institution must be prepared to sustain itself. This need to develop native leaders who would multiply the efforts of the American as teachers, printers, translators, or evangelists reconciled the missionary to his philanthropic activities.[50]

In one other matter the missionary-educator confronted a basic and enduring problem, that of the denationalized native. Whatever was done for or to the native must be such that he could return to his own people and pass on to them that which he had just learned. The experience in Syria indicated that at the secondary school level the continuing influence of the local environment often offset the values promoted by the mission school; alternatively, there was risk that the intense atmosphere of a boarding school made changes so radical in character that the student was alienated from his native community. The indicated solution was to make boarding school facilities correspond "in simplicity and cheapness" to the environment from which the student came and to which he should return. The most controversial question related to languages. Consistency required that mission schools teach students in their vernacular, and this they did without exception in the common schools. But expediency required that those natives from whom the mission and the native church would draw translators, editors, and biblical scholars must be able to use the large body of literature in English, which could not be translated economically. There was a risk in such a policy, for the bilingual Syrian was frequently tempted to seek employment with English firms or to migrate to England or America. Answers to these problems would have to be worked out in later years.[51]

Admittedly many of the impacts of the American school and the press were intangible. Yet there were evidences that their presence made a difference. In the 1840's John Bowring, investigating conditions in Syria in behalf of the English government, commented on the "high standard attained" by the American mission schools in Syria and observed that Syrian youths educated in the American schools were "more advanced than any other boys of their age in Syria." [52] The Americans, a Greek bishop admitted in 1859, "have done more for the diffusion of useful knowledge and literary advancement of Syria than had been accomplished by all the others during half a century." [53]

It is ironic that the missionary became the chief overseas philanthropist in the nineteenth century. The concept of the brotherhood of man might

[50] Whiting to Anderson, May 16, 1848, in *ibid.*, #27.
[51] S. Calhoun, 1855, in *ibid.*, #60; W. Bird to L. Bacon, June 27, 1856, in *ibid.*, #284; Calhoun to Bacon, July 2, 1856, in *ibid.*, #341.
[52] Quoted in Antonius, *The Arab Awakening*, 42, n.2.
[53] J. Williams to L. Cass, Dec. 28, 1859, in Despatches, Turkey, Vol. 16.

seem to contradict this view, but the missionaries of the American Board enlisted primarily to preach the gospel, and they manifested their concern for their brother men in that fashion. The sponsoring groups, Congregationalists and Presbyterians, had a tradition at home of church-related educational institutions which might incline the missionary to make use of the school as a reasonable instrument for furthering his religious activities. But as Fisk and Parsons departed, they were not guided by any *a priori* concepts. Rather they were to investigate the area and to suggest an appropriate course of action to authorities in Boston. The decision to operate schools and to prepare and publish teaching materials was pragmatic: missionaries in the field recognized a useful approach and followed it up. In undertaking such activities the missionary endeavored primarily to promote his evangelistic work. But it seems clear that the requirements for schools and books often resulted in emphasis on these activities. Thus, professional printers and teachers such as Homan Hallock and Rebecca Williams were recruited to supplement ordained personnel of the mission. The mission never unreservedly embraced these secular activities, but neither could it divorce itself from sponsorship. The product was tension.

As an organized body, the American Board had a continuity that was absent in the Greek relief movement. The Board and its sponsoring church bodies provided a source of funds and personnel. Its journals kept Americans aware of the Near East. At the same time it was the missionary abroad, rather than personnel at home, who developed a sensitivity to the need for social change and undertook to meet these needs. In relying on the schools and press, the missionary was not original, for he employed devices with which he and his patrons were familiar. Furthermore, these were agencies he could manage in conjunction with his ministerial duties.

As a part-time, pragmatic philanthropist, the missionary was not given to drafting formal statements of his concepts. His schools, while teaching Bible stories, differed from the existing native schools by teaching skills in reading, writing, and arithmetic. He adapted the American elementary school to the environment of the Near East, and he encouraged those who were so inclined to imitate him. Beyond this, the effectiveness of missionary philanthropy rested with the student. Presumably the "educated" man would proceed on his own initiative to employ his knowledge and talents in the Westernizing of society. Literate men would deal more imaginatively with the problems of the economy and the society. Philanthropy in this sense liberated the individual from the bonds of tradition but otherwise it was non-directive. The chief liability of this approach was the incapacity of the missionary to reach those who were suspicious of him or hostile to his evangelistic role.

III

Christian Philanthropists in Turkey, 1831-1861

IN TURKEY, as in Syria, it was the missionary who first played the role of philanthropist, establishing schools, operating a press, and undertaking limited medical work. Although these Americans had no political objectives, their activities contributed importantly to the cultural awakening and to growing social stresses and strains in Turkey. By 1861 and the death of Sultan Abdul Medjid, their schools and presses had become the bulwark of a small Protestant community that was widely dispersed across the Empire. During these years the American Board, which directed and supported the work, succeeded in perfecting an effective organization and in evolving a point of view toward philanthropy.

· I ·

In 1831 Turkey, then in the twenty-third year of reign of Sultan Mahmud II, was on the threshold of reform. A man with "a majestic form and carriage," piercing eyes and jet black beard, the Sultan was bent on introducing at least enough elements of European civilization to revivify his crumbling Empire.[1]

---

[1] Roderic H. Davison, *Reform in the Ottoman Empire, 1856-1876* (Princeton: Princeton University Press, 1963), 25 ff., succinctly summarizes the reforms of

A series of wars and revolts compelled Mahmud to bide his time. A rebellion in Serbia and war with Russia had occupied the early years of his reign. He had been obliged to summon his Egyptian vassal, Mehemet Ali, to put down the Wahhabis in Arabia; in the 1820's the Greek revolt, supported by the British and French, was accompanied by another war with Russia. As distracting as these events were, Mahmud in June, 1826, succeeded in destroying the Janissaries who, having lost their military prowess, had become a major barrier to reform. Once they were out of the way, Mahmud, in spite of other distractions, was able to root out abuses of power, restore royal authority in the provinces, and initiate a program of Westernization. He engaged German officers to train the new Turkish army. A handful of Turkish officers was sent to England to study. Military and medical colleges were opened at Constantinople. As signs of progress, such external symbols of Western civilization as the frock coat were adopted.

Only the first halting steps toward reform had been initiated when the American Board established its mission at Constantinople under the leadership of William Goodell, Harrison Gray Otis Dwight, and William Gottlieb Schauffler. In common with other early missionaries, Goodell was a product of rural New England. With more grit than funds, Goodell, his trunk strapped to his back, had hiked sixty miles to Phillips Academy hoping to be admitted as a bursary. As a student, he had attended the ordination of the first missionaries commissioned by the American Board. After graduating from Dartmouth College and Andover Seminary, Goodell enlisted with the American Board and was assigned to Beirut, where he commenced the study of Turkish. At the height of the Greek War he removed to Malta, where he oversaw publication of his translation of the New Testament in Armeno-Turkish (Turkish in Armenian characters). Thus, it was as a man of experience that Goodell arrived in June, 1831, in Constantinople, his home for the next thirty-four years. Energetic, warm, and out-going, Goodell was an effective leader who could infuse a spirit of cooperation into others.[2]

Goodell's associate, Harrison Gray Otis Dwight, was respected by colleagues as a man with "a fine mind excellently trained." [3] Along with Eli

---

Mahmud II. See also, Henry A. V. Post, *A Visit to Greece and Constantinople in the Year 1827–8* (New York: Sleight and Robinson, 1830), 342, 262–263; [James E. DeKay], *Sketches of Turkey in 1831 and 1832* (New York: J. & J. Harper, 1833), 237–238.

[2] Biographical sketches, arranged alphabetically, of all American Board personnel are to be found in Charles T. Riggs, "Near East Missionary Biographies," typescript, Istanbul, July 9, 1953, in Archives, UCBWM, Boston, Mass. See also, the DAB (21 Vols., New York: Charles Scribner's Sons, 1928–37), for sketches of Goodell, Dwight, and Schauffler.

[3] J. K. Greene quoted in Riggs, "Near East Mission Biographies."

Smith, he had just completed a survey of Asia Minor. Upon settling in Constantinople, Dwight continued the study of Armenian, a language which most Europeans regarded as "outlandish and barbarous in the extreme." [4] For many years he was one of the few Westerners who could use the language. Ordinarily reserved, he was possessed of a geniality and humor which enabled him to take "the discomforts, the strange notions, the unlooked obstacles, and the manifold absurdities of the oriental world . . . in a spirit that changed dross to gold." [5] His executive ability and sound judgment served the mission well.

The third member of the mission, William Gottlieb Schauffler, came from a German family that had migrated to southern Russia during the Napoleonic era. Recruited in the 1820's by an agent of the American Board, he made his way to Andover Seminary where he roomed with Dwight. An intense man, tall and erect, Schauffler was an accomplished linguist able to speak extemporaneously in six languages. Speaking with "percussive force," he moved audiences by his drive rather than by the eloquence of his delivery.[6]

Constantinople, the principal scene of mission work in Turkey in the 1830's, was a sprawling city with suburbs lining both sides of the Bosporus from the Marmara to the Euxine twenty miles distant. Americans sailing into the Golden Horn seldom failed to be impressed with the skyline, a "forest of domes, cupolas, and minarets." But the heart of the city, Stamboul, was closed to the Americans as a place of residence. Although this restriction was professionally inconvenient, it saved them from having to live in a quarter that was "dull and dreary, and disagreeable" where narrow, but paved, streets trapped the "pestiferous odors" of the city. The houses, generally of wooden construction, were jammed together, rendering the city vulnerable to devastating fires. Thus, American activity centered in the suburbs of Galata, Pera, Therapia and Buyuk Dere.[7]

Founded by traders from the Italian city states, Galata, across the Golden Horn from Stamboul, provided homes to many of the city's Greek residents as well as to foreign merchants. To the northeast of Galata, and separated from it by a stone wall with gates closed nightly, was Pera, dwelling place of the diplomatic corps and of most foreigners. Here, too, were the homes of many wealthy retired Armenian businessmen. By contrast, Therapia and Buyuk Dere were a dozen miles up the Bosporus on the European shore. "A dirty little Greek village prettily situated on a

4 H. G. O. Dwight to R. Anderson, July 17, 1834, in ABC 16.9, Vol. 2, #25, in American Board Papers, Houghton Library, Cambridge, Mass.

5 Cyrus Hamlin, *Among the Turks* (New York: Carter & Bros., 1878), 149.

6 "William G. Schauffler," in Riggs, "Near East Mission Biographies."

7 Post, *Visit to Greece and Constantinople*, 314–315; Edward Joy Morris, *Notes of a Tour through Turkey, Greece, Egypt, Arabia Petraea, to the Holy Land* . . . (2 Vols., Philadelphia: Carey & Hart, 1842), I, 41.

small bay," Therapia was the summer residence of Commodore David Porter, the American *chargé d'affaires*, who could not afford to live in the more fashionable village of Buyuk Dere where most of the European diplomatic corps maintained fine summer palaces.[8]

On his arrival in Constantinople, Goodell found the school his easiest entrée to the Christian community, and within six weeks he was organizing a large school on Lancastrian principles to serve the Greeks. A great fire in August, 1831, destroyed Pera and forced him to take quarters at Buyuk Dere, but he pushed ahead, encouraging the Greek community to found schools of its own. He discovered many Greeks moderately interested in promoting education and a few who were already familiar with the Lancastrian concept, a fact that facilitated his work immeasurably. Goodell particularly stressed the value of a school for girls in which "reading, writing, grammar, geography and arithmetic as well as needle work" should be taught, and in 1834 he was able to begin a girls' school at Pera, the first such in the capital. Despite a dearth of money and teachers, within a year over twenty Lancastrian schools were established by the Greek community with varying degrees of assistance from Goodell.[9]

In the role of educator, Goodell functioned chiefly as administrator and promoter and only incidentally as teacher. Recognizing that pervasive poverty limited the native's capacity to support schools, he sought supplementary funds from his mission board as well as from European diplomats and merchants residing in the capital. Indeed, he succeeded in getting both moral and financial aid from Commodore Porter, as well as from the Russian, Spanish, and British ambassadors. Generous support from Henry Eckford, an American shipbuilder in the employ of the Sultan, was cut off by his premature death in November, 1832. Goodell also performed a vital function by translating textbooks and editing teaching materials for the schools. During these years Goodell expressed a professional atttiude toward education. Though he exploited the novelty of such "philosophical apparatus" as orrerys and Leyden jars, he must be accounted a pioneer in introducing the elements of Western science to the Ottoman capital through a series of related public lectures using this equipment.[10]

Goodell was equally successful in establishing rapport with Turkish leaders. His previous experience in Beirut had taught him to avoid engaging natives in polemic discussions. As his arrival coincided with Mahmud

[8] [DeKay], *Sketches of Turkey*, 92, 102; Henry A. S. Dearborn, *A Memoir on the Commerce and Navigation of the Black Sea and the Trade and Maritime Geography of Turkey and Egypt* (2 Vols., Boston: Wells & Lilly, 1819), I, 173 ff.

[9] Goodell to Anderson, July 21, and Nov. 5, 1831, both in ABC 16.9, Vol. 1, #136 and #126; [DeKay], *Sketches of Turkey*, 398-399, is an eyewitness account by a visitor.

[10] Goodell to Anderson, Jan. 23, 1832, in ABC 16.9, Vol. 1, #129; [DeKay], *Sketches of Turkey*, 288.

II's efforts at introducing Western reforms into his army, the Turks were receptive to his techniques of education. When in October, 1832, the Seraskier Pasha, the Ottoman minister of defense, expressed interest in the Lancastrian system, Goodell responded by saying that he would "as readily provide globes, maps, etc., for them, as for the Christian sects." Nearly a year passed before the Turks established the first of several Lancastrian schools for their officers. Goodell, who by this time had a good knowledge of Turkish, reported he was "*pressed,* and *crowded,* and *urged on* by the Turks" to adapt lesson materials and textbooks from English to Turkish. The opportunity to be of service was so appealing that other mission personnel were pressed into service. As an adequate geography of Turkey did not exist, H. G. O. Dwight began to compile one in English from such reference books as were available locally. While one native assistant translated Dwight's manuscript into Armenian, another produced a version in Greek. Subsequently a third translator prepared a Turkish text from the Greek.[11]

Throughout the rest of the 1830's there was a high level of mutual respect and exchange between Turkish officials and the American missionaries. Ahmed Pasha, director of the Military Academy at Dolma Baktchè, and a colleague, Azim Bey, were pronounced "as fine young men, as I have ever seen," by Goodell. "They are very affable in conversation and gentlemanly in their appearance; and on the subject of education they are full of fire and enthusiasm." [12] Azim Bey reciprocated the goodwill. While he might have regarded assistance from Christians as offensive to his Moslem pride, he welcomed the aid, and he consulted on the methods of education. The officers were especially interested in the electrostatic machines, Leyden jars, and globes that the Americans made available. The Turks inquired as to how to present topographical features on maps and how to repair quadrants. Outwardly amused at their naïveté and inwardly pleased with the attention, Goodell observed: "They imagine that we know and are able to do almost everything." [13] While the Turks were proceeding along this path independently, their acquaintance with Western civilization was so slight that the help rendered by Goodell and Dwight must be reckoned as among the more important sustained cultural contacts with the West during the 1830's.

Simultaneously with this work among the Turks, Goodell and Dwight began laboring among the Armenians. Initially the Armenian leaders were polite but aloof, and the dislocations resulting from the 1831 fire added to the difficulties of reaching them. Not until 1834 were Goodell and Dwight

[11] Goodell, "Journal," Oct. 22, 1832, in ABC 16.9, Vol. 1, #131; Goodell to W. Schauffler, Aug. 27, 1833, in *ibid.,* #107; Goodell to Anderson, Oct. 2, 1833, in *ibid.,* #174.

[12] Goodell to David Urquart, Jan. 29, 1834, in *ibid.,* #180.

[13] Goodell, "Journal," Apr. 9, 1836, in *ibid.,* #118.

able to make a beginning among them. Their chief effort was directed toward organizing a high school, then still a novel institution in the United States. The school held its first session late in October, 1834, sharing quarters with the Goodell family at Pera. It boasted one large assembly hall (thirty-two feet by sixteen feet), where all the students assembled for morning and evening prayers and for general lectures, and five recitation rooms. The curriculum placed a heavy emphasis on languages: English, French, Italian, ancient Greek, Armenian, and Turkish. In addition, instruction was given in grammar, composition, arithmetic, geometry, and geography. In what would have been an innovation even in America, bookkeeping was taught, and lectures were given in the natural sciences. The students, exclusively boys, boarded at home. The faculty consisted of a variety of Europeans and natives who taught one or more courses. Dwight and Goodell gave the lectures on natural sciences and filled in at other courses as the need arose. By and large they hoped to "raise up" educated and enlightened teachers and clergy who would serve the next generation of their peoples. With pride the mission boasted that the school was more like a college than any other institution in Greece or the Levant.[14]

This "high school" was short-lived. The acclaim it won led the Armenian community in 1836 to organize a school at nearby Haskoy. Operating on Lancastrian lines with separate classes for boys and girls, the Armenian school accommodated nearly five hundred youth and was staffed in part by native teachers originally with the American school. As the new Armenian school functioned in sympathy with the educational and evangelical principles of the missionaries, the latter closed their high school in 1837. Then, to the chagrin of the mission, the Armenian hierarchy objected to the evangelical tone of the school at Haskoy and forced its closing in 1838. This experience indicated to the Americans that if they were to impart a lasting influence in Turkey, long-term American direction of schools was essential.[15]

Opportunities to work with the Armenians elsewhere in Turkey were followed up. As a result of the explorations of Dwight and Smith, mission stations and schools for Armenians in the interior of Asia Minor were projected. Existing native schools were judged "mere relics, the wrecks of better times." Their books were in classical rather than vernacular forms of the language; methods of instruction were regarded as "centuries" behind those in the United States. Accordingly each mission station was to

[14] Goodell and H. G. O. Dwight to Anderson, June 23, 1832, in *ibid.*, #103; Goodell to Anderson, Apr. 22, 1837, in *ibid.*, #123; H. G. O. Dwight, *Christianity Revived in the East* (New York: Baker and Scribner, 1850), 34. Schauffler, Goodell, Homes and Dwight to Anderson, Mar. 1, 1836, in ABC 16.9, Vol. 1, #119.

[15] Goodell to Anderson, Apr. 22, 1837, in *ibid.*, #123; Dwight, *Christianity Revived*, 52, 63.

develop "a model school" to be placed under the instruction of a well-educated schoolmaster sent from the United States; he was also to take the oversight of "a constellation of native schools." By the end of the 1830's, mission stations and supporting schools, all at the elementary level, were spread across Asia Minor from Trebizond at the eastern end of the Black Sea to Urumia, Persia, near the Turkish frontier, to Caesarea (Kayseri) in the interior of Anatolia and Tarsus in the South.[16]

A fourth group among whom the Americans began to work in the 1830's were the Nestorians. Located north of Mosul along the Persian-Turkish border between Lakes Van and Urumia, the Nestorians, numbering perhaps seventy thousand, were a church-centered ethnic group. Their language was Syriac, a dialect of ancient Aramaic. Some of them lived in Persia on fertile plains to the west of Lake Urumia; the greater number, however, lived hidden away amid the "inaccessible cliffs, deep hollows and precipitous rocks" of eastern Turkey. The chief figure in undertaking educational work among them was Justin Perkins.[17]

Characterized as being "uniformly polished" and possessing "courtly manners," Perkins had an "iron will and a robust constitution." He needed them. His voyage to Malta with his bride, Charlotte, was pleasant enough, marred only by the profanity of the crew, and the passage to Constantinople passed without incident. But the trip to Ooroomia (Urumia) proved a nightmare. An old American slaver that had been captured by the British carried the Perkinses through the Black Sea to Trebizond. Because the direct caravan route via Erzerum to Tabriz was imperiled by bandits, the Perkinses chose the longer way through Russian Georgia. Charlotte Perkins, no horsewoman and pregnant, must have been particularly uncomfortable as they jogged along for eight weeks. When at last the young couple reached the Russian frontier, they encountered the first of repeated acts of harassment by Russian officials. For two weeks they were assigned to quarantine, "a hollow, on the bank of a small muddy brook." The scarce food was often unpalatable, the milk generally sour and the eggs "far more than stale." Baggage inspection in the Tsarist custom house, "complete with a minute and ribald inspection of Charlotte's underwear," took a full day; after this inspection, a drunken inspector directed that most of the luggage would have to go back to Turkey.

With no choice but compliance, the Perkinses parted with their baggage and wearily hastened on to the Russian-Persian border, seven days away. At the border they learned their passports must be sent to Erivan,

16 Prudential Committee to W. Jackson *et al.*, Nov. 28, 1835, in ABC 8.1, Vol. 2, pp. 159.
17 Julius Richter, *A History of Protestant Missions in the Near East* (New York: Fleming H. Revell, 1910), 292–294; Eli Smith and H. G. O. Dwight, *Missionary Researches in Armenia: Including a Journey Through Asia Minor, and into Georgia and Persia* (2 Vols., London: George Wightman, 1834), II, 218 ff.

through which they had passed five days earlier, to be endorsed. While a messenger took the documents, the Perkinses camped. "Clouds of sand" sifted through "every joint and seam of our tent, upon our beds, our provisions, and ourselves," Perkins recorded. By paying an exorbitant price, he and his wife managed to obtain "bread and melons, once in two or three days." After seven days of deepening despair, the messenger returned with the passports endorsed. They crossed the Persian frontier. The British ambassador to Persia, Sir John Campbell, having learned of their plight, sent an English doctor to meet them and accompany them to Tabriz. Three days after their arrival Charlotte bore a daughter. Complications followed: convulsions and vomiting. Miraculously she recovered. The young husband noted: "It were grateful to offer a passing tribute to female fortitude in the missionary enterprise, might a husband be allowed to do it." [18]

For a year the Perkinses marked time in Tabriz until in the fall of 1835 they were joined by Asahel and Judith Grant. While Justin Perkins remained with the two women at Tabriz, Asahel Grant went on to Ooroomia to establish a home. At the end of November Grant summoned the waiting party. The Perkinses and Mrs. Grant arrived in a storm, wet and cold; their house, built of earthen bricks, was not yet finished. In the warmer of the sleeping rooms, barley from the straw mixed in the mud-bricks grew from the walls, while in the unheated rooms frost stiffened the bedclothes.[19]

Thus the mission to the Nestorians began. Perkins' first task, to master the native dialect, was a formidable one, for the Syriac vernacular had not yet been reduced to writing. In time he became one of the most eminent of Syriac scholars, producing some eighty works either as author or translator. A man of many talents, Perkins, in January, 1836, opened a Lancastrian school at Urumia, the first in that part of the Near East. Lacking slates and pencils, Perkins, with Yankee ingenuity, had his students write their letters with their fingers in boxes of sand and work arithmetic on an abacus. Like Goodell, Perkins aroused curiosity with a static electricity generator and a Leyden jar. With this equipment, supplemented by a microscope and orrery, he introduced the Nestorians to Western science.[20]

The achievements of the 1830's were uneven. Work with the Greeks and Turks was short-lived. In the former case the hostility of the Greek Orthodox clergy led to a breakdown between the Greeks and the Americans. Ironically, Americans responding to the Greek interest in education

---

[18] Justin Perkins, *A Residence of Eight Years in Persia Among the Nestorian Christians* (New York: M. W. Dodd, 1843), *passim*.

[19] Thomas Laurie, *Dr. Grant and the Mountain Nestorians* (3d ed., Boston: Gould and Lincoln, 1856) uses Grant's correspondence. See also, Perkins, *Eight Years in Persia*, 285.

[20] *Ibid.*, 250 ff.

were unable to sponsor schools which did not offend Greek sensibilities. Greek parents protested that while the American schools incorporated prayers in their programs, they omitted the sign of the cross. Goodell, adopting a laissez-faire policy, allowed his native teachers to cross or not to cross themselves as they pleased, but such permissiveness and his failure to enjoin students under pain of punishment "to keep the fasts, go to church, kiss the pictures, pray to saints, etc.," disturbed the Orthodox.[21]

At Smyrna, Greek clergy were even less cordial than in Constantinople, and as early as 1834 their hostility resulted in the closing of American schools. When missionary-teachers sought the intervention of the American legation, William Goodell counselled that such action would do more harm than good. The *coup de grace* came in March, 1835, when a new Greek patriarch accused his predecessor of being Protestant and of using Lancastrian schools to turn the Greek church in a Protestant direction. Such opposition generally was directed by and toward specific individuals and was sporadic. But in the early 1840's the Americans abandoned any concerted effort to work with the Greeks.[22]

Cooperation with the Turks died out gradually as both parties were diverted by other interests. Goodell in the late 1830's turned from educational work to resumption of the major activity of his life, translation of the Bible into Turkish. Having secured initial help for their schools, Turkish educators felt able to continue on their own. Furthermore, as Turkey was unable to enlist English aid against Mehemet Ali in the early 1830's, the country increasingly fell under Russian influence, and its interest in things "English" lessened. Close ties with the Greeks and Turks were never reestablished.

· II ·

The rapidly changing political and social milieu of the Ottoman Empire in the 1840's and 1850's substantially altered the position of American educational work during these two decades. Official interest in Western society was reflected in changes which were more apparent at Constantinople than in the interior. As streets were repaved, European phaetons came into wide use by men of rank who hitherto had gone abroad only afoot or on horseback. Steamships and telegraph lines began to link Constantinople with Europe, multiplying the frequency and intensity of contacts between East and West.[23]

[21] Goodell, "Journal," Dec. 20, 1832, in ABC 16.9, Vol. 1, #132.
[22] Goodell to Anderson, Mar. 6, 1835, in *ibid.*, #207; D. Temple to Anderson, Sept. 5, 1836, in *ibid.*, Vol. 3, #42.
[23] Joint Letter, Jan. 13, 1839, in ABC 16.7.1, Vol. 3.

Although Turkey was momentarily convulsed in 1839 by the annihilation of its army, the defection of its fleet, the bankruptcy of the state, and the death of Sultan Mahmud, reform continued to be the order of the day. Looking "faint and weary" and seemingly lacking the "original and noble traits" of Mahmud, Abdul Medjid, a sixteen-year-old youth, succeeded to the throne. The new Sultan was sympathetic to reform, in which he was encouraged by the English. Awaking to the importance of a friendly, independent Ottoman Empire, England took the lead in reestablishing the Sultan's authority in Syria and exerted strong pressure in behalf of reforms calculated to strengthen the Ottoman Empire. In 1839 Mahmud issued the Hatt-i-Sherif of Gulhané in which he promised to give equal treatment to all subjects and to bring the administration of justice and the collection of taxes into line with European practice. Further reforms, notably a new penal code and major educational measures, were instituted by Reshid Pasha, his Grand Vizier.[24]

The interest of the Ottoman government in reform should have facilitated the philanthropic work of the Americans. In fact the missionaries, in their evangelical role, provoked bitter opposition from the Armenian hierarchy. Although it was not the design of the missionaries to found a separate church, the reforms which they espoused threatened the traditions and practices of the Gregorian Church. In 1839 a small body of converts formed the Armenian Evangelical Union. While this group worshiped in the Protestant fashion, it was not formally organized as a Church. Efforts of the Gregorian hierarchy to suppress the evangelicals were delayed as attention was diverted by Turkey's political and military tribulations, but sporadic persecutions followed, during which the Americans enlisted the diplomatic assistance of Protestant governments to pressure the Porte into curbing the Gregorian Church. Finally, in 1846 the Armenian Patriarch at Constantinople excommunicated those Armenians who worshiped in the reformed fashion of the Americans. The excommunicated individuals, subjected to "expulsions from family, stripes, imprisonments, loss of property, banishments, etc.," [25] responded by organizing an Evangelical Church in July, 1846. Soon Protestant churches were founded elsewhere in Turkey and Syria and eventually in Persia. Thereafter American religious and philanthropic efforts were concentrated on this small, struggling Protestant minority.

The creation of a Protestant organization had immediate political reper-

[24] Cyrus Hamlin to Anderson, Nov. 1, 1839, in *ibid.*, Vol. 4, #232. Dwight, *Christianity Revived*, 80–81, presents a resident's recollection of these events.

[25] ABCFM, *Annual Report*, 1846, 95; Dwight, *Christianity Revived*, 189 ff. William G. Schauffler, *Autobiography of William G. Schauffler For Forty-nine Years a Missionary in the Orient*, ed. by his sons (New York: Anson D. F. Randolph & Co., 1887), 164.

cussions, for Ottoman Turkey had long administered the civil affairs of its Christian minorities through the agencies of their respective churches. If this Protestant community were to survive, the Turkish government had to be induced to provide for administration of its civil affairs. This was not easy to do without further offending the Gregorian Church or affording foreign powers an additional excuse for interfering in Ottoman affairs.[26]

Far from acknowledging the divisive effect of their activities, the American missionaries regarded themselves as champions of religious liberty in Turkey. Dabney Carr, the United States Minister to Turkey (1843–49), seeking to please the mission, gave wide currency to a passing remark of the Sultan that "Henceforth neither shall Christianity be insulted in my dominion, nor shall Christians be in any way persecuted for their religion." [27] This remark Carr interpreted as an unequivocal guarantee of religious liberty to American citizens in Turkey as well as to Ottoman subjects. If the statement did not distort the Sultan's view, it certainly went beyond the position his ministers were prepared to defend publicly, and the Porte sought unsuccessfully to deter Carr from distributing a circular publicizing this statement.[28]

The American government was too wrapped up in territorial expansion and slavery agitation to intercede in so remote an area, and a narrow, self-conscious application of the doctrine of separation of Church and State further restrained the State Department from championing the interests of the Protestant community. Unable to enlist their own government, the missionaries, led by William Schauffler and H. G. O. Dwight, spent a year courting the interest of the British Ambassador, Sir Stratford Canning. Once interested, Canning induced Abdul Medjid in November, 1847, to grant the Protestant Community the same rights hitherto enjoyed by the Roman Catholic, Greek Orthodox, and Armenian Gregorian minorities. Elated at this turn of events, American missionaries declared: "The gratitude of the Christian world is due to the English Ambassador, Sir Stratford Canning, for his intelligent, impartial and truly Christian course in relation to religious toleration in Turkey." [29]

The Ottoman government, while indifferent to the internal frictions within the Christian communities, looked with dismay at the rending of the political and social fabric of the State. That the Protestants depended

[26] Frank Edgar Bailey, *British Policy and the Turkish Reform Movement: A Study in Anglo-Turkish Relations, 1826–1853* (Cambridge: Harvard University Press, 1942), *passim.*

[27] D. Carr to J. Calhoun, Dec. 7, 1844, in Despatches, Turkey, Vol. 10, General Records of the Dept. of State, Rec. Group 59, National Archives, Washington, D.C.

[28] D. Carr to Calhoun, Mar. 5, 1845, in *ibid.*

[29] ABCFM, *Annual Report*, 1846, 97; see also, Schauffler, *Autobiography*, 186–187.

for protection upon Great Britain did little to sweeten the cause of religious liberty. Rather the Ottoman government protested officially that the American missionaries were subservient to British policy.[30] Consequently when the Gregorians and Orthodox vented their spleen in attacks on native converts, native schools, or American missionaries and teachers, the Turks manifested their frustrations by biding their time in bringing the malefactors to justice.

American educational work, though modified by this turn of events, continued and expanded. From being primarily an instrument with which to gain access to native homes, the schools became a prerequisite to the survival of the Protestant community. The Americans assisted the native congregations in organizing elementary schools, while they directly undertook to develop a generation of Protestant leaders in the secondary schools. Although the Americans were cut off from the Gregorian community generally, within the ranks of the Armenian evangelicals they functioned more intensively than ever before.

On Cyrus Hamlin fell the responsibility for directing the most important educational work of the American Board during the 1840's and 1850's. As a boy in Maine he had shared the "rigorous life" of his poor and religious farm parents. A term of apprenticeship as a silversmith left its impress, as Hamlin ever after took delight in mechanical gadgets. He was further differentiated from his colleagues in that he was a graduate of Bowdoin College and Bangor Seminary. Full of humor and anecdotes, Hamlin was as resourceful as he was indefatigable. He could also be quick-tempered and impulsive. Uncompromising in his methods, quick to assume responsibility, willing to try the unorthodox, and no less devoted to the gospel than his colleagues, Hamlin developed a broader, more incisive understanding of the role of education than they.[31]

Hamlin arrived in Turkey in the winter of 1838–39, at a moment when the American Board, strapped for funds by the depression, was redefining its views of missions and education under the strong leadership of Rufus Anderson, its secretary. Pointedly Hamlin was reminded that he would always be "a foreigner, an alien" in Turkey. "You can never become perfectly master of the idioms of their languages, nor of their habits of thought and feeling. You can never find the avenues to the heart like a native," Anderson added. As a corollary, Hamlin was instructed to watch for promising young men who might be trained for leadership. At the same time he was directed to improve the existing schools in preference to founding new ones. But the imperative need of schools congenial to evan-

---

[30] J. Brown to J. Buchanan, Mar. 1, 1846, in Despatches, Turkey, Vol. 10.

[31] Hamlin, *Among the Turks*, 207. As a student at Bowdoin, Hamlin designed and built a working model of a steam engine, reputedly the first steam engine in the state of Maine.

gelical doctrines led Hamlin and the mission to override the strictures of the Board.[32]

In the fall of 1840 Hamlin launched his first major educational venture, the Bebek Seminary. With the failure of the Armenian-operated school which had supplanted the one founded by Goodell, the mission felt a need for a school under its own control. A boarding school was preferred to a day school, since it kept students in an environment structured by the mission and isolated from secular forces that might vitiate mission influence. Furthermore, as Americans were excluded from dwelling in Stamboul, day students would need to commute such long distances to reach Pera that the ravages of heat and cold, storms and plague would preclude systematic instruction.[33]

The risk of invidious comparison with a small, newly founded, but well-financed Jesuit school further underscored the need for operating a quality institution. As American funds were scarce, Hamlin had to start his boarding school on a shoestring. The Board paid for his premises and his salary, but all the other expenses had to be met by student fees. Principal, teacher, housefather, and business manager, he felt the pressures of close confinement. So demanding were his young charges, he could not in good conscience leave the school for more than a few minutes at a time. Nor could he find time to perfect his command of the native languages or literature. Undaunted, Hamlin purchased a property at Bebek, a suburb some five miles up the Bosporus on the European shore, as a permanent site for his school.

Hamlin's institution was notable for its emphasis on mathematics, physics, and chemistry, as well as for thorough instruction in English. The curriculum also included Bible study, moral philosophy, history, and geography. Hamlin wrote or translated several of the texts, at least one of which was adopted for use by Ottoman schools. The program was physically demanding, the day starting with prayers at 5:30 A.M. and the first recitation at six o'clock. After breakfast at a genteel seven, recitations carried through the morning hours. Afternoons and evenings were generally taken up with study.[34]

Hamlin's interests and contributions could not be contained within the bounds of traditional academic programs. His interest in science and technology found expression in several ways. At the Bebek institution Hamlin introduced a self-help program, then fashionable in the United States. Securing funds from an English engineer in Constantinople, he established a shop in which students made sheet iron stoves, the first of their kind in

[32] Prudential Committee to Hamlin, Dec. 1838, in ABC 8.1, Vol. 3, #3.

[33] Hamlin to Anderson, Oct. 1, 1840, in ABC 16.7.1, Vol. 4, #216.

[34] Cyrus Hamlin, *My Life and Times* (Boston: Congregational Sunday School and Publishing Society, 1893), 246.

Constantinople, and other assorted metal articles. These were sold, the profits being used to clothe the poorer boys. With twenty-five boys in his school requiring financial assistance, Hamlin found that as a practical matter only one or two could be taught any single skill lest by competing with one another they would destroy their market. The need of teaching a variety of crafts made the program expensive. As the established forms of merchandising and crafts had been preempted by the orthodox Greeks and Gregorians, Hamlin directed his students toward crafts that were relatively new and not dependent for economic aid upon the established bankers. Thus, even though cut off from direct contact with the Turks, Greeks, and Gregorians, Hamlin became a force in introducing new technology to Turkey.[35]

To counteract the growing poverty among the Armenian Protestants, Hamlin afforded them relief by establishing a modern steam-powered flour mill and a bakery. The operation of flour mills and public ovens by educational institutions was a common practice in Constantinople, and Ottoman law exempted foreign institutions from the petty restrictions which hampered native-owned mills and bakeries. Because of Hamlin's inexperience, the capital requirements far exceeded his original estimate. Fortunately, some of the needed money was advanced by a British banker in Constantinople, while the remaining funds came as a personal loan by a member of the American Board. When the original fittings for the engine proved defective, Hamlin resourcefully cast his own. Having completed the mill and oven, he was balked temporarily by a series of circumstances which made operation of the mill financially prohibitive. This time the fortuitous outbreak of the Crimean War rescued Hamlin from his embarrassments, as the British military became the chief patron of his bakery. Ironically, Hamlin, an ardent temperance man, discovered his most successful product, a yeast bread, was known as *bira* (beer) bread. Demand varied, but production at times reached the rate of eight thousand pounds per day.[36]

Hamlin's contacts with British military personnel led him to other ventures. Appalled at the filth and discomfort which characterized the British military hospitals in Constantinople, Hamlin officiously decided to ease the condition of the sick and wounded by organizing a laundry that would rehabilitate their vermin-infested clothing and bedding. Opposition to this proposal from British hospital commanders was overcome by a successful appeal to higher authority. Hamlin's plan to provide employment to Armenian, Greek, and Turkish housewives nearly foundered when the women refused to touch the clothes and neighbors protested at the stench. The inventive Yankee saved the day by designing a washing

[35] *Ibid.*, 264–265.
[36] *Ibid.*, 296, 323.

machine fabricated from an old beer cask. Constructed and in operation within a day, the machine spared the sensibilities of the women and transformed the clothes.[37]

During the late 1840's and 1850's, Hamlin also assisted a handful of Armenians in going to the United States to seek specialized training. In general he preferred that natives remain at home, but when restive souls, frequently former students, indicated they were going abroad with or without his approval, Hamlin often went out of his way to assist. He advised on crafts they might profitably pursue and directed them to acquaintances in the United States who might arrange work-training for them. Fearing that American Board officials might look askance at his activity, Hamlin assured them that "Our young men must push boldly into the very forefront of the most difficult mechanical enterprises . . . or the community can never rise from its state of pauperism." [38]

Through his interest in technology, Hamlin reached the Turkish population as well as the Protestant Armenians. As early as 1839, Hamlin's study was the scene of a demonstration of Samuel F. B. Morse's still imperfect telegraph apparatus. Nearly a decade later, when J. Lawrence Smith, an American working for the Sultan, sought to demonstrate the telegraph instrument to the Sultan, Hamlin repaired the devices, which had been damaged in transit. With only three days' practice in mastering the code, he joined Smith at the Beylerbey Palace to demonstrate the instruments. With great delight Hamlin asked the Sultan for a chair in which he might sit while transmitting a message, leaving the amused Sultan standing and his attendants aghast. The demonstration led to the tending of an award to Morse, the first from a foreign government. But Ottoman officials, not eager to have their every action reported almost instantaneously to the Porte, blocked the construction of telegraph lines until the military requirements of the Crimean War outweighed their personal objections. Generally, the Turks' comprehension of Western ways was severely restricted; they had not yet embraced the idea of progress, and many regarded mechanical skill and machines as the work of Satan. Hamlin's identification with modern technology was sufficiently established in Constantinople that he was introduced by one Turk to another as "the most *Satanic* man in the Empire." [39]

The time and energy which Hamlin accorded to the scientific curriculum at Bebek and to his miscellany of projects troubled his colleagues. Although recognizing the service he was performing, the mission protested that the size of the investment and the need for supervision, which

[37] *Ibid.*, 355–364.
[38] Hamlin to Anderson, July 11, 1853, in ABC 16.7.1, Vol. 12, #244.
[39] Hamlin, *Among the Turks*, 185–194, 58. Davison, *Reform in the Ottoman Empire*, 78, n. 97, observes that the term also connotes "ingenious, cunning, devilishly clever."

only Hamlin could provide, were at the expense of the Seminary. Furthermore, the oven, mill, and laundry, while producing handsome profits, could not be manned by needy students. In fact, the demands on Hamlin's time varied considerably, and his colleagues exaggerated the amount of distraction, while Hamlin underestimated it. In the end the mission asked him to lease or sell the mill and ovens. Hamlin accepted the mission's decision with good grace. To the surprise of his colleagues he found little difficulty in negotiating a profitable lease. Without question he was relieved to slough off the burdens; to make the break complete, he sought a leave in the United States before returning to the administration of his school.[40]

Hamlin's conduct of the Bebek school also generated controversy, particularly over the use of English for instruction. His views were well-matured and balanced. He regarded mastery of one's native language as of the highest importance. It was the "chief instrument of thought and expression." He took special pride in the fact that his institution helped in refining the Armenian language at a time when it was undergoing relatively rapid change and standardization.[41] However, he also insisted that the well-being of the Protestant community required that their leadership be acquainted with the rich treasure of the English language. He pointed out that Turkey, in the midst of the Tanzimat reforms, was adopting "European principles and modes of art, of government or war" and that even its religious notions were being "shaken out of their place." With increasing numbers of Turks going abroad and returning with European tastes and ideas, the Protestants, to hold their own, needed leaders who were acquainted with Western thought. Never could the mission make available in translation a sufficient variety of books to do the job.[42]

Other members of the mission and the American Board remained unconvinced. American Board experience in India and at Beirut had revealed that students often feigned an interest in mission activities in order to acquire a smattering of English and thereby qualify for a lucrative job in business or government rather than use their bilingual skills to serve the evangelical cause. The arrival in Turkey during the Crimean War of large numbers of English officers who paid four and five times the going rate for translators seemed further evidence. Hamlin's associates believed that the most prudent course would be to teach only in the vernacular and to limit the curriculum to courses having immediate utility for church workers, thus minimizing the student's opportunity to seek other employment.[43]

[40] Hamlin, *Life and Times*, 299.
[41] *Ibid.*, 250.
[42] Hamlin, "Educational Institutions," in ABC 16.7.1, Vol. 12, #269.
[43] Hamlin, *My Life and Times*, 250. See also, H. G. O. Dwight to Anderson, Aug. 6, 1851, in ABC 16.7.1, Vol. 11, #140, and Rufus Anderson, *Memorial Volume of the*

In the 1850's, Hamlin was a prophet crying in the wilderness. His colleagues were willing to concede that mission-trained clergy might be taught sufficient English to read Biblical commentaries and glosses, but they objected to the use of mission resources to promote general education. The Board, its funds once again contracting with the approach of a domestic depression, was compelled to review its programs critically, giving the initiative to those who looked askance at Hamlin's views and practices. Accordingly, in 1856 the mission decided to operate the Bebek school as a seminary only, dismissing those students in the general curriculum who failed to give evidence of the piety expected of a candidate for the ministry. Subsequently, the mission decided to limit instruction to the vernacular.

· III ·

Mission-sponsored education moved ahead, though somewhat less dramatically in other parts of Turkey during the 1840's and 1850's. As new mission stations were organized, elementary schools followed. Increasingly, the teachers were natives who had been trained either individually by a missionary or at the Bebek Seminary and were supervised in varying degrees by an American missionary. By 1860, mission stations were transmitting American educational ideas into the interior of Asia Minor to Brousa, Aintab, Aleppo, Marsovan, Mosul, and Erzerum. A seminary was founded in southeast Turkey at Aintab (Gaziantep), which in the 1850's was the second largest center of Protestantism in Turkey. In accordance with the new mission policy, the Aintab school admitted boys who had completed their elementary schooling and gave them enough secondary training to permit them to undertake ministerial studies. Both the Prudential Committee and the mission professed to be pleased with this "vernacular system" of education, for these youth were content to stay in the towns and villages of the interior. The provincial schools, like those in the capital, reached chiefly the Armenian population of Turkey.[44]

Work also continued among the Nestorians. In the 1850's, for example, George Whitefield Coan, taking over from Justin Perkins, was able to spread the influence of schools over a wide area, superintending seventy-two village schools with some eleven hundred pupils. Although Coan reached a wider area than Perkins, necessarily his contact with any one school was minimal. His role was less that of the professional educator

---

First Fifty Years of the ABCFM (Boston: The Board, 1861), 323 ff. The American Baptist Mission in India had the same experience with the use of English and switched to the use of the vernacular.

[44] Prudential Committee to Clark, Dec. 19, 1852, in ABC 8.1, Vol. 2, p. 315.

than of a rural community coordinator urging and organizing villagers to undertake what they would not otherwise attempt.[45]

The efforts of Americans to afford educational opportunities to women was of special importance. American Board personnel quickly perceived the sharp contrast between the status of American as opposed to Eastern women. American visitors in Constantinople in the early 1830's were told that Armenian schools admitted girls, but no one reported seeing one in a classroom. The most pointed criticism came from a missionary wife who took exception to customs by which girls generally married by their fifteenth year: She objected that women had no higher purpose than to minister to their husband's wants and gratification; that there was no concept of mutual duties or privileges; and that betrothal and marriage occurred without the consent of the girl, either asked or given. As mothers, such girls could provide only minimal physical care to their offspring.[46]

A start in affording educational opportunities for girls was made at Pera in April, 1833. Founded by William Goodell, this school continued under his oversight after he had divested himself of other educational activities. By the 1840's it had evolved into a girls' boarding school located for a time at Bebek, then at Pera. The curriculum was less advanced than that of the Bebek Seminary, but it included arithmetic, geography, and history, as well as sacred music. In the early years, for the convenience of American teachers and as an inducement to native students, instruction was offered in English. But once the school was well-established, English was replaced by the vernacular. It was hoped that the girls who attended the boarding school would become either church workers or wives of native pastors and evangelists.[47]

More famous, at least in its day, was Fidelia Fiske's school at Urumia. A niece of Pliny Fisk, she had exhibited unusual religious precosity as a child, reportedly having "perused with interest, if not with full understanding," Cotton Mather's *Magnalia* and Timothy Dwight's *Theology* by the time she was eight years old. At seventeen she became a district school teacher. Later she attended Mount Holyoke Seminary, becoming a teacher there after graduation. In 1843 Justin Perkins recruited her. The devout Miss Fiske took over a day school started by Judith Grant and remade it into a boarding school. The girls, she discovered, were "coarse, passionate, and quarrelsome." All were illiterate, incredibly dirty, and with no scruples against lying or stealing. To make an impact upon such "students," Miss Fiske decided that it would be necessary to board the

[45] John Hewitt, *Williams College and Foreign Missions* (Boston: Pilgrim Press, 1914), 319-324.
[46] A. Pratt to Anderson, May 23, 1853, in ABC 16.7.1, Vol. 14, #314. See also, [DeKay], *Sketches of Turkey*, 398-399.
[47] Dwight, *Christianity Revived*, 46-47, 144.

children away from their parents so as to have them under the continuous and exclusive care and training of their teachers.[48]

The persistent Miss Fiske started with two boarding pupils in the fall of 1843. To her young charges she was teacher, nurse, and housemother. The school prospered. In June, 1850, she was ready to exhibit her students. Parents as well as leaders of the native community were invited to an all day program. Three hours of public "examination" in the morning were followed by dinner for the whole group, 175 persons. Again four hours in the afternoon were passed in exercises, twenty of the girls reading compositions written for the occasion.[49]

The establishment of boarding schools for girls encountered far more resistance than the establishment of similar schools for boys, for both parents and girls were indifferent to the value of female education. Furthermore, the Americans kept the girls in school until they were seventeen or eighteen years of age, well beyond the traditional age for marriage among the Nestorians. Although only a handful of girls was enrolled in the boarding schools either at Constantinople or Urumia, the supposition that it was reasonable to provide girls with even a simple course of study was revolutionary.

· IV ·

Missionary philanthropy also employed the press and medical work, thus broadening the aspects of American culture introduced to Turkey. The American Board had not originally envisaged itself as a producer of textbooks, but as in Greece and in Syria, the need to promote literacy among evangelical Christians proved irresistible. Goodell and Dwight, in fact, began their editorial labors while the mission press was at Malta. After they founded the mission at Constantinople; the press was removed to the mainland. Smyrna was selected because it afforded easy access to supplies from abroad, while its distance from the capital protected it from undue official molestation.[50]

The secular output of the press was surprisingly large. For the Lancastrian schools, Goodell and Dwight translated the necessary materials from English into Turkish, Armenian, and Armeno-Turkish. Before the removal of the press to Smyrna in 1833 the demand was so urgent that these materials were produced by hand. After Goodell founded a high school, a

[48] Daniel T. Fiske, *The Cross and the Crown, or Faith Working by Love as Exemplified in the Life of Fidelia Fiske* (Boston: Congregational Sabbath School & Publishing Society, 1868), 123–128. The family of Pliny Fisk dropped the "e" in the last name.

[49] *Ibid.*, 238–239.

[50] Goodell to Temple and Smith, Oct. 16, 1832, in ABC 16.9, Vol. 1, #156.

variety of textbooks in spelling, geography, arithmetic, and moral science was required. The books frequently carried the American impact further than the mission schools, for they were employed in schools operated both by the Gregorian church and by the Turkish government. At Goodell's insistence the mission press was equipped with fonts of type suitable for printing works on algebra, geometry, and trigonometry. To further work with young children, an *Infant School Manual* of some 120 pages, adapted from the pioneer work of Lydia Child and designed for teachers, was published in 1841. At times during the 1830's such publications took precedence over the translating and publication of the scriptures. Although the American Board operated larger presses in other corners of the world, the Smyrna press led in the variety of secular works published. While the missionaries acceded to the pressure to produce texts and other secular works, they often did so with a sense of guilt.[51]

The mission also recognized the need to provide leisure reading material suitable for adults. Much of this literature consisted of pious tracts and such books as John Bunyan's *Pilgrim's Progress*, and Legh Richmond's *Dairyman's Daughter*. The emphasis on the translation of Western literature was promptly disputed by some members of the mission staff, as well as by some natives who argued that such works were as "nearly unintelligible to the Greeks or Turks as a Pelham novel would be to 'Split Log' or to 'Black Hawk.' " The critics urged that stories should be composed on the spot, filled with local allusions, and with story lines naturally arising out of the scenes and manners of the Near East. Write more and translate less, was the admonition.[52]

Efforts to produce magazines for the general public led to creation of material more directly geared to native interests. A start was made in 1837 with the *Magazine of Useful Knowledge*. First issued in Greek as a monthly for Orthodox Christians, it subsequently developed into a weekly and was published simultaneously in an Armenian edition under the name *Avedaper* (The Messenger). Both papers reached wider audiences than either the mission's preaching or educational work. While these papers had a heavy religious content, perhaps half the material consisted of popular articles of an entertaining or scientific nature. Such an emphasis had the support of David Greene, a secretary of the Board. Far more liberal than Rufus Anderson, Greene argued that the press made possible a system of free schools and universal education. He further urged pouring the "treasures of science and thought and refined sentiment into the languages of the Asian nations." [53]

[51] "Historical Catalogue," in ABC 16.7.1, Vol. 2, #71. See also, Anderson, *Memorial Volume*, 375.

[52] [DeKay], *Sketches of Turkey*, 286–287.

[53] David Greene, "The Employment of the Press in Promoting the Missionary Work," ABCFM, *Annual Report*, 1840, 50.

The secular activities forced the officers of the American Board at home to formulate, in 1832, an attitude toward the employment of the school and the press. In speaking of the role of the "Christian Philanthropists," the Prudential Committee emphasized that they were bound to make the exerting of a religious influence their grand object. "Whatever tends not directly to this result falls without our proper sphere. We cannot found a college for literary and scientific purposes; we cannot publish an arithmetic or a grammar, or a geography, unless so composed as to exert a religious influence, or unless such books belong necessarily to a system of school books framed expressly with reference to the advancement of religion." [54]

A decade later, when the American Board was smarting from a decline in revenues occasioned by the 1837 depression, the Prudential Committee warned the mission against too much use of the press. American churchgoers, the source of mission funds, were more interested in the account of a single conversion than in the record of a million pages printed and circulated. But for the most part, so long as publication work did not seriously restrict preaching nor unduly tax mission funds, the Board imposed few restraints. [55]

At the same time, those responsible for publication work looked forward to transferring it to native Christians at the earliest possible date. One factor was that the mission could thereby limit its investment in manpower, presses, and inventory. Further, its publications could avoid the stigma attaching to foreign authorship. Finally, as a patron of the native press, the mission could encourage native printers to improve their style. These views reflected an overall goal of achieving self-direction of the overseas work by the native community, while the mission, serving as a catalyst, would precipitate social and cultural change among the people with whom it worked. It sought to avoid creating permanent American institutions. [56]

This attitude manifested ambivalence rather than confusion or contradiction. The Board at home had the example of the good works of the domestic churches to justify support of social reform, but necessarily it was primarily concerned with raising funds. The mission abroad, in intimate contact with the local culture, recognized problems whose solutions demanded their attention. Its response foreshadowed the Social Gospel movement which gripped America in the late nineteenth century.

In the 1840's and 1850's the output of the press was often restricted because of limited funds, but the publications of these years were more sophisticated than those of the 1830's. After William Goodell and H. G.

54 Prudential Committee to Thomson *et al.*, Oct. 24, 1832, in ABC 8.1, Vol. 10.
55 Prudential Committee to Perkins *et al.*, Feb. 25, 1843, in *ibid.*, Vol. 3, #15.
56 "Minutes," Mar. 14, 1836, in ABC 16.9, Vol. 3, #2.

O. Dwight turned their literary talents to translations of the Bible, Cyrus Hamlin became the chief source of textbooks, most of which were pitched at a more advanced level than those of the earlier years. In addition to volumes on mathematics and science, he produced works on ethics.

The press in the 1840's for the first time experienced serious, though passing, objections from the Turks. In one instance Turkish authorities took exception to a printer's ornament which resembled a cross. In another they took offense at a volume on "morals," a subject they regarded as reserved to Islamic scholars. In general, Turkish officials approved, if reluctantly, works in Arabic and directed at Christians, but they banned those in Turkish. To some extent the growing restrictions on the press were designed to exclude from Turkey books published in England or on the Continent that were derogatory toward Islam. The Americans were but the incidental victims.[57]

By 1860 the mission press in Turkey, now transferred to Constantinople, had published over 120 different items. Some were original; most were translations; and these were often revised in content to perfect the vernacular translation. But the future prospects were grim. The depression of the late 1850's had reduced funds, not only from the Board but from the supporting Bible and Tract societies, while the increasing controversy over slavery diverted the attention and energies of Americans to domestic issues. By 1858 publication of new works had halted as a means of conserving funds for schools and evangelism; prospects for resumption of publication were still uncertain in 1861.

The American Board's printing operations in India, Hawaii, and Ceylon were more extensive than those in the Near East. By 1860 the press in Turkey, with a production of 191,000,000 pages, far surpassed those at Beirut and Urumia, with outputs totaling 28,000,000 and 15,000,000 pages respectively. From a missionary viewpoint, production of the Arabic Bible was by far the most important achievement of the overseas presses.[58]

In the field of medicine the mission evinced an early, though superficial, interest. Sanitary conditions in the Near East were primitive, and large areas of the interior were completely lacking in medical facilities. The high death rate among mission personnel, particularly the wives and children, was a source of great concern to the Board. Many brides scarcely survived their honeymoons. Parents felt a sense of helplessness as their children sickened and died, the parents ignorant of the nature of their ailment and the nearest doctor as much as five hundred miles distant. Even

[57] "Journal," in ABC 16.7.1, Vol. 4, #209. "Report of Freedom of the Press," in *ibid.*, Vol. 3, #109. See also, ABCFM, *Annual Report*, 1844, 250.
[58] H. G. O. Dwight to Anderson, July 9, 1858, in ABC 16.7.1, Vol. 11, #286.

self-imposed quarantines lasting commonly from three to six months in a year proved ineffective.[59]

In an effort to protect mission personnel, medical doctors were assigned to the principal mission stations. Inevitably they were called upon to serve the local population, and gradually a concept of medical work as a form of philanthropy took shape. Asa Dodge, the first missionary doctor in the Near East, arrived in 1833 and was assigned to Syria. Before he died three years later, he had performed some fifty cataract operations.[60]

More important was the work of Asahel Grant, a colleague of Justin Perkins at Urumia. Believing that "the healing art . . . might procure favour and protection," the Board sent Doctor Grant to the Nestorians. He proved to be one of the most colorful figures in the mission movement. What he lacked in height, he more than made up in energy, enthusiasm, and daring. Much of his career hinged on his single-minded belief that the Nestorians were descendants of one of the Lost Tribes of Israel. His conviction was not shared by his colleagues, much less his critics, but it drove Grant repeatedly into the mountains west of Urumia to search out the main centers of the Nestorian people.[61]

In 1839, accompanied by two Persian Nestorians, a Kurdish muleteer, and a Turkish cavass, or guard, Grant entered the mountain fastness of the Nestorians on muleback. His medical skill enabled him to win the favor of a Kurdish chieftain who, a few years earlier, had murdered a European attempting to enter the area. Subsequently, Grant spent five weeks with the Nestorian Patriarch; on his departure he received a pair of scarlet *shahwars*, wide trousers trimmed with silk, and one of the ancient manuscripts of the country. Grant quickly became well acquainted with the customs and character of the Nestorians.

In his medical practice Grant sought to avoid competing with native doctors. Rather he gave them samples of his medicines, hoping that they would emulate his methods. He also lent some of his instruments to be used as patterns, so that they could be similarly equipped. Following the custom of the United States, Grant took a native youth as an apprentice in order to teach him the elements of Western medicine. In his use of poultices and bleeding in the treatment of patients, Grant was only a step or two ahead of Oriental medicine, but as a surgeon he brought dramatic relief to persons suffering from cataracts.

Grant reached large numbers of patients, ten thousand in his first year,

[59] For example, Prudential Committee to G. Whiting *et al.*, Jan. 18, 1840, in ABC 8.1, Vol. 3, #9; H. G. O. Dwight to Anderson, Aug. 22, 1853, in ABC 16.7.1, Vol. 11, #229.
[60] "Asa Dodge," in Riggs, "Near East Missionary Biographies."
[61] Asahel Grant, *The Nestorians: or the Lost Tribes* (New York: Harper, 1841), 17. This section also draws on Laurie, *Dr. Grant and the Mountain Nestorians.*

but professional life was hard. Patients, having received directions, asked a thousand questions: "Must the milk allowed for diet be that of a goat, sheep, buffalo, ass or cow; and if the latter, what must be her color?" For according to native lore, milk of a white cow was cold, and that of a red one, hot. For analogous reasons, they inquired what must be the sex of the chicken used to make the broth prescribed.[62]

Personal life was still harder. Though a sturdy man inured to hardship, Grant within a few weeks of his arrival contracted an "intermittent fever," followed shortly by a severe case of cholera from which he only partially recovered. His wife, Judith, an intelligent, well-educated girl with much to offer by way of leadership, was first blinded in one eye by ophthalmia and then died in January, 1839. Her twin daughters died a year later.

After the death of his wife and two daughters, Grant returned to the United States briefly. He found a foster home for his four-year-old son, Henry; tended to the last details of a book on the Nestorians; persuaded the American Board to found a new mission station at Mosul; and headed back to the Mountain Nestorians. Everything went wrong. Two couples, the Hinsdales and Mitchells, were to join him at Mosul, but the Mitchells both died en route to Mosul, and by the end of 1842 Abel Hinsdale was dead. Undeterred, Grant went ahead with plans to found a base in the Kurdish mountains. At Ashitha he bought a site and began building. But unfortunately his activities only increased the jealousy of Kurdish tribesmen, who had long-standing quarrels of their own with the Nestorians. Furthermore, Ottoman authorities, suspecting Grant of stirring a Nestorian separatist movement, gave their blessing to a Kurdish attack on the Nestorians. Grant managed to escape to Mosul before it was too late, but the Mountain Nestorians were decimated.

Grant was bitterly disappointed in his failure. Candidly, even eloquently, he recorded his feelings: "to return there [to the Mountain Nestorians] is in no way inviting to flesh and blood. All the romance of that field—if there ever were any—is now sober reality. There is no poetry in winding your weary way over rocks and cliffs, drifted snows or dashing torrents . . . I frankly confess that, when in peril, the thought that, should I fall, many will only say, 'I told you so,' and hand down my dishonored memory as the only heritage of my children, and an injury to the cause of Christ, has caused me much distress. But be it so." [63] But more disappointments awaited Grant. The young wife of his newest colleague, Thomas Laurie, died in December, followed early in the new year by the death of the infant son of the Hinsdales. And then on April 22, 1844,

[62] *Ibid.,* 64–65.

[63] Quoted in David H. Finnie, *Pioneers East: The Early American Experience in the Middle East* (Cambridge: Harvard University Press, 1967), 239–240.

Grant himself died of typhus brought into his home by Nestorian refugees.

Although Grant had demonstrated a means of disseminating to natives what he knew of Western medicine, his successors held back. Azariah Smith, trained at Yale Medical School as well as at Yale Divinity School, possessed catholic interests. For five years, 1843–48, he practiced in various towns of Turkey before settling down in Aintab. Bold and tireless, he made a special study of cholera, perfecting a remedy of his own that colleagues regarded as efficacious, although there is no evidence that it was widely adopted by others. It is a mark of this period that Smith, rather than focus his energies on the practice of medicine, traveled for a time with Austen Henry Layard on his pioneer archaeological surveys and that he wrote papers on meteorology, antiquities, and natural history for the *American Journal of Science*.[64] Likewise his successor, Andrew T. Pratt, trained at the College of Physicians and Surgeons in New York, while regarded as a good physician, developed into an outstanding Turkish scholar. Eventually he gave up medical work to concentrate his abilities on his translation of the Bible.[65]

Much the same course of events characterized medical work among the Nestorians. Henry Lobdell, an ordained clergyman and medical doctor, was assigned to Mosul, but he found it too much, suffering from fever three times during his first summer there and dying at that city three years later at the age of twenty-eight. In that brief span, however, Doctor Lobdell and a missionary associate, Dwight Marsh, kept alive the American contact with this remote spot and helped to acquaint Americans with it by transmitting to Amherst College a remarkable collection of coins, cylinders, bricks, and sculpture from Nineveh and Babylon, one of the first such collections in America.[66]

By and large the doctors followed the bidding of the American Board in playing down their medical skills. They were early enjoined to regard their medical practice "only as a means of furthering the spiritual objects of the mission." In taking this stand the Board expressed concern that extensive medical work attracted undue attention and questioned whether "great notoriety is ordinarily desirable" among a population which knows little of the real objects of the mission.[67] The chief value of the medical work was in gaining access to homes otherwise closed to the mission. In these circumstances, medical work never developed on the scale that

[64] "Azariah Smith," in Riggs, "Near East Missionary Biographies."

[65] "Andrew T. Pratt," in *ibid*. George F. Herrick, *An Intense Life: A Sketch of the Life and Work of Rev. Andrew T. Pratt, M.D., 1852–1872* (New York: Fleming H. Revell, [1890]).

[66] "Dwight Marsh," in Riggs, "Near East Missionary Biographies." Henry Lobdell, *Memoir of Rev. Henry Lobdell, M.D.*, W. S. Tyler, ed. (Boston: American Tract Society, 1859).

[67] Prudential Committee to Holladay *et al.*, Dec. 31, 1836, in ABC 8.1, Vol. 2, #194.

schools did, nor did any doctor during this period develop a professional pride in his specialty comparable to that of William Goodell, Cyrus Hamlin, or Homan Hallock in theirs.

· V ·

The growth of Christian philanthropy in Syria and Turkey was made possible by the development of a bureaucracy quite different from that which supported American relief work in Greece. As a pioneer in overseas philanthropy, the American Board quickly developed an organization that balanced the need for centralized policy-making with a high degree of local autonomy. The Board was incorporated in Massachusetts in 1812, and the ultimate authority lay with its Annual Meeting attended by clergymen and laymen from the three churches for which the Board acted: Congregational, Presbyterian, and Reformed. In practice, decision-making was generally exercised by the Prudential Committee, a body chosen by the Annual Meeting from among interested laymen and clergy living chiefly in the Boston area. In the very early days, meetings of this committee tended to be informal, being called on as little as one day's notice. Beginning in 1832 it met weekly. But while recognizing that it was only "*an agent* for its patrons," the Committee counselled that ordinarily the patrons "will be slow to condemn . . . and slower still to dictate what the proceedings will be." [68]

The day-to-day administration devolved upon several secretaries, who exercised a decisive influence both on the course of missionary work and on the philanthropic enterprises. They helped determine the priorities for the work, recruited personnel, and allocated funds. The secretaries drafted instructions for the new appointees, giving them detailed directions in the 1820's and 1830's. Delivered in the form of sermons at the commissioning of the missionary just prior to his departure, the instructions served to enlighten the public as well. The secretaries corresponded with the mission abroad and acted as purchasing agents for both the mission and its personnel. An important step in business-like management came in 1836, when the secretaries ceased to appropriate money request-by-request and began to set annual budgets for each station, requiring the stations to draw against their allocations. Fed information from a variety of missionaries abroad and supplemented by personal trips of inspection, the secretaries became a fount of authoritative data on these exotic areas.

By 1860 the American Board was a mature institution. Originally draw-

---

[68] The most useful discussion of the organization of the ABCFM is Anderson, *Memorial Volume*. Prudential Committee to H. G. O. Dwight and E. Beadle, June 9, 1839, in ABC 8.1, Vol. 3, #6.

ing its membership from New England and the Middle States, it drew on the Mid-West as well by the 1850's. In 1853 the Annual Meeting for the first time met west of the Appalachians. Whereas in 1820 and 1821 its offices were in the basement of its secretary's home, by 1838 it occupied its own building at Pemberton Square, Boston. While one secretary sufficed to manage affairs in 1820, by 1824 an assistant was needed. Yet the bureaucracy remained small, and in 1860 two full-time secretaries sufficed, one in charge of foreign affairs, the other of domestic.

The American Board proved a far more effective organization for raising money than the casual fund-raising committees that supported Greek relief in the 1820's. Because the Board had no authority to tax or otherwise assess the churches it served, it had to solicit voluntary contributions. As an agent for three churches, the American Board had an organized clientele that might contribute regularly to its support as a matter of duty. To raise additional funds, the secretaries traveled about New England urging individual churches to pledge support to specific projects. Trips of inspection to the Board's American Indian Missions permitted special fund-raising activities among Presbyterians in the South until the animosities generated by the anti-slavery crusade caused the Southern Presbyterians to withhold support in the 1840's. The *Panoplist* and the *Missionary Herald*, the official organs of the Board, kept contributors informed monthly as to what their gifts were achieving and of opportunities for doing yet more. Not uncommon were the personal accounts of such givers as "two pious ladies" who worked the afternoons of the first Monday in each month and contributed the proceeds to missions. Some contributions were made in goods, but the Board had a strong preference for cash; experience indicated that gifts in kind often precluded donations of money. The Board did not rely solely on the goodwill of the churches or the fruits of their own speaking and writing. They hired agents who were assigned specific territories in which to solicit funds. Beginning in the 1820's, the missionaries-to-be spent from a few weeks to a year promoting the cause of missions prior to their departure; once abroad, they maintained contacts with American churches via personal letters; and while on furlough in the United States, they renewed and enlarged their personal acquaintanceships. William Goodell, during a furlough exceptional for its length, traveled 21,000 miles, preaching or speaking four hundred times in formal engagements.[69]

The American Board was rewarded for its efforts by a continuing flow of funds in support of its work. This is not to say that it had an inexhaustible supply. At the moment when Parsons and Fisk went abroad, the

[69] S. Worcester to J. Evarts, Sept. 1, 1820, in ABC 11, Vol. 1; Evarts to Worcester, May 11, 1820, in *ibid.* As the two earliest officers of the American Board, Worcester and Evarts had enormous influence on the development of policy and procedures.

Board was experiencing the pinch created by the depression of 1819. Again in the 1830's and 1850's, domestic depressions seriously restricted the funds available to it. On the threshold of the financial crisis of 1837, the Board admitted that it had "probably overrated the amount of enlightened missionary spirit in the community." Although three-fourths of the Congregational churches contributed to its work, the average gift did not exceed fifty cents per communicant per year. Small as this may seem, no other agency, private or public, was prepared or able to raise as much year in and year out for overseas activities as were the mission boards. Receipts which were just short of $40,000 in 1820, when the American Board commenced its undertakings in the Near East, topped $100,000 in 1828 and surpassed $200,000 in 1837. After 1852, receipts never fell below $300,000. Of these sums over one-third had been expended on the work in the Near East.[70]

Credit for many of these achievements belongs to Rufus Anderson, the secretary of the American Board. Combining energy and skill with long tenure, Anderson's leadership was forceful, often paternalistic. Extended visits to the overseas missions added to his strength by giving him first-hand familiarity with the scenes of action. His "Instructions" to the new appointees wisely steered youthful missionaries through the first trying months. In appearance, Anderson was stern; in business affairs his decisions, once formulated, were not ordinarily to be questioned.

The mission stations abroad operated quite informally. Before he left home, the missionary was assigned to work with a specific group of people in a designated area. Most problems had to be resolved in the field in terms of his general instructions and by consultation with colleagues, if any. While the newcomers might expect to be guided by the older personnel, there was no hierarchy of authority.

Beginning in 1836, organization abroad was tightened. The mission at Constantinople was directed to appoint one of their number as a corresponding secretary and to keep the secretary in Boston informed of the general progress of the work. At this time the Prudential Committee and secretary began to assign each mission an annual budget, while the mission designated one member to act as treasurer and bookkeeper for all. Although the practice seems to have varied from place to place, the missionaries were on salary at least as early as 1837. These salaries were regarded not as "a compensation," but as providing "an economical support." In the early 1840's these salaries generally were about $750 per year. As the size of the enterprise expanded, the administrative work became more oner-

---

[70] A summary of the Board's total annual income and expenditures appears in Anderson, *Memorial Volume*, 183 ff. Prudential Committee to A. Holladay *et al.*, Dec. 31, 1836, in ABC 8.1, Vol. 2, p. 195.

ous, and as early as 1850, the mission at Constantinople asked that a layman be sent out as business agent.

The expressions of Christian philanthropy in Turkey differed from those in Syria in degree rather than in kind. The personnel in both areas shared a common background, were sponsored by the same organization, and operated under the general umbrella of Ottoman sovereignty. To be sure, there was a greater European presence in the Ottoman capital, but Turkish influences were stronger there than in Syria. In this environment, the conditions of the 1830's encouraged the missionaries to devote much time to educational activities, introducing both Armenian and Ottoman officials to American educational practices and teaching materials. But by the mid-1840's the direct contacts of the Americans were limited to the Protestant community, small, impoverished, and lacking in prestige and self-confidence. As in Syria, the American efforts succeeded in nurturing the Protestant community, but missionary sponsorship was not at this time and in this place an adequate vehicle for sustaining working relationships with groups of other religious persuasions.

The proliferation of activities ultimately provoked an examination of the nature and scope of "Christian philanthropy." The warm responsiveness of the first missionaries to the problems of native societies led the missionary board into secular activities not originally contemplated. Since the Near East was but one of several areas in which the American Board functioned, it became a matter of necessity to define the limits within which a missionary society might support "extra-curricular" activities. In 1842 David Greene, a secretary of the Board, formulated a statement. He was thoughtfully sensitive to the dangers of disrupting a traditional culture; he recognized that modern men live by bread as well as by the spirit; and he foresaw that the native society must be equipped to run its own affairs. Greene argued that the Christian philanthropist ought to teach the natives to use modern agricultural tools, to construct comfortable dwellings, to make decent clothes, and to supply their own wants while living in permanent settlements. To varying degrees his ideas were shaped by the requirements of societies in other parts of the world. So far as the Near East was concerned neither the American Board at home, nor the missionaries abroad were really prepared to go as far as Greene in directing deliberate changes in native cultures.[71]

The activities of Cyrus Hamlin stand out as an exception. Hamlin, one of the most self-possessed personalities among the missionary personnel, had brought an unusual range of interests and skills to the Near East, for

[71] David Greene, "The Promotion of Intellectual Cultivation and the Arts of Civilized Life in Connection with Christian Missions," in ABCFM, *Annual Report*, 1842, 69–75.

in addition to the usual liberal arts-plus-seminary training, he had served an apprenticeship as an artisan. Alone among missionary educators, he knew enough about tools and crafts to introduce vocational education in his school at Bebek. Because of America's rural background, one might have expected other educators to have attempted to improve the quality of native agriculture, but several factors precluded this. Even though these Americans came from farms and villages, none seem to have been farm operators before entering their formal studies; thus, they really had little agricultural skill to transmit. In addition, the role of the missionary abroad did not involve him in even part-time agricultural activities, so that he acquired no first-hand experience with agricultural conditions in the Near East. While David Greene had an insight into the nature of the problems of cultural change, the American Board was equipped to conduct only those activities that were incidental to the established programs of the overseas missions: the schools and press remained the principal vehicles for introducing Western ideas and practices. The Board was not yet prepared to venture into broader, unrelated activities. When the Sultan sought assistance in promoting Turkish agriculture or in developing Turkey's mineral resources, he requested the assistance of the United States Department of State in recruiting such experts, and they were placed on the payroll of the Turkish government.[72]

Native society, stimulated from within and without to accommodate itself to Western ways, was changing, too. While existing forms of philanthropy would continue, Americans both in Constantinople and Beirut felt that the time had come to introduce the Near East to the American college.

[72] Merle Curti and Kendall Birr, *Prelude to Point Four: American Technical Missions Overseas, 1838–1938* (Madison: University of Wisconsin Press, 1954), 22–24, treats the mission of James Bolton Davis and J. Lawrence Smith.

IV

Independent Colleges, 1863-1914

THE FIRST American colleges abroad, Robert College at Constantinople and the Syrian Protestant College at Beirut, were founded in the 1860's to offer the native Christian community a higher level of education than the mission schools could provide. A generation later the American College for Girls was organized at Constantinople. As an instrument for the transmission of Western culture, the college had potentials and limitations which were not possessed by the mission schools. As a form of philanthropy the college posed problems that required forms of administration and financial support different from needs that had been encountered either in the relief ventures in Greece or in the missionary activities of the American Board.

· I ·

Robert College, the first to get under way, although incorporated by a non-sectarian board of directors, owed its origins to the missionary movement. It was very much the product of the funds of Christopher Rhinelander Robert and the executive drive of Cyrus Hamlin. A New Yorker, Robert had joined a successful career as a businessman with an active interest in philanthropy. His fortune was accumulated primarily through importation of sugar, cotton, and tea. A deeply religious man, he had early in his career become an officer of the American Home Missionary Society as well as an important contributor to the support of Beloit and Hamilton colleges and of Auburn Theological Seminary. Ordinarily an unassuming man, Robert took his giving as seriously as he did his business affairs, exercising a paternal interest in his benefactions, investigating them thoroughly, and giving freely of advice and criticism.[1]

Robert first visited Constantinople in the spring of 1856, meeting the American missionaries there and inspecting their various undertakings. The city, filled with English and French officers going to or from the Crimea, was becoming more familiar with Western culture. On his return home, Robert was approached by James and William Dwight, sons of the missionary Harrison Gray Otis Dwight, who broached the idea of establishing an American-style college at Constantinople. Robert was receptive, but the project quickly aborted as there was no other support for such a thoroughly secular school as the Dwights proposed. Subsequently, Robert formulated a proposal of his own that would create a non-denominational Christian college. On approaching Cyrus Hamlin to learn if he were at all interested, Robert found him enthusiastic. Exasperated with the educational policies of the American Board under Rufus Anderson, Hamlin quickly threw in his lot with Robert.[2]

President of the school from 1863 to 1877, Hamlin brought experience and resourcefulness to his job. Since he had departed from Boston in 1839, he had learned much of Turkey and her problems. His educational theories reflected the experience of both classroom teacher and administrator. Like Robert, he was aggressive and decisive; the persistence of the two men saw the college through successive disappointments and reverses during a decade in which the college struggled for life. It was Hamlin's task to choose a site, raise funds, erect the necessary buildings, recruit students and faculty, and develop the educational policies of the college.[3]

Getting started proved particularly difficult. Prospective donors begged off putting pen to paper in support of the college until the presidential canvas of 1860 was concluded and then, in view of increasing tensions, asserted that "nothing can be done until this affair with the South shall be settled." [4] Only Robert's faith backed by hard cash permitted Hamlin to go ahead with the college. But even on his return to Constantinople he experienced difficulties in securing a site for the school. When at last a prime site was secured at Roumeli Hissar, up the Bosporus on the Euro-

[1] "Christopher Robert," in DAB (21 Vols., New York: Charles Scribner's Sons, 1928–37), XVI.

[2] William Gottlieb Schauffler, Autobiography of William G. Schauffler For Forty-nine Years a Missionary in the Orient, ed. by his sons (New York: Anson D. F. Randolph & Co., 1887), 226; Cyrus Hamlin, "Robert College, Constantinople," American Antiquarian Society, Proceedings, N.S. VI (Oct., 1889), 196–199. Robert's account is in Levant Times and Shipping Gazette (Constantinople), Nov. 9, 1870.

[3] Cyrus Hamlin, My Life and Times (Boston: Congregational Sunday School & Publishing Society, 1893), Ch. 13.

[4] Hamlin, American Antiquarian Society, Proceedings, N.S. VI (Oct. 1889), 197.

pean shore, permission to build was withheld. The resourceful Hamlin did not let these circumstances forestall opening of the college, however. Recognizing that, under Ottoman custom, an institution which had been established for a length of time acquired a prescriptive right to continued existence, Hamlin received permission from the American Board to use the empty premises of his old school at Bebek, and Robert College opened in 1863 without so much as a by-your-leave to the Ottoman government.

Hamlin derived his conception of a college from the New England college of the pre-Civil War era. The college was to promote character development in the student within a non-sectarian, but nonetheless evangelical, atmosphere. And he took pride in reporting in 1866 that there had been "serious thought and earnest, diligent study of the scriptures" which had produced "as great and gratifying a progress in the development of moral character and conduct as in scholarship." [5] Mandatory daily prayers were scheduled on campus, as was obligatory attendance at Sunday services at the church of the student's choosing. This religiosity, no greater than in comparable colleges at home, blended comfortably with the academic curriculum. Students studied mental and moral philosophy, logic, rhetoric, and natural history. As the New England colleges had regarded science as "a useful tool in demonstrating the wondrous ways of God," [6] and as Hamlin had long manifested an interest in science, he accorded ample attention to mathematics and the sciences. In view of the multilingual character of Constantinople, the curriculum allocated much time to the teaching of the languages—the native language of the student, Latin and Greek required for admission to European universities, and English, which was the principal vehicle of instruction.

Growth of student enrollments was slow. Though non-sectarian, the avowedly Christian character of the school deprived it of appeal to the Moslems, while Greek and Gregorian Christians for a time suspected it as an agency for proselytizing, and native Protestants could not afford the board and tuition of $200 per year. During the first two years, the small student body was recruited chiefly from youth of European extraction. But by the end of the second year native Christians overcame their fears, and thereafter enrollments swelled to the capacity of the facility, approximately seventy-two students.

Briefly in the late 1860's the future of the College was clouded by the appearance of two rivals, the University of Constantinople and the Lycée of Galata Serai. The former, organized in 1870, proved an ephemeral threat, for it closed after one year, not to reopen until the end of the Tanzimat era, when Robert College was a going institution. The Lycée,

[5] RC, *Report*, 1866, 4. NECA Archives, New York.
[6] Frederick Rudolph, *The American College and University: A History* (New York: Vintage Books, 1965), 226.

however, enjoyed French financial support and official Ottoman patronage. French in staff, language of instruction, and curriculum, the Lycée engendered the envy of the Americans for the "magnificent building" furnished throughout with "Parisian elegance and English solidity." Hamlin regarded these new schools as a challenge to be met by "a sounder and more thorough training" at Robert.[7]

Fortunately at this juncture, Hamlin secured permission to build at the Roumeli Hissar site, permitting Robert to parry the threat of the Galata Serai Lycée with a facility that was ample and even handsome. Like Thomas Jefferson at the University of Virginia, Hamlin was his own contractor, directing over two hundred workmen. Indeed, his part in the construction was so personal that he lost two fingers while operating a power saw. Of stone quarried and dressed on the site, the building formed a quadrangle 113 feet across the front, 108 feet in depth, and three full stories high. Built on a hillside, the structure, flying the American flag, looked across the Bosporus to the hills of Asia Minor. Just below the building was the fortress of Mohammed the Conqueror. Completed and occupied in the spring of 1871, the hall was dedicated publicly on the following Fourth of July by William H. Seward, the recently retired secretary of state.

Enrollments jumped immediately, reaching 180 before they levelled off. "Every nook and corner" was full, Hamlin observed with pleasure, allowing no room for additional scholars or teachers. The college dining room was as crowded as an "Irishman's gallows," he added.[8] Growth was not only rapid, but chaotic. Following the example of American colleges earlier in the century, President Hamlin made no effort to assign his students to classes. Rather, he let each pursue a course of study until in his opinion the student was ready to receive a degree.[9]

Hamlin did not long enjoy the fruits of his labor, for no sooner was his structure dedicated than he was called back to the United States to raise a $300,000 endowment fund for the College. But the times were out of joint. His ill-health, the business depression in the United States, and renewed agitation of the Eastern Question brought failure to his quests. At this point in 1877, Christopher Robert, discouraged and ill, broke with Hamlin, dismissing him summarily.

Direction of Robert College passed to George Washburn, in whose charge it remained until 1903. A product of an Amherst-Andover training, Washburn had served the American Board from 1858 to 1868 as treas-

[7] RC, *Annual Report*, 1867–68, n.p. Roderic H. Davison, *Reform in the Ottoman Empire, 1856–1876* (Princeton: Princeton University Press, 1963), 246–248 treats Galata Serai Lycée.

[8] RC, *Report*, July, 1867, n.p.

[9] George Washburn, *Fifty Years in Constantinople and Recollections of Robert College* (Boston: Houghton Mifflin Co., 1909), 26.

urer of the mission at Constantinople. During this time he also met, courted, and wed Henrietta Hamlin, eldest daughter of President Hamlin. After a year in the United States, he returned to Turkey to teach philosophy at Robert College, becoming director of the school in 1872 during the absence of his father-in-law and succeeding him as president in 1878.

Through long years of residence in Constantinople and contact with people of many nationalities, Washburn acquired distinction for his "statesman-like ability and broad outlook." [10] In later years he was a trusted counsellor to successive British ambassadors on the Eastern Question. He was twice decorated by the Bulgarian government. Keeping the College going and directing its expansion was no less a challenge than founding the institution, for he could scarcely have taken office under less auspicious circumstances. In addition to the depression at home and successive revolts and wars in the Balkan provinces of Turkey, Washburn had to face the problems growing out of the accession of Abdul Hamid to the throne. Washburn devoted much of his long tenure to problems of administration and curriculum.

Washburn's views on college organization and curriculum emphasized the traditional rather than the novel. He organized students into conventional classes and recruited a permanent faculty, the Americans drawn generally from missionary ranks. Intellectually he was far closer to the views of President McCosh of Princeton than of President Eliot of Harvard. Assuming the unity of knowledge which the college must purvey, Washburn affirmed that the student must have "four years of general discipline and culture, with no option as to what he will study." [11] The elective system, then making its introduction to American colleges, he rejected as inappropriate. His deprecation of the elective system was at least partly gratuitous, for Robert had too few students to permit on economical organization of alternative course offerings. A concomitant of Washburn's commitment to the ideal of the New England college of his youth was the consignment of technical and professional education to "a subordinate place" in colleges. Preferably, technical education ought to be offered by special schools. Washburn never questioned the practical value, but he explicitly denied that either a strictly commercial or scientific curriculum provided an education in any meaningful sense of the term.[12]

Washburn's traditionalism did not appreciably inhibit the quality of education in the sciences and mathematics. President Hamlin had already set

[10] "George Washburn," in Charles T. Riggs, "Near East Missionary Biographies," typescript, Istanbul, July 9, 1953, in Archives, UCBWM, Boston, Mass. E. J. Morris to H. Fish, Oct. 8, 1870, in Despatches, Turkey, Vol. 22, #377, commends Washburn's "rare endowments of mind and character." General Records, Dept. of State, Rec. Group 59, National Archives, Washington.
[11] Washburn, *Fifty Years in Constantinople*, 224.
[12] RC, *Report of the President*, 1891–92, 11–12.

a precedent. Robert continued to offer a sequence of courses in physics, chemistry, mineralogy, geology, astronomy, physiology, and zoology. Instruction was bookish rather than practical, and one instructor carried the responsibility for all the scientific courses. Not until the early 1890's did the College employ a second science teacher, and even then it lacked a permanent professor of mathematics. Compared with offerings of leading American institutions, Robert's curriculum was out-dated. But in Constantinople, where only a handful of military and civil functionaries had any direct exposure to European culture, the curriculum was intellectually as rich as the society could assimilate comfortably.[13]

While Turkey under Abdul Hamid was morbidly suspicious of Western influences, it could not resist the aggressive pressures of England, France, Russia, and Germany. German capitalists succeeded in pushing a railroad through the Balkans to Constantinople by 1888 and by the 1890's linked the capital with Ankara. Cheap transportation was a stimulant to the growth of agriculture and mining. A demand for engineers and technicians developed. Sultan Abdul Hamid on several occasions requested the assistance of the American Minister, Alexander Terrell, in recruiting American specialists to head or to staff Turkish schools of agriculture and commerce. Constantinople, its population nearing a million, lagged behind major cities of the West, its streets "fearfully bad," harbor facilities "signally inadequate" and public utilities non-existent. Although the spirit of change was in the air and Turkey required educated leadership, Turkish law prohibited Moslems from attending Robert College. By default, the nation had to depend either upon its Christian subjects or upon foreign engineers.[14]

Slowly, sometimes reluctantly, President Washburn made innovations in the curriculum of the College. In 1887, for example, calculus was added, while in 1893 Robert Academy, a preparatory school, was formally organized to direct the training of the pre-college youth. Finally, by 1900 Washburn was proposing to develop a commercial department in the College, though he was still chary lest the College "degenerate into a commercial school." He hoped also to make the science courses more practical "but not at the expense of disciplinary subjects." [15] New staff members were secured, and plans were laid for construction of a gym, a study hall, and a physical science laboratory as well as of faculty housing.

The execution of Washburn's plans was left to his young successor, Caleb Frank Gates, who assumed the presidency in the fall of 1903. Forty-five years of age when he became president, Caleb Gates had followed the

[13] RC, *Annual Report of the President*, Aug. 1, 1883, n.p.; *ibid.*, 1891–92, 11–12.
[14] A. Terrell to W. Gresham, Oct. 20, 1894, in Despatches, Turkey, Vol. 57, #326 and J. Angell to W. Day, July 25, 1898, in *ibid.*, Vol. 67, #160.
[15] RC, *Report of the President*, 1900–01, 14–15.

path of his predecessors by going first to the Near East as a missionary-educator of the American Board. In service at Mardin and Harpoot, he displayed a gift for languages that enabled him to reach natives easily in their own idiom. Gates' interest in athletics, tennis, and golf was too Western in flavor to be an effective avenue for approaching most Ottoman subjects, although it provided a common interest with the Westernized students at the College.

As president he brought fresh views and vigor to the direction of the school. As a first step Gates thoroughly overhauled the preparatory school, providing it with separate dormitories, class buildings, and faculty. His aim was to instill in the young students ideals of accuracy, neatness, industry, honesty, self-control, modesty, independent effort, initiative, brotherliness, and subordination of self to the good of the group. As enrollment in the Academy climbed, the school was able to dismiss the academically inferior students without crippling itself through the loss of tuition income.[16]

Although President Gates was no less interested than his predecessors in the spiritual development of his students, he enthusiastically embraced the concept of the university as a public service institution, then a new idea in American college circles. He affirmed that Robert College had a responsibility for promoting the economic development of Turkey. The Ottoman Empire desperately needed engineers to build railroads, bridges, and highways, to develop mines, to construct irrigation works and sanitation facilities, and to exploit the electric power potential of Anatolia. A timely bequest by John Stewart Kennedy, a Chicago banker and railroad financier, made available funds to begin an engineering school, and Professor John R. Alden of the University of Michigan was engaged to design the physical plant and to direct the construction of it. In 1912 Lynn A. Scipio of the University of Nebraska relieved Alden. He completed the building, hired the teaching staff, ordered textbooks, installed the shop equipment, and began classes. Thus, as Robert College approached its fiftieth anniversary in 1913, it had separate degree programs in the liberal arts, the sciences, and commercial studies. The engineering school was under construction with a prospect of supplying engineers for the Near East. With a total enrollment in the College of 475, Robert College was on the point of becoming a modern institution.[17]

[16] Caleb Frank Gates, *Not to Me Only* (Princeton: Princeton University Press, 1940), *passim*. RC, *Report of the President*, 1906–07, 10; *ibid.*, 1907–08, 14.

[17] Gates, *Not to Me Only*, 198–199; Lynn A. Scipio, *My Thirty Years in Turkey* (Rindge, N.H.: R. R. Smith, 1955), 59 ff.

· II ·

The Syrian Protestant College, chartered at the same time as Robert, operated in the mixed Islamic-Christian milieu of the Lebanon. Although Lebanon had been opened to Western influences first by Mehemet Ali and then through the intervention of the British and French, it remained without a college. Initiative for founding the Syrian Protestant College came from the Syrian mission of the American Board at its annual meeting in 1862. The mission agreed that the proposed school should strive to match the standards of "better" American colleges. Likewise, it agreed that the language of instruction should be Arabic. Most debated was whether the college should be managed by natives or Americans. A suggestion that the staff and President should be natives was rejected in the belief that the native community as well as foreign donors would have more confidence in the institution if it were operated by either Europeans or Americans. While the mission betrayed fears that the College might jeopardize its evangelistic work by competing with it for funds and personnel, it was more fearful that French Jesuits would gain prestige by founding a college in Lebanon first. The mission also decided that "all possible care" must be taken to assure that the students not be denationalized "by the acquisition of foreign and expensive tastes and habits." The College recognized that it would fail in its objectives unless its students were "prepared, adapted and disposed to mingle with their brethren in the duties and labours of life." Accordingly, the mission designated one of its number, Daniel Bliss, to return to the United States to secure independent support for a college.[18]

A native of Vermont, Daniel Bliss learned to work with his hands. When he was nine years old his mother died, and he went to live with relatives in Ohio. From the age of sixteen he supported himself by farming, tanning, and tree-grafting. His formal education was delayed; he was thirty-two when he completed his training at Andover Seminary. Strong-minded and physically robust, Bliss departed for Syria in 1855 as a missionary of the American Board. He spent his first two years at Abeih working with Simeon Calhoun—studying Arabic and teaching in the Academy. The next four years he and his wife conducted the Girls' Boarding School at nearby Suq al-Gharb. He was a younger, less experienced man than Cyrus Hamlin when he was chosen to organize a college.

18 F. J. Bliss, ed., *The Reminiscences of Daniel Bliss* (New York: Fleming H. Revell, 1920), 164–168; "Prospectus and Programme of the Syrian Protestant Collegiate Institute, Beirut," in ABC 16.8.1, Vol. 6, #110; Bayard Dodge, "The American University of Beirut; an Introduction to Beirut and the University," mimeographed, Princeton, 1952, 9–12.

Bliss' quest for funds was far more rewarding than that of Hamlin. The combination of Bliss' youthful aggressiveness in soliciting money and the location of the proposed college in an area under European tutelage made the proposal attractive to prospective donors. He raised $100,000 in America, but because of the Civil War the value of the money was depreciated. And so Bliss hit on the stratagem of investing it until it regained its value. Still in need of funds with which to open the school, Bliss went to England where between September, 1864, and February, 1866, he collected £3,397, a sum sufficient to meet the anticipated operating costs for three years.

The family of William Earl Dodge, Senior, shares with Daniel Bliss credit for the successful establishment of the Syrian Protestant College. A fortuitous encounter with David Stuart Dodge when Bliss was bound for America in 1862 marked the beginning of a continuing relationship with a family which was long the most important single factor in American philanthropy in the Near East. A partner in the successful metals-importing firm of Phelps & Dodge, William Earl Dodge, Senior, had been an active supporter of the American Board. To the proposed College he gave not only funds but two sons. One, David Stuart Dodge, served for a time as an instructor in the College and for the rest of his life as its business manager in America. The other son, William Earl Dodge, Junior, succeeded his father as a leading patron of the College.[19]

Instruction at the SPC, as the College was generally known, began in temporary quarters in December, 1866, and a permanent campus was occupied in 1873. Located west of the city of Beirut on the north side of Ras Beirut, the campus stretched a half mile along the Mediterranean, one hundred feet above the sea. In the distance on the land side stood Jebel Sannin, rising 8,400 feet and snow-covered half the year. The new buildings of buff limestone and sandstone, topped with red tile and landscaped with clumps of cypress and date palm, transformed a hitherto "wind swept, desolate place" into an attractive campus.[20]

The objectives of the SPC were much like those of Robert College. First, "to lead and control the higher education of the country," and second, "to train the largest number possible of pious teachers, translators, physicians and evangelists." In an environment where the population was almost evenly divided into Christians and non-Christians, the SPC had a better chance of making a significant impact on the native society than did her sister institution. The College recognized the underdeveloped state of the Syrian economy and hypothesized that "a course of instruction in the

19 "William Earl Dodge," in DAB; Carlos Martyn, *William E. Dodge; the Christian Merchant* (New York: Funk and Wagnalls, 1890).
20 SPC, *Annual Report*, 1906–07, 4–5; Dodge, "The American University of Beirut," 15.

higher mathematics, including Engineering and Navigation, will prove a great attraction to students, aid the growth and usefulness of the College and largely contribute to the development of the country." [21]

In most respects the SPC operated along the same lines as Robert College in terms of curriculum and staffing arrangements. As the students, whether Christian or Moslem, Syrian, Lebanese or Egyptian, all used Arabic, instruction was offered at first in Arabic. However, Arabic gave way to English as the language of instruction in order to assure ample supplies and selection of textbooks and to make use of English-speaking instructors. Not until 1903 did the College introduce the elective system, when enrollments, which had reached the seven hundred mark, made this economically feasible. The few senior faculty were generally Americans, natives being relegated to teaching Arabic or to preparatory courses. As early as 1898 an enlightened administration recognized the need for a limited sabbatical system, which would permit members of the medical faculty to spend a summer in Europe brushing up on their field.

As at Robert, the College found the operation of a preparatory school necessary to assure adequately trained youth for the college program, but it was a time-consuming and exasperating responsibility. In America, other institutions shared with the school in inculcating socially desired values. But abroad, because American educators were promoting values not widely shared by the native society, the school had to assume the whole burden. As a consequence, the problem of discipline was more troublesome abroad than at home. The faculty felt that strict discipline was necessary if the school were to inculcate American values in the short time the students were in its care. Yet as educators they recognized that, to develop the quality of self-reliance, students needed a generous degree of freedom. In resolving this dilemma the Americans operated in a state of uneasy tension in which discipline was too strict by their own standards, but too lax by native standards.

The unique feature of the Syrian Protestant College was its medical school, made possible by the presence of three unusual personalities, John Wortabet, Cornelius Van Dyck, and George Edward Post. Wortabet was an Armenian who had long been identified with the Syrian mission; his family had produced the standard Arabic-English dictionary. Van Dyck, an "impetuous, hot tempered man," had first made his mark as founder of the school at Abeih and as an Arabic scholar. A graduate of the Jefferson Medical College, he was the first to use the microscope for medical purposes in Syria. He taught internal medicine, general pathology, and ophthalmology, but he was not a medical researcher nor perhaps even a great physician. His great contribution was in joining his literary skill to his

[21] *The Syrian Protestant College* (Beirut, Syria, 1882), 2, 30.

medical training, writing Arabic texts in chemistry, natural science, internal medicine, and physical diagnosis among others.[22]

George Post was less flamboyant but, like Van Dyck, a man of many parts: ordained clergyman, college-trained medical doctor and dentist, botanist, and editor. His *Flora of Syria, Palestine and Sinai from the Taurus to Ras Muhammad and from the Mediterranean Sea to the Syrian Desert* has remained the standard work on the subject. Post taught materia medica but felt there was too much guess work with pills and powders. As a "bold, skillful and resourceful operator, very dexterous in his manipulations," he made his mark in surgery. By 1877 he was using Listerian methods of antiseptic surgery, though it is doubtful that he ever mastered rigorous asceptic methods. To keep graduates of the medical school abreast of the latest in medical science, he edited *Al Tabib* (The Physician.)[23]

The medical school was better able than the individual missionary-doctor to elevate the level of medical practice in the Near East. The College gave the student systematic training in basic sciences. The three-man faculty, although small, made teaching its first responsibility and developed at least limited areas of specialization. Most important, College medical students had access to the sixty-three-bed Prussian Hospital, the best medical facility in the Levant. From the start, the medical curriculum lasted four years, while most American colleges of the day had but a three-year program.[24]

The Syrian Protestant College experienced fewer growing pains than Robert College. Almost from its inception the SPC was stimulated to raise its standards by its rivalry with the College Saint Joseph, a French Jesuit school founded in 1874. The French institution also boasted a medical school, and from time to time the SPC had to acknowledge its superiority.[25] The existence of a medical school as a part of the SPC further served to strengthen the teaching of the sciences and to push the College in the direction of becoming a true university. Because medical work was once again in vogue as an instrument of evangelism, the College was able to expand its curriculum in areas related to medical science without a sense of having betrayed the College's Christian orientation. Thus, in the early 1870's when the medical faculty found itself handicapped by the lack of adequate drugs, the staff organized a two-year pharmacy program. Shortly thereafter, when an English friend presented the College with a small observatory and equipment for meteorological observation, Dr. Van

---

[22] Lutfi M. Sa'di, "Al-Hakim Cornelius Van Alen Van Dyck (1815–1895)," *Isis*, XXVII (1937), 20–45.

[23] Lutfi M. Sa'di, "The Life and Works of George Edward Post (1838–1909)," *Isis*, XXVIII (1938), 385–417.

[24] Dodge, "The American University of Beirut," 13, 23, 34.

[25] *Ibid.*, 27; SPC, *Annual Report*, 1898–1899, 11–12.

Dyck began systematic collection of weather data and offered instruction in astronomy. It was important, too, that Daniel Bliss, unlike George Washburn, did not regard technical or commercial education as out of place in a college. Rather he termed it, "one of our opportunities." [26] One of his acts as president was to create a two-year commercial course.

In the 1890's the College entered a new period of expansion. The building of a carriage road from Beirut to Damascus in the 1860's had opened Syria beyond the mile-high passes of the Lebanon and Anti-Lebanon mountains to limited trade. Beirut's trade expanded enormously in the nineties when the old carriage road was supplemented by a cogwheel railroad and a breakwater opened the port to sea-going vessels. As enterprising villagers flocked to the city and joined Beirut shopkeepers, awareness of need made interest in higher education grow apace. Equally important were the opening of the Suez Canal in 1869, the British occupation of Egypt in 1882, and the conquest of the Sudan, 1885–1899, all of which increased the demand for educated natives with a knowledge of English.

In meeting these needs new buildings were constructed, including a chapel, an observatory, and a chemistry laboratory. In 1900 the Preparatory School acquired its own building, the first structure of reinforced concrete in Lebanon. As Daniel Bliss stepped down as president in 1903 after forty years' service, the College enrollment stood at 610; the campus represented an investment of $645,000; and the endowment fund totaled $327,000.[27]

Under Howard Sweetser Bliss, the second president of the College (1903–20) and the second son of its founder, the College's role broadened. Born in Lebanon and educated at Amherst and Union Theological Seminary, Howard Bliss had taken post-graduate work at Oxford and Göttingen and was academically well-equipped for the post. Theologically, he was more liberal than his father, and he promptly ended the use of a "declaration of principles" which had committed the College to support of a fundamentalist creed. The younger Bliss, in common with his counterpart at Constantinople, Caleb Frank Gates, felt that the College must serve the community in ways which would actively promote community growth.

Howard Bliss undertook to strengthen the medical college and to explore new areas of education. When the facilities of the Prussian Hospital became too restricted, the College supplemented them by building pavilions for treating diseases of women and children as well as disorders of the eye and ear. As a result, two hundred beds were available. Two new schools were also established, a School of Nursing in 1905 and a School of Dentistry in 1911. At the outbreak of World War I, reflecting the contin-

26 *Ibid.*, 1900–01, 9.
27 Dodge, "The American University of Beirut," 29.

uing economic development of the Levant, the College was considering
the establishment of courses in agricultural engineering and the organization of schools of Engineering and Law.[28]

The College was the means of introducing to the Levant not only
Western science and medicine, but also Western-style recreation. The
idea of organized games seemed undignified to many Syrians and Lebanese. One father, experiencing a minor trauma on seeing his son freely
perspiring in a vigorous game of tennis, hastily assured College authorities
that he could afford a substitute to play in his son's place. In the early
years of the College, student activities had been limited to the "Urwat al-
Wuthqa" or Arabic Literary Society, and the "Students' Union," an English literary and debating club. Running events were introduced first, followed by soccer and swimming. It was 1898, however, before the school
acquired its first recreation field, which was devoted to track and field
events and gymnastics. An annual field day was started, which achieved
enough significance to merit the attendance of the provincial governor.
Tennis, field hockey, and basketball were also introduced about this time.
Finally, in 1913–14 the College built a student center.[29]

At the onset of World War I, the Syrian Protestant College was firmly
established with an impressive record of achievement behind it. The
teaching staff numbered eighty-one, of whom thirty held permanent tenure. Enrollment had passed nine hundred of whom over half were in the
collegiate program. After a half century the College counted nearly a
thousand degree-holding alumni, 364 in medicine, 195 in pharmacy, and
320 in the arts and sciences. Furthermore, most of these alumni had remained in the Near East, using their talents at home.[30]

· III ·

Higher education for women in Turkey had its origins in the formation
of the Home School for Girls at Constantinople. Given the subordinate
role of women in Eastern society, inevitably collegiate education for
women began later than for the men. As the few existing schools for
Turkish girls spared the young women "undue cerebral excitement," [31] it
was necessary to begin at the secondary level with a boarding school.

The impetus to found the Home School came from Cyrus Hamlin, who
thought a girls' school necessary to complete Robert College. Christopher

---

[28] Howard S. Bliss, "The Modern Missionary," *Atlantic Monthly* CXXV (1920),
664–675; SPC, *Annual Report*, 1904–05, 21; *ibid.*, 1910–11, 9–10; *ibid.*, 1913–14, 10–13.
[29] Dodge, "The American University of Beirut," 37–39.
[30] SPC, *Annual Report*, 1910–11, 19–20.
[31] Mary Mills Patrick, *Under Five Sultans* (New York: Century Co., 1929), 102.

Robert, resisting additional involvement, passed Hamlin's suggestion on to officers of the Woman's Board of Missions of the Congregational Church. The latter ultimately organized the school, selecting Miss Julia Rappleye as its principal.

A graduate of Oberlin, Julia Rappleye was an experienced teacher when she went to Constantinople in 1871 to organize the first classes at Stamboul. An intense, devoted teacher, she never gave a day "to mere recreation" but spent vacations making preparations for the next term and visiting parents of her pupils. An independent woman who resented unsolicited advice, she quarreled with her advisory board, on one occasion terminating an unsolicited visitation by throwing her watering pot. Before she resigned in 1875, she had seen the first class graduate and had moved the School to a permanent site at Scutari on the Asiatic side of the Bosporus.[32]

Clara Catherine Pond Williams, her successor, a widow with a Mount Holyoke training, was highly regarded for her "well-balanced mind and wonderful good sense." She was an able organizer and fund raiser. During the nine years that she directed the School, Mrs. Williams established English as the language of instruction, a move which made possible the recruitment of a cosmopolitan student body and simplified the procurement of adequate text books and competent teachers.[33]

On Mrs. Williams' retirement, responsibility for the Home School devolved upon Clara Hamlin and Mary Mills Patrick. Miss Hamlin, the daughter of Cyrus Hamlin, helped fulfill her father's dream of a girls' school as a counterpart to Robert College. She had spent her girlhood in Constantinople, going to the United States to complete her secondary education and to teach before joining the staff of the Home School. When Miss Hamlin married in 1889, direction of the School passed to Miss Patrick, alone, who guided its development until 1924. As an altruistic, unsophisticated girl of twenty-one, Miss Patrick had left her Iowa home in 1871 to teach in the American Board school at Erzerum in eastern Turkey. In 1875 she joined the faculty of the Home School. She was still young and immature when she became principal. In the years that followed, she matured into an able executive, a scholar, and an ardent feminist.[34]

Miss Patrick's first objective was to raise the Home School to collegiate rank. Its transformation in 1890 into the American College for Girls was more a declaration of intention than a recognition of achievement. The college aimed at combining "the highest moral and Christian culture with

[32] "Julia Rappleye," in Riggs, "Near East Missionary Biographies."

[33] "Clara Catherine Pond Williams," in ibid.; generally she was called Kate Pond Williams. Mary Mills Patrick, *A Bosporus Adventure Istanbul (Constantinople) Woman's College, 1871–1924* (London: Oxford University Press, 1934), 36–46.

[34] "Clara Hamlin [Lee]" in Riggs, "Near East Missionary Biographies; "Mary Mills Patrick," in *ibid.*

the most complete mental discipline." [35] As at Robert and the SPC, the students studied their native language and literature. While Greek and Latin were taught, they were not required; the young ladies acquired at least a veneer of culture through the study of drawing and art history. Equipped with a small zoological collection, an herbarium, and a three-inch telescope, the College exposed its students to a wider range of work in science than many liberal arts students receive today. Miss Patrick was more assiduous than either Daniel Bliss or George Washburn in keeping the curriculum of the College up-to-date. By 1894 she had introduced a choice of three baccalaureate programs: classical, literary, or scientific. Even so, the College did not match the academic standards of American colleges. An English resident of the capital compared it to an English or American secondary school. Its strong points, he said, were the "ideals of home life and purity." [36] Nevertheless, it was "the best organized and best equipped" school for women in the Empire.[37]

Transformation of the Home School into a college provoked a heated debate. Miss Patrick had scarcely assumed her responsibilities in 1883 when a change in officers of the American Board placed Dr. and Mrs. Judson Smith on the school's board of directors. Taking a narrow, evangelistic outlook, the Smiths resented both the autonomy of the Home School and its secular tone. Miss Patrick, on the other hand, increasingly regarded herself as an educator rather than a representative of sectarian religion, and she was determined to prevent the American Board from swallowing up the school. An uneasy truce prevailed until December, 1905, when fire destroyed the principal class building, Barton Hall, containing the science laboratories, classrooms, gymnasium, assembly hall, and dormitory. The fire brought to a boil the long-simmering differences of opinion. At the time of the fire, however, Caroline Borden, a long-time patroness of the school, and Charles Cuthbert Hall, President of Union Theological Seminary, were seeking an amendment to the college charter that would permit persons other than members of the Woman's Board of Missions to serve as directors of the College. An effort by Mrs. Judson Smith to dismiss Miss Patrick as head of the College failed, and in 1908 a new charter was secured, severing all ties with the Woman's Board.[38]

In the months immediately preceding World War I, the College planned, built, and occupied a new campus. By dropping the lowest three grades of its preparatory school, the College secured space in which to continue in spite of the fire and to expand its collegiate program. Encour-

---

[35] ACG, *Calendar*, 1889–90, 15. The ACG also called itself the Constantinople Woman's College.
[36] Edwin Pears, *Turkey and Its People* (London: Methuen & Co., 1911), 388.
[37] A. Terrell to W. Gresham, Dec. 30, 1894, in Despatches, Turkey, Vol. 58, #369.
[38] ACG, *Report of the President*, 1905–06, 18; *ibid.*, 1907–08, n.p.; Patrick, *A Bosporus Adventure*, 90–120.

aged by the growth of enrollment, Miss Patrick determined to rebuild. This decision was made easier by the Young Turk Revolution of 1908 and the subsequent removal of restrictions on the acquisition of real estate by foreigners. Shortly, a handsome park of forty-five to fifty acres with a commanding view of the Bosporus was secured at Arnaoutkeuy, located perhaps three miles from Robert College. Within a few months funds were in hand to commence building. Just as the war in Europe began in 1914, the College moved into its new quarters.

By 1914 the American College for Girls had recapitulated the experience of the two men's colleges. It was a non-sectarian college serving a multi-ethnic student population. Although a Christian institution, it had recognized the necessity of incorporating the sciences into its curriculum. Further, it was exploring new areas of possible service. Miss Patrick was interested in the possibility of creating a school of education, for she thought that America had a "freshness and power" in its methods and in the "high place given to moral and religious ideals." [39] Another proposal was the founding of a medical school for women. She felt this to be appropriate, since the girls' school served quite a different student body and area than did the Syrian Protestant College. These plans and proposals had to be shelved as Turkey entered the war. The College at this date had an enrollment of approximately two hundred, and its physical plant was the finest of the three American colleges in the Near East.

· IV ·

As instruments of cultural change, the colleges operated at a different level from the missions. The colleges reached fewer natives, to be sure, but those they reached had a far greater leadership potential because of the more advanced training they provided. Furthermore, the colleges were able to do their work in such a way that the greatest portion of their alumni were able to find places for themselves in local society, no mean feat when one keeps in mind that, until the Young Turk Revolution of 1908, Moslem Turks were discouraged or forbidden to attend the American schools. As students acquired new tastes and values, many found it difficult to return to the paternal hearth. This had the effect of disrupting the patriarchal family and of causing alumni who came from the rural areas of the Near East to remain in the more congenial urban centers. Thus, the colleges tended to accentuate the cultural differences between urban and rural areas.[40]

[39] ACG, *Annual Report,* 1911–12, 22.
[40] Mufidie Ferid, the Turkish novelist, made the impact of Western values on

The capacity of the colleges to reach the indigenous populations differed from that of the mission schools. The latter worked primarily among native Protestants, while the non-sectarian character of the colleges enabled them to reach non-Protestant Christians. Nevertheless, the Christian identification of the colleges minimized their appeal to Moslem Turks and Arabs until the Young Turk Revolution removed the bar on such enrollments. By requiring students to study their native language and literature, the colleges contributed to a sense of separateness on the part of the student which played into the hands of a divisive, often revolutionary, nationalism among the minority populations. Although Bulgarian nationalism had its own independent sources, Robert College contributed significantly to the small cadre of leaders who governed Bulgaria from the late 1870's to World War I. In fact, during World War I the Bulgarian minister to the United States, Stephen Panaretoff, was an alumnus of Robert and long-time member of the College faculty.[41] In the 1890's and after, Robert contributed to the growing national feeling of the Armenians. This contribution was cultural rather than political, and it was limited to Armenians in the Constantinople area. The American College for Girls may have aided and abetted the miniscule, but virulent, Albanian nationalist movement, as two of its alumnae, the Kyrias sisters, played a major role in creating the cultural environment in which Albanian nationalism grew to maturity.[42]

In Syria the College furthered the development of Arab cultural nationalism to which the mission schools had innocently contributed. About 1880, young students educated at the Syrian Protestant College founded a secret society that issued a flurry of patriotic sentiments. Placards posted surreptitiously about Beirut called for the people of Syria to unite, asked for autonomy for Syria, and sought recognition of Arabic as an official language. While the society reflected a growing political consciousness among Syrian Christians, it had an extremely limited impact. By 1883 it disbanded. Several of the most articulate Syrian nationalists removed to

---

students from rural areas of the Near East the subject of her novel *Pervaneler*. See Henry Elisha Allen, *The Turkish Transformation: A Study in Social and Religious Development* (Chicago: University of Chicago Press, 1935), 163. Henry Harris Jessup, *Fifty-three Years in Syria* (2 Vols., New York: Fleming H. Revell, 1910), II, 513.

41 RC, *Report of the President*, 1896–97, 6; George H. Huntington, "Report of the Principal of the Preparatory Department, 1908–09," in *ibid.*, 1908–09, 27. In the late 1870's and 1880's Bulgarian students outnumbered those of other nationalities at Robert College. S. Cox to T. Bayard, Jan. 1, 1886, in Despatches, Turkey, Vol. 45, #92; Cox to Bayard, Aug. 31, 1886, in *ibid.*, Vol. 46, #226.

42 The educational activities of the Kyrias sisters is outlined in Hester Donaldson Jenkins, *An Educational Ambassador to the Near East: The Story of Mary Mills Patrick and an American College in the Orient* (New York: Fleming H. Revell, 1925), Ch. 7. This topic is explored at greater length below [141–142].

Cairo, where they continued their campaign without hindrance from Turkish authorities.[43]

The role of the American colleges in nurturing nascent nationalism was tangential. The colleges did not expressly incite nationalist aspirations. The curriculums acquainted students with native languages, literature, and culture, and they provided an introduction to Western European political thought, which, of course, placed much emphasis upon national ideals. The intellectual environment of the college permitted a relatively free atmosphere in which these intoxicating ideals might be discussed. Such experiences made students receptive to the blandishments of political nationalism. While national feeling developed among many college students, similar feelings developed among those who had no affiliation with the colleges. Generally the American contribution was in helping to fashion a cultural self-consciousness that politically-oriented nationalists subsequently used to advantage in maneuvering for autonomy or independence.

The Woman's College made its unique impact by fomenting feminism and creating the first generation of female intellectuals in Turkey. Within the framework of standard college courses, women were inspired to strive for social, economic, and political equality with men. Students wrote essays which proclaimed that excessive domesticity thwarted development of the female mind and soul. They aspired to cultivate their minds by gaining the freedom to visit and study abroad.[44]

Many of the alumnae established new roles for women in the Near East as physicians, oculists, and pharmacists. Others made good marriages, and some women joined their husbands in significant educational and political work. Undoubtedly the most distinguished of the early graduates of the College was Halidé Edib, who in spite of Turkish laws attended the College and graduated in 1900. She achieved distinction as one of the most important writers in Turkey in the years just before and after World War I. She was active in the abortive reform movement of the Young Turks and served in the government of Mustapha Kemal. Aside from her

---

[43] George Antonius, *The Arab Awakening: The Story of the Arab National Movement* (Philadelphia: J. B. Lippincott Co., 1939), 79 ff. Zeine N. Zeine, *Arab-Turkish Relations and the Emergence of Arab Nationalism* (Beirut: Khayat's, 1958), 42–45; George E. Kirk, *A Short History of the Middle East* (London: Methuen, 1961), 103–105. Dodge, "The American University of Beirut," 24–25, notes that two Arab teachers were dropped from the College in 1882 "probably because of being connected with one of the secret societies which were beginning to ferment Arab nationalism." The two, Ya'gub Sarruf and Faris Nimr, migrated to Egypt where they achieved distinction for their newspaper and scientific publications. J. Dickson to F. R. St. John, Jan. 14 and 17, 1881, enclosed in St. John to Granville, Jan. 25, 1881, FO 78, Vol. 3274, #68, Public Record Office, London, attributes the disaffection to Moslem Arabs who regarded themselves as "ill-treated and oppressed by the Turks and desirous of an Arab caliphate."

[44] Jenkins, *An Educational Ambassador to the Near East*, 148 ff., reprints some student essays. See especially the essay of Stefka Obreshkova, 161–162.

personal example, she was active in opening opportunities to other women. Once Turkish women were legally free to attend the College, she aided in the selection of candidates for admission to the College for Girls. It was at a College commencement that she broke other precedents by speaking unveiled and before a mixed audience.[45]

· V ·

While the colleges assisted the native community in developing its leadership potential and in making use of elements of Western culture, they did not intend to evolve into indigenous institutions in the manner of the missions. From the first, the founders assumed that American funds should be employed to acquire a site, to construct and equip buildings, and to provide an endowment, but that student fees would cover most of the operating costs. Until the mid-1880's the colleges came surprisingly close to achieving this goal. But after 1885 operating expenses ordinarily exceeded income from fees, and American funds had to make up the accumulating deficits. Although the Near East had a long tradition of charitable support of health, education, and religion by wealthy men, local support was not forthcoming to the American schools.

Securing capital funds for the colleges in America proved a time-consuming chore. Unlike the mission schools, the colleges could not draw on the American Board for funds. Until the early years of the twentieth century the colleges were dependent upon the gifts of a few individual donors. Much of the responsibility for soliciting funds fell upon the college presidents, a task which took them away from their institutions for extended periods of time. Daniel Bliss, for example, was in England or the United States on five occasions between 1874 and 1899. Miss Patrick was in the United States on similar errands for as long as two years, while the last four years of Cyrus Hamlin's presidency were spent in the United States in an unsuccessful effort at fund-raising.[46]

The chief problem was in convincing Americans that a non-sectarian college abroad was a worthy object of philanthropic giving. Promoting Robert College proved particularly difficult, for men of means were not anxious to contribute to the support of an institution bearing another man's name. This was the more galling because the school had taken Robert's name, not to appease his vanity, but without his knowledge and because it was inoffensive and pronounceable in all the languages in use at

---

[45] *Ibid.*, Ch. 7. ACG, *Annual Report*, 1910-11, 18.

[46] This section is based on materials in the annual reports of the three independent colleges. See also, Hamlin, *My Life and Times*, 426; Patrick, *Under Five Sultans*, 55; Bliss, ed., *Reminiscences of Daniel Bliss*, 175-178.

Constantinople. But Christopher Robert had been a "loner" in his philanthropies, and business associates declined to support him at this juncture.

The newness of this form of philanthropy was likewise a deterrent to raising money. Americans at home were accustomed to supporting denominational colleges, but the non-sectarian school was still suspect. Abroad the propriety of even a denominational college was not yet established. When at last the American Board began to found mission colleges in Turkey, the independent colleges had to compete for the funds available. Caleb Gates noted that even the missionary had been confronted with selling the public the idea that non-evangelistic work was "important" and "interesting." Inevitably this led the missionaries to exaggerate the colorful aspects of their work and had led one to propose the rule that missionaries "should not lie any more than necessary" in raising funds.[47]

As a result, the cost of soliciting funds from a broad cross section of the American public was high, sometimes consuming two-thirds of the contributions. In the 1870's Hamlin reported expenses of $5,500 incurred in collecting $14,600. At a later date Washburn spent $3,600 in raising $5,100 for the college. Most dismal was the experience of Vice-President Long of Robert College, who collected but $200 while expending $2,300.[48] The presidents, living abroad and having major responsibilities abroad, lacked the time and contacts to create a broadly based organization to solicit financial support for the colleges in a manner comparable to the support afforded mission schools by the American Board.

Generally, the financial well-being of the Near East colleges devolved upon the benevolence of a few well-to-do men. Christopher Robert and the family of William Earl Dodge, Sr., provided the greater part of the initial funds for the two men's colleges. During his lifetime, Robert gave close to $100,000 to the College, part for its building fund and the rest for its endowment. At his death in 1878 he left property and funds in the amount of $140,000. The proceeds from the latter trickled in from 1878 to 1891, providing an income sufficient to offset the growing deficits incurred in operating costs but insufficient to permit additions to the physical plant or to the school's academic program. At the Syrian Protestant College, Dodge was a substantial contributor to the initial building fund, though Daniel Bliss did succeed in raising funds from a variety of persons both in the United States and in England. But until the end of the century David Stuart Dodge and his brother, William Earl Dodge, Junior, underwrote the cost of new buildings and repairs to existing structures.

By the 1890's a second generation of well-to-do patrons of the colleges appeared. As the colleges by this time were a quarter-century old and well

---

[47] Gates, *Not to Me Only*, 149.
[48] RC, *Report*, 1872, n.p.; *ibid.*, 1874, n.p.; *ibid.*, Nov. 1883, n.p.; *ibid.*, 1886, n.p.

established, they had an appeal hitherto missing. Washburn in 1890–91 was able to raise $62,815. Most of the gifts were modest in amount, but thirteen persons gave a thousand dollars or more. In the next few years Robert College reported gifts and bequests ranging from five thousand to twenty-five thousand dollars. Equally important, by 1896 Robert had acquired a new board of trustees headed by John Stewart Kennedy, a banker and railroad executive, and including Cleveland Hoadley Dodge, the son of William Earl Dodge, Junior. By pouring $190,000 of their own into the school and attracting additional money from others, the new trustees made possible the building program projected by President Washburn and executed by President Gates. At his death in 1909 Kennedy left a bequest of $1,500,000 to the College with which the Engineering School was founded.[49]

At Syrian Protestant College during the 1890's Morris Ketchum Jesup became an important patron. A banker for whom John Stewart Kennedy had once worked, Jesup had a variety of philanthropic interests, including the American Tract Society and Hampton and Tuskeegee institutes. Jesup was also treasurer of the John F. Slater Fund, one of the pioneer foundations, as well as a member of Rockefeller's General Education Board. In short, he was a man with his fingers on the pulse of modern philanthropy. Jesup and his wife made important contributions to the expansion and upgrading of medical work at Beirut.[50] At the American College for Girls, Grace Parrish Dodge, a sister of Cleveland Hoadley Dodge, made the funds of the Dodge family available to that institution as it freed itself from missionary control. These "second generation" patrons shared with those of the first generation a common background—fortunes made in trade or banking and strong evangelical interests through which they became interested in overseas philanthropy.

The last development in the financing of the independent colleges—and a foreshadowing of future trends—was the appearance of support from Mrs. Russell Sage and John D. Rockefeller. Once the Girls' College had secured permission to build anew, its future was assured by substantial gifts from the Sage and Rockefeller fortunes. Syrian Protestant College also enjoyed support from them. These new sources of funds placed the colleges in good financial condition, enabling them to bring their facilities up-to-date and providing them with modest endowments with which to meet current operating expenses.

In introducing the college to the Near East, the Americans had provided an indispensable institution of modern society. As a device for transmitting Western ideas and practices, the college was more sophisti-

[49] "John Stewart Kennedy," in DAB, X.
[50] "Morris Ketchum Jesup," in *ibid*. William Adams Brown, *Morris Ketchum Jesup: A Character Sketch* (New York: Scribner's Sons, 1910).

cated than the mission-sponsored school, for a college curriculum necessarily embraces a broader spectrum of knowledge than that of primary or
secondary schools. Operationally, however, the college, like other schools,
made its impact directly on individuals, enhancing their potential social
mobility, but relying on the student's initiative in utilizing the body of
knowledge to reconstruct his native society. At most, a talented teacher
might awaken a student's interest in a hitherto unrecognized problem and
inspire him to devote his abilities to its resolution. But colleges are not
designed institutionally to formulate systematic programs of social reform, nor are they equipped to administer broad reform programs. Their
social utility lies in equipping individuals with leadership potential.

The independent colleges broadened considerably the range of American philanthropy in the Near East. The colleges succeeded in reaching
directly youth who were outside the Protestant community, and after
1908 they began to reach a few Moslems. The independent, corporate
status of the colleges marked a step toward the secularization of overseas
philanthropy. The two men's colleges were always free of direct mission
control, and the woman's college became so; yet, like the church-related
colleges at home, these schools functioned in the protective shadow of the
mission societies. The funds, teaching staff, and pupils, by-and-large, came
from persons connected with the mission movement. The colleges could
not have functioned in the absence of the mission schools. But the degree
of independence was sufficient to allow a degree of professionalization not
ordinarily achieved by the mission-sponsored activities. The founding of
Robert College and Syrian Protestant College, while not novel in terms of
domestic American philanthropy, furnished precedents for establishing
other American colleges abroad, particularly in India and China. But perhaps equally important the precedent encouraged the American Board to
expand and broaden its own educational programs.

V

Philanthropy, Progress, and Nationalism, 1861–1914

BETWEEN 1861 and 1914 the paradox of mission philanthropy was more clearly revealed than ever before: the mission societies, still the only American institutions able to conduct programs in dozens of Near Eastern villages, succeeded in broadening the range of their philanthropic work and in achieving a high degree of professionalism, yet they remained unable to free their philanthropy from dependence on the evangelistic activities. Although Western ideas and practices gradually penetrated Ottoman society, the missionary philanthropists of this era—unlike Goodell and Dwight in the 1830's—were unable to reach across the barriers of religious and ethnic backgrounds. Growing friction between Turk and Armenian produced unrest and violence and ended by negating American efforts to make the native Christian institutions—schools, press, and medical work—self-supporting.

· I ·

The demands of the native Christians for better educational opportunities overcame the objections of American missionary leaders who in the 1850's had insisted that scarce funds should be concentrated on evangelical preaching. The building of macadamized roads and railroads linking the interior of Anatolia with the seaports and the consequent growth of commerce in the larger cities of the Near East made necessary secondary schools of higher quality if the Protestant community were to share in the opportunities thus opened. Armenian nationalists in Turkey, largely indifferent to the spiritual values of Protestantism, were primarily interested in opportunities to liberate themselves and their children from "the iron yoke of extreme poverty." [1] They complained that the well-trained, relatively rich Americans had made little effort to eradicate poverty.

Competition from rival missionary groups also spurred the Americans to expand their educational efforts. The main threat came from French Catholics; Jesuits, Lazarists, and Sisters of Charity began to organize numerous attractive schools among the Maronites after 1860. Expanded Russian missionary activity in Syria also caused concern. On the other hand, German, English, and Scotch Protestant societies which entered the Near East at this time seemed less menacing, for they worked on a smaller scale than did the Americans, and they shared enough in common so that a spirit of cooperation prevailed. Yet, the appearance of the well-staffed European schools charging little or no tuition served to undermine the American effort to make their mission schools self-supporting.

Division of the mission field between the Congregationalists and the Presbyterians in 1870 provided additional stimulus. Although the two

GROWTH OF MISSION WORK IN TURKEY[2]

Year	Missionaries	Native Workers	Churches	Members	Schools	Pupils
1845	34	12	—	—	7	135
1850	38	25	7	237	7	112
1855	58	77	23	584	38	363
1860	92	156	40	1,277	71	2,742
1865	89	204	49	2,004	114	4,160
1870	116	364	69	2,553	205	5,489
1875	137	460	77	3,759	244	8,253
1880	146	548	97	6,626	331	13,095
1885	156	768	105	8,259	390	13,791
1890	177	791	117	11,709	464	16,990
1895	176	878	125	12,787	423	20,496
1900	162	929	127	13,379	438	22,545
1905	187	1,057	132	16,009	465	22,867
1913	209	1,299	163	15,348	450	25,922

[1] A. L. Chapin and C. M. Mead, "Report of the Special Committee," in ABCFM, *Annual Report*, 1883, xliii; see also, Prudential Committee, "Memorandum: For the Missions in the Turkish Empire, and Recommendations," *ibid.*, 1882, lxx. E. J. Morris to W. Seward, Nov. 22, 1865, in Despatches, Turkey, Vol. 19, #131, General Records of the Dept. of State, Rec. Group 59, National Archives, Washington, D.C.

[2] Joseph K. Greene, *Leavening the Levant* (Boston: The Pilgrim Press, 1916), 108.

churches had long worked together through the American Board of Commissioners for Foreign Missions, the creation of a separate Presbyterian Board of Foreign Missions impelled both societies to greater efforts. The Presbyterians took over the work in Syria, Lebanon, and Persia. New mission stations at Tabriz, Salmas, Tehran, and Hamadan resulted in a tripling of school enrollments in Persia. Similarly, administrative reorganization of the mission field in Anatolia by the American Board promoted educational work. Altogether the number of American mission schools in Turkey jumped from 71 in 1860 to 464 in 1890 and then receded to 450 in 1913. In the same time intervals the number of pupils in Turkey climbed even more spectacularly from 2,742 to 16,990 to 25,922. In addition, at the latter date there were 2,900 pupils in Persia and 6,977 in Syria and Lebanon.

· II ·

Paradoxically, while eighty percent of the students in the mission schools were enrolled in the elementary grades, these schools absorbed only a small portion of the Americans' attention. For the most part they were staffed by natives and supported by the Protestant community, receiving only a modest degree of supervision from American missionary personnel. These schools continued to imitate American methods and practices. The Lancastrian system and the ungraded one-room school gave way in the 1880's to graded classes. Although schools in the smaller, more isolated villages, particularly among the Nestorians on the Ottoman-Persian frontier, were limited to teaching the barest essentials of reading and writing, many elementary schools added geography to the curriculum. The teaching materials were usually the product of the American mission press, and the language of instruction was the vernacular. Because of limited funds and the lack of strong supervision, the common schools were of uneven quality.[3]

The Americans lavished far more energy on their secondary schools. Although the first of these dated back to Cyrus Hamlin's school at Bebek, the founding of secondary schools accelerated in the 1880's, with boarding schools being established by each of the principal mission stations. By 1914 there were nearly sixty American secondary schools in Turkey, Syria, and Persia.

A major purpose of the secondary schools was to train teachers for the mission's elementary schools. The curriculums were revised by the intro-

[3] BFMPC, *Annual Report,* 1908, 362; Greene, *Leavening the Levant,* Chs. 10–11; G. E. White, "Report of the Western Turkey Mission Education Commission," July 7, 1908, in ABC 16.9.3, Vol. 27, #157, American Board Archives, Houghton Library, Cambridge, Mass.

duction of courses in pedagogy, methods, and school management. The mission school at Harpoot, Turkey, developed a normal department, while Gerard Institute at Sidon, Syria, required its seniors to observe the teaching of lower classes and to practice-teach in the day school prior to graduation. Quite a different tack was taken at Urumia, Persia, where the Protestant community organized a board of education to supervise its schools. The board's American-educated superintendent, in turn, utilized the teachers' institute as a means of raising standards through in-service training. To further strengthen their educational work, the secondary schools recruited single American women teachers to join their staffs.[4]

Another objective of the secondary schools was to provide terminal education for the Protestant community generally and college preparatory education for a select few. In these programs the curriculums were broader than those of the pioneer secondary schools at Bebek and Abeih. Botany, physiology, and chemistry were commonly included in the curriculums, and some schools offered courses in astronomy and philosophy. Girls' schools introduced courses in domestic science and art. A number of schools developed programs in vocal and instrumental music. Henry Jessup, who found the native music "monotonous and minor in its melody," discovered to his surprise that native children could learn Western tunes. The Central Turkey Girls' School at Marash offered a five-year course in instrumental music and by 1914 boasted a music hall complete with an auditorium and practice rooms. Other institutions were less ambitious, but many boasted glee clubs or choral groups and orchestras of as many as fifty pieces.[5]

An innovation that aroused considerable interest was manual training. It seemed to offer a means by which secondary students might learn a useful vocation while producing goods that would contribute to the support of the school. Optimistic mission educators argued that "intelligent and skilled labor will soon make a prosperous Christian community." The experiment was undertaken at Bardezag and Marsovan in Turkey, while Gerard Institute in Lebanon became the leading center for vocational training in Syria.[6]

Gerard's curriculum was designed to provide leaders for provincial villages. The mission was certain that the Syrian Protestant College was too sophisticated and expensive for such youth. Nor did the mission believe that SPC graduates would find the salaries paid in the villages attractive. Accordingly, the Institute trained youth as carpenters, tailors, shoemak-

[4] BFMPC, *Annual Report*, 1904, 352–353; *ibid.*, 1905, 291.

[5] Henry Harris Jessup, *Fifty-three Years in Syria* (2 Vols., New York: Fleming H. Revell, 1910), I, 251; Greene, *Leavening the Levant*, 187; "Minutes, 38th Annual Meeting, WTM," May, 1879, in ABC 16.9.3, Vol. 5, #7.

[6] N. G. Clark, "Two Unsolved Mission Problems," in ABCFM, *Annual Report*, 1893, xxii–xxiii.

ers, and farmers. In time this vocational program generated controversy within missionary circles, because the only teachers available were native craftsmen who were not evangelical Protestants, who lacked experience in teaching boys, and who were unacquainted with up-to-date European and American techniques.[7] There was growing realization that the ideal of self-support was a phantom.

Another innovation was the beginning of instruction for the blind and deaf. Although the desirability of such work was discussed in the 1860's, not until 1902 was a start made, when the Girls' School at Urfa began instruction for the blind under Mary Haroutunian, who had been trained for such work at the Royal Normal College in London. By 1914 thirty-two students were enrolled. In 1910 the Anatolia Girls' School at Marsovan organized the first class for deaf children with some fifteen children in the class. While these schools only scratched the surface in meeting the need for training the handicapped, they did demonstrate the possibility of educating this group.[8]

The most important single advance in secondary education was the organization of schools for girls. Although the mission's elementary schools had been open to them almost from the start, not until the 1860's and 1870's was much thought given to organizing secondary schools for girls. The inspiration for this move was derived in part from the feminist movement in the United States and the concomitant development of educational facilities such as Mount Holyoke and the Western Seminary for Women (Ohio), at which many missionary women had been trained. Conditions in the Near East provided more immediate motives. Several American missionaries had noted the low status of women in the region. In the judgment of Henry Harris Jessup, a long-time resident of Lebanon, Islam had "destroyed the family, degraded women, heaped ignominy and reproach on the girls." Secluded at home and veiled when abroad, women were without "training, veracity, virtue, or self-respect." Men despised them and they despised themselves, Jessup added.[9] Fearing that the missionary enterprise would be vitiated without trained women to share the work and to provide wives for Protestant leaders, the mission pioneered secondary schooling for girls.

Boarding schools for girls functioned in the 1860's at Constantinople, Harpoot, Marash, Marsovan, Mardin, Bitlis, Aintab, and Erzerum in Turkey, in addition to similar schools in Syria and Persia. Inevitably there were great variations between the schools. The Female Seminary at

7 Jessup, *Fifty-three Years in Syria*, II, 513–518. White, "Report," in ABC 16.9.3, Vol. 27, #157.
8 Greene, *Leavening the Levant*, 166, 180.
9 Rufus Anderson, *History of the Missions of the American Board of Commissioners for Foreign Missions to the Oriental Churches* (Boston: Congregational Publishing Society, 1873), II, 444–446; Jessup, *Fifty-three Years in Syria*, I, 224.

Beirut, organized in 1847 and reputedly the finest school for girls outside Constantinople, demonstrated the capacity of Syrian girls to pursue a liberal course of instruction. Like many other schools, it endeavored to introduce students to Western culture while keeping the girls "Syrian still in dress and manners." [10] The strength of these schools as purveyors of Western ideas lay in their reaching students in or near their home communities and in their native languages. All of them struggled to establish a firm financial base, for while the mission boards provided funds for salary, the presidents of the schools ordinarily had to find independent funds for building. The existence of educational opportunities for women in the Ottoman Empire prior to World War I was the product of American missionary schools.

An improvement in school equipment and facilities matched the development of the secondary curriculums. Classrooms, which in the 1860's could only be termed "primitive," were supplanted by well-lighted, spacious quarters and equipped with school desks, curtains, clocks, maps, pictures, and blackboards. Boarding schools, originally housed in a single dwelling, acquired separate faculty residences, dormitories, and classrooms. Although devoid of frills, the new buildings were often of brick or stone construction and rose three and four stories. The Anatolia Girls' School at Marsovan, for example, possessed by 1914 four modern buildings located on a modest four-acre campus.[11]

The same social and economic pressures which forced the missionary boards to found secondary schools also compelled them in the 1870's and 1880's to establish and support colleges. Native Christians desired advanced training, but Robert College and the Syrian Protestant College were too distant and too expensive for most youths. As the mission objected to enrolling secular-oriented youths in their theological seminaries, the mission offered collegiate education much as the Congregational Church had sponsored colleges in New England. Belatedly the insights of Cyrus Hamlin were vindicated.

Anatolia College, located at Marsovan in north central Anatolia, was typical of the mission colleges. It was an outgrowth of a theological seminary that had operated at a secondary level. The first step toward creating the College was to assign courses in the languages and sciences to a four-year high school, while the specialized courses in the Bible were retained by the seminary. Beginning with four students who met for classes in a basement room equipped with a table, four chairs, and a blackboard, the school grew, enrolling over eighty students by the end of its fourth year.

[10] Henry Harris Jessup, *The Women of the Arabs, with a Chapter for Children.* Charles S. Robinson and Isaac Riley, eds. (New York: Dodd & Mead, 1873), 80–82.
[11] BFMPC, *Annual Report,* 1883, 57; Bernhard Frederick Nordmann, "American Missionary Work Among the Armenians in Turkey (1830–1923)," Ph.D. dissertation, University of Illinois, 1927, 62.

At this point the high school was transformed into a "college" by adding a fifth year to its curriculum. When the school began life as Anatolia College in September, 1886, it was unincorporated, without funds, and without a building or campus of its own. For the time being the American Board pledged $1,200 per year to its operating expenses plus the full-time services of two missionaries.[12]

Growth of the school rested largely upon its president, Charles Chapin Tracy, whose task it was to breathe life into the project. A Pennsylvania farm boy who had been orphaned as a youth, Tracy prepared himself for college, entered Williams College as a junior, and graduated Phi Beta Kappa. After completion of his theological training at Union Seminary, he went abroad, spending most of the next forty-six years in Marsovan. "With its narrow dirty streets and not a tree or flower or bit of grass to be seen," his wife thought Marsovan "a dreary place in which to spend one's life." [13]

But the drive which Tracy had shown as a youth served him as an educator. During repeated visits to the United States, he raised funds for dormitories and classrooms. Of necessity the plant was not elaborate, although adequate by the standards of Anatolia. Dormitories were unheated, and students occasionally awoke with frost on their bed coverings. Meals were likewise plain, but wholesome and nourishing. In time a library of six thousand volumes was assembled. Discipline was "rather rigid, somewhat Puritanic." [14] Through the years the curriculum expanded to provide a four-year college program. Although in 1893 the college found itself in the center of Armenian revolutionary activity, with several of its students and teachers implicated, it weathered the storm. Finally, it incorporated as a college in 1894 and received imperial recognition in April, 1899. When President Tracy retired in 1913 at the age of seventy-five, the school was engaged in a building program to provide dormitories, a class building, and a museum-library. Most of the building funds came from a handful of philanthropists in the United States, including Mrs. John Stewart Kennedy, whose husband was an active supporter of Robert College, and Arthur Curtiss James, an intimate associate of Cleveland Hoadley Dodge, who shared Dodge's philanthropic interests in the Near East. Student fees took care of five-sevenths of the operating expenses of the school. Enrollment in the school had passed four hundred, mostly Greeks and Armenians.[15]

---

[12] George E. White, *Adventuring With Anatolia College* (Grinnell, Iowa: Herald-Register Publishing Co., 1940), 12 ff.

[13] "Myra Park Tracy," in Charles T. Riggs, "Near East Missionary Biographies," typescript, Istanbul, July 9, 1953, in Archives, UCBWM, Boston, Mass.

[14] *Missionary Herald*, XCVI (1900), 223–228; *ibid.*, XCV (1899), 184–186; Greene, *Leavening the Levant*, 213–215.

[15] George E. White, *Charles Chapin Tracy, Missionary, Philanthropist, Educator,*

By analogous steps six other mission colleges were founded in Turkey prior to World War I. Two of these, the American Collegiate Institute at Smyrna (f. 1888) and the Central Turkey Girls' College at Marash (f. 1882) were for women. The Armenian College (f. 1878), later renamed Euphrates, at Harpoot was unique in that it was coeducational. The college at Sivas (f. 1880) was designated a Teacher's College. The other institutions, Central Turkey College at Aintab (f. 1874) and Urumia College (f. 1881) at Urumia, Persia, were for men only. By 1914 the largest institution, Euphrates College, had 505 students; the smallest, Central Turkey Girls' College, had but 136. The total college enrollment for 1913–1914 was 1,748. In Persia the seminary for boys was raised to "collegiate" status, an expression more of aspiration than of achievement.[16]

The Americans who directed the educational work were a far more homogeneous lot than their counterparts in the United States. They shared common religious convictions and educational experience, being generally better educated than the average American secondary school teacher of the period. While some educators followed the well-trod path to Amherst and Andover, those educated at midwestern schools such as the University of Michigan, Grinnell, or Beloit were increasingly numerous. Furthermore, the mission personnel of the late nineteenth century were frequently united by ties of family, as children of pioneer missionaries returned to the Near East upon completing their education in the United States, took up posts in one or another of the mission stations, and married into other mission families. By 1914 the Riggs family, for example, was related to the Barnum, Dwight, Trowbridge, Shephard, Tracy, and Goodell families. While this inbreeding provided a degree of cohesiveness which strengthened the mission in the troubled times of the late nineteenth and early twentieth centuries, it also reduced the flow of fresh personnel into the missions.

Stability was also the product of the long tenure of many of the educators. Men such as Robert Chambers at Bithynia High School, Charles Tracy and George Emmons White at Marsovan, Crosby Wheeler at Euphrates College, Tilman Trowbridge at Central Turkey College, and Thomas Christie and Alexander MacLachlan at St. Paul's Institute, Tarsus, gave much of their adult lives to the cause of education in the Near East. So, too, did many of the women teachers. Charlotte and Mary Ely, financially independent sisters educated at Mount Holyoke, gave their adult

---

First President of Anatolia College, Marsovan, Turkey (Boston: The Pilgrim Press, 1918), *passim*.

16 *Missionary Herald*, XCV (1899), 529–533; *ibid.*, C (1904), 50–52; Greene, *Leavening the Levant*, 185–188, 200–228; BFMPC, *Annual Report*, 1882, 53; *ibid.*, 1900, 201; Julius Richter, *A History of Protestant Missions in the Near East* (New York: Fleming H. Revell Co., 1910), 306.

lives to founding and operating a girls' school at Bitlis near the Persian frontier. Although Charlotte possessed "an extremely nervous temperament and delicate physique" and her sister was yet more frail, they supervised the building of their school, made furniture, planted gardens, and rehearsed their choirs, besides teaching classes in domestic science, drawing, and composition. At the height of the 1895–96 disorders, they were the only foreigners in Bitlis for over a year. Nor was their long service unique, for at random one can point to Laura Farnham who served thirty-seven years at Adabazar, Corina Shattuck who began teaching at Aintab and subsequently founded girls' schools at Urfa and Kessab during a career stretching over thirty years, or Isabel Frances Dodd who gave forty-five years in Constantinople.[17]

· III ·

In contrast to the vitality of the schools, the mission presses, except at Beirut, were in the doldrums much of the time between 1860 and 1914. They continued to produce translations of English books and to produce teaching materials for the mission schools. But the presses, particularly the one at Constantinople, also imported and distributed materials printed abroad. During these years the secular activities of the presses were subordinated to the religious work of the mission.[18]

Textbooks and magazines constituted the chief secular output of the presses. While they published some primers and geographies for use in the elementary schools, much of their catalogue consisted of texts in mathematics and the sciences. The press at Beirut specialized in medical texts. But as the colleges and secondary schools made increasing use of English as the language of instruction, they turned to American and English publishers who could offer a broader choice of works. As the mission press lost its market for texts, it retrenched; early in the present century the selection of texts available from the press at Constantinople was so inadequate that the schools had no choice but to import books from abroad.[19]

[17] Sketches of the American educators can be found in Greene, *Leavening the Levant*, 170–174 (Ely sisters), 164 (Farnham), 165 (Fritcher), 174–181 (Shattuck). George F. Herrick, "Educational Work at Marsovan Station," ABCFM, *Annual Report*, 1887, 71–74; Crosby H. Wheeler, *Ten Years on the Euphrates* (American Tract Society, 1868); Caleb Frank Gates, *Not to Me Only* (Princeton: Princeton University Press, 1940). White, *Charles Chapin Tracy, passim.*

[18] Thomas Laurie, *The Ely Volume; or, the Contributions of Our Foreign Missions to Science and Human Well-being* (Boston: ABCFM, 1881), 196 ff. "The Publication Department's Report," in ABC 16.9.3, Vol. 28, #183, reviews the financial history of the press.

[19] ABCFM, *Annual Reports*, 1860–1914, *passim.* White, "Report," in ABC 16.9.3, Vol. 27, #157.

The production of the mission magazine, *Avedaper,* consumed more time and provoked more debate than the text books. Founded in 1854 as a semi-monthly printed in Armenian, *Avedaper* was published in an Armeno-Turkish edition as well, starting in 1857. Its contents included articles on religion, modern science, and general news. *Avedaper's* circulation seldom exceeded two thousand, but nevertheless it had the largest circulation of any periodical in the Ottoman Empire prior to 1914. This paper was the means of conveying Western ideas to natives beyond the direct reach of the mission schools or independent colleges.[20] Yet its course was seldom smooth, for the cost of production, much to the distress of the American Board, usually exceeded subscription income. Repeatedly the Board suggested that either the paper be transferred to native ownership and operation, or that it be discontinued. But the mission could not find natives in whom it had confidence to whom it could transfer the paper, nor could it bring itself to suspend publication.[21]

The hostility of the Ottoman government also inhibited the Constantinople press. Beginning in 1864, the Ottoman government interfered with the distribution of books, severely limiting the places of sale. Ottoman legislation adopted in the 1870's and 1880's introduced censorship. Although directed chiefly at religious publications, censorship so demoralized the mission that it was discouraged from pursuing its publication work vigorously.[22]

Preoccupation of the mission translators and editors with religious publications also restricted the secular output of the Constantinople press. Although the various editors—Henry S. Barnum, Joseph K. Greene, Edwin E. Bliss, Isaac G. Bliss, and George F. Herrick—were competent linguists, they were all ordained clergymen, and many of them were primarily interested in the production of vernacular editions of the Bible. During much of this time the Constantinople press was staffed by only one full-time man, Elias Riggs. Displaying a precocious aptitude for languages as a child, Riggs from 1832 until his death in 1901 made a distinguished record as a linguist and translator. His *Manual of the Chaldee Language* was the

---

[20] H. O. Dwight to S. Cox, Aug. 25, 1886, in Cox to T. Bayard, Sept. 10, 1886, Despatches, Turkey, Vol. 46, #234.

[21] "The Avedaper," in ABC 16.9.3, Vol. 28, #179; "Minutes, 26th Annual Meeting, Western Turkey Mission," May, 1866, in *ibid.,* Vol. 1, #29; "Minutes, 30th Annual Meeting, WTM," May, 1870, in *ibid.,* #33; "Minutes, 32d Annual Meeting, WTM," May, 1872, in *ibid.,* Vol. 5, #1; "Minutes, 43d Annual Meeting, WTM," May, 1884, in *ibid.,* Vol. 9, #5; "Minutes, 40th Annual Meeting, WTM," May, 1881, in *ibid.,* #1; "Minutes, 41st Annual Meeting, WTM," May, 1882, in *ibid.,* #2. Rufus Anderson, Secretary of the American Board, did not share the enthusiasm of overseas personnel for the continuation of *Avedaper.* See, ABC 16.9.3, Vol. 1, #29.

[22] E. Morris to W. Seward, July 18, 1865, in Despatches, Turkey, Vol. 18, #103; O. Straus to T. Bayard, June 8, 1888, in *ibid.,* Vol. 47, #87; S. Hirsch to J. Blaine, Mar. 31, 1890, in *ibid.,* Vol. 49, #104.

standard treatise in American theological seminaries for a half century.[23] A master of the Armenian vernacular as well as Greek, Turkish, and Bulgarian, he devoted his linguistic skills chiefly to making translations of the complete Bible into Armenian and Bulgarian and in revising the Turkish Bible in both Arabic and Armenian characters. An accomplished hymnologist, he also translated from one hundred to five hundred hymns into Greek, Armenian, Turkish, and Bulgarian. His work was characterized by "painful exactitude, patient research, sincere fidelity and a wonderfully consistent style." [24] These were accomplishments enough for one lifetime, but they left little time for the secular work of the press.

A particularly noteworthy achievement of the mission, though accomplished independently of the press, was the production of the still-standard Redhouse English-Turkish dictionary. Funds for the original edition were raised by William Gottlieb Schauffler, who commissioned the English lexicographer, James William Redhouse, to do the work, the mission retaining the copyright. The first edition was printed in England in 1861.[25] Subsequently Henry Otis Dwight, son of the pioneer missionary, devoted six years to the preparation of a new edition that appeared in 1890.[26] The dictionary was of utility wherever English-speaking persons worked with Turkish language materials.

The presses at Urumia and Tehran, of secondary importance, were even less active than that at Constantinople. At Urumia, a translation of *Pilgrim's Progress* was prepared in Syriac, but because of the limited capacity of the printing equipment, the government press was engaged to do the work. At Tehran the press functioned at the editorial level only, for it proved cheaper to use native print shops, and this arrangement entailed fewer difficulties with the official censor.[27]

---

[23] Elias Riggs, *A Manual of the Chaldee Language* (Boston, 1832).

[24] Richter, *Protestant Missions*, 109; Riggs also published *Notes on the Grammar of the Bulgarian Language* (Smyrna, 1844); *A Brief Grammar of the Modern Armenian as Spoken in Constantinople and Asia Minor* (Smyrna: W. Griffitt, 1847); *A Vocabulary of Words in Modern Armenian but not Found in the Ancient Armenian Lexicons* (Smyrna: W. Griffitt, 1847); and *Outline of a Grammar of the Turkish Language As Written in the Armenian Character* (Constantinople: A. B. Churchill, 1856). See *British Museum General Catalogue* for his translations of the Bible.

[25] James William Redhouse, *A Lexicon, English and Turkish* . . . (London: B. Quaritch, 1861). A second edition of this work was published at Constantinople in 1877. William Gottlieb Schauffler, *Autobiography of William G. Schauffler for Forty-nine Years a Missionary in the Orient*, ed. by his sons (New York: Anson D. F. Randolph & Co., 1887), 232. The funds for the 1861 edition were given by William Wheelwright, an American residing in England. "H. O. Dwight," in Riggs, "Near East Missionary Biographies."

[26] James William Redhouse, *A Turkish and English Lexicon* (Constantinople: A. H. Boyajian, 1890). A new impression of this edition was made at Constantinople by H. Matteosian in 1921 for the American Board.

[27] BFMPC, *Annual Report*, 1908, 360; Richter, *Protestant Missions*, 320.

The Beirut press, alone, grew significantly during these years. It benefitted from the ability of the Presbyterians to concentrate their resources
on the one press, as well as from the decidedly freer atmosphere of Beirut.
In 1871 the press acquired a new building; by 1900 its staff numbered
forty-five, and its equipment included a variety of presses in addition to an
electrotype apparatus and a type foundry that produced matrices in Arabic for print shops as far off as India, making it unquestionably the "most
far-reaching agency" of the mission. It was the largest Arabic printing
establishment in the world.[28]

After 1900 the mission presses enjoyed a renaissance. At Constantinople
the American Board increased the proportion of its budget allocated to
the press, while John D. Rockefeller, Sr., made a modest contribution to
its support. In Persia, which was exposed to Western influences from Russia and Great Britain, the Presbyterian Board stirred their press to renewed
activity. An example of its work was *Poor Boys Who Became Famous*, a
potpourri of biographical sketches including Abraham Lincoln, Horace
Greeley, Booker T. Washington, John Bunyan, and Giuseppe Garibaldi.
When a group of Urumia men sought to found an Assyrian national
paper, the mission press contracted to do the printing.[29]

· IV ·

Medical philanthropy, which had been introduced in the 1830's, enjoyed
only a sporadic interest in the 1860's, but it became a major activity of the
mission in the 1880's and thereafter. The main emphasis was on general
practice, individual mission doctors taking their skills into the provincial
towns of Turkey, Syria, and western Persia. In the early years of the
twentieth century their work became institutionalized as they established
small hospitals. Simultaneously, several doctors formed small classes of native students, training them in elements of Western medicine. In general
the mission's medical work focused on the patient, bringing him personal
relief not otherwise available. But at the same time, by acquainting residents of provincial villages with elements of Western medicine, mission
doctors brought hope that pain and suffering need not be a way of life.
In creating a market for medical service, the mission facilitated the work
of the Syrian Protestant Medical School.

Illustrative of the role of a mission doctor in the 1860's and 1870's were
the diverse activities of Henry S. West. Small, nervous, and modest, West

[28] BFMPC, *Annual Report*, 1900, 267; *ibid.*, 1882, 49; *ibid.*, 1884, 58; Greene, *Leavening the Levant*, 144; H. Maynard to W. Evarts, May 18, 1880, in Despatches, Turkey,
Vol. 36, #396.
[29] BFMPC, *Annual Report*, 1908, 360; ABCFM, *Annual Report*, 1906, 73; "Report of
the Publications Department," in ABC 16.9.3, Vol. 28, #190.

had spent two years at Yale College before undertaking medical studies at the College of Physicians and Surgeons in New York. He went abroad for the American Board in 1859, locating at Sivas in western Turkey. The first medical missionary in Anatolia who was not also an ordained clergyman, West, nevertheless, preached the gospel, distributed tracts, and taught Sunday School in addition to practicing medicine, a profession he loved passionately. In his home he established a clinic where he met patients, had an operating room, and conducted a post-operative ward. His specialty was surgery, and during his seventeen-year career, he performed fourteen hundred operations on the eyes and 250 lithotomies. A tireless worker, he also traveled, serving a radius of a hundred miles from Sivas, though of course on a chance basis. While at Sivas, Doctor West took a total of nineteen native youths into his home and clinic where he gave them formal medical instruction for an hour or two a day over a period of three to four years. Much as other Americans seeking to share a part of their culture and civilization with the Near East, West encountered difficulties and misunderstandings. Patients all but frustrated his best efforts in their behalf by consuming all of a prescription at one time in the hope of obtaining quicker relief, by taking the wrong medicine, or by refusing altogether to carry out orders. In 1876 he died of typhus fever at the age of forty-nine.[30]

The career of Joseph Plumb Cochran, a pioneer of Western medicine in Persia, was surprisingly similar to that of West, although Cochran began his work a generation later. Typical of medical missionary personnel in the late nineteenth century, he was a college-trained doctor. Although he may have given much time to Christian evangelism, Cochran and other doctors after 1880 made fewer references to such activities than Henry West and other early doctors. Cochran, the only skilled physician within a 120-mile radius of Urumia, built the first regular, fully-equipped hospital in Persia. While the Presbyterian Board gave its blessing to his venture, Cochran had to raise the major portion of the necessary funds himself. This he did chiefly through contacts with churches at home, inducing a specific congregation to adopt his hospital as a special object of giving.[31]

Even the building of a hospital did not entirely solve Cochran's problem, for there was no pharmacist in the area, and the doctor had to compound his own medicines. He had no orderly, no nurse, and often no colleague. Servants and even schoolboys were pressed into service to administer chloroform. During operations the doctor's attention was diverted by the necessity of taking the patient's pulse, listening to his

[30] *Missionary Herald*, LXIII (1867), 270–272, 309–312; Greene, *Leavening the Levant*, 146 ff. "Henry S. West," in Riggs, "Near East Missionary Biographies."
[31] Robert Speer, *"The Hakim Sahib" The Foreign Doctor, A Biography of Joseph Plumb Cochran, M. D., of Persia* (New York: Fleming H. Revell, 1911), 61–63, 322.

breathing, and selecting the instruments as they were needed. When an operation was over, Cochran had to help carry the patient to his bed. In serious cases he had to sit up all night with the patient or at least make several nocturnal visits. Because facilities were inadequate and native confidence in modern surgery was not yet established, he was loath to attempt any operation when a successful outcome was at all doubtful. Cochran frankly confessed that dispensing pills and making one-visit calls made little impact on the overall state of native health.[32]

In Persia, where Moslems were less familiar with Christians than were their co-religionists in Anatolia and Syria, the Americans were compelled to confine their ministrations chiefly to the Christian population. The ceremonial cleanliness of the Moslem and the "uncleanness" of the Christian made it most difficult for the Moslem to turn to a Christian doctor. As late as 1914 many Persian Moslems could scarcely force themselves to enter the house of a Christian doctor, much less allow themselves to be touched by his hands or to swallow medicines prepared by him. Yet the Presbyterian mission engaged in medical work at Urumia, Tabriz, Tehran, Hamadan, Resht, and Kazvin.

By 1900 the role of the medical missionary in Turkey and Persia was changing. On the one hand, American medicine was abandoning the primitive and often ineffective methods of the early nineteenth century in favor of procedures based on modern science. More than ever before it had much to offer the Near East. On the other hand, increasing numbers of native doctors possessed a "considerable knowledge" of Western medicine. The American doctor found himself called in as a consultant in "difficult" cases to confirm the diagnosis of a native physician and to advise on up-to-date methods of treatment. Both the American and the Presbyterian boards displayed vigor in recruiting medical missionaries. As opportunities presented themselves, the doctors opened dispensaries or small hospitals. These were seldom more than a large house that contained separate wards for men and women, an operating room, a pharmacy, and an outpatient clinic, as well as living quarters for the staff. After 1900 specially designed hospital buildings were constructed in several centers, and by 1914 there were nine mission hospitals operating in Turkey. In four of these—Van, Marsovan, Talas (Caesarea), and Aintab—the facilities were reasonably up-to-date.[33]

---

[32] *Ibid.*, 329–331.

[33] BFMPC, *Annual Report*, 1887, 81; *ibid.*, 1900, 192; *ibid.*, 1908, 368–369; see also, John G. Wishard, *Reminiscences of a Doctor: A Personal Narrative* (Wooster, Ohio: Collier Printing Co., 1935), the account of a Presbyterian missionary doctor at Tehran.

· V ·

Although the American mission, ever since the founding of the Protestant community, had aimed at creating an autonomous, self-supporting native church, it was unsuccessful. Responsibility for this failure lay partly with the Americans, partly with the native Christians, and partly with the Ottoman government. As a consequence the schools, press, and medical work remained precariously dependent upon continuing American financial support.

In the years from 1860 to the mid-1880's the impact of the Americans was vitiated by continuing differences between the missionaries and their native converts over the organization and financing of the native churches and companion institutions. The difficulty originated with the reorganization of the mission in the early 1860's. The American Board, which previously had assigned its personnel to work with members of a specific ethnic group, reorganized on geographical lines, organizing East, Central, and West Turkey missions. In any one community all Protestants were to be served by a single congregation. These changes, however meritorious in terms of Christian brotherhood, ignored the imperatives of emerging nationalism. As self-esteem required that each ethnic group retain its language and culture, native Protestants resisted efforts at forced integration. The new policy occasioned little difficulty in the elementary schools, which enrolled children from ethnically homogeneous neighborhoods. But efforts to implement the policy in the boarding schools, which drew students from several ethnic groups, provoked bitter controversy and resistance. Greek Protestants ordinarily declined to attend schools in which the predominant element was Armenian, and vice versa. Nor did native Protestant faculty or students welcome those few Kurds or Turks who braved censure from co-religionists to enroll in mission schools. Thus a "brilliant future" for Euphrates College was threatened when well-to-do Armenians, who had just begun to support the school, objected to the admission of Moslems to the student body.[34]

Questions of finance also produced protracted, divisive controversy between the Americans and native Protestant leaders. At issue was the mission's policy of expecting the native community to assume support and control of the various institutions. While much of the argument involved ecclesiastical affairs, the secular program was also involved. Native leaders complained that the paternalism of the Americans had thwarted growth of native self-reliance. They proposed that the Americans restrict them-

[34] Alford Carleton, "The Development of Missionary Policy in Turkey," Thesis, Hartford Theological Seminary, 1930, 16.

selves to making grants-in-aid and leave the administration of the programs to native leadership. From the mission's point of view, continued
American direction was justified on the grounds that as the Americans put
up the funds, they should set policy. Furthermore, American direction
was indispensable if the schools, press, and medical work were to demonstrate American values and techniques effectively.[35]

As the issue came to a head in the 1880's, the American Board sent President A. L. Chapin of Beloit College and Professor C. M. Mead of Andover
Seminary to conduct an inquiry. They reported that although numeri-
cally the natives carried much of the leadership burden, they had been
restricted to subordinate positions. They recognized, too, that the limited
incomes of the natives did not allow sufficient funds to support schools at
the standards set by the Americans. Moreover, the missionaries, who lived
well by native standards, had generated discontent by restricting their
social life to other mission families and by remaining aloof from the native
community. Subsequently a formula was worked out for transferring responsibility and control of the enterprises to the native community, but it
was contingent upon increased native support of the work.[36]

Despite good intentions this plan failed. The financial hardships of the
native community were accentuated in the 1880's by the flight of many
men to seek their fortunes in America, leaving behind wives, children, and
the aged to shift for themselves. By the start of the twentieth century as
many as one person in four had left numerous Protestant communities for
the United States. Losses of life, money, and property in the massacres of
1895 and 1909 intensified these financial problems and prevented realization
of autonomous Protestant institutions, the key to the success of the whole
enterprise. Try as they might, the Americans never extricated themselves
from the necessity of directing and subsidizing their philanthropic ventures.[37]

No less a deterrent to the conduct of the American philanthropies in
Turkey was the intensity of animosities between various ethnic and religious groups, resulting occasionally in civil disorders. At such times the
Americans had to suspend their ordinary activities and turn to administration of relief. Such was the case in 1860 when Syria was gripped by civil
war between the Maronites and Druzes. Ottoman authorities, rather than
suppress the protagonists, sided with the Druzes, a sect which if not orthodox Moslem was not Christian either. As a result the conflict was pro-

[35] "Minutes, 48th Annual Meeting, WTM," July, 1889, in ABC 16.9.3, Vol. 9, #14;
"Minutes, 40th Annual Meeting, WTM," May, 1881, in ibid., #1.
[36] Prudential Committee, "Memorandum: For the Missions in the Turkish Empire,
and Recommendations," in ABCFM, Annual Report, 1882, lxvii ff.; "Deputation to
Turkey," in ibid., 1883, 15–18; Chapin and Mead, "Report of the Special Committee,"
in ibid., xix–xxxvii.
[37] Ibid., 1903, 65; BFMPC, Annual Report, 1902, 233.

tracted, and by the time the Turks restored order later in the year some six thousand Maronite Christians had been killed in the Lebanese villages plus five thousand more in Damascus.[38]

Appalled by the "desolation and death," missionaries at Beirut issued a circular in August, 1860, describing the events and soliciting relief funds locally as well as in England and the United States. Americans with religious or philanthropic interests in the Near East responded by organizing a fund-soliciting committee under the leadership of William A. Booth, a New York merchant who later served as a trustee of the Syrian Protestant College. Although the Beirut committee sought $240,000, it received but $100,000 of which one-quarter came from the United States. This sum was less than that raised by the philhellenes in behalf of the Greeks, but the distraction of the presidential canvas and the growing animosities between North and South may well explain the failure to raise more in the United States.[39]

In dispensing alms the missionaries utilized much the same techniques employed by Samuel Gridley Howe and associates in Greece. A local committee, styled the Anglo-American Relief Committee and headed by the British Consul-General for Syria, Nevin Moore, provided general administrative oversight. Initially, assistance took the form of food and medical care. But "in order not to encourage idlesness," recipients of aid were required to work for the help rendered. Able-bodied men were put to work repairing the principal roads in the area. Approximately one-fourth of the relief monies were employed in this fashion. Far the largest part of the funds was used to furnish villagers grain with which to sow their lands and again become self-supporting. Ultimately, the committee reported that 75,000 persons had been assisted.[40]

· VI ·

Before World War I the Americans had little personal contact with the Moslem peasants and made little direct impact on them. The Anatolian peasant remained gripped tight by "the tyranny of history." [41] Remedies

---

[38] "Civil War on Mt. Lebanon," Aug. 1, 1860, in ABC 16.8.1, Vol. 6, #105.

[39] H. Jessup to R. Anderson, Jan. 27, 1861, in *ibid.*, #19; "Statement of Anglo-American Relief Committee," Aug. 23, 1860, in *ibid.*, #102; Lord Bulwer to Lord Russell, Nov. 11, 1860, in FO 78, Vol. 1513, #738, Public Record Office, London.

[40] "Statement of Anglo-American Relief Committee," Aug. 23, 1860, in ABC 16.8.1, Vol. 6, #102; see also, *ibid.*, #105, 106, and 278. Jessup, *Fifty-three Years in Syria*, I, 213. Jessup published thirty articles or letters on the situation in the *New York World*, 1860–61.

[41] Lewis V. Thomas and Richard N. Frye, *The United States and Turkey and Iran* (Cambridge: Harvard University Press, 1951), 38–39; Hans Kohn, *Western Civilization in the Near East* (London: George Routledge & Sons, 1936), 75–76; Barbara Ward, *Turkey* (London: Oxford University Press, 1942).

for treating the sick, elements of diet, the role of the family, the structure and furnishing of homes, the style of clothing and tools, and techniques of work remained the product of inherited folkways. The physical isolation of the peasant and the contempt in which he was held by the Ottoman ruling class minimized the possibilities of change. The Americans made no concerted effort to reach him.

Nor, except in the 1830's, did they have much direct impact on Ottoman intellectuals or officials. Most Turkish intellectuals and officials made their acquaintance with the West by reading European books; others did so by traveling or living in Europe. France, close, prestigious, and eager to oblige, provided the chief source of Turkish acquaintance with Western culture during the 1860's. While reforms of the Tanzimat era often rendered little more than lip service to Western liberalism, in the 1860's the atmosphere was conducive to the publication of Turkish journals, which flooded the country with Western ideas. Primarily at French insistence and with some French aid, the first hesitant steps were taken toward creating a state school system. In no important way did the missionary philanthropists serve as a means of directly Westernizing the Moslem Turk.[42]

If the Americans made no direct impact on Moslem peasants, intellectuals, or officials, American philanthropy was subject to the political environment of Ottoman Turkey and in turn affected that environment. Goaded by the British, Abdul Medjid had issued the Hatt-i Humayun in 1856, pledging Turkey to accord all subjects equal liberties. During the 1860's the powers of government were exercised chiefly by Aali Pasha and Fuad Pasha, both committed to preserving Ottoman sovereignty by reorganization and Westernization, by secularization and Ottomanization. While the Western Powers were preoccupied with the emergence of Italy and Germany as national states, and while Russia was recovering from her defeat in the Crimean War and was attempting far-reaching internal reforms, Turkey enjoyed a respite from unwanted foreign interference.

Turkish receptivity to Westernization during the 1860's provided no stimulation to American philanthropy. First, Aali and Fuad were captivated by French civilization, not Anglo-American, and the Turks adopted French educational systems and absorbed Western culture through French writers. Second, the Turks, aspiring to bridge ethnic and religious differences and create a common Ottoman loyalty, would tolerate but not encourage parochial institutions serving a minority group.[43]

[42] Carl Brockelmann, *History of the Islamic Peoples*, Joel Carmichael and Moshe Perlmann, translators (London: George Routledge & Kegan Paul, 1949), 389 ff.

[43] Fuad had lived in France and England; Aali had been ambassador in London (1842–45) and had taken part in the Congress of Vienna (1855) and the Congress of Paris (1856).

Paradoxically, American missionary philanthropy, in disseminating Western ideas, added to the difficulties of Fuad and Aali in the realization of Ottoman goals. By their educational efforts, the Americans promoted among the Armenians and Arabs an awareness of their distinctive cultures. Armenians who had been assimilated by the Turks to the degree that they spoke only Turkish began to learn and use their native tongue. The standardization of the Armenian vernacular promoted by the American mission press permitted Armenians in all parts of Ottoman Turkey—Constantinople, the Caucasus, or Cilicia—to communicate more easily with one another. The American contribution to Armenian and Arab nationalism was cultural, not political, but it was no less effective in making these persons less receptive to the Ottomanization desired by Fuad and Aali as a means of uniting the disparate subjects of the Sultan.[44]

The American educators, editors, and doctors also opposed some specific measures which in Turkish eyes were designed to strengthen Ottoman sovereignty. By treaty and custom, Westerners living in Turkey enjoyed special privileges under Ottoman law. These capitulations, originally granted freely by the Porte to a handful of Christian traders, were widely abused during the mid-nineteenth century, and Turkish statesmen regarded them as objectionable limitations on Ottoman sovereignty and as barriers to future development. As it seemed unlikely that the Western Powers could be persuaded to abandon these privileges, Fuad and Aali attempted to attack them piecemeal. In legislation regulating the press in 1864, Turkey permitted foreigners to publish only on condition that they become subject to the jurisdiction of Turkish law and Turkish courts. In 1867 Turkey carried out promises in the Hatt-i Humayun to permit foreign ownership of real estate. But again the Porte insisted that, in their role as property owners, foreigners must foreswear their capitulatory privileges by conforming to Ottoman police regulations, submitting to the jurisdiction of Ottoman civil courts, and paying the usual taxes. The Americans, in common with the Europeans, protested that the Turks were not to be trusted and enlisted the aid of the American government to oppose this infringement of their "rights." [45]

Not all Ottoman officials and intellectuals were enthusiastic about the blessings of Westernization. To some it seemed that Turkey was "camped on a volcano." One writer, reviewing the principles and policies which

[44] Roderic H. Davison, *Reform in the Ottoman Empire, 1856–1876* (Princeton: Princeton University Press, 1963), 88 ff.

[45] Nasim Sousa, *The Capitulatory Regime of Turkey: Its History, Origins, and Nature* (Baltimore: Johns Hopkins University Press, 1933) and Leland J. Gordon, *American Relations with Turkey, 1830–1930: An Economic Interpretation* (Philadelphia: University of Pennsylvania Press, 1932) treat these innovations from the perspective of American diplomacy; Davison, *Reform in the Ottoman Empire*, 260 ff., places the issues in the broader perspective of Ottoman reform. See also, E. Morris to W. Seward, July 25, 1868, in Despatches, Turkey, Vol. 20, #265.

had made European states powerful, paid tribute to the importance of Western technology, commerce, and education. He recognized, too, that in Western Europe the "strength and safety of the State" rested on the "equality of all citizens before the law" in the enjoyment of their rights to life, liberty, and property as well as on guarantees against the exercise of arbitrary power. But if Ottoman Turkey were to adopt these Western principles, the benefits would accrue to Christian minorities to the detriment of the Turks. Public instruction, which had promoted progress elsewhere, would not save Turkey for the Turks, for the Christians in Turkey had "twenty times the start." Neither would reliance on political liberalism, for the Christians, far from being grateful for their newly acquired rights, were exasperated because of those still denied them. To open public service to the Christians would likewise fail to solve Turkey's problem, for a Christian would "attain to power not as a Turk, but as a Greek, an Armenian, or Schlave [sic]." The Ottoman dilemma was a bitter one: "how to go on without reforming, and yet how to reform without perishing." [46]

In 1871 the winds of change began to blow from another direction. French prestige in Turkey faded visibly as Prussia crushed the Second Empire, while the deaths of Fuad in 1869 and Aali in 1871 left Turkey with no one to continue their enlightened policies. A "period of chaos" ensued as Abdul Aziz concentrated power in the Palace and frittered away his energies and public funds on a spate of eccentricities. Abandoning the policy of uniting all ethnic and religious groups in a common Ottoman nationality, the Sultan hoped to employ Islam as the bond that would hold his fragmented empire together. As this new policy downgraded Westernization, Henry Harris Jessup recorded, "Hostility to foreigners, and jealousy of their presence and operations of every description, commercial, educational, and religious are on the evident increase." [47]

The deposition first of Abdul Aziz and then of Murad V in 1876, the abortive effort to institute constitutional government by Midhat Pasha, and the coming to power of Abdul Hamid II, resulted in official policies still less receptive to American philanthropy. Abdul Hamid promptly dismissed Midhat Pasha, his liberal Grand Vizir, and, after allowing the new Ottoman parliament to assemble, prorogued it, not convening it again until 1908. Adopting pan-Islamic policies, he condemned the Christian minorities to continued second-class citizenship. Hamidian policies became increasingly repressive and capricious, as the Sultan successfully shifted power from the Porte to the Palace. Except in the realm of military affairs, his regime was less receptive to reform than those of his predeces-

---

[46] "Turkish Reforms from a Mussulman Point of View," *Levant Herald*, May 1, 1867, in Morris to Seward, May 3, 1867, in *ibid.*, #205.
[47] Jessup, *Fifty-three Years in Syria*, II, 438.

sors. The new restrictions interfered with the philanthropic activities even more than with the evangelistic work. As a result, American philanthropists clashed repeatedly with Ottoman regulations and requested the assistance of the United States and Great Britain to oppose Ottoman regulations.

Of least effect were restrictive regulations involving the doctors. Regarding the issuance of a medical diploma as a state rather than an academic function, the Porte categorically declined to permit the Syrian Protestant College to certify the eligibility of its graduates for a diploma, without which a doctor risked prosecution for malpractice. Even in reaching an accommodation the Porte agreed only to let graduates travel to Constantinople at their own expense to stand examination by officials of the Imperial Medical College.[48] Individual mission doctors, though licensed abroad, were required to meet Ottoman standards. Viewing these regulations as designed to harass foreign doctors rather than as bona fide measures to protect Ottoman subjects from unqualified practitioners, many mission doctors flouted the laws. Although these regulations were more vigorously enforced against Americans than against other foreigners, the American *chargé d'affaires* at Constantinople advised compliance with the law.[49]

In similar fashion Americans continued to run afoul of capriciously designed and enforced regulations of the press. Initially, American publications were made to share the opprobrium with foreign religious publications, which offended Moslem sensibilities by labeling the Prophet Mohammed an "imposter" and his religion a "matter of abhorrence."[50] But the Turks also feared secular materials which promoted a sense of nationalism among the minority populations. Exception was taken to a Turkish-English lexicon because of references therein to Armenia, Albania, and the short-lived constitution of Midhat Pasha.[51] The enforcement of censorship regulations compounded difficulties, for the Turks employed a dual standard by which works certified as acceptable in the capital were subject to

[48] H. Fish to J. Brown, July 31, 1871, in Instructions, Turkey, II, #7; Brown to Fish, Aug. 22, 1871, in Despatches, Turkey, Vol. 23, #16 and Feb. 16, 1872, in *ibid.*, #50.

[49] L. Wallace to F. Frelinghuysen, Apr. 23, 1883, in *ibid.*, Vol. 40, #207; June 5, 1883, in *ibid.*, #228; July 18, 1883, in *ibid.*, #247; Apr. 11, 1884, in *ibid.*, Vol. 42, #370. British subjects faced the same difficulties. W. White to Lord Salisbury, Aug. 17, 1888, FO 78, Vol. 4102, #318. White protested Turkish regulations and declined to require British doctors to go to Constantinople to stand examination by the Imperial Medical Council. Bending to foreign pressures, the Turks agreed that foreign doctors already practicing in Turkey as of Sept. 21, 1888 might submit their diplomas only; doctors arriving after that date would have to appear in person. White to Salisbury, Dec. 6, 1888, in *ibid.*, Vol. 4106, #482.

[50] Aali Pasha cited in Brown to W. Seward, July 23, 1864, in Despatches, Turkey, Vol. 18, #8.

[51] H. O. Dwight to Wallace, Aug. 4, 1883, enclosure to Wallace to Frelinghuysen, Aug. 14, 1883, in *ibid.*, Vol. 41, #265.

seizure in the provinces. After much protest by the Americans, the Turks agreed to formulate a single standard of acceptability. In practice, provincial officials continued their capricious actions. Consequently, there was little certainty that printing schedules could be maintained or that published materials would reach their intended audience.[52]

The mission schools encountered the most persistent difficulties. As Abdul Hamid centralized power in his own hands, his means of frustrating the activities of the American educators increased. One means was to forbid, or at least delay, the transfer of property or the granting of a building permit for a new school. Another technique, employed widely in the 1880's and 1890's, utilized newly adopted school laws which, like those in America, established standards for teacher certification, the curriculum, and the physical facilities of the school. These laws were not inherently objectionable and formed part of a legitimate effort to strengthen the state school system. In some cases Ottoman dissatisfaction with foreign schools was triggered by the French schools, and the Americans were caught in the backlash; in other cases rival Roman Catholic and Greek Orthodox clergy encouraged Moslem authorities to object to the American schools. But whatever the cause, provincial officials, hostile to the Protestant community or to the mission, would collect for examination the teaching certificates of all members of a school's faculty, whereupon local authorities, conducting an independent check, would close the school because the teachers could no longer produce their credentials.[53]

Resolution of these problems proved most difficult. The Americans complicated matters by assuming a high-handed position that they were free to operate schools as soon as their teachers, textbooks, and curriculums met Ottoman standards and that they need not await the issuance of an official permit attesting to that fact. Furthermore, the missionaries claimed the right to unrestricted operation of three categories of schools: those owned and taught by American citizens; those owned and directed by Americans but taught by natives; and those owned and taught by na-

[52] J. Blaine to G. Heap, June 6, 1881, in Instructions, Turkey, Vol. 3, #36; Assim Pasha to Wallace, Nov. 15, 1881, in Wallace to Blaine, Nov. 18, 1881, in Despatches, Turkey, Vol. 38, #27; Assim to J. Longstreet, Apr. 16, 1881, in Longstreet to Blaine, Apr. 29, 1881, in *ibid.*, Vol. 37, #26; H.B.M.'s. Consul Everett cited in Frelinghuysen to Heap, Aug. 19, 1884, in Instructions, Turkey, Vol. 4, #220.

[53] "Provisions Additional to Regulations Concerning Public Instruction," in O. Straus to T. Bayard, Dec. 27, 1887, in Despatches, Turkey, Vol. 47, #47; Heap to S. Cox, July 3, 1886, in Cox to Bayard, July 13, 1886, in *ibid.*, Vol. 45, #191; Wallace to Heap, Jan. 27, 1885, in Wallace to Frelinghuysen, Feb. 6, 1885, in *ibid.*, Vol. 43, #471; Straus to Blaine, Mar. 28, 1889, in *ibid.*, Vol. 48, #187 and May 27, 1889, in *ibid.*, #196. A. Terrell to W. Gresham, Nov. 15, 1893, in *ibid.*, Vol. 56, #106. W. White to Earl of Iddesleigh, Jan. 8, 1887, FO 78, Vol. 4172, #13. See H. C. A. Eyres to White, Feb. 7, 1887, in White to Salisbury, Mar. 19, 1887, in *ibid.*, #106; White to Salisbury, Apr. 16, 1887, in *ibid.*, #42; and E. Thornton to Lord Rosebery, June 5, 1886, in *ibid.*, #291.

tives with a subsidy and some supervision from Americans. Lacking confidence in the willingness of Ottoman officials to enforce the school laws fairly, missionary educators declined to abide by the regulations.[54]

The American legation vigorously defended the rights of schools in the first category, while it held that schools in the third group, which comprised the majority of the "American" schools in the Near East at this date, had no recognizable rights which could be protected by the United States government. The "rights" of the second group of schools remained obscure. The legation further agreed that newly organized schools should submit their programmes of study, their textbook lists, and the diplomas or certificates of their teachers to examination by the Turkish authorities. Existing schools, however, on the assumption that they had acquired a prescriptive right to operate, were directed not to apply for permits, lest this imply the right of the Ottoman government to deny a permit.[55] By 1893 affairs had reached crisis proportions, and American diplomats spent the better part of the decade resolving the issues. The heart of the matter was that Abdul Hamid believed his government threatened by revolutionary activities of the Armenians with whom the Americans had been identified.[56]

An incident at Anatolia College in Marsovan in 1893 lent credence to the growing fears of the Sultan. On January 6, the Gregorian Christmas Day, posters proclaiming a revolution and calling for the deposition of the Sultan appeared on mosques, churches, and school houses. After preliminary investigation by Turkish authorities established that these revolutionary placards had been printed at the College, a student and two native faculty members, Thoumayan and Kayayan, were arrested and charged with revolutionary activity. At the end of January a newly completed college building burned, whereupon the acting president, George F. Herrick, accused Husref Bey, the ranking Ottoman official in Marsovan and "a known robber and murderer," with setting the blaze.[57]

This incident occasioned an outburst of anti-Turkish sentiment that soured American-Turkish relations for years. An investigation by American officials confirmed that the placards had been printed at the College,

---

[54] P. King, to Bayard, Jan. 11, 1887, in Despatches, Turkey, Vol. 46, #276.

[55] Straus to Bayard, Feb. 18, 1888, in *ibid.*, Vol. 47, #61; A. MacLachlan and H. S. Jenanyan to King, Aug. 24, 1888, in King to Bayard, Sept. 15, 1888, in *ibid.*, Vol. 48, #111; Straus to Blaine, Mar. 16, 1889, in *ibid.*, #179. American educators, on occasion, were overbearing in their demands. The founders of St. Paul's Institute (Tarsus), while asking more privileges than those conferred hitherto on foreign institutions, declined to observe Ottoman administrative procedures in filing their application.

[56] Occasionally essays by native students expressing seditious sentiments came to the attention of Ottoman officials. For example, see White to Salisbury, Aug. 17, 1888, in FO 78, Vol. 4102, #317 and Dec. 29, 1888, in *ibid.*, Vol. 4106, #517.

[57] G. Herrick to D. Thompson, Feb. 4, 1893, in Thompson to J. Foster, Feb. 25, 1893, in Despatches, Turkey, Vol. 54, #37; see also Thompson to Foster, Jan. 25, 1893, in *ibid.*, #17.

though without the knowledge of American personnel; that the two native professors were indeed members or officers of an Armenian revolutionary group; and that Husref Bey was responsible for setting the fire.[58]
But American educators, long frustrated by capricious Ottoman regulations, sounded off. Cyrus Hamlin, in retirement but widely identified with
American activities in Turkey, charged that the missionaries were being
"insulted, mobbed, imprisoned, their dwellings and schools burned, their
property seized and confiscated. . . ." [59] President Herrick stirred still
more anti-Turkish feeling on a speaking tour of England.[60] But missionary
attacks on the Ottoman government reached their widest audience in the
revelations of William W. Peet, the American Board treasurer at Constantinople, who appeared in print in both the *Daily News* and the *Daily
Telegraph* of London charging that the disorders had been carried out at
"the order of the Sultan himself." [61]

In 1895 the smoldering hostility between Turk and Armenian burst
into open rebellion by the Armenians. For a time Americans at Marash,
Hadjin, Aintab, Bitlis, and Urfa feared for their lives. Although early reports described the Armenians as victims, later evidence established that
the Armenians were more often the aggressors. Furthermore, it became
clear that the greatest danger to American lives and property came from
Armenian revolutionaries, most of whom were Gregorians, who resented
the neutrality of the American missionaries.[62]

Although the European powers blustered, they failed to agree on any
common policy. The Russians, according to Judge Terrell, the American
Minister to Turkey, opposed any intervention until they were given *carte
blanche* in the Caucasus. The French, like the Turks, regarded the American missionaries as the chief cause of the disturbances, while only the
British and Germans exhibited any sympathy for the work of the Americans. Convinced that the Turks were trying systematically to drive out

[58] H. Newberry to Thompson, Apr. 12, 1893, in Thompson to Gresham, Apr. 24,
1893, in *ibid.*, Vol. 55, #78 is the authoritative report. See also dissenting views, W. W.
Peet cited in Newberry to Gresham, May 9, 1893, in *ibid.*, #86 and Terrell to
Gresham, July 20, 1893, in *ibid.*, #13.
[59] Cyrus Hamlin, "The Relations of Missionaries in Foreign Lands to Their Government," *Missionary Review of the World*, cited in A. Terrell to W. Gresham, July 14,
1893, in *ibid.*, Vol. 55, #7.
[60] Terrell to Gresham, Aug. 11, 1893, in *ibid.*, #34.
[61] Terrell to Gresham, Jan. 26, 1895, in *ibid.*, Vol. 58, #409. See *Daily Telegraph*
(London), Jan. 14, 1895.
[62] British views of the rebellion are to be found in FO 78, Vol. 4629, #562-793.
American missionary views are Everett P. Wheeler, *The Duty of the United States to
American Citizens in Turkey* (New York: Fleming H. Revell, 1896); Cyrus Hamlin,
"America's Duty to Americans in Turkey: an Open Letter to the Hon. John Sher-
man," *North American Review*, CLXIII (Sept., 1896), 276-281; and Frederick D.
Greene, *The Rule of the Turk, and the Armenian Crisis* (New York: G. P. Putnam's
Sons, 1897).

the missionary philanthropists by "burning them out and securing their departure by intimidation," Judge Terrell called for the dispatch of American naval vessels to Turkish waters. At the same time he urged missionaries in remote areas to move to coastal areas or at least to send their wives and children to places where they might be protected.[63]

Refusing to abandon their varied enterprises, the Americans held on and again provided relief to natives in distress. The missionary establishment abroad became the channel through which relief funds from a multiplicity of sources were administered. Mission stations and schools became centers for the distribution of food and clothing. Shelter was provided the homeless. At some centers, such as Trebizond, women were employed in making quilts and jackets, shirts, and other garments for distribution to the needy. Plows, hoes, forks, and other simple farming implements were manufactured to replace those lost or destroyed. Likewise, seed corn was distributed. Forty orphanages cared for as many as fifty thousand children at the height of the crisis; this resulted in the organization of permanent orphanages at six major mission stations. Altogether relief was afforded some half-million victims of the uprising.[64]

A concomitant of the relief work abroad was the raising of funds at home. Unlike earlier crises among the Greeks, Syrians, and Armenians, this time there was a small, vocal group of Armenian expatriates in the United States, headed by the Armenian Hentchak Revolutionary Federation, to echo the cries of their countrymen. A committee formed, public meetings were scheduled in Malden, Andover, and other Armenian centers in Massachusetts, and resolutions were dispatched to Congress. "Habitual humanitarians" such as Robert Treat Paine, William Lloyd Garrison, Jr., and Julia Ward Howe, widow of the great philhellene, were enlisted in support of the United Friends of Armenia, which reached Americans inaccessible to the Armenian expatriates. Numerous local relief committees in the Midwest and East formed a loose confederation, the National Armenian Relief Committee, headed by United States Justice David J. Brewer and supported by Spencer Trask, Chauncey Depew, Leonard

---

[63] Terrell to R. Olney, Nov. 28, 1895, in Despatches, Turkey, Vol. 60, #695; Terrell to H. O. Dwight, Dec. 27, 1895, in Terrell to Olney, Dec. 29, 1895, in *ibid.*, Vol. 61, #742. H. O. Dwight, "American Missions in Turkey and their Protection," in Terrell to Olney, Dec. 29, 1895, in *ibid.*; and H. O. Dwight, "Memorandum on the Denial of Treaty Rights to American Citizens in Turkey who are Missionaries," Oct. 18, 1893, in Terrell to Olney, Dec. 10, 1896, in *ibid.*, Vol. 64, #1099.

[64] Straus to J. Hay, Jan. 25, 1899, in *ibid.*, Vol. 67, #40. Fuller accounts are in "Armenian Relief Fund," FO 78, Vol. 4792–4794, *passim.* Funds from the committees headed by the Duke of Westminster and the Duke of Argyll and transmitted through the British Embassy exceeded £50,000 during 1896. Duke of Westminster to T. H. Sanderson, Nov. 7, 1896, FO 78, Vol. 4794. See P. Currie to Lord Kimberley, June 19, 1895, in *ibid.*, Vol. 4693, #257, for details on organization of the committee.

Woolsey Bacon, and Frederick D. Greene. Another loud, anguished voice was raised by the American Board. Through sermons and church publications the "unspeakable Turk" was assailed; Armenian virtues were sung, their sufferings exposed.[65]

Yet another campaign was launched by T. DeWitt Talmadge, a popular Brooklyn preacher, and his associate, Louis Klopsch of the *Christian Herald*, the most widely circulated religious paper in the English-speaking world. Fresh from promoting Russian famine relief, Klopsch was experienced in the ways of converting sympathy to gifts. In fifteen years as editor, Klopsch subsequently reported he had raised over $3,000,000 for various causes, extracting an average of $2.75 per donation in return for graphic, on-the-scene accounts of misfortune and misery. To this hue and cry the newspaper press added reports "almost week by week of further massacres, mutilated children, and ravished women." [66]

The horror stories, while initially effective in opening purses, provoked reaction. "Much harm has been done by painting the subject in colors so black as to paralyze all effort to relieve it and even to make such an effort absurd," Frederick Greene, an old Turkey hand, warned fellow fund raisers.[67] Indeed, enthusiasm to support Armenian relief was inhibited by successive demands for Russian, Armenian, and Cuban relief and compounded by a continuing depression in the United States. As atrocity was added to atrocity, some Americans began to suspect that the stories were exaggerated; others concluded that political turmoil in Turkey precluded wise use of funds. By December, 1895, various fund raisers, including Louis Klopsch and the American Board, desired to broaden the base of support and lessen responsibility for distribution of funds by drawing the American Red Cross into the act.[68]

Reluctantly Clara Barton, already in her mid-seventies and still smarting from accusations of dictatorial conduct of the Red Cross, after receiving unanimous support of local groups and assurance of funds, lent her know-how to Armenian relief. Taking five assistants, "skilled, practical helpers," she went to Turkey. Despite the irksome attacks of the American press, the Ottoman government ultimately allowed Miss Barton to send five expeditions into the interior. Leaving the feeding of the masses to others, Miss Barton concentrated her resources on getting the victims of the disorders back to work. In spite of "colossal difficulties" encountered in Tur-

[65] Merle Curti, *American Philanthropy Abroad: A History* (New Brunswick: Rutgers University Press, 1963), 119 ff.; Ernest R. May, *Imperial Democracy: The Emergence of America as a Great Power* (New York: Harcourt, Brace & World, 1961), 27.

[66] Charles M. Pepper, *Life-Work of Louis Klopsch: Romance of a Modern Knight of Mercy* (New York: The Christian Herald, 1910), 28 ff. See New York *Tribune*, Nov. 13, 1895; Philadelphia *Record*, Mar. 13, 1896.

[67] Frederick D. Greene to Herbert Welsh, Jan. 16, 1896, cited in Curti, *American Philanthropy*, 123.

[68] *Ibid.*, 125.

key, compounded by criticism and misunderstanding at home, "her achievement was remarkable." [69]

Yet relief was not enough. The "tide of beneficence" could not be sustained. As early as October, 1895, British fund raisers felt there was no solution short of administrative reforms in the Ottoman government that would safeguard life and property. In America, as during the Greek War for Independence, humanitarians called on Congress to intercede. Senator Wilkinson Call of Florida in December, 1895, introduced a concurrent resolution calling on the American government to end the Armenian disorders by negotiation if possible, by force if necessary. The resolution went on to urge creation of an independent Armenian state guaranteed by the major powers. Rejecting Call's resolution as too sweeping, Senator Shelby Moore Cullom, chairman of the Senate Foreign Relations Committee, proposed a more restrained substitute. He would assure the President of Congressional support for any measure he might take to induce the parties to the Congress of Berlin to respect their treaty obligations to the Armenian people. In fine, the United States would recognize the necessity of a political settlement, but others should direct the settling. [70]

In the ensuing debate, sympathy for the Armenians was general. Many Senators and Representatives pointed out, however, that the Cullom resolution afforded neither relief nor protection. And in the House, Charles Henry Grosvenor of Ohio expressed his contempt for its pusillanimous tone. "They have asked us for bread, and we are giving them a stone. They have asked us for the fish of a Christian nation's powerful protest, and we have given them the serpent of an abject falling down and apology at the feet of the Turkish government." [71] Outside the halls of Congress, clergymen were quick to affirm that the American government should act "promptly and effectively." The Methodist *Western Christian Advocate* suggested that Turkish rule must be overthrown by force. When the disorders spread to Constantinople in August, 1895, there were demands that the navy be dispatched at once to deal justice. But this bellicosity soon exhausted itself. Scholars protested the distortion of fact, and the conservative press dissented from the proposals for American involvement. In the end sympathy for the Armenians was not enough to persuade Congress to intervene, and both Senate and House agreed only to the mild proposal of Senator Cullom. [72]

[69] Clara Barton, *The Red Cross: A History of this Remarkable International Movement in the Interest of Humanity* (Washington: American National Red Cross, 1898), 279–280; Curti, *American Philanthropy*, 129.

[70] *Congressional Record*, 54 Cong., 1 Sess., 1896, 108, 959–961, gives the background of the Call and the Cullom proposals.

[71] *Ibid.*, 1000–1016.

[72] May, *Imperial Democracy*, 28–29. H. O. Dwight, "Report of the Constantinople Station, 1896–97," in ABC 16.9.3, Vol. 18, #80.

Even this resolution proved but an empty gesture. Despite pleas from William E. Dodge, Jr., the philanthropist, and Andrew D. White, distinguished university president, President Cleveland declined to act. Rather he took his cues from Oscar Straus, former minister to Turkey, who advised that official intervention would succeed chiefly in irking the Ottoman government and in disrupting relief efforts. Yet the incident was not without consequences. The relief effort was an enterprise of major magnitude. To the $73,000 raised by the *Christian Herald* were added other large sums including $107,000 from the Red Cross. American groups collectively provided at least $300,000, while organizations in England added even more money, so that by mid-1897 $1,116,896 in relief funds had passed through the hands of the American Board's treasurer in Constantinople. A new generation of Americans had been introduced to the Eastern Question in terms describing Turks as barbaric oppressors and Armenians as hapless victims. The policy of non-involvement adopted at the time of the Greek War for Independence had been set aside for a mild resolution in which Congress recognized that political intervention was a necessary condition for reestablishment of stability in Turkey.[73]

As both the Turks and Armenians exhausted themselves in acts of violence, the crisis in Turkey burned itself out. Subsequently Judge Terrell, the American minister, pressed the claims of those American institutions which had sustained damage, but the Ottoman government, recognizing that acquiescence to American demands for reparations would expose it to still greater demands from other powers, resisted settlement. Years of continual goading by successive American diplomats were required before the Sultan agreed to an indemnity. Even then, the school question went unresolved. Only a threat to recall the American minister entirely persuaded the Ottoman government to come to terms.[74]

Although the Americans made little direct contribution to the Westernization of the Ottoman ruling classes during the reign of Abdul Hamid, the Sultan could not stem the growth of Western ideas among his European-trained officers, who became the most cohesive Westernized element in government circles. Organized as the Committee of Union and Progress, but popularly known as Young Turks, the officers reestablished the constitution of Midhat Pasha in 1908 and deposed Abdul Hamid the next year.

Under the Committee of Union and Progress, Turkey eagerly embraced elements of Western liberalism, and Moslems for the first time

---

[73] Curti, *American Philanthropy*, 125.

[74] For example see, L. Griscom to Hay, Dec. 26, 1900, in Despatches, Turkey, Vol. 69, #302; Leishman to Hay, July 28, 1902, *ibid.*, Vol. 72, #239; and Feb. 9, 1903; in *ibid.*, Vol. 73, #351. A naval demonstration from September, 1903 to January, 1904, proved unavailing. Instructions, Turkey, Vol. 8, *passim.*

became free to attend the American schools and colleges if they so desired. The Americans were delighted with the change. But pyramiding internal and external problems frustrated the ambitions of the Young Turks. Difficulties in Tripoli and Albania shattered the hopes of the CUP to create a strong state on the principle of political equality for all subjects. Although Christians were allowed to hold public office and the press was freed from capricious censorship, goodwill was not enough. Animosities among the various minorities were too deeply ingrained to permit unity. Moslems retained an "invincible repugnance" to taking orders from those whom they could not regard as other than giaours, infidels.[75] Furthermore, the rank and file of the Young Turks did not share their leaders' interest in the Westernization of Turkey, and they emphasized the nationalistic elements of the party's program. Increasingly the Young Turks were driven to embrace pan-Islamism, denying the Christian minorities any hope of sharing Turkey's future, just as had Abdul Hamid. The Young Turks foundered on "the reef of nationalism," [76] as Turkey became involved successively in disastrous wars in Tripoli and the Balkans. World War I brought the denouement.

· VII ·

By 1914 more than a thousand American missionaries, educators, editors, and doctors had served in the Near East. This area ranked alongside India and China as a major center of American missionary philanthropy abroad. Within the Near East the American effort far surpassed that of any other Protestant nation and was rivaled only by that of Catholic France. By reputation the American schools and colleges equalled or surpassed other schools operating in the Ottoman Empire or Persia.

At the elementary level the Americans reached a large proportion of the Protestant community of the Near East, while at the secondary and collegiate levels, they reached the few from whom the Protestant community drew its leaders. The American schools were influential in promoting knowledge of the vernacular languages and of modern science. The leading ideas of Western culture were presented in the native tongues. Far more than the independent colleges, the mission schools carried Western ideas into the provincial towns. But it must be underscored that the energies of the mission institutions were largely concentrated on low-prestige Protestants.

[75] Brockelmann, *History of the Islamic Peoples*, 67. See also, Harry Luke, *The Old Turkey and the New: From Byzantium to Ankara* (London: Geoffrey Bles, 1955), 141–142.
[76] Ward, *Turkey*, 30.

Indirectly the mission schools and press had an impact that reached beyond the Protestant community. As the mission schools were the earliest Western-type institutions, they served as models for other parochial schools as well as for the first Ottoman state schools. Religious rivalry spurred other religious groups to intensify their educational work. American textbooks and American-trained teachers were frequently employed by Orthodox, Gregorian, Roman Catholic, and Ottoman schools. The American example in affording opportunities for the education of women spurred emulation by others and contributed to the cause of feminism.

In retrospect, the drama of American philanthropy in Turkey to 1914 exhibited elements of classical tragedy. Like other multi-ethnic states of the nineteenth century, Ottoman Turkey was threatened with disintegration should a minority group conclude that its ethnic or religious ties weighed more heavily than its loyalties to the Ottoman state. Because Protestant evangelists of the 1830's and 1840's failed to find a common ground for cooperation with the orthodox churches, native Protestants and orthodox Christians wasted endless energies in recriminations that added to the internal disorder within Turkey. Similarly, Protestant Christian sponsorship of schools and presses precluded their making major direct contributions to the Westernization of Turkey under the liberal regimes of Fuad and Aali in the 1860's. By their concentration of efforts on the Arabs and Armenians, the Americans strengthened the sense of separateness of these minority groups, thus adding to the difficulties of assimilating all the subjects of the Sultan within a framework of Ottoman loyalty. Unintentionally, the Americans intensified the forces of nationalism and separatism within Ottoman Turkey.

By providing better educational opportunities than were otherwise available in Turkey, the Americans aroused aspirations that their Armenian and Arab protégés could not realize under the pan-Islamic policies of Abdul Hamid. The limited training in English and the exposure to Western ideas generated by the American institutions gave many natives hope that by migrating to England or America they might achieve success denied at home. The flow of Armenians beginning in the 1880's was small in comparison to the numbers of eastern and southern Europeans entering the United States, but it was thoroughly disruptive to the Protestant community in the Near East. The Ottoman government was greatly offended when Armenian émigrés, returning to Turkey armed with American citizenship, claimed the right to live again in Turkey as Americans entitled to special treatment under Ottoman law. From 1880 to 1914 the status of such Armenians was a major source of controversy in American-Turkish relations.[77]

[77] J. Barton to O. Straus, Jan. 26, 1888, in Despatches, Turkey, Vol. 47, #66; Gordon, *American Relations with Turkey*, 305–355.

Missionary benevolence had its chief strength in its ability to mobilize resources and personnel to conduct sustained educational and medical work abroad. Its chief weakness was its inability to transcend religious barriers and develop a sustained relationship with non-Protestants. As a consequence its direct impact was upon minority groups that in the context of Ottoman and Persian politics could not perform as an effective leaven of general reform.

While the Americans were pursuing, adapting, and enlarging their activities in Turkey, Syria, Lebanon, and Persia, the American Board was undertaking new ventures in the Balkans.

CHAPTER

VI

New Ventures in the Balkans, 1858–1914

A CONCOMITANT of the American Board's expanded activities in Ottoman Turkey was its entrance into the Balkans. Mission stations and a supporting apparatus of schools, medical work, and publications were initiated among the Bulgarians in 1858, and educational work was begun among the Albanians in 1889. Among both groups, the Americans unintentionally contributed to the development of emerging nationalism. Before World War I engulfed the Balkans, the mission also undertook a pioneer venture in agricultural education.

· I ·

Bulgaria, along with present-day Macedonia, Yugoslavia, and Albania, was subject to Ottoman authority during the middle of the nineteenth century. As with the Armenians, the primary agency and symbol of common feeling among the Bulgarians was their church, Orthodox in doctrine, but Greek in the language of the service and in leadership. Since the 1830's the Bulgars had entered the orbit of Western thought and culture. As a by-product, Bulgarians organized schools that disseminated the doctrines of nationalism in the form of history and folklore. In the 1860's, during the progressive administration of Midhat Pasha, the Bulgars prospered, gaining self-confidence in their capacity to run their own political affairs better than their Turkish overlords and their religious affairs better than Greek clergymen.[1]

American awareness of the Bulgars began with the literary activities of Elias Riggs, the great missionary linguist, who composed an elementary Bulgarian grammar (1847) for use by English-speaking students. In his work, first at Smyrna and then at Constantinople, Riggs worked closely with Constantine Photinoff, one of the leaders of the Bulgarian literary renaissance. Using the mission press, Photinoff issued in 1842 a magazine, *Luboslovie,* thus beginning the periodical press of Bulgaria. This cooperation continued to the degree that of the first hundred books printed in modern Bulgarian, some seventy were printed by the American mission press. Riggs also worked with Petko R. Slaveikov, famous for his collections of proverbs and folklore. Together they established the Thracian dialect as the standard literary form. Riggs' success in this effort rested partly on his choice of a dialect that Bulgarians were willing to accept, his association with independently influential Bulgarian literary figures, and his access to one of the few presses working with Bulgarian materials.[2]

As Riggs and his associates pursued their editorial labors, the mission at Constantinople began exploring the prospects for undertaking missionary work among the Bulgarians. Cyrus Hamlin, visiting England in the late fall of 1856, sounded out British church leaders to ascertain their views. Encouraged, he toured Bulgaria the next spring, visiting Rodosto, Adrianople, and Philippopolis.

Hamlin was lyrical in his enthusiasm for Bulgaria. It was "a beautiful region waiting for the taste and intelligence of virtuous industry to make it a paradise. . . . The fields, clothed in the highest verdure of spring, gave promise of unsurpassed abundance. . . ." Although the houses, often windowless, were constructed of wattle or wicker work plastered with mud, the inhabitants therein were "the cleanest people in the world," industrious, unembarrassed, humble, and kind. Obviously Hamlin was impressed. So, too, were other Americans who shortly made similar tours of Bulgaria.[3]

Hamlin recognized the existence of a "great national movement" among

[1] Sydney Nettleton Fisher, *The Middle East: A History* (New York: Alfred A. Knopf, 1959), 325–326.

[2] William Webster Hall, Jr., *Puritans in the Balkans: The American Board Mission in Bulgaria, 1878–1918* (Sofia, 1938), 32 ff., is based on printed and manuscript records of the mission. A contemporary Bulgarian nationalist has commented that the American translation of the Bible into the vernacular meant "the resuscitation of the Bulgarian nation from the fetters of Hellenism. . . ." Constantine Stephanove, *The Bulgarians and Anglo-Saxondom* (Berne: Paul Haupt, 1919), 300.

[3] Cyrus Hamlin, *Among the Turks* (New York: Carter & Bros., 1878), 262–273. Hamlin, letter of May 18, 1857, in *Missionary Herald,* LIII (1857), 292–298; see also, E. E. Bliss, in *ibid.,* LIV (1858), 72–76; and Charles F. Morse, in *ibid.,* 286–287.

the Bulgarians to free themselves from Greek (clerical) domination. Bulgarians told him: "We have no books in our language and are not allowed to print any for ourselves. We are without a literature, without schools, and, you may say, without a language." [4] From this Hamlin inferred that the Bulgarians would welcome American aid in establishing schools, in preparing textbooks, and in providing the complete Bible in the Bulgarian vernacular. The prospects of realizing national independence Hamlin regarded as hopeless, and he counted on this failure to increase the receptivity of the Bulgarians to American efforts.

Hamlin and his colleagues in Constantinople urged the American Board to inaugurate work in Bulgaria immediately. The Board was further encouraged to do so by British churchmen. Unable for political reasons to undertake mission work of their own, these churchmen believed that if the American Board failed to do so, the Bulgarians would fall under the spell of French and Austrian Catholics. The Turkish Missions Aid Society, a British organization which Hamlin had helped organize, offered support; accordingly, in 1858 a mission was authorized. [5]

Ironically, work among Bulgarians began just as the American Civil War forced the Board to retrench elsewhere. Mission stations were established at Adrianople (Edirne), Eski Zagra (Stara Zagora), and Philippopolis (Plovdiv), and sometime later at Samokov, Monastir (Bitolj), and Salonika, all primarily in the area south of the Balkan Mountains. Following the by-now-traditional course of action, the mission promptly organized schools. The Reverend James F. Clarke started a school for boys at Philippopolis in the fall of 1860. A small man, Clarke more than compensated for his size by his doughty spirit and a passionate devotion to the school he led for twenty-eight years. His task was facilitated by a gift of three hundred pounds from English friends and the eagerness of many Bulgars to secure an education. Beginning modestly with four students, enrollment in the school grew to about thirty during the next decade. Thirty-five dollars sufficed to keep a student for a year. Three years after the start of the boys' school, Theodore L. Byington organized a school for girls at Eski Zagra. While not the first in Bulgaria, the girls' school was a pioneer. The two schools contributed to the small number of Bulgarians acquainted with Western European thought. [6]

[4] C. Hamlin to R. Anderson, May 18, 1857, in ABC 16.7.1, Vol. 12, #270, in American Board Papers, Houghton Library, Cambridge, Mass. The British Ambassador, Henry Bulwer, confirmed Hamlin's assessment of Bulgarian dissatisfaction with Greek clergy. Bulwer to Lord Russell, Dec. 5, 1860, in FO 78, Vol. 1514, #816, Public Record Office, London.

[5] C. Hamlin to R. Anderson, Nov. 10, 1856, in ABC 16.7.1, Vol. 12, #262 and H. G. O. Dwight, "European Turkey as a Field of Christian Missions," [1858], in ABC 16.7.1, Vol. 11, #284.

[6] Robert Carlton Delk, "The History and Influence of American Education in the Near East, 1823-1914," typescript, 1949, in Archives, UCBWM, Boston, Mass. The

Both schools encountered difficulties. The main objective of the Americans had been "to raise up reliable native helpers to preach the gospel to the Bulgarians." But it appeared that many Bulgarians intended "to get as much secular and as little religious instruction" [7] as possible. In spite of this attitude, the respective school principals succeeded in creating an intensely religious atmosphere within the schools, much as Amherst and Andover had done early in the century. Clarke reported some of his students were in tears at the thought of their "lost condition." "Room prayer meetings" and a "week of prayer" became regular features of school life. Students in the boys' school went out by two's as colporteurs and preachers during vacations. But in shaping the religious conduct of their students, the educators often irked those parents who rejected the evangelical doctrines of the Americans. [8]

The start of American educational work with Bulgarians coincided with the rise of a determined, organized Bulgarian opposition to the Greek Orthodox hierarchy. Encouraged by the Hatti-i-Humayun (1856) and prodded by Bulgarian refugees in Odessa and Bucharest, Bulgarian nationalists petitioned Sultan Abdul Medjid for the same ecclesiastical privileges enjoyed by the Greeks and Armenians. In 1860 several Bulgarian bishops renounced their allegiance to the Patriarch. Then followed a decade-long contest between Greeks and Bulgars for control of churches and schools in Bulgaria, Macedonia, and Thrace. Bulgarian nationalists, regarding their nation as bound together by their religion, often felt that acceptance of Protestantism meant separation from the nation. As the evangelistic activities increased, bitterness and persecution increased. In one village a member of the town council was removed from office because of his evangelical leanings; the use of public ovens for baking bread was denied the evangelicals; their cattle were barred from the common pasture. At the girls' school a native teacher was kidnapped, and when the teacher escaped her captors and returned to the school, a crowd of Orthodox Bulgarians, angry at the teacher's return to the school, rioted and stoned the school. In 1867 the parents of some of the girls, offended by the religious atmosphere of the school, withdrew their daughters. Protestant sponsorship in the minds of these Bulgars offset the value of the otherwise highly-prized academic training. The school closed until 1871, when it was reopened in Samokov. [9]

The environment within which the Americans operated changed mark-

---

annual reports of the principals of the schools and related materials are in the records of the European Turkey Mission, ABC 16.9.

7 Theodore Byington quoted in Hall, *Puritans in the Balkans,* 30, 31.

8 Quoted in *ibid.,* 31.

9 "Report," Feb. 5, 1861, in ABC 16.9, Vol. 4, #56, and Letter of Mar. 12, 1870, in *Missionary Herald,* LXVI (1870), 221.

edly in the 1870's. As early as 1863 the mission had resolved to defer as long as possible the formation of a separate Protestant community. In July, 1868, three Bulgarian adherents went before Turkish authorities and declared themselves Protestants, but not until the summer of 1871 was an Evangelical church organized. At the same time, American activities in Bulgaria were separated organizationally from the Western Turkey Mission. Functioning henceforth as the European Turkey Mission, the Americans had to operate their schools to nurture the small Protestant community. Of far greater importance was the action of the Sultan in 1870 freeing the Bulgarian church from Greek control and placing it under a Bulgarian Exarch residing at Constantinople.[10]

Having secured autonomy for their church, Bulgarian nationalists in the 1870's turned to the pursuit of political independence. When the Turks reacted slowly to a revolt begun in July, 1875, in neighboring Herzegovina, Bulgarian revolutionists took advantage of the diversion. Noting that "young Bulgaria" was "on fire to be up and fighting for the fatherland," the American educators cautioned their impatient charges "against connection with any revolutionary schemes." [11] During the first months of 1876, there was much behind-the-scenes activity as the European powers, particularly Britain and Russia, sought to maintain the status quo in the Balkans without becoming directly involved. But to no avail; in May, 1876, Bulgarian nationalists deliberately killed some two hundred Moslem officials. The Turks, responding quickly, retaliated savagely by killing twelve thousand Bulgarians, the reprisals centering on the town of Batak a few miles west of Philippopolis where an estimated five thousand people in a population of seven thousand perished.[12]

In the months that followed, the American philanthropists, though generally onlookers, played a minor but significant role in the events which precipitated Bulgarian autonomy. In the first instance Albert Long and George Washburn, both of Robert College, having received detailed accounts of the massacres from former students, passed these reports on to Sir Henry Elliot, the British ambassador, and to Edwin Pears, resident correspondent of the London *Daily News*. Because the details had been gathered by Americans, the accounts had a credibility they would not

[10] "The Bulgarian Question," *Saturday Review* (London), Apr. 17, 1869, quoted in ABC 16.9, Vol. 4, #57. Julius Richter, *A History of Protestant Missions in the Near East* (New York: Fleming H. Revell, 1910), 168.

[11] Hall, *Puritans in the Balkans*, 40; H. G. O. Dwight and J. F. Clarke, "The Suffering in Bulgaria," Oct. 17, 1876, ABC 16.9, Vol. 5, #36. George Washburn of Robert College claimed that Bulgarian students at the College were almost unanimously opposed to the insurrection. H. Layard to Lord Derby, May 12, 1877, in FO 78, Vol. 2571, #440.

[12] Walter G. Wirthwein, *Britain and the Balkan Crisis, 1875–1878* (New York: Columbia University Press, 1935), 84 ff., is a review of British opinion as presented by the press.

otherwise have commanded, and the story was published while it was still timely.

Disraeli, then Prime Minister, was committed to upholding Turkey and thwarting Russian policy in the Near East. Assured by his ambassador that Pears' "immensely exaggerated" accounts emanated from American missionaries who were "very good men but ultra Bulgarians," [13] Disraeli dismissed this first report as "mere coffee house babble." [14] A second, more explicit report, passed by Long and Washburn to Pears and urging an official investigation, forced the reluctant prime minister to act. Indeed, three investigations were made. The British government chose Walter Baring, second-secretary of the embassy at Constantinople. Alarmed that the British had selected the least experienced member of the embassy staff for their investigation and fearing that the Turks would be whitewashed, George Washburn persuaded the American minister, Horace Maynard, to send Eugene Schuyler, the consul-general, to make an independent investigation. In addition the *Daily Mail* commissioned the American journalist, Januarius Aloysius MacGahan. Within a week Baring's preliminary report alerted the prime minister to the truth of Pears' accounts, but his report was not published until September 19, 1876.[15] So far as the public was concerned, any doubts as to the veracity of Pears' stories were removed when, on August 30, Schuyler's report was published in English newspapers along with the first in a series of stories by MacGahan.[16]

Confirmation of the atrocities, after Disraeli's efforts to pooh-pooh them, enhanced public interest in the Bulgarians and intensified the reaction against Turkey. No other developments in the crisis gave the Eastern Question the emotional intensity or personal quality imparted by the Bulgarian atrocity stories. Newspapers, including the *Times* which had at first doubted the stories, thundered against the iniquities of Turkish rule,

[13] H. Elliot to Derby, July 6, 1876, in FO 78, Vol. 2460, #716. Elliot discounted the atrocity accounts because they stemmed from Russian and Bulgarian sources. H. Elliot to Lord Tenterden, July 14, 1876, in FO 78, Vol. 2460, private and July 20, 1876, in *ibid.*, Vol. 2461, private. See H. Maynard to H. Fish, Nov. 21, 1876, in Despatches, Turkey, Vol. 30, #106 for an American view of the affair. General Records of the Dept. of State, Rec. Group 59, National Archives, Washington, D. C.

[14] Hall, *Puritans in the Balkans*, 41.

[15] W. Baring to Elliot, July 22, 1876, in Elliot to Derby, July 25, 1876, FO 78, Vol. 2461, #788.

[16] E. Schuyler to Maynard, Aug. 10, 1876, in Elliot to Derby, Sept. 5, 1876, FO 78, Vol. 2463, #964. This letter also transmits Baring's final "Report on the Bulgarian Insurrection of 1876." Elliot, still defensive about his reports to the Foreign Office, impeached Schuyler's report, alleging that he spoke neither Turkish nor Bulgarian, that he had relied completely on a Bulgarian interpreter, and that as he had just arrived on post, he lacked the necessary background to evaluate the accounts. Elliot to Derby, Sept. 5, 1876, in *ibid.*, #965. Schuyler claimed he could converse in Bulgarian. Edwin Pears, *Forty Years in Constantinople: The Recollections of Sir Edwin Pears, 1873–1915* (New York: D. Appleton, 1916), 12–24.

while clergymen, both Anglicans and dissenters, inveighed against the Turk from their pulpits. In early September William Ewart Gladstone, long a partisan of evangelical Christianity, placed himself at the forefront of the cause, publishing *The Bulgarian Horrors of the East*. His pamphlet, selling fifty thousand copies in five days, demanded that the Turks be evicted "bag and baggage . . . from the province they have desolated and profaned." Meetings throughout Britain raised anti-Turkish feeling to a fever pitch.[17]

While the details of the atrocities leaked out, the crisis in the Near East broadened. Riots at Salonika in May led several European governments to dispatch warships to the mouth of the Dardanelles; the deposition of Sultan Abdul Aziz on May 30 brought his gentle-minded nephew, Murad V, to the throne. After Serbia declared war against Turkey in early July, Murad became insane, and he was in turn deposed on August 31, in favor of his brother, Abdul Hamid II. Exploiting Turkey's distracted state, Russia threatened late in September to join the war against Turkey unless the latter agreed to peace terms.

As Disraeli faced this widening crisis, public reaction to the Bulgarian atrocity stories limited his freedom of action. His policy called for support of Turkey against Russian pressure. But by the end of August, 1876, the Foreign Office recognized that publication of the atrocity stories had "completely destroyed" popular sympathy for Turkey. The feeling was "universal and so strong" that even if Russia were to declare war against the Porte, popular sentiment would make it "practically impossible" for Her Majesty's Government to interfere.[18] In early October Sir Henry Elliot told the new Sultan, Abdul Hamid, that Turkey had forfeited British support. Nor did Britain act to support Turkey when Russia declared war on Turkey the following April.[19]

While turning the English against the Turks, the atrocity stories promoted growing sympathy for the Bulgarians. This first expressed itself in a great outpouring of relief funds. Exploiting the reports of Pears, Schuyler, Baring, and MacGahan, a plethora of English committees solicited funds for the Bulgarians. The Bulgarian Fugitives' and Orphans' Relief Fund and Viscountess Strangford's Bulgarian Peasant Relief Fund were among the first. The Turkish Missions Aid Society of England, long a patron of the American missions and schools, organized the Bulgarian Re-

---

[17] Elliot to Derby, Aug. 29, 1876, FO 78, Vol. 2462, #922, denounces the British press for trying to force the government to abandon its traditional policy of preserving the Ottoman government in favor of protecting the Christian minorities. Wirthwein, *Britain and the Balkan Crisis*, 84 ff.

[18] Derby to Elliot, Aug. 29, 1876, FO 78, Vol. 2451, #528 and Sept. 5, 1876, in *ibid.*, #546.

[19] Elliot to Derby, Oct. 4, 1876, FO 78, Vol. 2465, #1102 and Oct. 7, 1876, in *ibid.*, #1118.

lief Fund. Of the greatest importance was the Mansion House Eastern War Sufferer's Relief Fund sponsored by the Lord Mayor of London. These monies, channeled through the British Ambassador at Constantinople, were administered by James F. Clarke, principal of the American school at Philippopolis and the only English or American resident of the stricken region. During the fall and winter of 1876–1877, Clarke gave full time to dispensing relief. Hospitals were established, food distributed, and wool given to be worked into clothing. Oxen and horses were hired, implements furnished, sawmills constructed, and rose oil stills rented in order to help the victims become self-supporting once more. Clarke estimated that forty-five thousand Bulgarian sufferers had been relieved.[20]

While Clarke exhausted himself in the distribution of relief, George Washburn of Robert College became an unofficial adviser on Bulgarian affairs to the British ambassador, a role Washburn continued to play to the end of the century. The basis for his position was the dearth of Englishmen familiar with the Balkans and his extensive contacts in Bulgaria through alumni of the college. Although years later Washburn claimed much credit for Robert College in the creation of an independent Bulgaria, in 1876 he opposed independence. Writing to Ambassador Elliot in September, 1876, Washburn expressed doubt that the peoples of the European provinces were ready for autonomy, even if the Turks could be forced to grant it. Rather he suggested that Christians be incorporated into the military and police forces in the Balkans. Acknowledging Washburn's "exceptional acquaintance" with Bulgaria, Elliot passed his ideas on to the Foreign Office.[21] Washburn's ideas were most fully stated in a "Memoir of Reforms in Turkey," which he presented to Elliot in advance of the Constantinople Conference of December, 1876. In it Washburn reiterated his suggestions of September, but he sketched a rounded reform program designed to make tolerable Bulgarian existence within the Ottoman empire. In place of Moslem religious courts he proposed a civil code administered by civil courts; he would open administrative appointments to Christians and Turks alike; the farming of taxes, an age-old evil, would be abolished with taxes reapportioned and paid in cash; each nationality would run its own schools; absolute religious liberty would be guaranteed; equality of representation of Christians and Moslems would prevail in the Ottoman legislature. Elliot thought Washburn's suggestions deserved "consideration" but were not "practical." [22] Washburn's proposals set a precedent that American philanthropists followed repeatedly in later

[20] J. House to N. G. Clark, Dec. 7, 1876, in ABC 16.9, Vol. 6, #26 and J. Clarke to N. G. Clark, Feb. 9, 1877, in *ibid.*, Vol. 5, #306; see also *Missionary Herald,* LXXIII (1877), 370, 397.

[21] G. Washburn to Elliot, Sept. 10, 1876, in Elliot to Derby, Sept. 23, 1876, in FO 78, Vol. 2464, #1048.

[22] Elliot to Derby, Nov. 9, 1876, in *ibid.*, Vol. 2466, #1264.

years, emphasizing that the best efforts of philanthropy could never offset
the effects of capricious misgovernment.

An orderly, negotiated settlement was not to be; in the spring of 1877
Russia, championing Bulgarian interests, declared war on Turkey. In the
year-long war, April, 1877, to March, 1878, the Russians overran much of
Bulgaria. At Eski Zagra the two American families were protected by
Turkish neighbors, although the town was completely destroyed and
many of the males were killed. Samokov, site of the two American
schools, was spared a similar fate as the Turkish army withdrew. In
March, 1878, the war ended; the Turks were defeated. In the final settlement at the Congress of Berlin, "Bulgaria" was separated into three parts.
Northern Bulgaria became an autonomous Principality, nominally under
the suzerainty of the Sultan. Eastern Rumelia, south of the Principality,
was autonomous, while Macedonia or Western Rumelia remained under
Turkish rule. Thus, Samokov was within the Principality; Philippopolis
was in Eastern Rumelia; and Monastir, the newest mission station, remained within Turkey.

With peace restored in the Balkans, the Americans returned to their
educational activities. The chief center of such work from 1871 to World
War I was at Samokov, a flourishing community thirty-five miles south of
Sofia. Located on a small plain at the foot of the Rila Mountains and more
than three thousand feet above sea level, the town enjoyed a splendid climate and scenic beauty. It was here that the girls' school was reestablished in 1871 under Esther Maltbie, who presided over it in regal fashion
for the next thirty-eight years, "making of it an expression of her dominant personality." [23]

A graduate of Oberlin College, Esther Maltbie was as much concerned
with the spiritual life of her students as with the progress of their studies.
She prayed with and for her teachers and students, often arising in the
night to do so. Displaying the same intensity of energy in the conduct of
school affairs, she took her graduates and trained them as teachers according to her own methods and theories. Because of her dictatorial attitude
she was unable to draw and hold competent American associates, a matter
of concern to the mission. Yet for all her shortcomings, she was loved and
respected; and perhaps because of her iron will, the school enjoyed stability.[24]

From 1871 to 1881 the Boys' School functioned solely as a theological
school, receiving only "hopefully pious students" who were to become
workers in the Protestant movement. After repeated requests for admission from youth who did not expect to become preachers, the mission in
1881 opened enrollment to boys of good character and added a scientific

[23] Hall, *Puritans in the Balkans,* 137.
[24] *Ibid.,* 143–144.

curriculum to the school's program. To clarify this new orientation, the school was restyled the American Collegiate and Theological Institute. In fact, only a few students ever enrolled in the theological program. Instruction was given in Bulgarian during the first two years and in English during the third and fourth years. French was taught as a second foreign language. To enable Bulgarian students to defray the costs of education, a manual training program was organized. Work was offered in printing, carpentry, and gardening, each boy receiving aid being expected to work three hours a day. This work-study program drew its inspiration not from that directed by Cyrus Hamlin at Bebek Seminary in the 1850's, but from that at Dwight L. Moody's Northfield Schools.[25]

Overall, the political environment of the newly autonomous Principality weakened the thrust of the American's work. Although on several important occasions successive Bulgarian rulers assisted the Americans, as Hamlin had perceived, Bulgarian aspirations were bound up in their national church. As a result, the Americans never succeeded in spreading a network of schools across Bulgaria as they had done in Turkey and Syria. The schools were harassed. The administrators were required to file time-consuming reports. Students in the American schools were not exempt from military service as were those who attended the state schools. Yet such American presence as existed in Bulgaria prior to World War I was largely the product of the missionary philanthropists.[26]

The most persistent problem encountered by the American educators revolved about the academic level of the Samokov schools. With the encouragement of Prince Ferdinand (1887–1918), Bulgarian state schools "popped up like mushrooms." As in many Western countries, the state asserted supreme control over education. The Bulgarian state schools, enjoying more financial support than government schools in Turkey, created stiff competition for the Americans. But Bulgarian use of the German gymnasium as a model for its secondary schools proved the most formidable problem. Academically the gymnasium was more than a high school, for it pursued some work which in the United States was relegated to the college. Because the schools at Samokov were not organized as gymnasiums, their graduates were excluded from entering professional schools and from professional or governmental employment.[27]

The mission forthrightly observed that "the advance in popular education" in Bulgaria threatened its schools, but it lacked the requisite funds to transform its two secondary schools into gymnasiums. The depression of

---

[25] "Minutes, 10th Annual Meeting, ETM," June 9, 1881, in ABC 16.9, Vol. 7, #45.
[26] L. Wallace to F. Frelinghuysen, Sept. 26, 1883, in Despatches, Turkey, Vol. 41, #282.
[27] Delk, "American Education in the Near East," 18 ff. *Missionary Herald*, LXXXIX (1893), 13–14.

the 1890's affected the American Board even more adversely than the general economy, so that mission funds remained sparse even after the return of prosperity following McKinley's election in 1896. As a result the mission was limited to reforms that did not require major additional expenditures. The scientific course in the Boys' School had been extended from five to six years in 1889; the Girls' School lengthened its program to six years in 1894. Within the limits of available resources, Robert Thomson, who became director of the Boys' School in 1898, codified school regulations, introduced supervised study and written examinations, assigned students to graded classes, and established closer ties between teachers and students. While these changes strengthened the quality of education, the school still was a high school, not a gymnasium.[28]

Before a solution to this problem could be found, the mission was distracted by the sensational Ellen Stone kidnapping. While traveling from Bansko to Salonika, Miss Stone, an American missionary, and her companion Madame Katerina Tsilka, the American-educated wife of Gregory Tsilka and a teacher in the American school at Korcha, were seized by "brigands." The kidnapping took place early in September, 1901, but not until late in the month did the kidnappers make contact with Miss Stone's friends, demanding a ransom of £T 25,000 ($110,000). For nearly six months the kidnappers, traveling at night, moved their victims from hiding place to hiding place, pausing briefly in early January when Mrs. Tsilka gave birth. As time passed, it became clear that the "kidnappers" were Bulgarian members of a Macedonian revolutionary committee seeking publicity and funds for their cause. Negotiations for the release of the victims proved difficult, as the Bulgarian government refused to permit negotiation for their release on Bulgarian soil lest it become implicated in the affair, while the brigands feared capture if they remained in Turkish territory. Finally, in February, 1902, John Henry House, a missionary educator, negotiated the ransom payment and effected the release of the two women and the baby.[29]

Because of the protracted negotiations, the incident focused enormous attention on Bulgaria's claim to Macedonia. Miss Stone added to this publicity on her return to the United States by inflammatory speeches and articles denouncing the Ottoman government for the conditions which drove the Bulgarians of Macedonia to rebellion. The American minister to

---

[28] ABCFM, *Annual Report*, 1893, 31; "Minutes, 33d Annual Meeting, ETM," May 9, 1904, in ABC 16.9, Vol. 15, #5.

[29] N. O'Conor to Lord Landsdowne, Feb. 14, 1902, in FO 78, Vol. 5189, #64 is a British account of the kidnapping. J. Leishman to J. Hay, Feb. 6, 1902, in Despatches, Turkey, Vol. 71, #134 is an American summary. H. Haskell, "Samokov, Annual Report, 1901–02," in ABC 16.9, Vol. 16, #107 is by the recipient of the ransom letters. Ellen M. Stone, "Six Months Among Brigands," *McClure's Magazine*, XIX (1902), 3–16; 99–109; 222–231; 291–300; 464–471; 562–570, is by the victim.

Turkey and the Ottoman government came to believe that if Miss Stone were not privy to her own kidnapping, Gregory Tsilka and other members of the Protestant community were. The incident intensified Turkish suspicions of the mission schools, and it caused John Leishman, the American minister, to oppose any expansion of the American Board's educational work in Turkey except on lines acceptable to the Ottoman government, a policy with which William Peet, the Board's business manager in Constantinople, agreed. The affair further underscored the degree to which loyalty to the revolutionary movement took precedence over everything else in the minds of the Bulgarians.[30]

In 1904 the leadership of the Collegiate Institute devolved upon Leroy Ostrander, a former tutor at Robert College and nephew of Robert Thomson. Of "a modest, scholarly, demeanor, quiet and efficient, cool in judgment, fair-minded, temperate, and firm," [31] Ostrander was well-equipped to tackle the problems confronting the school. The mission was agreed to create a school able to play a commanding role in the life of the nation, a school attracting Protestants and non-Protestants alike. While this meant transforming the schools into gymnasiums, Thompson insisted that the mission must do so not simply to match its competitor but to satisfy its conscience that it was doing "the thorough work that is expected of us." [32] Ostrander promptly committed the school to a gymnasium curriculum, introducing the first four classes in 1905. The Girls' School remodeled its curriculum to conform to the pedagogical course in the state gymnasiums. To secure qualified instructors, the mission made loans to prospective teachers so that they could complete the university training required of teachers under Bulgarian school regulations.[33]

The strengthening of the curriculum and the teaching force cost money. Student fees provided approximately half of the operating costs aside from the salaries of the Americans. The remaining funds came from the American Board, which was still unable to increase its subsidies to the school. Finally, the Board authorized the school to raise money on its own, provided the funds came from sources not already supporting the mission.

Additional relief came unexpectedly from the John D. Rockefeller donation to the American Board. This gift occasioned a storm in the United States from critics who argued that acceptance of the money implied approval of Rockefeller's business practices. James L. Barton, the Board Secretary and former mission educator in Turkey, who had solicited the gift, defended Rockefeller as "an earnest Christian man." But even if the

---

[30] Leishman to Hay, May 17, 1905, in Despatches, Turkey, Vol. 77, #1065 and Nov. 30, 1903, in *ibid.*, Vol. 75, #647; W. Peet, to J. Barton, Mar. 30, 1908, in ABC 16.9.3, Vol. 36.
[31] Hall, *Puritans in the Balkans*, 191.
[32] *Ibid.*, 194.
[33] *Ibid.*

charges against him were true, Barton favored doing "everything that I can to convert money into service for the Kingdom of God." The conversion of money, he concluded, is "in a large measure commensurate with the conversion of man." [34] The Board accepted Rockefeller's money, $100,000, and distributed it in support of a variety of projects, affording temporary help to the Samokov schools.

At last the Samokov schools met the academic requirements of the Bulgarian government, but a prolonged campaign was necessary to win official recognition of this fact. As had happened in Turkey, the reluctance of the government to recognize the American school seemed less a manifestation of hostility to the Americans than an unwillingness to set a precedent that would require the sanctioning of schools operated by other foreign groups, in this instance by the Greeks.[35] Aware that at least two foreign schools, although not organized according to Bulgarian standards, had nonetheless secured official recognition through diplomatic intercession, Ostrander decided to follow the same tactics. His overtures to the American Minister, R. K. Harvey, came to naught when the minister declined to act, contending that the "most-favored-nation" principle extended only to questions of mutual pecuniary and commercial advantage. Harvey offered, instead, to make a personal, unofficial approach to the government.[36]

The issue took a new turn, however, when the Bulgarian government sought to escape from the onerous capitulatory regime inherited from the days of Ottoman rule. After consultations between officers of the American Board and the State Department, the latter agreed to the abrogation of the capitulatory privileges and instructed the American minister to seek of the Bulgarian government "the most extensive and liberal application of the most-favored-nation treatment," including religious and philanthropic interests.[37] The negotiations halted as Bulgaria became enmeshed in the problems growing out of the disastrous Balkan wars. Finally, the mission, resorting to direct representations, persuaded the Ministry of Public Instruction to recognize the schools as gymnasiums on a par with the national schools. The Girls' School won the coveted status in June, 1914; the Boys' School, a year later.

To take advantage of their new position, the directors of the Samokov schools decided on a radical reorganization. Samokov, an idyllic location for the schools in the 1870's and 1880's, had become a cultural backwater. Meantime Sofia had become the leading city and the capital. A decision to

[34] *Ibid.*, 197.
[35] *Ibid.*, 211 ff. United States Department of State, *Papers Relating to the Foreign Relations of the United States, 1913* (Washington: GPO, 1920), 76–78; Delk, "American Education in the Near East," 26 ff.
[36] *Foreign Relations, 1913*, 76–78.
[37] P. Knox to Jackson, Feb. 12, 1913, quoted in Hall, *Puritans in the Balkans*, 217, n. 3.

relocate the Girls' School was taken in early 1915. Because of Bulgaria's involvement in the war, implementation was delayed. At the war's end the mission decided to combine the two schools. At this point the Bulgarian National Assembly interceded, voting to present the combined schools with a fifty-acre campus on the outskirts of Sofia.[38]

A unique enterprise of the Americans in Bulgaria was the introduction of the kindergarten. At least as early as the 1830's missionary wives in Syria and Turkey had operated classes for children of pre-school age, but in 1900 Elizabeth Clarke, the daughter of the first principal of the Boys' School, opened a combined kindergarten and kindergarten teachers' training school in Sofia. A graduate of Mount Holyoke who was trained in the methods of Friedrich Froebel, she first started a kindergarten at Samokov. But the tradition-minded townspeople were so hostile to her project that she removed to Sofia. Here she deliberately avoided identification with the Protestant community and so served an upper class clientele. Enrollments grew; in 1905, through the generosity of her aunt, a spacious school building was erected; and in 1907, a second kindergarten was set up in a poorer district of Sofia. Although Miss Clarke's kindergarten was not the first in Bulgaria, her training program for teachers was the only such course in the country until 1934. Directly and indirectly through her students Miss Clarke greatly influenced the course of child-training in Bulgaria.[39]

As in other areas of the Near East, the educational activities of the mission schools were supplemented by the mission press. At the secular level the most important instrument of the mission press was the journal, *Zornitsa*. Begun in 1864 as a monthly, *Zornitsa* established a reputation for "accurate news and the high character of its comment." [40] It was the more highly prized as there were no papers in Bulgarian published in what is now Bulgaria. The paper, changed to a weekly in 1876, had at that time a circulation of about one thousand, reaching subscribers in more than a hundred towns. The great majority of these readers were not Protestants. Despite the hindrances of the Russo-Turkish War, Bulgarians were so starved for news that subscriptions to *Zornitsa* reached 2,500. With the coming of Bulgarian autonomy, an independent Bulgarian press arose, but *Zornitsa* continued to grow, reaching a circulation of four thousand by 1882. Theodore L. Byington, founder of the Girls' School, who edited the paper from 1874, brought to his labors training and practice in law as well as theology. His legal training and judicial cast of mind especially equipped him for treating public issues perceptively. Prior to the liberation of Bulgaria he sought to "educate the people to a just view of their

[38] *Ibid.*, 216–217.
[39] *Ibid.*, 186.
[40] *Ibid.*, 35.

political rights, while not neglectful of the interests of the Gospel." [41] Afterwards he pursued a conservative, non-partisan course. In 1885, Byington resigned, a sick man. He was replaced by Robert Thomson, a young Scot, an able man but somewhat narrower in his interests. Lacking Byington's grasp of secular affairs, Thomson thought the paper overweighted with political and scientific news. It was not the business of the missionary editor "to take an active part in the politics of the country." Under Thomson *Zornitsa* preferred "articles less learned, more short and pointed, appealing rather to the conscience than to the intellect . . . ." [42] The paper reached its widest audience under Thomson.

Until 1897 *Zornitsa* served as one of the few journals accessible to all Bulgarians. It was edited and printed in Constantinople and hence was subject to Turkish censorship. Turkish censors, discovering objectionable political overtones in a prayer which used the word *Czar* to convey the idea of *king*, urged that the term be translated as *Sultan*. On one occasion publication was suppressed for nearly six months, supposedly for referring to acts of brigandage in Macedonia and for requesting better police protection. As officious as Turkish censors were, the editors thought they would encounter greater obstacles if they attempted to publish within the Principality. By publishing in Turkey, the paper could circulate in Macedonia and Thrace as well as in the Principality; should it publish in the Principality, the Turks would bar it from areas under their jurisdiction.

By the early 1890's the equation changed. Most Bulgarians lived within the Principality, which by this time had annexed Eastern Rumelia, and the number of Bulgarian newspapers and magazines had increased greatly. All were free of censorship; some were subsidized by government agencies. Beginning in 1892 the Bulgarian Exarchate published its own paper, *Novini* (News); Bulgarian priests, major subscribers to *Zornitsa*, were expected to subscribe to *Novini* and to act as distributors. The contest was unequal, and circulation of *Zornitsa* dropped from a high of 4,500, the largest of any paper published in Constantinople, to a thousand. In 1893 the paper incurred an operating loss. The Americans determined to hold on, partly because nine-tenths of the readers were non-Protestants and otherwise beyond the reach of the mission, but also because the journal afforded a forum in which Bulgarians might discuss church, school, and other questions with a freedom not permitted in other journals. When the American Board proved unable to sustain the continuing losses, the mission staff pledged the necessary funds from their own salaries. But finally in 1897, faced with the possibility of losing both the paper and the Boys' School, the mission suspended *Zornitsa* in an effort to save the school.

In the first years of the new century, the mission resumed publication of *Zornitsa*. The paper was revived under Bulgarian leadership, the new editor being A. S. Tsanoff, long the senior Bulgarian teacher at Samokov. Published in cooperation with the Bulgarian Evangelical Society, it was now printed in Bulgaria. To assure broad appeal, the paper generally divided its space equally among political news, scientific features, and religious topics. Circulation crept slowly upwards from eight hundred in 1903 to thirteen hundred in 1907. As a result of the Young Turk revolution in 1908, the paper was permitted to circulate among the Bulgarians of Macedonia once again. As before, a substantial majority of the subscribers were non-Protestants. Necessity, as it turned out, led the mission to achieve a long-standing objective, the devolution of responsibility for American-initiated institutions upon native leadership.[43]

The medical work of the Americans in Bulgaria was inconsequential compared with similar activities in Syria, Turkey, and Persia. Not until 1881 did the American Board send its first and only medical man to the Balkans, Frederick L. Kingsbury, a graduate of Dartmouth College and the University of Vermont Medical School. Like other medical missionaries, Kingsbury gave much time to "the saving of personal souls." [44] And on his first furlough to the United States he was ordained as a minister.

Bulgaria in the 1880's and the 1890's provided Kingsbury minimum encouragement. Upon his arrival in Samokov, a city without a hospital, he was denied the right to practice or dispense medicine. Only after three years and the intercession of the British consul-general in Sofia was he able to begin his practice. Peasants came to him, often trudging twenty, even forty, miles to seek his advice. Kingsbury recognized, however, that given Bulgaria's development, his contribution as a general practitioner was limited. He hoped to establish a children's hospital or a medical school. His colleagues authorized him in 1884 to solicit funds for a hospital, and out of the fees received from his medical practice he supported two youths in the Samokov school in expectation that they would study medicine with him. But Kingsbury never enjoyed the satisfaction of achieving his goals. He tried to raise four thousand dollars in England and America with which to build and equip a modest hospital and to maintain it through its first year, but without success. Frustrated, hampered by the lack of medical facilities and suffering from rhumatism, Kingsbury resigned in 1898. His final report he termed the "Decline and Fall of the Hopes of a Medical Missionary." [45]

Whether or not Kingsbury's mission was a failure is a moot point. Measured in terms of his aspirations, he failed. But it is also true that

43 *Ibid.*, 176 ff.
44 *Ibid.*, 86.
45 *Ibid.*, 133–134. When Kingsbury arrived in Bulgaria there were three hospitals in Sofia and one in Philippopolis. There were numbers of state-paid doctors, most of whom served the army. Bulgaria had no medical school.

Bulgaria, far more advanced and self-sufficient than Persia, Syria, or rural Turkey, had less need of the services of a foreign doctor. Furthermore, Bulgarian national pride derived more satisfaction from the provision of medical services by its own people than it did from the medical skills offered by benevolent foreign doctors.

By 1914 the Americans had a half-century of experience in Bulgaria. The mission could fairly claim to have contributed decisively to the awakening of Bulgarian national consciousness. American activities in the 1860's and 1870's reinforced the efforts of Bulgarian nationalists to develop a distinctive language and literature, thereby forestalling the assimilation of their compatriots by the Greeks. *Zornitsa*, published at Constantinople, had acquainted its subscribers with the affairs of the Western world, while the mission press provided Bulgarians with a medium of communication. After the attainment of Bulgarian autonomy, *Zornitsa*, although challenged by numerous rivals within the Principality, retained a unique character in providing a common bond between Bulgars in Turkish Macedonia and countrymen in Thrace and Bulgaria proper. In the troubled years 1876–78, American educators brought the disaster in the Balkans to the attention of the West, succored the distressed, and generated a climate of opinion favorable to the Bulgarians.

After 1878 the Samokov schools attracted the main energies of the Americans. By 1914 the Samokov schools had produced a thousand male and eight hundred female graduates. The importance of these schools must be viewed in terms of the state educational system, which as late as 1910 operated but twelve gymnasiums. Whereas Robert College furnished Bulgaria with ministers of state, mayors, and professional leaders, the Samokov schools reached into levels of Bulgarian village society untouched by the College and provided Bulgaria with middle-level leadership which, though it more often achieved local rather than national renown, was indispensable to the smooth functioning of a modern state. Nowhere else during these years were the Americans so successful in reaching beyond the bounds of the small Protestant community. Although struggling to meet the requirements of Bulgarian school laws, the American schools were commended for their pragmatic way of dignifying labor by combining academic with manual skills.[46]

[46] Stephanove, *The Bulgarians and Anglo-Saxondom*, 273. William Miller, *Travel and Politics in the Near East* (London: T. F. Unwin, 1898), 452–454.

· II ·

The European Turkey Mission also served Albania, one of the least known corners of Europe. By virtue of their isolation in the mountains along the Adriatic Sea, the Albanians enjoyed a considerable degree of freedom from control by the Porte prior to the administration of Abdul Hamid II. Yet the spirit of nationalism began to penetrate even this area in the late 1870's. Resentment at the transfer of "Albanian" soil to Montenegro by the Congress of Berlin (1878) served as a catalyst in precipitating a sense of national consciousness. Taking advantage of Turkey's preoccupation with the Russo-Turk War, Albanians called a congress in Constantinople and elaborated a phonetic alphabet, mainly Latin, for their language. They also founded the first Albanian society, Bashkim (The Union), whose aim it was to publish books and periodicals in Albanian. American educational work in the Balkans contributed to the growth of Albanian nationalism, and the American-assisted schools were used by Albanian nationalists to serve their own ends.

American philanthropy was focused on two Albanian schools, both at Korcha (Korçë) in southeastern Albania. The initiative in founding the schools was taken by members of the Kyrias (Qirias) family, among the first Albanians to secure a Western education. In 1888 Gerasim, the eldest, founded a boys' boarding school with financial aid from the American Board. This arrangement was unorthodox in that the school was not under the immediate superintendence of an American. For Gerasim Kyrias this relationship had a substantial advantage in that he was free of supervision, yet the tenuous affiliation with the Americans exempted his school from a ban placed by the Porte only two years before on the use of Albanian dialects in printed works or in schools. The relationship also shielded his school from the hostility of local Greek Orthodox prelates, a hostility that culminated in an unsuccessful attempt to assassinate Kyrias. Despite determined opposition, Gerasim Kyrias in 1891, joined by his sister, Sevasti, who had just completed her formal education at the American Home School in Constantinople, opened a girls' boarding school at Korcha.[47]

From the viewpoint of the American Board and of the American Girls' College, the activities of the Kyrias family were much to be praised. In an area in which illiteracy was almost universal, the schools introduced the basic prerequisites to cultural and technical progress. In an area which

---

[47] Christo A. Dako, *Albania, the Master Key to the Near East* (Boston: E. L. Grimes Co., 1919); Hester Donaldson Jenkins, *An Educational Ambassador to the Near East: The Story of Mary Mills Patrick and an American College in the Orient* (New York: Fleming H. Revell, 1925), Ch. 7.

afforded women a minimum of opportunities for self-expression, Sevasti Kyrias was a noteworthy feminist, exhibiting drive and self-reliance. When Gerasim died in 1893, Sevasti carried on, assisted by her sister, Paraskevi, also a graduate of the Home School. Although in 1903 they were forced to give up the boys' school, the two sisters kept the girls' school in operation. When printed books were unavailable, the sisters produced texts by hectograph. When Turkish officials attempted to seize her Albanian language materials, Sevasti faced them down in a four hour verbal duel. Such harassment, promoted by Greek clergy and Ottoman officials, only rendered her cause the more romantic, and funds to save her school were contributed by the Womans' Board of Missions of the Interior (Congregational) and the Bible Lands Missions Aid Society of London.[48]

But the operation of Albanian-language schools was not a wholly innocent educational enterprise. It had important nationalistic overtones. Because of Albania's isolation, Albanians used two principal dialects and six different alphabets, each serving to identify one or another partisan group and effectively barring national unity. Furthermore, Greek Orthodox clergy aspired to Hellenize the Christian Albanians as a means of including them within an expanded Greek state. Although Albanian nationalists organized schools at Constantinople and Bucharest, the Kyriases' schools at Korcha were until after 1900 the only institutions in Albania using the Albanian language. They were major instruments for the introduction of the Albanian language written in Latin characters and for the frustration of Greek efforts to Hellenize and assimilate the Albanians. The extent to which the schools preached political nationalism is uncertain. Prior to 1908 the Albanians aspired only to autonomy within the Ottoman Empire, but it is also clear that Paraskevi Kyrias was a militant leader in that movement. Finally, in 1907 the Turks closed the school at Korcha.[49]

In the wake of the Young Turk revolt of 1908, Albanian nationalism took hope that it could find expression in partnership with the Young Turks. It aimed still at cultural autonomy rather than political separation and independence. Meeting in Congress at Monastir (Bitolj, Yugoslavia), Albanians renewed their efforts to create a unified language. Albanians with American ties ranked high among the leadership of this Congress. George Kyrias, the younger brother of Sevasti and Paraskevi, an alumnus of Robert College, served as vice president of the Congress and presided over its early sessions. Other Albanian nationalists with American ties who were active in the Congress were Gregory Tsilka, whose wife had been kidnapped along with Ellen Stone and who himself was an instructor in

---

[48] Joseph Swire, *Albania, the Rise of a Kingdom* (London: Williams and Norgate, 1929), 64–65.

[49] Federal Writers' Project, *The Albanian Struggle in the Old World and New* (Boston: The Writer, Inc., 1939), 33.

the school at Korcha, and Christo Dako, an acquaintance of the Kyriases and a student at Oberlin College who returned home in 1909. The alphabet, the Congress was told, was the "soul of the nation and the only instrument by which the nation will progress." As members of the committee on the alphabet, George Kyrias and Gregory Tsilka used their influence to secure the adoption of the Latin alphabet, which had long been used in the schools at Korcha and by the American mission press.[50]

While the Albanians threshed out their own problems, the European Turkey Mission of the American Board took a hard look at the work in Albania. They decided to reopen the school at Korcha under the control of an American, the Reverend Phineas B. Kennedy, and to transfer the title to the school property to the mission. Young, ambitious, and impulsive, Kennedy aspired to turn the school at Korcha into a full-blown college at a time when the Ottoman government was reluctant to give him even a permit to travel to Korcha. Ambassador Leishman urged personal caution on Kennedy; William Peet, the American Board's agent at Constantinople, counselled the Board to proceed slowly, but Kennedy went to Korcha.[51]

Simultaneously the American Board was persuaded to institute a second center of educational work in the northern part of the country. Initiative for this new venture and responsibility for its execution was assumed by C. Telford Erickson, a free-wheeling American Board missionary who had just come to Albania from India in search of a climate suited to the health of his ailing wife. Erickson made his headquarters at Tirana where, in the absence of an American consul, he placed himself under the protection of Austrian officials and thereby became suspect as an Austrian spy. He further aroused the ire of Ottoman officials by his efforts to introduce Albanian language instruction and by his identification with Albanian nationalists. In 1909 Turkish officials expelled him from Tirana on grounds that they could not guarantee his safety there. As relations between Moslem Albanians and the Young Turk government deteriorated in 1910 and 1911, Erickson was subjected to repeated harassment. He was assaulted on the street by local police; he was driven peremptorily from the country along with his invalid wife and four children. Persistent, Erickson returned to Albania in 1912 and was again arrested and expelled late that year. In part, Erickson's difficulties stemmed from Turkey's own difficulties in maintaining political control in Albania; but without question he compounded his difficulties by his avowed championing of the Albanian nationalist cause. As early as 1909 he urged the mission, as a means of

---

[50] "Report of the Albanian Congress Held in Monastir," Nov. 14, 1908, in ABC 16.9, Vol. 16, #5.

[51] Leishman to W. Peet, Mar. 19, 1908, in ABC 16.9.3, Vol. 3; Peet to J. Barton, Apr. 27, 1909, in *ibid*.

"planting and rooting" Protestantism, to promote the use of the Albanian language and the development of an Albanian literature. By unifying the people and giving them a national consciousness and national ideals, Erickson believed the Albanians would become more receptive to Protestantism. The political implications of such a policy he ignored.[52]

American philanthropy also impinged modestly on the political resolution of the Albanian question. In 1911 Christo Dako, a youthful nationalist who had interrupted his studies at Oberlin to return to Albania at the time of the Young Turk rebellion and to marry Sevasti Kyrias, met Charles R. Crane, the Chicago industrialist and trustee of the American College for Girls at Constantinople. Dako conducted Crane on a tour of disaffected parts of northern Albania. For his pains Dako was arrested and jailed at Scutari by local officials, but he was released shortly as a result of Crane's intercession at Constantinople. The experience led to a warm, continuing relationship through which Crane became an influential advocate of the Albanian cause. In 1911 he issued a public statement on the Albanian revolt, the first by an outsider, which focused public attention on the tribulations of this area. The following year the Albanians forced Turkey to grant them autonomy. But the Greeks made successive attempts to acquire control of Korcha. As the great powers sought to unravel the tangled interests and claims, Crane personally championed the claims of the Albanians to the Korcha area and in the mind of Dako, at least, was primarily responsible for the inclusion of the province within the territorial bounds of an independent Albania by the Ambassadorial Conference in London in 1913. Albania's future in 1914, however, was most uncertain, for the Greeks were unwilling to give up the Korcha area and the Albanians were unable to hold on to it. In July, 1914, Dako, his wife, and his sister-in-law fled Korcha for their lives, abandoning for the time the girls' boarding school.[53]

· III ·

Potentially the most significant venture of the European Turkey Mission was the Thessalonika Agricultural and Industrial Institute established in 1903 at Salonika. The school was founded to serve Bulgarian youth living in the Macedonian area of Turkey. These youth were deterred from attending the mission's schools at Samokov by Bulgarian regulations that made them subject to military service if they entered Bulgaria. Further-

---

[52] See file on Erickson, SDNF 367.112 Er4, National Archives, Washington. Erickson to ETM, Mar. 29, 1909, in "Minutes, 38th Annual Meeting, ETM," in ABC 16.9, Vol. 15, #10.
[53] Federal Writers' Project, *The Albanian Struggle*, 56 ff.

more, the costs of attending the Samokov schools were beyond the means of most Macedonians. Though the mission had recognized the need for a separate school at Salonika in the 1890's, a shortage of funds precluded the organization of such a school for a decade.[54]

The initiative in founding the school was taken by Edward B. Haskell and John Henry House. The son of a missionary, Haskell was born in Bulgaria and went to the United States for college and seminary training. Through a friend his attention was directed toward the educational program of Hampton Institute in Virginia. The latter, founded by the son of an American Board missionary, had pioneered in combining academic education with in-the-field farm training. In Haskell's view the methods of Hampton, which stressed "self reliance and usefulness to others," were ideal for Macedonia. After securing the reluctant consent of his colleagues, Haskell acquired a tract of fifty-three acres of barren land with "not a tree on the place, no water and scarcely a sign of life." [55] He began construction of a combination dormitory-class building and a barn. He further engaged a native couple to take immediate charge of the farm and of ten orphan boys who were to be the first students. Haskell also incorporated the school in New York with a board of trustees including Josiah Strong, one of the foremost proponents of Social Gospel, and H. B. Frissel, President of Hampton Institute. At this point Haskell, whose wife had died, passed the leadership of the school to John Henry House. A man in his late fifties, House, who had gone to Bulgaria in 1872, brought to this task three decades of experience as a teacher.

As with many other work-study programs, the achievement fell short of the aspiration. The boys did much work on the farm facilities, cutting cash costs to the minimum, but adding nothing to cash income. Thanks to sums of money remitted periodically by the Bible Lands Missions Aid Society in London, from students at Hampton Institute, and from ex-missionary Ellen Stone, the school was able to continue. In time the services and goods produced by the students added modestly to the school's income. But money was never plentiful, and repeatedly only the timely action of Leander T. Chamberlain, chairman of the school's trustees, procured critically needed funds.

The problems of the school reflected the revolutionary turmoil of the Balkans. The student body was exclusively Bulgarian, which was well enough so long as the Turks retained sovereignty over Macedonia. At the same time Macedonia, in a severely depressed state economically and psy-

---

[54] E. Haskell, "Report of the Salonika Station for 1902–03," Apr. 13, 1903, in ABC 16.9, Vol. 16, #75.

[55] *Ibid.*; J. M. Nankivell, *A Life for the Balkans: The Story of John Henry House of the American Farm School, Thessaloniki, Greece* (New York: Fleming H. Revell, 1939), 144.

chologically after 1903, was also a revolutionary center for disgruntled Young Turks. In addition, Greeks and Bulgars engaged in a tug of war in behalf of their respective "fatherlands" for political control of Macedonia. As hopes for the pacification of the country or for the improvement of conditions of life died out, large numbers of Macedonians migrated to the United States. Although Salonika was a center of the revolutionary events of 1908 and 1909 which culminated in the deposition of Sultan Abdul Hamid, the school survived these crises wihout difficulty. The great crisis came at the conclusion of the Balkan Wars of 1912–13 when Macedonia was wrenched loose from Turkey and was assigned by the Treaty of Bucharest to Greece. The Bulgars, who had endured Turkish rule, moved across the border into Bulgaria rather than pass under Greek jurisdiction. As a result, in 1913, House was confronted with the necessity of recruiting a new student population from among the Greeks, of changing the language of instruction, and of cultivating the support of Greek officialdom. This transition was complicated by the coming of World War I.

Of the school itself several qualities stand out—the simplicity, even stark quality of its plant and the extreme dependence of the school upon the sacrificial leadership of House, his wife, and his daughter. In the absence of any endowment, make-do was the order of the day. The first structure was of adobe, housing in one room the caretaker and his wife, the other room doubling as a combination dormitory and classroom. Here the boys slept on mats, rolling them in daytime as they would do at home, and turning the space into a classroom. In 1906 when a larger, permanent structure was erected, the boys did much of the less skilled manual labor. But it remained a simple facility. The oven, like those of the American colonial era, was heated by burning fuel in a brick enclosure. After the coals were swept from the oven, bread was placed within to bake on the hot brick floor. When the Houses—husband, wife, and daughter—moved in, the outside doors had not yet been hung. Even after this was done, their privacy was minimal. They lived under the same roof as their young charges. Mrs. House and her daughter periodically had sole responsibility for their physical welfare and always were responsible for overseeing the cleanliness and repair of their clothing. Nor were the students invariably charming little tykes. "With little discipline in their homes, they very often ran wild with the cattle from the time they were big enough to wander from the village." Yet in time they responded to training and care. From Mrs. House's standpoint the work was "a hard life, but a good one." Slowly the barren site began to blossom.[56]

American philanthropy in Bulgaria, Albania, and Macedonia operated

[56] *Ibid.*, 160. Reports of E. B. Haskell and J. H. House are in ABC 16.9, Vols. 15 and 16. Thessaloniki Agricultural and Industrial Institute, *Annual Reports*, begin in 1907.

under quite different conditions. Bulgaria, though backward by Western standards, was progressive, advanced, and affluent by Albanian or Macedonian standards. Americans entered these areas at a critical moment, when nationalism was in its formative stage. In both Bulgaria and Albania the Americans contributed to the fashioning of standardized vernaculars, a factor of enormous importance in overriding the regional attachments that accompanied various local dialects and in nurturing the growth of national self-consciousness. But the Bulgarians, once they had achieved autonomy, had the talents and resources to develop their own press, medical services, and educational institutions; the Albanians, remaining a subject people, were far more dependent upon the Americans for reading materials and schools. The opportunity for missionary philanthropy to assist seemed inversely proportional to the state of development of the local culture. There is a fine irony in this, for at the operational level a persistent restraint on mission philanthropy was the unrest that accompanied unfulfilled national aspirations and the capricious regulations of Ottoman administrators who had to tolerate the foreign educators, editors, and doctors. Yet when national autonomy was achieved, the climate of operation did not significantly improve, for the quality of Bulgarian nationalism required self-sufficiency in matters of medical care and education. In the field of medicine, an American doctor as a general practitioner added by one to the total number of doctors practicing in Bulgaria, but he was not able to perform significantly better than a European-trained native doctor. By contrast, in the less developed areas of Turkey, Syria, and Persia the Americans often provided the only medical service available. Instinctively, Frederick Kingsbury recognized the heart of the problem: the American could be useful when he introduced specific services or techniques that the native community could not yet provide for itself. Kingsbury could see a role for an American doctor who specialized in childhood ailments or who founded a medical school. Unable to follow either path, he retired from the field. The attraction of the Samokov schools to Bulgarian students and parents centered in their emphasis upon character-building and ethical conduct and in the willingness of the schools to admit students excluded by bureaucratic regulations from entering the state gymnasiums. Elizabeth Clark made a long-term impact with her kindergarten and teacher-training school. The Thessalonika Agricultural and Industrial Institute was another imaginative innovation. In these specialized roles the Americans found opportunities to function constructively without provoking invidious comparisons that offended native sensitivities or arousing hostilities.

World War I, which disrupted American activities throughout the Near East, wrenched American philanthropy out of its established patterns.

CHAPTER

VII

Near East Relief, 1915–1930

WORLD WAR I brought a halt to American philanthropy in the Near East, as the cataclysm altered the lives of the inhabitants and the political structure of the governments. The war unloosed long pent-up passions in which the Christian minorities of the Ottoman Empire were subjected to a degree of persecution far exceeding the earlier incidents. Untimely death came to at least 600,000 Armenians and varying degrees of suffering to another 1,400,000. In connection with Mustapha Kemal's rise to power in the 1920's nearly 1,100,000 Greeks residing in Turkey were uprooted and compelled to seek new homes in Greece. To mitigate the suffering visited upon the Armenians and Greeks, the American missionaries and educators suspended most of their usual activities to devote full time to disaster relief.

· I ·

The first disorders occurred on the Ottoman-Persian frontier. In October, 1914, Kurdish tribesmen led by Turkish officers raided a Russian garrison stationed at Urumia (Rizaiyeh) in northwest Persia, killed a few villagers, and then withdrew. After Turkey formally entered the war in December, 1914, the Russian garrison withdrew to the Caucasus. In January, 1915, the Kurds again raided the Urumia plain, sending 15,000 peasants scurrying to the American Presbyterian mission for protection. There was no

housing or food for these people. Sanitation facilities were inadequate.[1]
Food shortages complicated by the war brought suffering to Syria.
When local grain supplies were exhausted in 1914, the Turkish rail network, overloaded by mobilization, proved unable to import foodstuffs
from other regions. These conditions, which continued into 1915 and
1916, were intensified by a plague of locusts that reduced grain production in Syria. Prolonged shortages of food and high prices created acute
distress.[2]

The worst calamities befell the Armenians of Anatolia. Early in April,
1915, the Turkish government, which had long suspected the loyalty of its
Armenian subjects, began deporting Armenians living at Zeitoun in antici-
pation of an Allied landing at nearby Mersin (Icel). The deportees were
sent into the vilayet of Konia and the arid regions of Der-el-Zor. Soon
other Armenians from Adana, Brousa, and Izmid were also deported. Notice of impending deportation was brief, leaving the Armenians little time
to prepare. Nor did the Turks ease the hardship of the forced move. As
the military had first claim on the railroads, there were overcrowding,
uncertainty, and long delays. In the eastern provinces of Angora, Sivas,
Trebizond, Erzerum, and Marmouret-ul-Aziz, where there were no railroads, the rigors of travel were especially severe. For women and children
on foot, the trip from Harpoot to Urfa meant a month-long trek in an
area where water holes were sometimes several days apart and food was
often unavailable. To the discomforts stemming from the lack of facilities
were added the misconduct of the undisciplined troops that guarded the
travelers and the attacks of marauding bandits. Reports reaching the
American embassy in Constantinople alleged that women and girls had
often been robbed, raped, and murdered. Males fifteen years old and over
were being massacred, while the "poor exiles" who survived had been
"clubbed and beaten and lashed along as though they had been wild animals. . . ."[3]

[1] Mary Edna Lewis, *The War Journal of a Missionary in Persia*, Mary Schauffler
Platt, ed. (BFMPC, 1915); William Walker Rockwell, *The Pitiful Plight of the
Assyrian Christians in Persia and Kurdistan Described From the Reports of Eye-
Witnesses* (New York: ACASR, 1916); William A. Shedd cited in Arnold J. Toyn-
bee, ed., *The Treatment of Armenians in the Ottoman Empire 1915–1916* (London:
H. M. Stationery Office, 1916), #100; Francis B. Packard, *The Story of Our Missions
in Persia* (BFMPC, 1920).

[2] Margaret McGilvary, *The Dawn of a New Era in Syria* (New York: Fleming
H. Revell, 1920).

[3] R. F. Leslie to J. B. Jackson, June 28, 1915, SDDF 867.4016/92; "Report of Leslie
A. Davis, American Consul Formerly at Harput, Turkey," Feb. 9, 1918, SDDF 867.-
4016/392 in General Records, Dept. of State, Rec. Group 59, National Archives,
Washington. James L. Barton, *Story of Near East Relief (1915–1930) An Interpreta-
tion* (New York: Macmillan, 1930); Clarence D. Ussher, *An American Physician in
Turkey* (Boston: Houghton Mifflin, 1917); Grace Knapp, *The Tragedy of Bitlis*

The missionaries abroad assisted the victims from their limited supplies and requested financial aid from the mission boards in the United States. In March, 1915, a Persia War Relief Fund was started by officers and laymen connected with the Presbyterian Board of Missions. A few weeks later a Syria-Palestine Committee was organized by Presbyterians and Jews. Because censorship as well as the isolation of the Armenians delayed reports on the Armenian persecutions, not until September, 1915, did Ambassador Henry Morgenthau, Sr., ask that relief funds be sent for them. In the United States representatives of the American Board and of the independent colleges promptly organized the Committee on Armenian Atrocities.[4] Shortly thereafter when the Committee solicited $20,000 from the Rockefeller Foundation, the latter contributed, but it virtually stipulated that further aid would be contingent on the merger of all relief committees functioning in the Near East.[5]

In response to this ultimatum the three committees merged in November, 1915, as the American Committee for Armenian and Syrian Relief. Chairman of the new organization was Dr. James L. Barton, the senior secretary of the American Board and one-time President of Euphrates College at Harpoot. In day-to-day command of the Committee was Samuel T. Dutton, treasurer of the Constantinople Woman's College. Later, as the relief work grew, the ACASR took over the offices and staff of the Laymen's Missionary Movement with Charles Vernon Vickrey replacing Samuel Dutton as the executive secretary. Long-range planning for the ACASR rested with a committee composed of Dr. Barton and representatives of various mission boards and schools interested in the Near East. Unquestionably the most important of these representatives was Cleveland H. Dodge, who had helped organize the Armenian Atrocities Committee and had contributed generously to the ACASR.[6]

During the war years, 1915–18, relief work was carried on by missionaries and educators who were in the area. Given the magnitude of the disorders, the relief workers often could do little more than give temporary shelter, simple first aid, and enough food to sustain life a day longer. Because conditions varied from place to place, relief techniques varied, too.

(New York: Fleming H. Revell, 1919); William Walker Rockwell, ed., *The Deportation of the Armenians Described from Day to Day by a Kind Woman Somewhere in Turkey* (New York: ACASR, 1916).

[4] H. Morgenthau to R. Lansing, Sept. 3, 1915, in USDS, *Papers Relating to the Foreign Relations of the United States: 1915, Supplement* (Washington: GPO, 1928), 988.

[5] R. H. Kirk (of the Rockefeller Foundation) to G. T. Scott, July 27, 1915, PML, File 1067–1915, in PML, New York City.

[6] Barton, *Story of Near East Relief, passim*. Robert L. Daniel, "From Relief to Technical Assistance in the Near East," Ph.D. dissertation, University of Wisconsin, 1953, 5–28.

In Persia, and later at Van and Bitlis in southeastern Anatolia, the mission compounds, surrounded by high walls and topped by the American flag, gave a semblance of physical safety to refugees, but it was often debatable whether the besiegers without or disease and malnutrition within were the more devastating. At Urumia, for example, four thousand refugees died of starvation or disease in the mission compounds during the five-months-long siege. When its cash reserves were exhausted, the mission appropriated some $75,000 in coin which native merchants had left with it for safekeeping. The mission was to make restitution from funds raised in the United States.[7]

The return of Russian troops raised the siege, and the mission concentrated its efforts on helping the natives to become self-supporting. To get grain into cultivation once more, the mission distributed sickles, spades, plows, oxen, and cows. The effort failed, for in the fall of 1915 the Russians again abandoned Urumia. Native Christians, fearful of what might happen, fled from their fields without harvesting their crops.[8]

Undeterred by this setback, the mission employed similar techniques in 1916. Seed was loaned to the natives rather than given outright. For each unit of grain borrowed the native was to return one and one-half units. The extra half unit was to recompense the mission for its losses and overhead. The mission sought unsuccessfully to introduce millet in lieu of wheat, as its great yield would feed more people for the same labor. Small cash loans were made to keep native vineyards in cultivation. In 1917 to reduce the cost of direct relief, which was still necessary, the mission bought a tract of grain land measuring eighteen miles by twelve miles. Refugees were employed to harvest the grain, which the mission used to feed the masses. While the land produced much needed grain, this arrangement did not reduce relief costs as anticipated.[9]

In Syria, where hardship was created by high prices and a shortage of grain, the greatest source of assistance came from Syrians who had settled in the United States. The ACASR arranged for the remittance of funds to Syria, often through the Standard Oil Company, to be disbursed to the designated beneficiaries by the personnel of the American Mission Press in Beirut. American entry into World War I necessitated other arrangements, and lists of beneficiaries were secreted in packets of money carried into Syria by courier. Americans withdrew from conspicuous positions of

[7] Persian War Relief Fund, *Bulletin*, No. 12, Apr., 1915, and No. 13, July, 1915, PML.
[8] Persian War Relief Fund, "Bulletin Letter," Oct. 8, 1915, *ibid.*
[9] E. T. Allen, "Brief Statement of Needs for Relief Work Urumia and Salmas, Persia, Oct. 29, 1916," William W. Rockwell Papers in Union Theological Seminary Library, New York; R. M. Labaree, "Report," June 29, 1915, in Persian War Relief Fund, "Bulletin Letter," Aug. 31, 1915, PML; G. T. Scott to "Friends of H. A. Muller," Sept. 26, 1916, in *ibid.*; W. Shedd to C. V. Vickrey, Sept. 15, 1917, in *ibid.*; W. Shedd to C. Vickrey, Oct. 12, 1917, *ibid.*

leadership in Syrian relief, and a German banker, Ernst Schoemann, took formal responsibility for distributing funds. By 1919 some 300,000 remittances had been transmitted to Syria.[10]

The arrival in Syria in 1915 of 110,000 Armenian refugees from Anatolia made soup-kitchen relief necessary. In areas where food supplies were available the refugees were given a cash dole; in other areas the mission imported food stuffs, and American consular officials supervised their distribution. Work relief was provided a few women by giving them raw wool to spin in their homes. The woman kept a part of the product as a wage, while the remainder was collected and sold by the missionaries to provide more raw materials. In addition, some six to seven thousand homeless children were cared for on the premises of the scattered mission stations during the balance of the war.[11]

The principal relief task was to assist the Armenians in Anatolia and the Caucasus. Initially Ambassador Morgenthau suggested that the Armenian refugees be brought to the United States. Although he secured assurances from the Ottoman Minister of War that the refugees would be permitted to leave Turkey, his plan was rejected as unfeasible by the American committee to which he referred it. As a result, in Anatolia the main reliance was on disaster relief directed by the American Board personnel and their native assistants. Mission hospitals, schools, and homes were pressed into service to house the ill. Food, clothing, and blankets were procured locally and distributed as far as they would go around. There was little chance of returning the refugees to their homes or helping them reestablish roots until the war ended.[12]

Administration of relief was even more difficult in the Russian Caucasus, where some 300,000 Armenians from eastern Turkey drifted to secure the protection of the Russian armies. Three American missionaries accompanied them, remaining until the collapse of the Czarist regime in 1917 made their continued stay untenable. Thereafter the relief work was largely in the hands of natives. Effective supervision by two overtaxed American YMCA workers, John Elder and James Arroll, who stayed behind when the missionaries left, was impossible. Chaotic political conditions in the Caucasus prevented the flow of relief supplies from the United States until the middle of 1919. Even then, because it was impossible to properly supervise the distribution of supplies, "corruption and thievery were beyond belief." [13]

The story of the persecutions was current, dramatic, newsworthy, and

[10] McGilvary, *Dawn of a New Era in Syria*, 104, 129–130, 163.

[11] *Ibid.*, 196–197.

[12] Morgenthau to Lansing, Sept. 3, 1915, *Foreign Relations, 1915, Supplement*, 988; Polk to Morgenthau, Sept. 22, 1915, *ibid.*

[13] Herbert C. Hoover, *The Memoirs of Herbert Hoover: Years of Adventure 1874-1920* (5 Vols., New York: Macmillan, 1952), I, 386.

emotionally appealing to Americans. The press releases of the American Committee for Armenian and Syrian Relief not only made the front pages of the sensational press but those of the New York *Times* and the *Christian Science Monitor*. Editors of the *Literary Digest,* the *American Review of Reviews,* and the *Independent* served as trustees of the ACASR and offered the facilities of their journals to raise funds for Armenian relief. In one emergency the *Literary Digest* loaned the Committee over $100,000. Protestant, Catholic, and Jewish churches obligingly employed their services and publications to publicize conditions in the Near East. Those who contributed to the organization were put on the mailing list of the *News Bulletin* and its slick paper successor, the *New Near East,* a monthly periodical of the relief committee. As the ACASR became better known in 1917, it was able to command the speaking services of nationally known political figures such as Henry Morgenthau, Sr., Oscar Straus, Abram Elkus, Charles Evans Hughes, and William Howard Taft.

Relief work during the war years cost far more than the $100,000 requested by Ambassador Morgenthau in September, 1915. This initial sum was contributed largely by the laymen who organized the Committee on Armenian Atrocities. By the end of 1915 the American Committee for Armenian and Syrian Relief had raised $176,000. During 1916 and 1917 it raised two million dollars each year. Receipts climbed to seven million in 1918 and reached a peak of more than nineteen million in 1919.[14]

A nationwide fund-raising organization was created by 1917, and with the help of presidential proclamations creating Near East Relief Days the fund-drives acquired a semi-official character. Food and clothing were collected at fire houses, police stations, and public schools. A concerned public gave personal jewelry, family heirlooms, and wedding presents. Money was sought from all conditions of men through schools, fraternal societies, Sunday Schools, and by door-to-door solicitation, but much money, half or more, came from community war chests and the American Red Cross. Never before had overseas philanthropy enjoyed such a broad base.

· II ·

Inevitably the ACASR as well as the missionaries and educators were concerned with American-Turkish relations. These had been severely strained in September, 1914, when the Ottoman government, bowing to the growing force of Turkish nationalism, unilaterally repudiated the Capitulations under which American residents in Turkey were exempt from trial in Ottoman courts. The American government denied the right of

---

[14] Abstract of Minutes of ACASR, Jan. 22, 1918, Rockwell Papers; Barton, *Story of Near East Relief,* 408–409.

Turkey to do so, but neither government was prepared to make a major issue over the question during the early months of World War I. The American declaration of war against Germany in April, 1917, brought demands by the British, French, and Italian governments, along with the Supreme War Council, that the United States declare war on Turkey as well. Secretary of State Lansing reported that all of the Republican members of the Senate Foreign Relations Committee and many of the Democratic members favored such a move.[15] For his part, President Wilson admitted to Congress that Turkey might properly have been included in the American declaration of war.[16] On the other hand, the ACASR as well as the missionary and educational organizations had a vested interest in keeping the peace with Turkey. As a foreign group their "rights" to operate effectively in the Ottoman Empire rested upon the sufferance of the Ottoman government. The problem of the ACASR was to prevent, if it could, the use of anti-Turkish, pro-Armenian feeling to push the United States into war with Turkey.

The absence of provocation by the Turks unquestionably helped to preserve the peace. The Ottoman government had entered the war in 1914 as an ally of Germany. Early in 1917 Talat Pasha, the Ottoman Minister of Foreign Affairs, expressly assured Abram Elkus, who had succeeded Morgenthau as ambassador, that there was no reason why Turkey and the United States should not continue to enjoy friendly relations, even though the United States should go to war with Germany.[17] Although the Ottoman government severed diplomatic relations with the United States in mid-April, 1917, it was careful to give no cause for offense, a point the anti-war party in the United States repeatedly stressed.[18]

The unwillingness of the Congress to declare war in the absence of a positive request by the President to do so also served to keep the peace. President Wilson was no jingoist, but more important was the fact that well before the United States entered World War I, Cleveland H. Dodge, his close personal friend, had explained the importance of maintaining neutrality with the Ottoman Empire in order to safeguard the mission property, the independent colleges, and the relief work. In February,

[15] Lansing to W. Wilson, May 2, 1918, *Foreign Relations: Lansing Papers, 1914–1920* (2 Vols., Washington: GPO, 1939–1940), II, 121 ff. Lansing to Wilson, May 8, 1918, *ibid.*, 125–126. The topic is more fully explored in Robert L. Daniel, "The Armenian Question and American-Turkish Relations, 1914–1927," *Mississippi Valley Historical Review*, XLVI (1959), 252–275. A. Rustem to W. Bryan, Sept. 10, 1914, *Foreign Relations, 1914* (Washington: GPO, 1922), 1090.

[16] Ray S. Baker and William E. Dodd, eds., *The Public Papers of Woodrow Wilson* (6 Vols., New York: Harper & Bros., 1925–1927), V, 14.

[17] A. Elkus to Lansing, Mar. 2, 1917, *Foreign Relations: Lansing Papers*, I, 787.

[18] Lansing to Wilson, May 2, 1918, *ibid.*, II, 121 ff.; Elkus to J. Tumulty, Mar. 30, 1917, Woodrow Wilson Papers, Division of Manuscripts, Library of Congress.

1917, the President assured Dodge that he hoped to "manage things so prudently" that the lives of Americans in the Near East would not be endangered. In April, 1917, when the United States was entering the war, Dodge went to the President and restated the case for neutrality, and President Wilson's war message explicitly called for war only with Germany.[19]

The question of war with Turkey remained dormant until December, 1917, when Wilson asked for a declaration of war against Austria-Hungary. There was some Congressional feeling that the United States should include Turkey in the declaration, and outside Congress a few persons, notably Theodore Roosevelt, favored such a policy. But there was no organized effort to bring about a declaration of war. President Wilson spiked any disposition to include Turkey in the declaration of war by insisting that while it might be logical to do so, there were certain controlling reasons—which he did not state—that made such a course of action undesirable. Although there was some grumbling, Congress acquiesced.[20]

During 1917 and 1918 Cleveland H. Dodge and Dr. James L. Barton campaigned quietly to head off any move to declare war on Turkey. They argued that militarily a war with Turkey was undesirable because the United States could not mount an attack on Turkey without weakening its war effort against Germany. Diplomatically, a declaration of war would tend to bind Turkey and Germany closer at a time when they seemed to be drifting apart. To these arguments was added the humanitarian consideration that adoption of a war resolution would halt American relief work and subject mission and college property in Turkey to destruction or expropriation.[21] These arguments were employed both by Congressional opponents of war with Turkey and by Secretary of State Lansing. The arguments sufficed to kill off the final efforts to declare war on Turkey when the issue was revived in the spring of 1918 by Senatorial malcontents who charged the President with keeping the Senate in "as dense ignorance about our foreign relations as the Common Council of Keokuk." [22]

The question of United States-Bulgarian relations, less critical than

[19] Wilson to C. H. Dodge, Feb. 6, 1917, Cleveland H. Dodge Papers, Firestone Library, Princeton University. Hearsay testimony that Dodge went to the President in April, 1917, is given in New York *Times*, June 25, 1926 and Stephen B. L. Penrose, Jr., *That They May Have Life: The Story of the American University of Beirut, 1866–1941* (New York: Trustees of the AUB, 1941), 162–163; the occurrence of the meeting is confirmed by Dodge's son, Cleveland E. Dodge to author, Sept. 9, 1959. For the importance of the Dodge-Wilson relationship see Robert L. Daniel, "The Friendship of Woodrow Wilson and Cleveland H. Dodge," *Mid-America*, XLIII (1961), 182–196.

[20] Baker and Dodd, eds., *Public Papers of Woodrow Wilson*, V, 136.

[21] See for example, ACASR, "Worker's Bulletin 11," ca. Jan. 1918; also, J. Barton to H. C. Lodge, Dec. 10, 1917, ABC 3.2, Vol. 333; J. Barton to T. Roosevelt, May 9, 1918, in *ibid.*, Vol. 336, p. 258; New York *Tribune*, June 23, 1918, III, 5.

[22] Sen. Brandegee quoted in *Cong. Record*, 65 Cong., 2 Sess., 5473 (Apr. 23, 1918).

those with Turkey, followed much the same pattern. More than a year before the United States entered the war, the Bulgarian government gave assurances that mission interests would not be molested. Again in the spring of 1917, both the mission and the American consul-general hastened to assure their respective headquarters that Bulgaria would not declare war on the United States. Bulgaria, indeed, managed its affairs with skill. Unlike Turkey it did not break off diplomatic relations with the United States. Its wartime minister to the United States was Stephen Panaretoff who had been associated with Robert College for forty years.[23]

Representatives of Greece and Serbia continued to exert strong pressure on the Wilson administration to declare war on Bulgaria. Although President Wilson had indicated his unwillingness to include either Bulgaria or Turkey in a declaration of war, the administration had to make its case clear. In 1918 two members of the mission in Bulgaria, R. H. Markham and Edward B. Haskell, returned to the United States, their homeward trip facilitated by the Bulgarian government, in order to lobby against a declaration of war. Their energetic defense of Bulgaria provoked an admonition from William Phillips, the Assistant Secretary of State. Markham and Haskell offered no apology, and they stressed that American interests would be best served by cultivating Bulgarian goodwill and by seeking to detach her from her alliance with the Central Powers. Senate leaders, then discussing a proposal to declare a state of war with Bulgaria, professed to being impressed by the Markham-Haskell argument. The proposal was dropped, and four months later Bulgaria sued for peace.[24]

· III ·

The end of the war in Europe brought hope that the missionary-relief workers could finish their job and resume their mission work. Conditions in the Near East, far from becoming settled, became more confused as a result of conflicts between the Soviet Union and Turkey over control of

[23] William Webster Hall, Jr., *Puritans in the Balkans: The American Board Mission in Bulgaria, 1878–1918* (Sofia, 1938), 257 ff. is the fullest discussion of the mission's role. See also, *Foreign Relations, 1917 Supplement I*, 16, 137–138, 172; *Foreign Relations, 1917, Supplement II*, 67.

[24] E. B. Haskell, "Bulgaria Points the Way," *Asia Magazine*, XVIII (1918), 918–924; James L. Barton, letter in Boston *Evening Transcript*, Apr. 16, 1918; "Bulgarian Minister Says His Land is not Our Foe," New York *Times*, Dec. 9, 1917. The Boston *Evening Transcript* editorially urged an American declaration of war on Bulgaria, Apr. 12, Apr. 25, Apr. 27, and May 9, 1918. "Should We Declare War on Bulgaria?" *Independent*, XCIV (May 25, 1918), 310–311; R. A. Tsanoff, "To Pry Off Bulgaria," *New Republic*, XIV (Mar. 23, 1918); "Balkan States May Shock Hun," New York *Globe*, May 21, 1918. See also, *Foreign Relations, 1918, Supplement I*, 3, 65–67, 147, and 262–264.

the Caucasus, the civil war within Turkey during which Mustapha Kemal destroyed the Sultanate, and the intervention of various European governments in Turkish affairs. As the need for relief continued, hope gave way to frustration.

One of the first steps taken by the ACASR to meet the continuing need for relief was to reorganize and incorporate under a Congressional charter as the Near East Relief. Corporate status was sought primarily to give the organization the "prestige and unity essential for the efficient administration and distribution of funds." The organization was charged with providing relief and assisting in the "repatriation, rehabilitation and reestablishment of suffering and dependent people of the Near East." [25] Incorporation in itself brought no fundamental changes in the work. Sponsorship continued to come principally from those groups with interests in the Near East —the American Board, the Presbyterian Board, and the independent colleges, and to a lesser extent from Methodists, Episcopalians, Roman Catholics, and Jews. The Laymen's Missionary Movement, the Church Peace Union, and the Federal Council of Churches of Christ also participated actively.

Relief activities overseas were reorganized and hastily expanded. Civilian relief workers were recruited in the United States, while abroad United States Army officers were placed on detached service to direct the relief efforts. By the end of 1920, Near East Relief's staff numbered 270 newly recruited lay workers in addition to an equal number of missionaries. The employment of laymen created personnel problems. The military tended to measure their own achievements in terms of the amount of money expended rather than the number of people helped. The officers were transient, and this meant frequent interruptions in the administration of the work. Civilian employees were often more interested in seeing the world than in devoted service to the refugees. Misappropriation of funds occurred, and six relief workers were apprehended by American consular officials. In view of the task confronting the relief workers—it was estimated that there were four million refugees of whom 400,000 were children separated from their parents—it is surprising that the complaints were not more numerous and more serious. [26]

Efforts to conduct relief work in northwest Persia indicated the inter-

[25] Barton, *Story of Near East Relief*, 432-437. A bill to incorporate the ACRNE was passed unanimously Dec. 12, 1918, by the Senate but was defeated in the House. Opponents feared that the Committee had ulterior motives. Objections to a new bill, introduced in 1919, emphasized that incorporation was unnecessary and that Elihu Root and Charles Evans Hughes, trustees of the committee, were concession hunters. Notwithstanding these arguments the charter was approved. See *Cong. Rec.*, 65 Cong., 3 Sess., 340-341, 675-677, 836-838; *ibid.*, 66 Cong., 1 Sess., 2545-2548, 3012-3013, 3151-3154.

[26] J. Barton to H. C. Jaquith, Dec. 17, 1919, ABC 3.2, Vol. 345, p. 357. New York *Times*, Sept. 12, 14, and 15, 1920; E. A. Yarrow, "American Relief Activities in the Caucasus. Historical Memoranda," Sept. 3, 1919, ABC 16.9.7, Vol. 5, p. 274.

dependence of political conditions and the need for relief. After two relatively quiet years, the Urumia plain was again thrown into turmoil in the
summer and fall of 1918. During the summer of 1918 Urumia was caught
between a British expeditionary force moving up the Tigris River and
Turkish troops to the west of the city. A British officer was busy in the
area recruiting an army of refugees to assist the British against the
Turks, and indiscreet American missionaries diverted some $100,000 in
relief funds to support this "Christian army." One of the missionary-relief
workers, William Shedd, also the American vice consul at Urumia, seriously compromised the American government by signing in his capacity
as vice consul an offer to pay the bills of the Christian army. He also
issued orders summoning "every young man who has a rifle" to join the
Christian army "without any delay or excuse," an action which Shedd
admitted was "directly in contravention" of orders of the State Department.[27]

Neither the British nor the "Christian army" was able to prevent the
Turks from occupying Urumia on July 31, 1918, and although the latter
withdrew in mid-October, civil war followed when the Persian government attempted to reassert its control over the area. As a result of this
effort, the Kurds attacked the mission compound in May, 1919, destroyed
the property, and drove the refugees to Baghdad, Kermanshah, and Hamadan. Presbyterian missionaries in the latter two communities attempted to
continue relief work, but Near East Relief sought to disengage itself from
the area, letting local Armenians and Assyrians care for their own.

In other areas of the Near East the most urgent task seemed to be caring
for the hundreds of thousands of children who were drifting about. Starting early in 1919, Near East Relief herded thousands of children into mission stations and other facilities used for relief work. Since many of these
were under five years of age, Near East Relief assumed a responsibility to
develop a program of child care until the children reached the age of self-
support. As thousands of the children had trachoma, scabies, or favus (a
contagious skin disease), a mass prophylaxis program was required; it was
also necessary to provide vocational education for older children. Manifesting pride in the American achievement, Near East Relief saw its "orphans" settling down to "absorb American ideals of wholesome living and
to grow into useful manhood and womanhood according to American
standards and by American methods." [28]

In Turkey and Syria, work with children centered about mission sta-

[27] Mary Lewis Shedd, *The Measure of a Man: The Life of William Ambrose Shedd,
Missionary to Persia* (New York: George H. Doran, 1922), 243 ff. Augustin Ferrin to
Sec. of State, Nov. 6, 1926, SDDF 891.00/1396; *ibid.*, Dec. 21, 1926, SDDF 891.00/1400;
ibid., Feb. 21, 1926, SDDF 891.00.
[28] *New Near East*, VII (June, 1922), 6.

tions of the American Board. The work at Marash, a town of sixty thousand in the foothills of the Taurus Mountains, was illustrative. Here five orphanages and a hospital were organized to care for over a thousand children. Christian girls "rescued" from Moslem harems were placed in special homes to facilitate their readjustment. When the most immediate physical needs of the children had been provided, "industrial" training was begun. Trades such as shoemaking, baking, tinsmithing, and tailoring were taught the older boys. In some places children were sent out to work with artisans to learn a trade; in other places craftsmen gave instruction at the orphanages. This training not only prepared the boy to become self-supporting, but it provided the orphanage with some or all of its shoes, utensils, baked goods, and clothing. Girls were taught carding and spinning, sewing and mending, and child care.[29]

The largest orphanages were in the Caucasus, where there were no mission stations to serve as nuclei for orphanages. Arrangements were made with Soviet authorities to concentrate the children at Alexandropol in former army barracks of the Czarist regime. The Kazachi Post with ninety buildings, adequate water, and a rail spur, was suited to housing large numbers of children. Grammar schools were set up for nearly 4,400 younger children, while vocational education was offered to nearly as many older youth. The Seversky Barracks in another quarter of the city were rehabilitated by Near East Relief in the fall of 1921 for use as a medical center. The Barracks housed six thousand children undergoing treatment for trachoma. A special school, the first of its kind in the area, was organized for those already blinded by the infection. These children were given an elementary education, taught braille, and instructed in mat and basket weaving.[30]

In Constantinople, prosperous and orderly in spite of the turmoil in the hinterland, Near East Relief carried on a varied program. Some fifteen thousand children were cared for here, but the native community was persuaded to assume substantial support of the work. Near East Relief organized day nurseries for the children of widowed mothers and treatment centers for victims of tuberculosis and trachoma. Under an American social worker, Frances McQuaide, a start was made in introducing child welfare work in the city, and in the summer of 1921 a six-week summer school was held to help train orphanage teachers from the interior in civics, hygiene, manual arts, domestic science, kindergarten work, and pedagogy.

[29] A. J. Culler, "The Day's Work in Marash," *News Bulletin*, IV (Oct., 1919), 10 ff.; "Starting Again At Their Beginnings," *New Near East*, V (June, 1920), 3–15.

[30] "Trachoma at its Worst, Worsted," *ibid.*, VII (Apr., 1922), 14; "Schools for the Blind," *ibid.*, VII (Sept., 1922), 16–17.

Of necessity much energy was still devoted to feeding and clothing adults. Dr. Barton, on an inspection tour in the Caucasus in March, 1919, found adults wearing "the rags they have worn for four years" and saw hungry women stripping flesh from a dead horse with their bare hands. Improvised soup kitchens sustained over a half million persons during the winter and spring of 1919–20. Over 300,000 persons were clothed from some 1,500,000 pounds of used clothing shipped from the United States. The need in the Caucasus was such that Barton estimated it would cost thirty million dollars in 1920 alone to provide food and clothing to the distressed.[31]

During the peak of the post-war emergency, Near East Relief had substantial assistance from the American Relief Administration, the United States Grain Corporation, and the Commonwealth Fund. The American Relief Administration, financed by Congress, shipped $8,075,000 in foodstuffs to the Near East, while the United States Grain Corporation, another government agency, sent flour worth $4,725,000. The Commonwealth Fund appropriated $750,000 to help feed the children. With wartime altruism still alive and local war chests still active, Near East Relief raised $4,802,000 to finance the orphanages and their staffs, for a total of $19,485,000. But in mid-1920 the American Relief Administration and the U. S. Grain Corporation wound up their activities, leaving Near East Relief on its own. At the same time the total revenues of Near East Relief declined. As a result its soup-line became a breadline, dispensing a half-pound of bread per person per day. These retrenchments were not enough, and in March, 1922, a twenty-five percent cut in operations was ordered. In effect this meant dismissing twenty-five thousand children from the orphanages to secure food, shelter, and clothing for themselves.[32]

In 1919, with Turkey defeated and presumably unable to inflict further hurt on her Christian minorities or on American institutions there, Near East Relief abandoned all restraints in defaming the Turks in order to raise money. The image Americans were shown garbed Turks in evil black, the Armenians in saintly white. The general tenor of the propaganda was that the Turks had initiated the persecutions without provocation. Ambassador Morgenthau charged that the Turk was "psychologically primitive," and a "bully and a coward." Others contrasted the "ruthless Turk" with the "250,000 homeless little children" he had orphaned, and reported that Turks had placed Christian girls in their harems, that fourteen- to eighteen-year-old girls were being sold into slavery or were compelled to live

---

[31] James G. Harbord, "Conditions in the Near East: Report of the American Military Mission to Armenia," Oct. 16, 1919, *Senate Docs.*, 66 Cong., 2 Sess., No. 266, p. 8; Barton to Vickrey, Mar. 14, 1919, ABC 16.5, Vol. 6, p. 89.

[32] Barton, *Story of Near East Relief*, 399–415, discusses financial arrangements.

"naked for months," and that others were being forcibly tattooed "on the forehead, lips, and chin to mark them as Moslem women." [33] The climax of these lurid charges came in a movie version of the experiences of one refugee girl, Aurora Mardiganian, suggestively titled, "Ravished Armenia." [34]

Vilification of the Turk was matched by idealization of the Armenian. William Howard Taft's evaluation of the Armenians as "the backbone of the Ottoman Empire" was typical. In an otherwise unlovely place they had "made the valleys bloom as the rose." [35] Also much was made of the point that the Armenians were the "oldest Christian nation." They were identified with Noah and as the people who had given "more martyrs to the Christian faith than all the others combined." [36] Again the Armenian was pictured as a seeker of freedom, a lover of education. Abstract qualities were personified. At one instant the Armenian was a pathetic child. "Eager, burning-eyed boys and girls, in their shoeless feet, shivering with cold and often weak from hunger," were proof of the "true quality and worth of this nation. . . ." The next instant he was a romantic, desperate warrior whose "sparkling black eyes bespeak resolution and intensity of purpose." [37]

While such publicity helped to raise money, it did not contribute to an understanding of the problems of the area. The divorcement of the events then taking place in the Near East from the past precluded an appreciation of the complexity of the issues. Such publicity permitted the American public to remain largely unaware of the barriers to internal political reform posed by the intermittent interference of European powers in the affairs of the Ottoman Empire. It exploited the religious differences between the Turks and the Armenians without disclosing that during much of the nineteenth century the Christian subjects of Turkey had enjoyed a degree of religious freedom that was not accorded to dissenters from the established faith in some of the more enlightened kingdoms of Europe. It overlooked the existence of an active Armenian revolutionary party and left unmentioned the doubts entertained by the Ottoman government as to the loyalty of the Armenians. It failed to point out that many of the Armenians had lived in a theater of war or that Moslem Turks were also suffering. The publicity was so distorted that Americans who went to the Near East at the end of the war were repelled by the Armenian of reality. Mark Bristol, the American High Commissioner to Constantinople, com-

---

[33] Henry Morgenthau, *Ambassador Morgenthau's Story* (Garden City: Doubleday, Page & Co., 1918), 236, 275; New York *Times*, June 1, 1919 and Feb. 1, 1920.

[34] *Ibid.*, Feb. 15, 1919 and May 12, 1919; New York *Tribune*, Feb. 17, 1919.

[35] New York *Times*, Jan. 16, 1919.

[36] *New Near East*, VI (Mar., 1921), 3.

[37] *Ibid.*, VI (Oct., 1921), 7, 12.

mented tartly that the Armenian was neither Christian nor capable of self-government.[38] Indeed, Dr. Barton of Near East Relief admitted privately that many American relief workers had returned to the United States wondering whether the Armenian was worth helping.[39]

At the end of World War I, with the missionary-relief workers anxious to terminate the relief work and the mission boards eager to resume full-time mission work, philanthropists once again urged political solutions to the Near East problem. Wilson's Fourteen Points had implied international control of Constantinople, a national state for the Turks, and autonomy for the Armenians. Presumably the images of the vicious Turk and the helpless Armenian should have been a potent force in securing American support for a mandate for Armenia. Although officers and trustees of Near East Relief played a major role in the effort to organize a mandate, they were unable to make effective use of the images or to win Congressional approval.

American philanthropists generally thought in terms of organizing the Armenians into a mandated state, but they did not agree on the specific form the mandate should take. Dr. James Barton favored creation of a federation of six states administered by a single power. In this arrangement Armenia would form one of the states.[40] Henry Morgenthau likewise proposed a mandate for the whole Empire, but he proposed to divide it into three units for administrative purposes: Constantinople, Anatolia, and Armenia.[41] James W. Gerard, another trustee of the Near East Relief and a friend of the Armenians, assumed that the Armenians were ready for self-government, and he suggested a short-term mandate for Armenia alone to get the new government underway; but he vigorously opposed any plan placing the Armenians and Turks in the same jurisdiction.[42] In contrast, Oscar S. Straus, a former ambassador to Turkey and a trustee of Near East Relief, rejected American acceptance of a mandate for Constantinople or any other part of the Near East as a "barbed wire-entanglement" of the most dangerous variety. America, Straus concluded, should restrict herself to financial aid to the Armenians and leave the administration of a mandate to the League of Nations.[43] Straus excepted, the

[38] M. Bristol to Barton, Mar. 28, 1921, ABC 16.9.1, Vol. 6, p. 235.

[39] Barton to J. Bryce, Sept. 15, 1920, ABC 3.2, Vol. 350, p. 538.

[40] Barton to F. Dixon, Jan. 27, 1917, *ibid.*, Vol. 327, p. 473; "Suggested Possible Form of Government for Area Covered by the Ottoman Empire at the Outbreak of the War, Exclusive of Arabia, but Inclusive of the Transcaucasus," ABC 16.9.1, Vol. 4, p. 313.

[41] Draft of a speech, Dec. 2, 1918, Henry Morgenthau Papers, in Division of Manuscripts, Library of Congress, A 482, Box 11; also, Henry Morgenthau, "Mandate or War?" *New York Times Magazine*, Nov. 9, 1919, 12.

[42] James W. Gerard, "Why America Should Accept Mandate for Armenia," New York *Times*, July 6, 1919; reprinted in American Committee for the Independence of Armenia, *America as Mandatary for Armenia* ([New York], 1919), 3–10.

[43] Straus cited in New York *Evening Post*, May 29, 1919, and May 8, 1920.

proposals of Near East Relief's officers and trustees were generally in accord with the President's Fourteen Points.

These views were not carried to the public in the name of Near East Relief. Dr. Barton restricted himself to discussing his ideas with friends. While Straus, Gerard, and Morgenthau reached a limited public through the New York City press, Gerard also circulated his ideas through the instrumentality of the newly organized American Committee for the Independence of Armenia, thus publicly identifying himself with the Armenian nationalist movement rather than with American philanthropy. The Near East Relief published but two proposals of a political nature. Both studies emphasized what ought to be done within Turkey by way of political, economic, and social reform; neither argued the case for American acceptance of a mandate; neither was widely circulated by the relief committee. Dr. Barton for his part was disposed to keep the relief committee out of politics.[44]

In their private capacities the philanthropists worked with the Wilson administration in finding a solution to the complex Near East problem. Howard Bliss, president of the Syrian Protestant College, perhaps more than anyone else persuaded President Wilson to send a neutral, inter-allied commission to make a field study and to propose policy recommendations for the Near East. Henry Churchill King and Charles R. Crane, both trustees of Near East Relief, were appointed by President Wilson as the American members of the commission. When the British and French failed to appoint their delegates, King and Crane made the study alone. After a working-tour of Palestine and Syria and extensive interviews in Constantinople with persons representing all shades and varieties of opinion, the commission made its report in August, 1919. King and Crane recognized that the administration of a mandate for Armenia would entail serious responsibilities. One of these would be the large-scale relocation of Armenians from other parts of Anatolia into the new Armenia and the removal of non-Armenians from it. Compounding this problem was a conflict between those who were content with an Armenian state located in eastern Anatolia and those who sought to expand the boundaries to include Cilicia. King and Crane recommended the formation, under a mandatory, of an Armenian state completely separated from Turkey, an International Constantinopolitan state, and a Turkish state, all three mandates to be administered by the United States. They explicitly rejected the inclusion of Cilicia within an Armenian state.[45]

---

[44] William H. Hall, ed., *Reconstruction in Turkey* (ACASR, 1918); Harold A. Hatch and William H. Hall, *Recommendations for Political Reconstruction in the Turkish Empire* (ACASR, 1918). Hall drew up the proposals; Hatch financed the research.

[45] "Report of the American Section of the International Commission on Mandates in Turkey," USDS, *Papers Relating to the Foreign Relations of the United States,*

Even before King and Crane completed their report, the Wilson administration took additional steps to facilitate the creation of an Armenian homeland. Henry Morgenthau, whose distress call in 1915 had led to the organization of the Armenian Atrocities Committee, shared with Herbert Hoover the responsibility for initiating the preliminary studies. As a stopgap they appointed Colonel William Haskell to direct all relief work in the Caucasus, where famine and political chaos were rampant. Next, they induced General James Harbord, chief of staff to General Pershing, to make an estimate of the operating costs of the proposed mandate. Harbord's report, completed in mid-October, 1919, was hard-hitting. Acceptance of the mandate, he estimated, would cost $756,104,000 for the first five years. Nevertheless, Harbord judged that it was "imperative from every standpoint of peace, order, efficiency, and economy" that one power assume a mandate for the whole of Anatolia.[46] Because the contents of the Harbord and the King-Crane reports reached the White House after Wilson's breakdown, neither exerted a significant influence on public policy. Indeed, the King-Crane Report was not published until December 2, 1922.

Official action to undertake a mandate was delayed, however, while the Senate debate over the peace settlement with Germany and acceptance of the League Covenant dragged on through the closing months of 1919 and the early part of 1920. While Congress debated, conditions in the Caucasus deteriorated rapidly. An Armenian Republic established in the Caucasus in 1917 had become so shaky by May, 1918, that such peace and order as existed was maintained by British troops operating from Batum and Baku. In August, 1919, President Wilson acknowledged that the only way to help the Armenian Republic effectually was by sending armed forces, but that in view of the "temper of Congress" approval of such action seemed too remote to be worth the asking.[47] After the Senate finally rejected the Versailles Treaty in March, 1920, the United States was no longer in a position to deal with the Armenian question on the basis of membership in the League of Nations, although the way was still open for direct action. The President remained hopeful that Congress could be persuaded to approve the mandate, if it could be shown that the American people demanded it. Thus, in asking Congress officially in May, 1920, to accept the mandate, he interpreted the generous response to appeals for

1919: Paris Peace Conference 1919 (13 Vols., Washington: GPO, 1942–1947), XII, 751–863, especially 841–48. See Harry N. Howard, *The King-Crane Commission: An American Inquiry in the Middle East* (Beirut: Khayats, 1963) is authoritative.

[46] Harbord, "Conditions in the Near East," 14, 24–29.

[47] Wilson to Dodge, Aug. 14, 1919, and Wilson to J. S. Williams, Aug. 12, 1919, both in Wilson Papers; Wilson to W. Phillips, Sept. 23, 1919, SDDF 860J.01/92. A congressional resolution to authorize the President to use American military forces in the Armenian Republic was defeated later in committee.

relief funds as evidence that the American public desired the United States to protect the Armenian state and assist it in achieving political and economic stability.[48]

Ultimately President Wilson undertook unsuccessfully to enlist the aid of relief and missionary groups in bringing pressure on Congress. While some of the philanthropists, Dodge, Morgenthau, and Crane, had ties to the President, they had no influence with members of the Senate who had to vote on the measure. Nor was Near East Relief prepared to lead a public fight for the mandate, for the bonds which linked the contributors to the relief committee were those of humanitarian concern for human suffering, not political consensus. Leadership in the campaign for a mandate shifted to Armenian-American organizations, but they, too, were unable to sway popular opinion. It came as no surprise in June, 1920, when the Senate "respectfully declined" to accept a mandate for Armenia, 52–23.[49]

Failure to secure Congressional approval of a mandate added to the frustrations of the philanthropists who frantically advocated a spate of political solutions to the Near East problem. First the philanthropists urged a unilateral declaration by President Wilson to regard any attack on the Armenian Republic as an unfriendly act against the United States.[50] Wisely, the President refused. Next they sought a loan of United States funds to the Armenian Republic. Dr. Barton secured the support of Senator Lodge, who had some Armenian-American constituents; then Barton and Dodge induced the President to ask Congress to authorize such a loan, which the latter did in his annual message to Congress in December, 1920. Again Congress declined to act.[51]

When control of the federal government passed to the Harding Administration, the philanthropists lost much of their pull with the executive branch of the government, but the campaign of private letter-writing to Congressmen continued. Exasperation reached such a point in 1922 that the Near East Relief urged its constituency to write their Congressmen about conditions in Turkey. The board of trustees "in behalf of at least 20,000,000 of the people of the United States who have contributed to American relief work in the Near East" officially appealed to Congress to exert pressure on the war-time allies and on Turkey to end the "state of anarchy" in Anatolia.[52] Shortly thereafter Near East Relief and the mis-

[48] *Cong. Record,* 66 Cong., 2 Sess., 7533 (May 24, 1920).

[49] Wilson to Dodge, Apr. 19, 1920, Dodge Papers; *Cong. Record,* 66 Cong., 2 Sess., 8073 (June 1, 1920).

[50] Barton and others to Wilson, June 18, 1920, Wilson Papers.

[51] Wilson to Dodge, Dec. 2, 1920, Dodge Papers; Baker and Dodd, eds., *Public Papers of Woodrow Wilson,* VI, 520. J. Barton to H. Morgenthau, Dec. 3, 1920, ABC 3.2, Vol. 352, p. 153.

[52] New York *Times,* May 26, 1921.

sionary group made common cause with Armenian-American leaders in an unsuccessful effort to bring about the recall of Admiral Bristol as American High Commissioner in Constantinople on the grounds that his pro-Turkish viewpoint made him unacceptable to the friends of the Armenians.[53]

· IV ·

The September, 1922, victory of Mustapha Kemal over his adversaries, both domestic and foreign, created a new crisis of major proportions for the Near East Relief. Paradoxically it brought peace to the Near East, permitting a gradual termination of emergency relief work. The last stroke of the Turkish War for Independence resulted in the burning of Smyrna. On the evening after the fire, September 13, 1922, there were 260,000 homeless refugees, mostly Greeks. American and European residents of the burned city gave such immediate aid as was possible, while an *ad hoc* committee begged, borrowed, and commandeered enough shipping to evacuate the women, children, and aged to offshore islands beyond reach of the hostile Turks. Although the Near East Relief had been attempting to extricate itself from adult relief work in order to concentrate its energies on child care, it resumed disaster relief work on a major scale. Promptly it sent relief supplies from Constantinople.[54]

In this crisis, Near East Relief received help from the American Women's Hospitals, a group founded in 1917 by women doctors desiring a share in the "glory" of overseas medical relief work. When Smyrna burned, the organization's moving spirit, Dr. Esther Lovejoy, went directly to the city and joined other American relief officials in arranging the immediate relief and evacuation of the refugees. Other personnel of the American Women's Hospitals were posted to the Greek islands and the mainland to receive them. Subsequently Dr. Lovejoy returned to the United States to raise a half million dollars in support of medical relief. American Women's Hospitals assumed full medical responsibility for all orphans and NER work in Greece, the AWH paying the salaries of medical personnel as well as costs of medicine and medical supplies. NER met the larger costs of feeding and housing the children.[55]

When other organizations declined responsibility for some eight thousand refugees quarantined on "bleak, barren" Macronissi Island, Dr. Mabel

[53] Barton to G. Montgomery, Dec. 19, 1921, ABC 3.2, Vol. 358, p. 543.
[54] Bristol to Phillips, Sept. 22, 1922, USDS, *Foreign Relations, 1922* (2 Vols., Washington: GPO, 1938), II, 431–432; U. S. Navy Department, *The United States Navy in Peacetime* (Washington: GPO, 1931), 168–169.
[55] Esther Pohl Lovejoy, *Certain Samaritans* (New York: Macmillan, 1927) and Mabel Evelyn Elliott, *Beginning Again at Ararat* (New York: Fleming H. Revell, 1924) are by two of the women doctors.

Elliott committed the AWH to accept complete responsibility. "It simply *had* to be done," she informed Dr. Lovejoy. Dr. Ruth Parmelee, born in Turkey of missionary parents, organized medical work for the AWH at Salonika, including clinics, a one-hundred-bed hospital, and a nurses' training course. Another AWH doctor, Marian Cruikshank, was sent to Crete. Armed with a delouser, vaccine, soap, and a *carte blanche* from island authorities, she vaccinated twenty thousand refugees and deloused fifteen thousand, arresting incipient epidemics of typhus and smallpox.[56]

When Turkey settled her differences with Greece at Lausanne, an exchange of populations was negotiated whereby nearly all the remaining Greeks and Armenians living in Turkey were sent to Greece, and 300,000 Turks hitherto residing in Greece were sent to Turkey. Although this was a League of Nations operation, Near East Relief personnel were put in charge of feeding and housing the refugees until they were put aboard ship at ports of embarkation in Turkey, Syria, the Greek islands, and Thrace. Most of this work was completed in 1923, but the last group of twelve thousand Greeks was not repatriated until 1925. The American Women's Hospitals worked closely with Near East Relief in providing medical care for these refugees. Once the repatriated Greeks arrived on the mainland of Greece, the American Red Cross assumed responsibility for relief. Through the winter of 1922–23 the American Red Cross fed some 860,000 refugees daily.[57]

Efforts in the United States to raise an emergency fund for refugee relief were not successful, and neither the American Red Cross nor the Near East Relief was able to maintain its level of expenditures. As refugees were evacuated from Asia Minor the strain on the Near East Relief lessened, but as the Greek economy could not provide the refugees with work, the burden on the Red Cross increased steadily. Unable to stand the drain on its resources, the Red Cross withdrew in June, 1923, shifting the burden to the Greek government and the League of Nations. The Near East Relief provided limited assistance in Athens by organizing Near East Industries, an adaptation of the Goodwill Industries' workshop. Some refugees were hired to rehabilitate used clothing shipped from the United States for use of the refugees. Other refugee women were engaged to produce fancy needlework, which was sold to tourists and in Near East Relief offices in America. The income from the sale of these goods reached as high as $100,000 a year and was used for further relief work.[58]

[56] Lovejoy, *Certain Samaritans*, 197, 241–245.

[57] *Ibid., passim;* C. Hughes to A. Geddes, Mar. 31, 1923, USDS, *Foreign Relations, 1923*, (2 Vols., Washington: GPO, 1938), II, 329–330; NER, *Annual Report, 1923*, in *Senate Docs.*, 68 Cong., 1 Sess., No. 111, p. 9.

[58] NER, "Summarized Report to Executive Committee," Sept. 27, 1923, Talcott Williams Papers, Union Theological Seminary Library; J. B. Payne to Phillips, Mar. 1, 1923, *Foreign Relations, 1923*, II, 321–322.

Lesser crises in Syria and the Caucasus also demanded temporary renewal of disaster relief work. In Syria, Shiite terrorists in the Jebel-ed-Druze and dissatisfied groups in Damascus revolted against French control in 1925. When Lebanese Christians volunteered to fight against the rebels, Arabs sympathetic to the revolt subjected Christians all over Syria to abuse or persecution. Near East Relief supplied used clothing and limited financial aid to sustain these latest refugees, principally Armenians from Damascus. In the Caucasus, after a series of severe earthquakes in 1926 left many homeless, Near East Relief opened an emergency hospital for the injured and shipped thousands of square feet of wallboard and roofing material along with tons of used clothing to provide shelter and clothing. The Armenian General Benevolent Union, a world-wide Armenian organization, collected over $100,000 in the United States, which it sent through the Near East Relief for assistance. As nearly as it could, Near East Relief limited itself to giving temporary assistance to adults in order to maximize its work with children.[59]

The turmoil in Turkey in 1922 led Near East Relief to evacuate its orphan charges from Anatolia. Some were taken to Syria, where the children were housed in or about mission stations. Many were removed to the Greek island of Syra, where facilities for twenty-five thousand children were constructed, the older boys doing some of the work. As in other NER orphanages, the children were taught various trades and crafts. The children were cared for until they were about sixteen. Thereafter a few of the ablest were assisted in furthering their education. Most of them, however, were discharged. To assist their adjustment to the adult world, a Near East League was organized in the larger cities where the youth were most likely to congregate. Low cost shelter was made available, and organized recreation and social programs were led by a part-time director. Ultimately the League developed night schools. By 1930 most of the orphans in Greece had reached the age of self-support.[60]

In the Caucasus the Near East Relief continued to work with Armenian children. Special efforts were made to train the boys in farming. The Soviet government made available seventeen thousand acres on which to graze dairy and beef cattle and to raise food crops needed for the children. Four agricultural specialists headed by Leonard Hartill, one-time head of the Horticulture Department of the New York Institute of Applied Agriculture, operated the farm as an agricultural school. Older boys worked a

---

[59] Laird Archer, "Annual Report, Foreign Department," in NER Board of Trustees, Annual Meeting, Jan. 18, 1927, Williams Papers. "Statement Concerning Refugee Relief in Syria, Aug. 1926," in NER, *Docket*, Nov., 24, 1926, Williams Papers.

[60] NER, *Annual Report*, 1923, in *Senate Docs.*, 68 Cong., 1 Sess., No. 111, p. 17; *ibid.*, 1926, in *Senate Docs.*, 69 Cong., 2 Sess., No. 229, pp. 15–16; NER, *Docket*, May 28, 1925, Williams Papers; Barton, *Story of Near East Relief*, 293.

half day and attended classes the other half day. When the boys proved their capabilities as farmers, they were assigned tracts of land of their own. Each boy was to submit a plan for its use. Near East Relief provided him with seed and fed and clothed him until his first crop was in. Thereafter he was expected to support himself from his labor.[61]

At the end of three years the land and equipment were to be his. The plan did not work out, for in 1924 the Soviet government seized the land. Although it shortly returned the land to Near East Relief, the experience led Near East Relief to close the project and give the land back to Soviet authorities. Orphanages, however, were operated until 1930. At this time the organization found itself caught in the Stalin-Rykof rivalry. The flood of antagonism toward foreigners in Russia engulfed the organization's native staff, of whom forty were arrested and several executed for no apparent offense other than association with a foreign agency. As quickly and gracefully as it could, Near East Relief terminated all work in the Caucasus.[62]

Near East Relief was important for its magnitude. Together with its predecessors, NER operated for nearly fifteen years and oversaw the distribution of more than a hundred million dollars in relief supplies. Only the American Red Cross and the American Relief Administration performed on a larger scale. In so far as it ministered to the immediate needs of the victims of disaster, NER followed techniques of relief work that Samuel Gridley Howe had initiated in Greece nearly a century before and that missionaries had periodically utilized since in times of trouble.

The special contribution of NER was in broadening the base of support of American philanthropy in the Near East. The magnitude of the disasters in the Near East attracted the attention of the general public, and this in turn enabled the founders of Near East Relief to create a broadly based committee in support of relief work. The protracted character of the distress forced the relief committee to go beyond the *ad hoc* level of organization that had characterized all earlier efforts to solicit relief funds outside the circle of givers to the missionary boards. The repeated solicitations produced a "clientele" whose successive gifts gave them a "stake" in the final resolution of the disorders. Yet even in this relief work, the mission boards that had been the common denominator of philanthropy in the Near East still provided much of the active leadership. As time passed

---

[61] NER, *Annual Report, 1922, Senate Docs.*, 67 Cong., 4 Sess., No. 343, pp. 10–11; *New Near East*, VII (Dec., 1921), 7; "The Transcaucasian Farm Plan," *ibid.*, VII (Mar., 1922), 6; William A. Biby, "Repopulating the Garden of Eden," *ibid.*, VII (Dec., 1921), 16–17.

[62] Barclay Acheson, "NER Interstate Communications," Mar. 10, 1931, NER, *Docket*, 67–69; Acheson, "Report," NER, *Annual Meeting*, Feb. 4, 1932, 70, Williams Papers; NER, *Minutes*, July 8, 1930, 28–29; *ibid.*, Nov. 24, 1930, 33–34.

without a distinct improvement in the condition of the Armenians and Greeks, the mission boards became increasingly frustrated by the continuing demands upon their overseas staffs to engage in relief work. Finally, in the middle 1920's they took the initiative in reexamining the objectives and methods of their varied overseas projects.

VIII

Philanthropy in Transition, 1920–1930

THE 1920's were years of adjustment and transition for the Near East and for American philanthropy. The Ottoman Empire, defeated in war, disintegrated in peace. Under the leadership of Mustapha Kemal an intensely nationalistic Turkey emerged, and the vigorous new republic made great strides toward Westernization. New jurisdictions appeared in other portions of the defunct Ottoman Empire as Great Britain organized mandates in Iraq, Palestine, and Transjordan, while the French administered mandates in Syria and Lebanon. In Persia a strong man, Reza Khan, came to power. After crushing a Russian-inspired separatist movement in northwest Persia, he overthrew the Kajar dynasty, became Shah, and instituted a reform program akin to that of Mustapha Kemal. For the Christian philanthropist this changing political scene meant retrenchment in some activities and occasioned substantial changes in others.

· I ·

The operation of mission schools was marked by serious problems for both the missionaries and the native governments. In general the native governments of the Near East were by no means convinced that the mission schools were desirable. In the past the foreign school had seemed to be a front for subversive political movements sponsored by one or another European government. While the American schools had never knowingly supported subversion, Near Eastern governments could not grant Americans rights to operate schools and deny similar privileges to citizens of other nations. Another objection was that foreign schools, including the mission schools, had contributed to the cultural self-consciousness of minority groups. Furthermore, the American schools represented a foreign cultural influence that taught from foreign textbooks and from foreign viewpoints. Turkish critics argued that inasmuch as only the well-to-do could afford to send their children to the school, these "class" schools were harmful to the growth of Turkish democracy.[1] On the other hand, there were cogent arguments for permitting a few foreign schools to operate, for the new regimes did not yet have sufficient funds or enough competent teachers to staff an adequate school system. Besides, there was something to be learned from the American school. Joseph Grew reported in the late 1920's that the Turks were coming to respect the driving energy of the Anglo-American institutions, hoping that some of this drive would rub off on themselves.[2]

As a first step toward strengthening national control over all schools functioning within their jurisdictions, both Turkey and Persia imposed bans on compulsory Christian instruction for Moslem students attending mission schools. The mission boards questioned whether the spiritual character of their schools could be retained in the absence of formal religious instruction, which they regarded as one of the major contributions of their schools. They were generally agreed that unless their schools made a spiritual impact on the student, the mission should stop operating schools. Among the missionaries abroad, the liberals affirmed that formal religious instruction was not essential; the fundamentalists remained doubtful. The spirit of the times was on the side of the liberals who derived substantial support from the Laymen's Foreign Missions Inquiry, a study directed by William Ernest Hocking that strongly advocated irenic methods in lieu of the repent-and-be-saved approach of the fundamentalist.[3] Accordingly, mission boards accepted the terms laid down by the native regimes and continued to operate schools.

In Turkey some of the older missionaries found it difficult to accept the new pattern. When Miss Edith Sanderson, a teacher in the American Board school at Brusa, persisted in having Moslem children read the Bible,

[1] *Hayat* quoted in J. Grew to F. Kellogg, May 8, 1928, USDS, *Papers Relating to the Foreign Relations of the United States, 1928* (3 Vols., Washington: GPO, 1942–1943), III, 976.

[2] *Ibid.*, 977.

[3] Laymen's Foreign Missions Inquiry, *Re-thinking Missions: A Laymen's Inquiry After One Hundred Years* (New York: Harper & Bros., 1932), *passim.*

she and two of her colleagues were arrested, and the school was closed. Joseph Grew, the American ambassador, ultimately persuaded the Turks to regard this as an isolated incident—the act of an over-zealous teacher rather than a product of mission policy—and while the Brusa school remained closed, the incident did not become an excuse for closing other mission schools in Turkey. Thereafter American educators were careful to observe the letter of Turkish law, and there were no further disagreements of major import between the mission schools and the Turkish government.[4]

Gradually a national school system emerged in Turkey, but foreign schools, both elementary and secondary, were permitted to function as long as they observed the standards prescribed by the state. The most important of these regulations required that beginning in 1932 the teaching of history, geography, and civics be carried on by Turks, in Turkish, and from Turkish textbooks. Of lesser importance was a requirement that mission schools hold sessions on Sunday, which, of course, was just another weekday for the Moslem. The Turks also required equal pay for American and Turkish teachers irrespective of differences in training.[5]

Enrollment in mission schools after World War I was much smaller than before the war. As the American Board's schools had served primarily the Armenian Protestants of Anatolia, who had either died or been driven out, few of their schools reopened. By the fall of 1923 the student population stood at 2,800 compared with twenty-four thousand in 1912. Thereafter enrollments rose, leveling off at five thousand students. Many mission colleges in Anatolia—largely boarding schools operating at a secondary or junior college level—either quietly closed their doors or followed the Armenian refugees to Syria or Greece.

Affairs in Persia ran even less smoothly. The government first prohibited the use of the Bible with Moslem students and then required that all Moslem students be instructed in the Koran and Islamic law, a regulation which Presbyterian educators protested vigorously. The government temporarily retreated, but the continuing efforts of Armenians, Kurds, Assyrians, and Turks living in Persia to retain their national identities led it in 1928 to forbid foreigners to operate any schools in Azerbaijan province. The government promptly reimbursed the Presbyterian Board for its properties in Urumia and announced that it might carry on "charitable and educational work" elsewhere on the condition that "it contravenes neither the public order nor the laws and regulations of Persia." [6]

---

[4] Grew to Kellogg, Jan. 22, 1928, in *Foreign Relations, 1928,* III, 964–965; *ibid.*, Feb. 8, 1928, III, 970; *ibid.*, Feb. 1, 1928, III, 966–969.

[5] This policy was announced in 1928. Grew to Kellogg, May 8, 1928, *ibid.*, 979.

[6] Arthur Judson Brown, *One Hundred Years: A History of the Foreign Missionary Work of the Presbyterian Church in the U. S. A.* (New York: Fleming H. Revell, 1936), 530.

Thereafter the major focus of the Presbyterian's educational work was the American School at Tehran. The Boys' School, started in 1887 as a grade school, had progressively upgraded itself, becoming a high school in 1900 and a junior college in 1913. Because of Persia's physical isolation from Europe, those Moslems desiring a Western education enrolled in the American school. Even in 1900, sixty percent of the students were Moslems. In 1924 the school developed a college department, fulfilling an ambition of two decades. The joy was short-lived, however, as Persian nationalism continued to gain strength. In 1932 the government enacted laws reserving to Persian schools the elementary education of all Persian subjects, an act seriously reducing the number of students adequately prepared for work in the American school. In this less friendly climate, funds available for support of the school dried up, compounding the problems. Despite the threatening signs, the mission exhibited an attitude of optimism. It pointed to the increasing enrollments of Moslems and the willingness of the government to hire its graduates. To play down its American character, the mission renamed the school Alborz College after the mountain range north of the capital. To no avail, for in 1940 the government closed all foreign schools and expropriated the property. These steps reflected no specific disagreement with the American schools but rather a continuing effort to create a national school system and to assimilate the minority populations. The decision may also have reflected efforts to avoid granting Russian nationals permission to operate schools in Persia.[7]

Syria and Lebanon, both under mandate to France, erected the fewest barriers to the continued operation of schools by foreigners, but there were major shifts in the pattern of schools. French political control much enhanced the prestige of the French-operated lycées and added to the demand for courses in the French language. At the same time the Americans turned most of their primary schools over to the native Protestant communities and concentrated their energies on the remaining secondary schools. As a result, enrollments in the Presbyterian schools dropped from a pre-war level of seven thousand to 3,700 pupils in the mid-1920's.[8]

Because of developments in Turkey, several of the American schools moved their seat of operation to the calmer environment of Syria or Lebanon. The Girls' School at Marash, Turkey, moved to Aleppo and merged with the Presbyterian school there, forming the American High School for Girls. It operated a kindergarten, six primary grades, and five second-

[7] C. Engert to Sec. of State, Aug. 14, 1939, USDS, *Foreign Relations, 1939* (5 Vols., Washington: GPO, 1956-57), IV, 525-526; Memorandum of W. Murray to S. Welles, Aug. 21, 1939, *ibid.*, 530-531; Engert to Sec. of State, July 19, 1940, USDS, *Foreign Relations, 1940* (5 Vols., Washington: GPO, 1957-61), III, 701-702. See also, BFMPC, *Annual Reports.*

[8] Roderic D. Matthews and Matta Akrawi, *Education in Arab Countries of the Near East* (Washington: American Council on Education, 1949), 325.

ary grades. Of its five hundred students, the largest number were Moslems.[9]

The major American school in Syria in the 1920's and 1930's was Aleppo College. Founded as Central Turkey College at Aintab, it had been disrupted by World War I. Transferred to Aleppo, it reopened as a high school in 1924. In 1927 it merged with the North Syria High School for Boys and became Aleppo College. It operated elementary, secondary, and junior college classes. Well-housed on a new campus overlooking the city, the college possessed the best science laboratories of any secondary school in Syria. Many of its students completed their education at the American University of Beirut.[10]

The organization of the American Junior College for Women at Beirut and the transfer of the International College to that city changed the pattern of American mission education in Lebanon. The Junior College, organized in 1924, was an outgrowth of the American School for Girls. The purpose of the Junior College was to prepare girls for admission to the American University. Housed for a time in temporary quarters, the school by the 1940's acquired a modest campus consisting of a dormitory and a classroom building.[11]

The International College, originally at Smyrna, moved to Beirut in 1936 to become a preparatory school for the American University. It operated three separate programs: an intermediate section that offered a junior college program; a preparatory school, fashioned after an American-type high school; and the Section Secondaire, a French-type secondary school. The preparatory school operated a boarding department that received students from Palestine, Transjordan, Iraq, Bahrein, Iran, and Ethiopia. The Section Secondaire served primarily Syrian and Lebanese students who were preparing for the French-designed Lebanese examinations.[12]

In other respects the American mission schools continued as before. The American School for Girls at Beirut which could, with interruptions, trace its history back to the days of Sarah Lanman Huntington Smith, offered a secondary program. The School for Girls at Tripoli continued to serve students in northern Syria and Lebanon, while the Girls' School at Sidon served a student population to the south of Beirut. The latter school gave special attention to home economics. Secondary education for

[9] General Committee of the Near East Survey, *The Near East and American Philanthropy*, Frank A. Ross, C. Luther Fry, and Elbridge Sibley, eds. (New York: Columbia University Press, 1929) provides succinct resumés of the various schools in the 1920's. Hereafter cited in the name of the authors, Ross, Fry, and Sibley.

[10] Matthews and Akrawi, *Education in Arab Countries*, 402–404.

[11] *Ibid.*, 498–499; Francis P. Irwin, "American Junior College for Women in Beirut," *Junior College Journal*, VI (1935), 17–20.

[12] Matthews and Akrawi, *Education in Arab Countries*, 488–490. See also, AUB, *Report of the President* for appropriate years.

boys continued at Tripoli, where the school occupied a fine site overlooking the old city, and at the Gerard Institute at Sidon. Because of parental and student pressure the curriculum had shifted from its original emphasis upon vocational work to college preparatory work. Each of these schools was headed by an American principal and was staffed by a few American teachers, while the majority were Syrian or Lebanese.[13]

While American mission-sponsored schools were relegated to a minor role by 1930, the native governments turned to American educators for advice. John Dewey was engaged by the Turkish government to study educational practice and philosophy in Turkey. He recommended the creation of a national school system in which Church and State were completely separated.[14] Paul Monroe, Dewey's colleague at Columbia and a specialist in comparative education, performed a similar mission for the government of Iraq.[15] Monroe further taught and counselled natives of the Near East who studied at the International Institute of Teachers College. One of his students, Mohammed Fadhel Jamali, helped place Western influence on Near Eastern education in perspective. He argued that the West, like the East, was in transition; that it had unresolved problems; and that it had a heterogeneous culture. The Iraqi educator encouraged his countrymen to retain portions of their traditional culture and to infuse it with congenial elements of the new.[16]

American and Near Eastern educators agreed that American schools operating in the Near East must work with, rather than oppose, rising forces of nationalism. They agreed that the schools must be discriminating and selective in adjusting the "new education of the West" to the "traditional social structure of the East. . . ." [17] They spoke of "vitalizing and enriching Eastern culture with the best which the Occident has to offer." [18] Another aim was to provide the "eager, earnest future leaders of the Near East." [19] Finally, they spoke of using the schools as demonstration centers in the fields of home economics, agriculture, medicine, and engineering.[20]

[13] Matthews and Akrawi, *Education in Arab Countries,* 484–486.
[14] John Dewey, "Foreign Schools in Turkey," *New Republic,* XLI (1924–25), 41. *The John Dewey Report* (Ankara: Ministry of Education, Research and Measurement Bureau, 1960).
[15] Government of Iraq, *Report of the Educational Inquiry Commission; Survey Directed and Report Edited by Paul Monroe* (Baghdad, 1932).
[16] Mohammed Fadhel Jamali, *The New Iraq: Its Problem of Bedouin Education* (New York: Teachers College, Columbia University, 1934), 103.
[17] Paul Monroe, "The Educational Situation in the Near East," *News Bulletin of the Institute of International Education,* XII (Oct., 1936), 4.
[18] Bayard Dodge, "The Middle East and Modern Culture," *ibid.,* XXIII (June, 1948), 50.
[19] Howard Bliss, "The Modern Missionary," *Atlantic Monthly,* CXXV (1920), 674.
[20] Lee Vrooman, "Issues in Missionary Education in the Near East," *International Review of Missions,* XXII (1923), 54–56.

· II ·

In this changing milieu the independent colleges found continuing opportunities to work in the area. Their secular sponsorship permitted them to escape Moslem hostility toward the mission-sponsored school, and because they enrolled only college-age students, there was less fear that students would succumb to foreign influences. In addition, the poverty of native governments and the greater cost of collegiate education combined to make the independent colleges acceptable.

While World War I brought difficult problems, the independent colleges survived. In October, 1914, the Ottoman government revoked the Capitulations, but it made no rash move to assert its newly claimed rights. American diplomatic and consular officials expressed interest in the continued well-being of the colleges by visiting them frequently and by establishing temporary offices on their campuses. The colleges did their part in nurturing good relations with the Ottoman government. The Woman's College and the Syrian Protestant College carried on modest relief programs for wounded Turkish troops. As a concession to Turkish nationalism, the Woman's College issued its diplomas in Turkish as well as the traditional Latin. Although other foreign schools were closed, threats to close the American schools after the United States entered the war were not carried out, and at the end of the war the American colleges were still open and their property intact.[21]

Operation of the colleges during the 1920's, though often frustrating, proved possible. As the Christian population in Constantinople and Syria had not been subject to deportation, the independent colleges were spared the loss of their students. Furthermore, they attracted increasing numbers of Moslem and Jewish students. Depressed economic conditions temporarily cut total enrollments in the early 1920's, and the Greek-Turkish War proved unsettling to students, but the most pervasive problem in Turkey arose out of the Nationalist revolution. The colleges were subjected to strict regulation by the Ministry of Public Instruction, the curriculum, textbooks, and teaching staff all requiring ministerial approval. Although President Gates of Robert College believed that the Nationalist leaders earnestly desired "a new era of progress and development," [22] frequent

21 Bayard Dodge, "The American University of Beirut; An Introduction to Beirut and the University," mimeographed, Princeton, 1952, 41–51; Mary Mills Patrick, *Under Five Sultans* (New York: Century Co., 1929), 312–320; Mary Mills Patrick, *A Bosporus Adventure; Istanbul (Constantinople) Woman's College, 1871–1924* (London: Oxford University Press, 1934), 171–192; CWC, "President's Report," in *Bulletin,* 1915–1916, 20; Caleb Frank Gates, *Not To Me Only* (Princeton: Princeton University Press, 1940), 216–240. See also, RC, *Report of the President,* 1914 through 1918.

22 Caleb Gates in *ibid.,* 1922–23, 11.

changes in the personnel of the Ministry of Public Instruction proved irksome, as did the necessity of traveling to Ankara to discuss matters with public officials. Patience and forebearance were rewarded, however, for in 1927 Robert and the Woman's College secured the right to hold property in their corporate names, while two years later the Engineering School at Robert College won official recognition from the government.[23]

Executives of the Syrian Protestant College noted apprehensively that France reputedly dealt sternly and uncompromisingly with foreign institutions in her dependencies. Yet for reasons of state French officials left the College alone, as they had the mission schools. Although French officials were cool, but correct, neighboring governments positively courted SPC. The Shah of Iran visited the school, as did educational officials from Iraq, Palestine, and the Sudan. The latter three governments, in fact, began to send scholarship students to the school in 1924. In 1927 President Bayard Dodge of the Beirut school was appointed to the Conseil Superieur de l'instruction Publique to study all general questions relating to education in Lebanon. By the middle of the decade there was no doubt that all three colleges could continue to function, though major problems remained.

Numerous administrative changes took place in the colleges. In 1920 the Syrian Protestant College began to transform itself from a non-denominational college to a full-fledged university, restyling itself the American University of Beirut. Plans to expand the school were delayed by the death of President Howard S. Bliss. Nearly three years passed before his son-in-law, Bayard Dodge, was named his successor. The new president, an ordained minister, was the son of Cleveland Hoadley Dodge and a nephew of David Stuart Dodge, both of whom had given the college funds and guidance. Under the Dodge regime native members of the faculty were finally admitted to the governing board of the University. Salary differentials between native and American teachers were eliminated, and promotion was placed on the basis of ability. In 1924 the University became coeducational. The organization at Beirut of the American Junior College for Women in 1924 and the relocation of the International College at Beirut in 1936 permitted the University to concentrate all its energies on college work.[24]

Elsewhere administrative changes were less significant. The Woman's College underwent a change in leadership when Mary Mills Patrick retired in 1924 in favor of Kathryn Newell Adams, who had joined the faculty in 1920 as head of the English Department. Robert College alone went through the postwar decade without a change in command.

Major attention was given to revising the curricula in all the colleges.

23 *Ibid.*, 1926–27, 5; *ibid.*, 1928–29, 1.
24 AUB, *Report of the President*, 1921–22, 2; *ibid.*, 1928–29, 30.

As Turkish schools raised their standards, the American colleges felt obliged to raise their entrance requirements and to demand more mature work for the A.B. degree. Honors programs and comprehensive examinations for graduating seniors were instituted. Modest beginnings were made in setting up graduate studies. Conscious efforts were made to induce the student to think for himself rather than to passively memorize textbooks.

By the middle 1920's, major changes were underway at Beirut to strengthen existing academic programs and to extend them into new fields. The major beneficiary was the medical school. First it lengthened its program to five years; then it reorganized its laboratories and erected new buildings. New apparatus and an expanded medical library were secured. Arrangements were made to permit the younger teaching faculty to study abroad. In the dental school, entrance requirements were stiffened by making two years of college prerequisite to admission. As the dental curriculum was changed to provide more emphasis on laboratory and clinical work, the bachelor's degree was dropped for the doctorate of dental science.

The Arts and Sciences acquired no new buildings during the period, but existing buildings were remodelled to permit greater emphasis on laboratory work in the natural sciences. President Dodge urged the departments of sociology, education, economics, and commerce to establish "living contacts" with village and urban life so that the school might better serve the community. He felt it a "fair criticism" of his institution to say that "the work has been too pedantic in the past and too far removed from practical problems of life. . . . In the East, it is essential that university-trained men and women should not be made too proud and aloof to interest themselves in the lowly problems of the masses." He added, "In a period of reconstruction, higher education may become a curse, if it breeds social climbing and political violence. On the other hand, it may become an invaluable blessing, if it trains leaders how to adjust themselves to social changes and how to adapt themselves to modern methods of business and professional life." [25]

Academically Robert College was forced to mark time during the 1920's. First, the Turkish War for Independence made it difficult to plan ahead or to secure the funds. Subsequently the intensity of Turkish nationalism raised questions as to whether the College would be permitted to operate. Thus, one wing of the engineering building remained uncompleted at the end of the twenties, although the structural steel for it lay on the ground. School officials devoted much time and energy to soliciting permission for graduates of the School of Engineering to practice as engineers in Turkey. The nationalistic Turks were reluctant to rely on foreign-

[25] AUB, *Report of the President*, 1928–29, 30.

ers to train their engineers, but also they regarded the standards of their own Turkish School of Engineering as higher than those of Robert College, for the Turkish school required its students to graduate from a lycée prior to entering professional training, while Robert College admitted students from the equivalent of an American high school. Even though the government granted graduates of Robert College the right to practice as engineers in 1928, it still regarded them as having less training than graduates of the Turkish University.[26]

The College stressed public service. The Engineering School operated a Bureau of Testing throughout the decade, testing the properties of cement, brick, coal, coke, acids, and the like for business and industrial firms operating in the Near East. In 1926 the School instituted a two-year, non-degree program to train skilled workmen and foremen for engineering firms. Instruction was given in Turkish to enhance the utilitarian aspects of the course, which encompassed civil, electrical, and mechanical engineering. The program was immediately filled, the Turkish government sponsoring twenty-some men.[27]

In an effort to be of further service in the late 1920's, the College established an agricultural department, preparatory to creating a college of agriculture. The department was to identify crops especially suited to Turkey and incidentally to provide the college with some of its food supplies. A Robert College graduate who had taken advanced work in agriculture at Cornell University directed the program. Livestock, chiefly milk cows and swine, were secured from Near East Relief. Lack of funds and probably lack of adequate administrative know-how prevented vigorous prosecution of the plan.[28]

The Woman's College, too, encountered barriers to its plans. It had always placed much emphasis upon languages: Greek, Latin, Armenian, Bulgarian, Turkish, English, French, and Italian. Generally it emphasized the ancient forms of these languages and the classical literature. Immediately after the war it shifted the emphasis to the vernacular in order to "fit the women of the different classes for educational and literary work in their own languages." The project was snagged when the Turks expelled a large proportion of their Christian population, and the Nationalists required all citizens of Turkey to study Turkish and forbade their remaining Armenian and Greek subjects to study their traditional languages. President Adams conceded that the new requirements were reasonable, but as late as mid-1928 the College lacked a head for its Turkish language department.[29]

[26] RC, *Report of the President*, 1924-25, 5, 23-24; *ibid.*, 1928-29, 1; Lynn A. Scipio, *My Thirty Years in Turkey* (Rindge, N.H.: R. R. Smith, 1955), 226.
[27] RC, *Report of the President*, 1926-27, 15-16; *ibid.*, 1927-28, 16-17.
[28] *Ibid.*, 1926-27, 12-15.
[29] CWC, *Bulletin*, 1919-20, 26; *ibid.*, 1924-25, 19; *ibid.*, 1927-28, 23.

The keenest disappointment lay in an unsuccessful effort to establish a medical program. Plans had been discussed prior to World War I, and in 1919 steps were taken to create the medical school. Dr. Alden R. Hoover was selected to organize the institution, and a sum of $100,000 was in hand to provide the necessary building and equipment. The Near East Relief and the American Red Cross lent assistance. By the fall of 1920 the American community in Constantinople had established a hospital to serve both American civilians and naval personnel. Three navy surgeons were assigned to the hospital, as was a U.S. Public Health Service physician. Instruction began with a freshman class of nineteen students. The founding of the American Hospital and of a medical school made it possible to organize a school of nursing. But Turkish nationalists were even more zealous to monopolize medical education than engineering, with the result that the school was ordered closed in April, 1924.[30]

The Woman's College felt a new crisis was at hand when in the summer of 1926 the government asked it to receive free of charge twenty-five Turkish girls to be chosen by the government. Although the demand was regarded as brazen and as slighting what the College was already doing, the Trustees agreed to take ten students provided they met the academic standards of the College. By the end of the year, however, the College decided it had misinterpreted the Turkish motivation and that the "affront" was in reality an indication of recognition of the value of the College program by the Turks. This was confirmed by "friendly and encouraging" conversations held with Turkish education officials and by the further requests the College received from the government for assistance or advice in its educational planning.[31]

Both the independent colleges and the surviving mission secondary schools tried to introduce American concepts of the wholesome use of leisure time by inaugurating the American system of extra-curricular activities. The major emphasis was on athletics as a means of breaking down the Oriental antipathy to physical exertion. At the Woman's College fencing, archery, and rowing were introduced, while the men's colleges began interscholastic athletics. Both Robert College and the American University furthered the cause of sports by organizing track and field meets for secondary schools in their respective areas. The Aleppo Girls' High School introduced gymnastic drill and basketball. The most far-reaching recreation program, however, was developed in 1926 at Adana, where the mission school conducted playground work for the surrounding community. The municipality gave free space, and by 1928 a field house that offered dressing facilities as well as rooms for reading and listening to a

[30] Patrick, *Under Five Sultans*, 331 ff. See also, CWC, *Bulletin*, 1922–23, 44–48; *ibid.*, 1923–24, 24, 47–50.
[31] *Ibid.*, 1926–27, 18–19.

phonograph had been built. By 1931 this recreation center had over 4,300 members, and it had developed a separate social service center.[32]

For the cultivation of the mind, the colleges introduced Western music and drama. An Institute of Music, organized by the American University of Beirut, won recognition by the École Normale de Musique of Paris. Robert College and the Woman's College sponsored various concerts, ranging from performances of Gilbert and Sullivan to Latin Masses, in order to cultivate a taste for Western music. The Woman's College, concerned less with developing professional skill in the dramatic arts than with affording opportunities to become familiar with the work of great playwrights, produced famous Greek and French plays.[33]

The organization of clubs in science, literature, and music also enriched the curricula. Beginning in 1923 several girls' schools organized chapters of the Girl Reserves, a YWCA program. By 1930 schools at Aleppo, Smyrna, Brusa, Beirut, Athens, and Salonika had either a Girl Reserve organization or a chapter of the YWCA. National literary societies, which had existed prior to the war, were forbidden by the Turks after 1924 lest they become centers of anti-Turkish movements.[34]

Probably as important as any single change made during the 1920's was the effort to secure adequate financial support for the independent colleges. Prior to World War I a few affluent Americans sufficed to support these schools, providing funds for building and endowment and periodically making up the difference between tuition income and the cost of operation. In the postwar decade, however, inflation and the ambitious new programs of the colleges raised costs of operation beyond the means of the few devoted contributors. To meet these higher operating costs, the colleges organized a common fund-raising agency with offices in New York City.[35]

A common business office for the three independent colleges, established in 1920 under the direction of Albert Staub, supervised the procurement of supplies and the solicitation of funds for the schools. To liquidate the debts incurred during the war and to secure adequate operating funds for the next five-year period, the colleges organized a coordinated

---

[32] Stephen B. L. Penrose, Jr., *That They May Have Life: The Story of the American University of Beirut, 1866–1941* (New York: Trustees of the AUB, 1941), 286; ABCFM, *Annual Report,* 1928, 74 ff.; RC, *Report of the President,* 1930–31, 29; Tedford P. Lewis, "Health, Physical Education, and Recreation in Lebanon and the Near East," *Journal of the American Association for Health, Physical Education and Recreation,* XX (1949), 211–212.

[33] Penrose, *That They May Have Life,* 254–255; the plays for 1930–31, for example, were Houseman's "Prunella," and Moliere's "l'Avare," NECA, *Animal Report,* 1930–31; 20; RC, *Report of the President,* 1928–29, n.p.

[34] ABCFM, *Annual Reports,* 1923 through 1930, *passim.*

[35] Penrose, *That They May Have Life,* 222–223; see also, "Hall Bequest," NECA, *Annual Report,* 1928–29.

fund drive. The International College at Smyrna and the reorganized American College at Sofia also joined this collective enterprise. Finally, in 1927 the joint office formally incorporated as the Near East College Association. Within its first decade of operation it raised the endowment of the member colleges to fifteen million dollars.

Behind this successful quest for money lay the effort of Cleveland Hoadley Dodge and the generosity of several endowed foundations. Dodge had inherited a family interest in all three of the independent colleges. His father and grandfather had played a role in founding and financing the Syrian Protestant College; one son, Bayard, was President of the American University; his daughter, Elizabeth, was the wife of George Huntington, vice-president of Robert College; his sister, Grace, had been an officer of the Woman's College; and Dodge himself was past President of the Trustees of Robert College; it was asserted eulogistically at the time of his death in 1926: "He *was* Robert College." [36] It was at his behest that the Near East College Association was organized. While he did not live to see NECA incorporated, another son, Cleveland Earl Dodge, pushed the matter to a speedy conclusion.

Without the financial support of the endowed foundations, the physical and academic growth of the 1920's could not have been achieved. Generous grants from the Commonwealth Fund and the Rockefeller Foundation materially assisted the independent colleges in extricating themselves from debt in the early 1920's. Thereafter the Rockefeller Foundation, which was particularly interested in promoting medical education, made repeated grants to the American University of Beirut for the development of both the medical and dental schools. Funds were appropriated for buildings and equipment. To assure continuity of these new ventures, the new operating costs were capitalized by making major additions to the endowment. The Laura Spelman Rockefeller Memorial supported work in the social sciences, assisting both the American University and the Constantinople Woman's College.[37]

By 1930 the independent colleges were relatively well-off financially. Old buildings had been replaced or repaired, and new structures had been completed. The staff of the colleges had been strengthened. The AUB, which had but one person with permanent tenure in the Arts and Sciences in 1918, had nineteen such professors a decade later. Despite grave political and economic upheavals in the Near East, student enrollments in the colleges had increased. In general, preparatory school enrollments declined so that the gain in collegiate enrollment was very large, and for the first

[36] RC, *Report of the President*, 1925–26, 8. New York *Times*, June 25, 1926, Sept. 13, 1926.
[37] See *Annual Reports* of the Commonwealth Fund, the Rockefeller Foundation and the Laura Spelman Rockefeller Memorial for the 1920's; Penrose, *That They May Have Life*, 224–228.

time a majority of the students were in the college programs. At the same time the nationality mix of the students had changed; at Robert College, for example, Turks, who in 1920 had constituted but ten percent of the enrollments, composed fifty percent of the student body by 1928. The AUB was the major university serving the Arab-Moslem Near East.[38]

· III ·

While the mainstream of the evolution of American philanthropic practice flowed from missionary philanthropy to the independent colleges and the Near East Relief, there were other tributaries. Here and there during the 1920's other American organizations conducted programs, which if not in the mainstream, nevertheless contributed to the impact of American philanthropy on this region.

The Young Men's Christian Association and the Young Women's Christian Association, with American funds and leadership, promoted educational and social work for students and urban youth in Sofia, Athens, Salonika, Constantinople, Beirut, and Jerusalem. Educators organized the first YMCA's at the Syrian Protestant College, Central Turkey College, and Robert College, perhaps as early as 1886. As the Hamidian regime regarded all student groups as potentially seditious, YMCA-YWCA programs formally connected with the American YMCA did not develop easily until the Young Turks came into power. In 1910 the International Committee of the North American YMCA appointed the first salaried secretaries for Constantinople, but the successive distractions of the Balkan Wars, World War I, and the Turkish War for Independence again retarded development of YMCA-YWCA work until after the return of peace in 1922.[39]

The programs of the 1920's and 1930's, whether in Sofia, Athens, Constantinople, Beirut, or Jerusalem, stressed recreation, youth club work, discussion groups, concerts and lectures, and adult education classes, of which the latter was perhaps the most important activity. The subjects—languages, typing, and bookkeeping—were those particularly useful to working youth in the multilingual cities. These courses reached hundreds of youth beyond the range of the American mission schools or of the independent colleges. Hostels operated by the Y's afforded a decent shelter to young people, some new to city ways, while they put down roots. Leadership was provided by one or two Americans supplemented by a

[38] AUB, *Report of the President*, 1928–29, 18–20; RC, *Report of the President*, 1920–21 and 1928–29.

[39] This section is based on Kenneth Scott Latourette, *World Service: A History of the Foreign Work and World Service of the Young Men's Christian Associations of the United States and Canada* (New York: Association Press, 1957), 341–345.

larger number of natives, some of whom in Constantinople, Beirut, and Jerusalem were Moslems. Financial support came partly from America, but half and sometimes nearly all of the operating funds were raised locally.[40]

An outgrowth of this YMCA work was the organization of the American Friends of Turkey. The term *Christian* to a Turkish nationalist connoted not religion but members of hated minority groups. To avoid offending the Turks, some Americans proposed to drop the word *Christian* from the title of the organization. When the YMCA rejected this proposal, Asa K. Jennings, an American YMCA secretary, formed the American Friends of Turkey. Jennings' new organization enlisted the support of John H. Finley, Albert W. Staub, Mary Mills Patrick, Cleveland E. Dodge, and Admiral Bristol, most of whom had long been identified with the mission schools, the independent colleges, or Near East Relief. Arthur Nash, a Cincinnati clothing manufacturer widely known as "Golden Rule" Nash, guaranteed the needed funds.[41]

The American Friends of Turkey, manifesting the irenic spirit of the day, was to be "international, interracial, non-sectarian, and non-political." [42] To coordinate the overseas activities of the group, Jennings organized a board, a majority of whom were Turks. They promoted prenatal, baby, and dental clinics, playgrounds, libraries, and sports clubs. They also supported Dr. Beryl Parker's kindergarten and primary work in Ankara and cooperated with the Turkish Educational Association in translating and publishing literature in the new alphabet. Jennings' group also assisted Turkish students studying in the United States. Although Jennings died prematurely in 1933, his work was well-grounded, and it continued under other leadership.

Meantime the formal YMCA-YWCA programs in Turkey encountered periodic difficulties. When the depression of the 1930's cut the funds available in the United States as well as in Turkey, the YMCA in Constantinople disposed of one of its properties to a Turkish social and cultural organization. Thereafter it conducted a limited program in Stamboul. After Turkey banned all organizations founded on religion, the YMCA, late in 1939, closed. However it shortly reopened under the name Amerikan Lisan ve Ticaret Dersanesi (American School of Languages and Commerce) and continued the educational and recreation programs. It estab-

[40] Ross, Fry, and Sibley, *Near East and American Philanthropy, passim,* treats the educational activities.

[41] Robert W. Bruère, "Mr. Nash Does Unto Others," *The Survey,* LV (1926), 412–13. "Mr. Nash Behind New Christian Enterprise in Turkey," *Christian Century,* XL (1925), 592–593.

[42] "American Friends of Turkey," pamphlet, May 25, 1931, quoted in John A. DeNovo, *American Interests and Policies in the Middle East, 1900–1939* (Minneapolis: University of Minnesota Press, 1963), 271.

lished good rapport with Turkish authorities, and there has been a rapid growth in indigenous leadership. Aside from its contribution to individuals enrolled in its classes, the YMCA promoted wholesome recreation by introducing basketball and volleyball, which became nationwide school sports. The Turkish government adopted the YMCA pattern of camps for boys and utilized Association personnel to train leaders for them.

The YMCA work in Jerusalem developed in an extremely troubled environment. Although YMCA work began there in 1890, American participation started in 1919 when the American YMCA sent Archibald C. Harte to Jerusalem. Harte wanted a "systematic work" combining traditional YMCA educational programs with rural work such as that done at Hampton Institute. He raised the needed funds and started construction of a YMCA facility, the most elaborate outside the Anglo-Saxon world. But Harte's vision was unfulfilled. He had to leave YMCA work before the building was finished. During the 1930's the YMCA was subjected to successive, debilitating quarrels. Even so, it conducted a substantial recreation program, affording one of the few places in that troubled land where Jews and Moslems mixed socially.[43]

In Constantinople the American community rescued the American Hospital and its school of nursing that the Woman's College had founded. Through the appeals of Ambassador Joseph Grew and a contribution of $300,000 by John D. Rockefeller, Jr., the hospital obtained a satisfactory financial base. In 1939 it was able to construct a modern three-story, sixty-bed facility. During the 1930's and 1940's, the hospital increasingly served the Constantinople community. In 1945, its twenty-fifth anniversary, the hospital was renamed for Admiral Mark Bristol, the even-handed American High Commissioner to Turkey.[44]

Throughout this period the medical director had been Dr. Lorrin A. Shepard, the son of American Board missionaries. Ordinarily he was assisted by one other American, his superintendent of nurses, and a staff of perhaps six Turkish doctors. The hospital was incorporated in New York and shared office space with the Near East College Association. Income from patients and endowment generally covered the operating costs of the hospital, but the School of Nursing proved a continuing drain on its resources. While its medical influence was less broad than that of the medical school at Beirut, it was a means of illustrating American standards and methods of medical care in Turkey's largest city.

In the shifting currents of the day, American educational activities in Greece increased. Anatolia College of Marsovan relocated in Salonika in 1925. Assisted by the Charles Hall bequest, the struggling school was able

43 Latourette, *World Service*, 325–357.
44 *The Admiral Bristol [Hospital]* (New York, 1954). Ross, Fry, and Sibley, *Near East and American Philanthropy*, 169–170.

to build on its new campus overlooking the Aegean. Operating now as a Greek gymnasium, the school prepared students for the Greek universities. The American Collegiate Institute, a girls' school originally at Smyrna, reorganized as Pierce Junior College for Girls at Athens. But most significant was the founding of Athens College. Still smarting from the expulsion of their co-religionists from Turkey, Greek alumni of Robert College sought a Greek counterpart of Robert College. They solicited American support from such men as John Huston Finley, associate editor of the New York *Times,* and Edward Capps, one-time American ambassador to Greece. The American response was prompt and sympathetic, and the school was chartered by the New York regents in 1926. An American president shared responsibility with a Greek co-director. Funds to support the school were raised in nearly equal amounts by Greeks and Americans. A ten-year program, starting at the equivalent of the American fourth grade, continued through junior college.[45]

The thrust of American educational work was carried into corners not reached by the older mission organizations. The Friends (Quakers) operated five elementary schools for girls and a high school for boys at Ramallah, a short distance north of Jerusalem. Founded in 1901, the boys' school prepared students for the American University of Beirut. The latter, however, continued to exert great influence in Palestine as the chief source of secondary school teachers. American Methodist influence was focused on a Girls' School at Lovech in northern Bulgaria. Begun in 1880, the school had over two hundred students in the mid-1920's. Although the facilities of the school were doubled during the decade, the school still turned away nearly a hundred applicants a year. The American Reformed Presbyterian Mission operated two high schools, one for boys and one for girls, in Latakia in northern Syria. In the 1920's, following a practice the American and Presbyterian boards had long since abandoned, the schools in Latakia provided tuition, food, and clothes to its two hundred or so pupils. These schools fit into the general pattern of American-operated institutions by preparing students for the University at Beirut.[46]

Several American mission societies supported schools in Iraq. The oldest, the American School for Girls at Mosul, had been founded by the American Board and subsequently passed from sponsor to sponsor until the Mesopotamian Mission, a joint project of the Presbyterians, the Reformed Church in America, and the Reformed Church in the United

[45] George E. White, *Adventuring with Anatolia College* (Grinnell: Herald-Register Publishing Co., 1940), 130–154; Abul H. K. Sassani, "American Institutions of Higher Learning in the Near East," *Higher Education,* VI (Sept. 15, 1949), 17–18. Homer Davis, "Athens College," *News Bulletin of the Institute of International Education,* XI (Nov., 1935), 10–11.

[46] Ross, Fry, and Sibley, *Near East and American Philanthropy,* 105, 221–223; Matthews and Akrawi, *Education in Arab Countries,* 401.

States, assumed responsibility for it. The most notable feature of this school was its training class for kindergarten teachers.[47]

The Mesopotamian Mission also supported the American Boys' School at Baghdad, begun in 1924 by the Reverend and Mrs. Calvin Staudt. It offered both elementary and secondary work. Its student population of 240 was so distributed that one-quarter each were Moslems and Jews and one-half were Christians. Because of British influences in Iraq, the English language curriculum of the secondary school was a great attraction. In a companion Girls' School, founded in 1925, an Iraqi supervised the elementary program, but an American directed the secondary curriculum. English was the language of instruction in the upper classes, and students prepared to complete their education in English or American colleges or universities.

The American School for Boys at Basarah differed greatly from the school at Baghdad. Founded in 1921 by Dr. John Van Ess, it was supported by the Arabian Mission of the Reformed Church. Its classes, at both elementary and secondary levels, served a largely Shia Moslem student body. The language of instruction at all levels was Arabic. Like Robert College in the days of Cyrus Hamlin, the school was non-graded, each student advancing at his own pace subject-by-subject. Dr. Van Ess discouraged his students from going to the American University at Beirut or from seeking a government sinecure. Rather, he wanted his students to work within the framework of their own society, a view perhaps colored by his experience as the first Director of Education under the British occupation of Iraq in 1915.

In 1932 American Jesuits founded a secondary school, the Baghdad College for Boys. This was the first school undertaken in the Near East by American Catholics. Functioning as a secondary school, Baghdad College enjoyed the most modern school plant in Iraq with well-equipped laboratories and extensive areas for athletic fields. Its enrollment in 1945 exceeded four hundred. A majority of the students were from the Christian minority in Iraq. Most of the students, Christian and otherwise, were from upper-middle class families.

The most isolated areas in which American educators and medical men functioned were the Persian and Oman gulf areas of the Arabian peninsula. Starting in 1889, personnel of the Reformed Church in America organized centers at Bahrein, Muscat, and Kuweit. At each, a modest hospital was the focal point for the mission's medical work. In keeping with mission practice, medical care was combined with evangelism as mission personnel toured outlying villages. Perhaps the leading development of the

[47] This section draws on *ibid.*, 211–213; and Ross, Fry, and Sibley, *Near East and American Philanthropy*, 193–195. See also John Van Ess, *Meet the Arab* (New York: John Day, 1943).

transitional 1920's was the expansion of medical work for women. In 1927 a new women's hospital was built at Bahrein, and one of the women doctors was invited to treat women regularly at Ibn Saud's palace at Riyadh. In 1934 the Reverend Dr. Dirk Dykstra, following the example of Cyrus Hamlin, designed and constructed a fine new hospital at Matrah just outside Muscat. With financial assistance from Charles R. Crane, whose gifts had helped the colleges in Constantinople and various projects in Albania, Dykstra was able to make his hospital "the most livable building in Muscat." [48]

From these bases on the eastern coast of Arabia, medical missionaries periodically penetrated the interior of Saudi Arabia. Dr. Paul W. Harrison, at the invitation of Ibn Saud, first went to Riyadh in 1917 to treat the sick, and he made a second trip in 1919. Subsequently Dr. Louis P. Dame made repeated trips through the interior. On his tour of 1924, for example, he treated 6,552 patients and performed more than a hundred major operations. In 1933, his last trip, the doctor was accompanied by his wife, who was given the rare privilege of visiting the royal harem. Saudi Arabia in the 1930's was still primitive and forbidding when Dr. Harold Storm traversed Arabia from Bahrein via Riyadh to the Red Sea and thence counterclockwise along the coast to his starting point. It was an experience in the tradition of Eli Smith and Harrison Gray Otis Dwight in Armenia, Dr. Asahel Grant in Kurdistan, and Justin and Charlotte Perkins en route to Urumia. For more than three weeks Dr. Storm shared the hut and life of the poorest Arab, harassed by locusts and scorpions. At another juncture a swordfish-thrust sank his boat. Again traveling by native steamer, he shared space with a cargo of sheep, while another leg of the trip was a thirty-three-day sailing voyage. Back "home" after ten months, the doctor calculated that he had treated 10,406 patients and had performed 224 operations.

American medical work in Arabia was not a carbon copy of earlier work in other remote areas of the Near East. The American doctors of the 1920's and 1930's were far more skilled and sophisticated than Asa Dodge or Asahel Grant. Unlike American doctors working in late nineteenth century Turkey or Syria, the Americans in Arabia had no native competitors whose jealousy or fears might provoke opposition. In the absence of any school system the doctors of the Arabian mission had to rely on naturally bright but illiterate youths to train as operating room assistants. But the doctors made no attempt to train these youths as medical doctors after the manner of Henry West or Joseph Cochran. These

[48] Quoted in DeNovo, *American Interests and Policies in the Middle East*, 356. The activities of the mission are treated in Alfred D. Mason and Frederick J. Barny, *History of the Arabian Mission* (New York: Board of Foreign Missions of the Reformed Church in America, 1926). See also, Paul W. Harrison, *Doctor in Arabia* (New York: John Day, 1943).

Americans made their impact by demonstrating the power of Western medicine to relieve suffering and to bring cures. They accustomed native communities to the presence of Christians and by their exemplary conduct and their reputation as healers made it easier for other Americans and Europeans to follow.

· IV ·

While the educators of the mission schools and the independent colleges were re-examining the role of education in the Near East, the Near East Relief was laying the groundwork for a new approach to philanthropy. At the end of World War I the sponsors of Near East Relief were increasingly frustrated by the never-ending need for disaster relief. Furthermore, their initial venture in operating temporary soup kitchens had turned into a task of feeding, housing, and educating thousands of homeless children. But as the decade progressed, income declined. Accordingly, the NER explored ways by which it could make a permanent contribution to the reconstruction of the Near East.

The first steps leading to a redefinition of its mission were taken by Paul Monroe, an internationally known specialist in comparative education, and Rudolf R. Reeder, an expert in child welfare work. After extensive travel in the Near East in 1924, the two men urged Near East Relief to concentrate its energies to make its temporary institutions for orphan care the nuclei for permanent institutions. They also felt that Near East Relief could contribute to the advancement of vocational education, public health, and the rehabilitation of the handicapped. This meant the organization of some new institutions and the modification of existing ones. Monroe saw in the orphanage trade schools a means of changing the Near Eastern attitude toward manual labor. He insisted that such education be practical, and he particularly deprecated teaching English to children who would never live in an English-speaking area. Chemistry and physics, he argued, should be taught as household arts rather than as academic disciplines. In this respect he warned against using elaborate laboratory equipment and urged the use of illustrative materials from ordinary life. Such a school would prepare youth for conditions they would meet in the Near Eastern environment. Furthermore the cost would be low enough to permit vocational education to be incorporated into the native school system. Monroe's advice was followed, and in 1930 Near East Relief was able to transfer its trade school on Syra to the Greek government which transformed it into a polytechnical school, the first in Greece.[49]

[49] Paul Monroe, R. R. Reeder, and James I. Vance, *Reconstruction in the Near East* (New York, 1924), 16–18.

As might be expected of an educator, Monroe gave attention to the need for teacher training. As he surveyed the Near East, he saw few opportunities to conduct such work in Syria, since the orphans were Armenian and the native population largely Arab. But Soviet Armenia and Greece seemed to offer ample opportunities. Accordingly, small training schools were founded in Soviet Armenia and on the island of Syra. The Greek government was especially cooperative and provided financial support for the school. The schools at Leninakan and Syra each graduated twenty-five or more teachers a year. By 1930 over 260 teachers had graduated, some of whom went on to do additional work at one of the American colleges in the Near East, usually at the American University of Beirut. Of the two schools, only the one in Greece had a lasting impact, for Near East Relief ran into political difficulties with the Soviet authorities, and the school at Leninakan never fulfilled its initial promise.[50]

Monroe placed special emphasis on the need for institutions to promote public health. In June, 1921, for example, Near East Relief was caring for twenty-five thousand children in Armenia, fourteen thousand of whom were infected with trachoma. There were no hospitals, doctors, or nurses to care for them other than those provided by Near East Relief. Necessarily, medical work began with treatment of chronic disorders. Monroe argued that permanent cure and avoidance of reinfection depended more upon health education than on medical treatment. At his suggestion the schools operated by Near East Relief prepared texts in hygiene and sanitation for use by school children. The next step was the establishment of a school for public health workers. A beginning was made with the Edith Winchester School for nurses at Leninakan, where training was given by American doctors and nurses in the orphanage hospital. Girls seventeen or older who had completed the eighth grade were eligible for the three-year course that included ward work as well as classroom instruction. A second school was founded in Greece, which at the time reportedly had but seven graduate nurses in the whole country. Less than a year after its founding, this school began supplying nurses to the Polyclinic Hospital in Athens, and at the end of the second year the hospital assumed direction of the school. A third school was then organized at Syra. By 1930 Near East Relief had trained 197 nurses.[51]

Special institutions, organized by NER, assisted handicapped children, of whom there were some two hundred blind and over sixty deaf mutes.

[50] George M. Wilcox, "Education in Soviet Armenia," in *Journal of Educational Sociology*, II (1929), 310–318; James L. Barton, *Story of Near East Relief (1915–1930) An Interpretation* (New York: Macmillan, 1930), 227–250.

[51] Elsie L. Jarvis, "Edith Winchester School for Nurses," in NER, *Docket*, Feb. 11, 1927, 77–86, Talcott Williams Papers, Union Theological Seminary Library, New York; "Foreign Department Notes," NER, *Docket*, Nov. 20, 1924, n.p.; *ibid.*, Nov. 24, 1926, 17–18; Barton, *Story of Near East Relief*, 314.

A braille code was developed for the use of the Armenian children; scholarships were granted to selected Greek teachers to send them to the Perkins Institute or the Clark School for training. The personnel thus trained returned to Greece to organize instruction for handicapped children. As Near East Relief liquidated its work in 1930, the special schools for the blind and the deaf were transferred to the Greek government. The latter provided new buildings and appropriated funds to continue the schools permanently.[52]

The idea of demonstrating new types of educational institutions was not original. Officers and missionaries of the American Board had made such proposals in the mid-nineteenth century, but rising opposition from Orthodox and Moslem leaders and the inhibiting influences of the American fundamentalists had prevented the missionaries from fully employing this technique of philanthropy. The Near East Relief, however, was free to explore and, indeed, the burden of educating tens of thousands of children motivated it to experiment. The idea of helping others to help themselves had been practiced by social settlement workers, agricultural extension agents, and philanthropic foundations long before the organization of Near East Relief. What was notable here was that this group, organized for the purpose of administering disaster relief, was able to develop its program so that, in the process of caring for children, it could also establish model institutions. It went one step farther still and initiated the first significant rural reconstruction programs to be conducted abroad.

The origins of rural reconstruction work had two roots: the Country Life Movement and the missionary movement. Founded early in the twentieth century, the Country Life Movement was an expression of concern over the impact of industrial society on agriculture. It was marked in part by efforts to glamorize rural life, but far more significant was a recognition that by instituting changes in agricultural technology, farming could be made more profitable. The basic problem was to formulate a program by which the best current knowledge of farming practice might be transmitted from the agricultural scientist to the dirt farmer.[53]

The Country Life Movement had an immediate impact on the missionary societies. In India a Presbyterian missionary, Sam Higginbottom, seeking to raise rural incomes and levels of living, had founded the Allahabad Agricultural Institute, while in the Balkans John Henry House, an American Board missionary, had established the Thessalonika Agricultural and

---

[52] George M. Wilcox, "America's Part in Near East Education," *New Near East*, X (June, 1926), 16–17; "Near East Work in Greece," *Volta Review*, XXXII (1930), 290; "Foreign Department Notes," NER, *Docket*, Feb. 11, 1927, 16; *ibid.*, Nov. 24, 1926, 18; NER, *Annual Report*, 1926, in *Senate Docs.*, 69 Cong., 2 Sess., No. 229, p. 33.

[53] Benjamin H. Hunnicutt and William Watkins Reid, *The Story of Agricultural Missions* (New York: Missionary Education Movement of the U.S. and Canada, 1931), 16.

Industrial Institute in 1902. The founding of these two institutions helped focus the attention of mission executives on the problems of underdeveloped agrarian economies.[54]

Through the influence of Kenyon L. Butterfield, a prime mover in the Country Life Movement, James L. Barton, the senior secretary of the American Board and a major figure in the Near East Relief, became interested in agricultural missions. Advising Barton on the agricultural problems of the American Board, Butterfield urged him to adapt the experience of the Country Life Movement to the missionary program. When the Near East Relief was organized, Butterfield was appointed to its agricultural advisory committee. This was intended to be a fund-raising committee, but Butterfield used it as a platform to proclaim that ameliorative relief work was inefficient. "You cannot help people very long by giving them food," he asserted. "You must teach them to produce it through fundamental industries, of which agriculture is the first." [55] By 1925 Dr. Barton, receptive to Butterfield's prodding, confessed to the latter that he was becoming a "crank on the subject of the rural approach." [56] The American Board, however, was not ready to undertake a major rural reconstruction program, since it was still trying to divest itself of relief work and to reestablish its educational and evangelistic programs in the Near East. Nor were the Presbyterians any better prepared to undertake rural work. They had similar problems in the Near East, and they were bitterly divided over continued support of the Allahabad Agricultural Institute in India. Dr. Barton expressed his interest in rural reconstruction through the Near East Relief.

Almost from the very start in 1915, relief workers had indicated a concern over the state of native agriculture. Missionaries in Persia had sought to substitute millet for wheat, since its greater yield would feed more people for the same labor. Another reflection of concern appeared in a book, *Reconstruction in the Near East*, published in 1918 by the American Committee for Armenian and Syrian Relief, in which George E. White, President of Anatolia College, outlined a program for agricultural reform. White appreciated that the introduction of new agricultural techniques in the Near East required the training of native farmers and that such training would have to begin with familiar tools and procedures. He advocated the founding of thirty agricultural schools with demonstration farms of a thousand acres. That the problems of farming a thousand-acre estate differed substantially from those of tilling the small tracts common in most of the Near East, White did not consider. Nor did he consider

[54] [Charles L. House], "Report of the Director to the Board of Trustees, 1930–31," American Farm School, Salonica, 61–62, in ABC 16.5, Vol. 16, p. 516.

[55] NER Form Letter, June 2, 1925, William W. Rockwell Papers, Union Theological Seminary Library, New York.

[56] J. Barton to K. Butterfield, Nov. 13, 1925, ABC 3.2, Vol. 381, p. 55.

whether the students trained on such demonstration farms would be free to employ "new-fangled" notions in a patriarchal society. White envisaged his program as one to be undertaken by the mandatory power that he expected would control Turkey after the war rather than by either the missionary societies or the Near East Relief.[57]

The first concrete proposals for a rural improvement program to be undertaken by Near East Relief were contained in the critique of Near East Relief's work by Paul Monroe and Rudolf R. Reeder. The latter told the organization that its objective ought to be to help people "through their own agencies rather than directly by an American organization." [58] The report additionally suggested the introduction of public health nurses into the "dark, unsanitary, dreary abodes" of Near Eastern villages. To correct these conditions he proposed to build a model house of materials at hand to serve as a center of operations for "workers whose business it shall be to lift the life of the village to the level of this home." [59]

Another person who focused the attention of the Near East Relief on agricultural work was Ora S. Morgan, a professor of agriculture at Columbia University and an adviser to the relief committee. Morgan took as a basic premise the argument that farming was done incompetently in the Near East. He was prepared to use formal education to improve agricultural techniques, and he advised Near East Relief to operate its own agricultural school in conjunction with its orphanages and to send selected students to native agricultural colleges or to American institutions. However, he warned that students would learn more on native farms than on school farms, that "plowhandle farmers" needed the aid of extension workers to bring the findings of the experiment station out to the fields.[60]

The most important individual in reshaping the philosophy of philanthropy in the Near East was Thomas Jesse Jones. He brought to the Near East Relief years of experience in working with Hampton Institute and as Director of the Phelps-Stokes Fund. This experience led him to question the universal efficacy of formal education. Furthermore, Jones, who had experience in extension education work, was on the point of formulating his ideas on philanthropy in a systematic statement of principles. When these were published in 1929, he declared that "merely to feed the hungry is . . . a wasteful form of charity except as a temporary help in special cases. Sound charity aims to guide the needy to self-support, and still more to remove the conditions that caused the misfortune." This was best

[57] George E. White, "Tentative Plan for an Anatolian Demonstration Farm," in William H. Hall, ed., *Reconstruction in Turkey* (ACASR, 1918), 163–169.

[58] Monroe, Reeder, and Vance, *Reconstruction in the Near East,* 36–37.

[59] *Ibid.,* 30.

[60] O. S. Morgan, "Summary of Agricultural Program for Near East Relief," NER, *Docket,* Feb. 11, 1927, Williams Papers.

done when the philanthropist limited his participation to "initiation, stimulation, or illustrations of types of service." [61]

By 1926 Near East Relief was prepared to investigate actively the problems of undertaking a rural development program. As a first step it commissioned Frank A. Ross, Luther Fry, and Elbridge Sibley to make a systematic survey of economic and social conditions in the Near East. Other American organizations operating in the Near East joined in the sponsorship. Chief among them were the American Board, the Presbyterian Board, and the independent colleges. The survey would help all these agencies plan their future operations. To make the report as useful as possible, Dr. Thomas Jesse Jones and Dr. James H. Dillard of the Jeanes and Slater Fund went to the Near East to confer with the field workers while the survey was underway. Finally, the rough draft of their report was submitted for criticism to representatives of American social, educational, and religious agencies in the Near East. The final document gave the most complete picture of the Near East then available.[62]

The Near East portrayed by the report was backward, often primitive. Its mineral and agricultural resources, its transportation and communications facilities, and its manpower were under-utilized or underdeveloped. Most of the region had considerable potential, but the problems of development varied markedly from place to place. In Turkey, for example, it was apparent that much arable land was only partially utilized because of primitive methods of cultivation. The native plow, a crooked stick tipped with metal and drawn by a water buffalo or oxen, was inefficient and precluded deep plowing. The practice of burning manure as fuel and the non-use of artificial fertilizers held production of wheat to as low as six bushels per acre. In the Caucasus, where agricultural practices were much the same, the limited amount of arable land, two and one-half acres per capita, retarded development. Iraq, while favored by soil of better quality, was arid and dependent upon irrigation. Oppressive absentee landlords, crop pests, and inadequate capital also afflicted Iraq. Conditions in Syria were a composite of those in Turkey and Iraq—parasitical landlordism, underpopulation of arable regions, and primitive methods of cultivation.

In Albania, a Moslem country in part, rural conditions were similar to those of Asia Minor. Subsistence agriculture was conducted at so primitive a level that it could not produce funds necessary for schools, hospitals, and public health work. By contrast, Bulgaria and Greece had developed public school systems, including agricultural schools. The Greeks even had a rudimentary agricultural extension service. This is not to say

[61] Thomas Jesse Jones, *Essentials of Civilization: A Study in Social Values* (New York: H. Holt & Co., 1929), 196, 216.
[62] Ross, Fry, and Sibley, *The Near East and American Philanthropy, passim.*

that conditions in either Bulgaria or Greece were idyllic. Bulgaria was in a state of economic exhaustion from her defeat in the War; Greece had not yet recovered from its disastrous war with Turkey. Both nations had major refugee problems; in both, the peasant was an inefficient farmer by Western standards, though much better than his counterpart in Asia Minor.[63]

Conditions in the home were as unfavorable as those in the field. Especially noticeable was the lack of adequate health practices. Maternal death rates were high; infant mortality rates, astronomic. In Constantinople, an urban community, one-half of all children born died before reaching five years of age. Generally the whole population was subject to endemic disorders—malaria, tuberculosis, trachoma, and intestinal diseases. Precise figures were lacking, for only an occasional city kept records. In the Mardin district, hard hit by malaria, one-third of the population was infected. In Constantinople tuberculosis caused one out of six deaths. Trachoma, which often blinded its victims, had affected eighty percent of the population in Malatia. Such conditions reflected the lack of understanding of the simplest procedures of sanitation and preventive medicine, as well as the poverty of the people. In part, this was attributed to the low status of women; by and large, they were confined to domestic duties in the home, and in many areas Moslem women were still veiled. Conditions in Bulgaria and Greece were somewhat better, for there were facilities for training doctors and nurses. Public health services, though inefficient, existed.

Clearly no one program would suffice for all areas of the Near East. While methods of extension education would promote increased productivity, fundamental political and economic reforms would be necessary before arid lands could be irrigated. Work among women would be difficult, for it would be necessary to change their status before one could begin to teach them new methods of child care and home management. Before better health facilities could be realized, the reluctance of native girls to become trained nurses or midwives had to be overcome. Likewise, it would be necessary to overcome Moslem fatalism before natives would make use of existing hospital facilities which were regarded as the "ante chambers of death."

The difficulties of introducing change into the Near East were further complicated by widespread illiteracy. In Turkey ninety percent of the population was illiterate, while in other countries of the Near East the proportion was similar. Consequently most of the population was cut off from much knowledge of the outside world. Inadequate preparation of the few who aspired to receive a secondary or collegiate education depressed the academic level of these institutions. This in turn limited the

[63] *Ibid.*

caliber of native leaders who might be used in a rural reconstruction program. The tendency of many natives to regard academic education as a means of escaping manual labor still further reduced available native leadership.

While it was not the assignment of the Ross-Fry-Sibley team to formulate a program, it was evident from their critique of the past efforts of American philanthropy in the Near East that a rural improvement program was in order. The report indicated that American philanthropy was affecting only a select segment of the population. Most of the institutional work was being conducted in urban centers, especially along the Mediterranean coast. Even here the philanthropists worked almost exclusively among the middle classes. The urban proletariat and the rural fellahin and peasants were largely unreached. Little was done for the Moslem majority. Fewer and fewer graduates of American schools were returning to their home communities.

In suggesting alternative solutions the report did not ignore education. Ross, Fry, and Sibley took the position that while American organizations might demonstrate techniques of progressive education, they should not compete with native governments in the operation of primary and secondary schools. In the area of higher education the report emphasized the need for the education of leaders with an emphasis upon quality rather than quantity, particularly in such fields as engineering, industrial chemistry, and commerce. The final report of the survey committee reinforced the emphasis of Monroe, Reeder, Butterfield, Barton, White, Morgan, and Jones that American philanthropy had neglected agricultural work. Reflecting the influence of Thomas Jesse Jones, no doubt, the survey committee pointed to the work of the Jeanes and Slater Fund among Negroes in the American South as a model of the methods philanthropists ought to follow. "Mass education of a simple, direct sort, carried to the people in their fields and workshops," was the ideal solution to the problem of uplifting an underdeveloped area. For personnel the philanthropist should rely upon natives. When methods of formal education were found useful, they should be employed, otherwise the philanthropist should innovate. In general the accent should fall on "helping to do" rather than "doing for." Since many of the needs of the Near East, especially the rural needs, could not be met by existing agencies, the survey committee recommended the creation of a new organization.[64]

At the end of the twenties, American philanthropy stood at a critical turning point. The missionary philanthropist, for a century the chief representative of American ideals and institutions in the Near East, had been compelled to retrench to such a degree that he could no longer perform a major role. The independent colleges, having established their non-

[64] *Ibid.*, 8.

denominational character, succeeded during the twenties in serving an ever-increasing proportion of non-Protestant Christians and Moslems. By broadening their educational programs and expanding their financial support, the colleges were able to function more effectively in training future professional, educational, and business leaders for the Near East. The experience in Turkey and Persia underscored that, however much leadership trained in Western ideas and methods might be desired, militant nationalism often intertwined with xenophobia could frustrate the best efforts of American educators. Withal, in 1930 the colleges were in a stronger position than ever before to serve natives who might look forward to positions of leadership in their own countries.

The turning point in American philanthropy came with Near East Relief. Its transcendent achievement was its pioneer work in vocational education, nurses training, the education of the handicapped, and in inducing the native governments to take over and expand these institutions. Finally, Near East Relief deliberately surveyed the needs of the Near East and sought new forms of philanthropic enterprises that might permanently improve the environment of the rural populations, approaches that could reach across the barriers of religion and nationality that had so often frustrated the missionary philanthropist.

CHAPTER

IX

Near East Foundation, 1930–1940

ONCE THE Ross, Fry, Sibley survey was completed, Near East Relief moved swiftly to initiate a broad program of rural reconstruction in the Near East. To do so it organized the Near East Foundation, which during the 1930's pioneered agricultural extension services, home demonstration and social service work, and sanitation and public health projects, becoming the first American organization expressly designed to undertake technical assistance work abroad. Simultaneously, Near East Foundation reorganized the refugee centers which it inherited from Near East Relief so as to transform them into model social welfare programs. In all cases the Foundation sought to avoid conducting service programs per se; rather it aimed at inducing local governments to assume the responsibility for them and to duplicate them elsewhere.

· I ·

Without waiting to create a new organization, in 1928 Near East Relief set up an experimental program of agricultural technical assistance. The initial problem was to decide where the demonstration should take place. The militant nationalism of the newly independent regimes in the Near East ruled out some areas. Although Turkey had adopted the Roman alphabet, Western legal codes, and the public school, it was determined to direct its own reform program. A similar situation existed in Persia, where

Reza Khan, although no Kemal Ataturk, was clearly on the side of change and of Westernization. As in Turkey, Westerners were restricted in their actions by nationalistic sentiments. In other independent areas of the Near East there was no climate of reform. Well into the 1920's Husein of the Hejaz and Ibn Saud of Saudi Arabia carried on intermittent warfare over Husein's pretensions to being the "King of the Arab Countries." These monarchs were too preoccupied with establishing their dynasties to show interest in improving the standards of living of their subjects.

In Palestine, Lebanon, Syria, and Iraq continued European control created an environment in which it was doubtful that a successful reform program directed by Americans could be carried to fruition. Native groups were preoccupied with wresting political control from their British or French overlords. Although in some cases the Europeans were favorably disposed toward reform, the exigencies of maintaining control in these areas often required that the status quo be undisturbed. In Iraq, for instance, the British bought the loyalty of traditional tribal chieftains by granting them subsidies and supporting them against their rivals. While this system kept law and order, it precluded any effort to reform the social order in the tribal areas. In Syria and Lebanon, French control had been instituted despite the report of the King-Crane Commission that the natives much preferred either American or British rule. Syrian discontent culminated in an uprising in 1925 and 1926 that the French crushed, in part, by an aerial bombardment of Damascus. Clearly the French were in no position to inaugurate reforms, and the natives were busy with other matters. In Palestine a poorly organized, often primitive, Arab majority found itself challenged by an aggressive, rapidly growing Jewish population. The British mandatory regime, which had made conflicting promises to both sides, was caught in the middle. Ultimately the Arabs adopted a program of non-cooperation with the British authorities and turned to terrorism to forestall further Jewish immigration and acquisition of Arab soil. Although the Near East desperately needed better health practices, more enlightened mothers, and better farmers, political conditions were not favorable for the successful conduct of enterprises whose ultimate success depended upon the financial support of the local government or close cooperation between the people and their governments.[1]

Largely by default, the Near East Relief began its demonstrations in Greece among Armenian and Greek refugees from Asia Minor. Far more than the Asian countries, Greece had imbibed the idea of progress. It had a public school system, even a rudimentary extension system, and its officials understood and appreciated the benefits to be derived from a rural

[1] George Lenczowski, *The Middle East in World Affairs* (Ithaca: Cornell University Press, 1952).

village improvement program. Furthermore, the Near East Relief had had a program for orphan children in Greece. As a point of departure it decided to work among those orphan children who had come of age and settled in Macedonia.

The task of organizing the program was assigned to Harold B. Allen, NER Educational Director in the Caucasus. Reared on a farm in Albion, New York, Allen had experience as a country school teacher, an instructor of vocational agriculture, and a college professor. In his quest for methods suited to the requirements of the Macedonian peasant, Allen had a variety of choices. In the nineteenth century the American search for effective media for the dissemination of technical information to farmers produced in turn the county fair, the agricultural and mechanical college, and the agricultural experiment station. The county fair had depended upon the participation of farmers whose achievements would be admired and whose methods would be emulated by the less skilled. It foundered in commercialization, horse racing, and sideshows. As for the nineteenth century agricultural and mechanical college and the experiment station, Seaman A. Knapp, one-time president of the Iowa State Agricultural College, observed that the "A & M" school too often was "academic and military," while the experiment station had a "three mile limit" on its influence.[2]

Extension education, a means of increasing agricultural efficiency, first found wide acceptance in the United States in the twentieth century. The essence of the plan developed by Seaman A. Knapp was to send the expert from the agricultural school or experimental farm out into the fields to induce the dirt farmer to carry on a small demonstration on his own farm. The ultimate goal was to lead the farmer to adopt a variety of practices that would increase productivity and generally increase farm income, permitting a higher level of living, including better housing and new schools. This type of agricultural education, first undertaken as a private venture, was expanded as a joint effort of the General Education Board, the United States Department of Agriculture, and local groups of farmers and businessmen. The enactment of the Smith-Lever Act in 1914 provided a nationwide extension service.[3]

Another widely used technique to upgrade agricultural practices was the vocational agricultural program of the Smith-Hughes Act of 1917. Aimed at secondary school youth, it provided for formal agricultural courses in the high school supplemented by demonstration projects carried on at home under the auspices of the school or of the 4-H club. This

[2] Russell Lord, *The Agrarian Revival; A Study of Agricultural Extension* (New York: American Association for Adult Education, 1939), 70–71.
[3] *Ibid.*, 54–85.

vocational program was designed to supplement the extension system, the experimental farm, and the agricultural college by acquainting the prospective farmer with the potentialities of scientific agriculture.[4]

Allen's approach to agricultural education in the Near East was thoroughly pragmatic. He was under no specific directives as to the methods he should employ, although there was a presumption that Near East Relief did not want to found a formal agricultural school. For his part Allen was anxious to get into the field, "to do something—anything—with the idea of formulating more permanent plans as the exploration proceeded, then to scrap these early beginnings and to build a solid structure upon the foundations of experience thus laid." [5] By way of beginning, a staff was recruited from the ranks of Greek government agriculturists and agricultural teachers. Hired on a part-time basis, each worker was scheduled to hold a series of twelve classes in a specified village. For the most part these lectures were to be directed at the youth whom Near East Relief had cared for in their orphanage program and who had now reached young manhood.

The exploratory period taught Allen much. On the whole his plan, an adaptation of the Smith-Hughes program, was not especially successful. Allen found that his teaching staff, although graduates of Greek agricultural schools, preferred office work to contact with the dirt farmer. During the first winter usually not more than one teacher at a time functioned on schedule. The flimsiest excuses served to cancel a scheduled meeting: inclement weather, failure to arrange for light or heat, or difficulties in arranging transportation. Only by a *tour de force* did Allen succeed in having fifteen courses of twelve lessons each taught in fourteen villages. Thereafter he resolved to recruit men on the basis of personal qualities and to rely on in-service training to develop their technical competence.[6] Allen also decided to redirect his program at farm owners rather than youth who were still too young to have acquired farms of their own and who had little opportunity to experiment.

While Allen organized his course of lectures, he assigned Demosthenes Economou to serve as an extension agent in three Macedonian villages near the Bulgarian border. A native, Economou had a farm background and had attended the Thessalonika Agricultural and Industrial Institute. Although his technical knowledge was limited, he had enthusiasm, an at-

---

[4] Alfred Charles True, *A History of Agricultural Education in the United States, 1785–1925* (Washington: GPO, 1929), 370–382.

[5] Harold B. Allen, *Come Over Into Macedonia: The Story of a Ten-year Adventure in Uplifting A War-torn People* (New Brunswick: Rutgers University Press, 1943), 39–40. Allen's book is more detailed than the official records retained by the NEF for the work in Macedonia.

[6] *Ibid.*, 48–52, 66. See also, Allen, "Macedonian Rural Life Improvement," in NEF, *Basic Project Reports*, 1932, 37–49.

tractive personality, and a desire to learn. Economou occupied himself full-time in the villages, talking with farmers informally, holding meetings, visiting schools, and giving service wherever he could. This pattern, based on the agricultural extension system of Seaman Knapp, proved much more successful; Allen adopted it for future use in Macedonia.[7]

In reshaping his program, Allen used full-time demonstration agents as intensively as their personal resourcefulness permitted. Initially each agriculturist was assigned nine villages, giving instruction two days a week in each of two or three villages for two months, then repeating the process in other villages until all nine villages had been covered. This activity occupied the agent from October through March. The other half year was devoted to "follow up." A variety of activities for school children, young people, and adults was organized. All were counseled as needed. Through the employment of six agriculturists, fifty-four villages in a concentrated area were served.[8]

Until January, 1931, the emphasis was on perfecting the agricultural work. One important task was to equip the staff suitably. Popular leaflets written in a simple vocabulary were secured from the Hellenic Agricultural Society. Pruning shears, saws, budding knives, syringes, grafting material, and instruments for demonstration purposes or for emergency services were fitted out in a portable box. To these were added sports equipment, especially footballs and volleyballs. Experience also directed a reduction in the number of villages served, for Allen found that his best men were able to create so many opportunities for service that they could efficiently serve but six villages.[9]

Training the native staff was another major task of the early years. Allen first had to overcome the impact of poor and inadequate teaching on his demonstrators. In elementary school they had learned by rote, and in secondary school they had endured the lecture system, but they had never experienced instruction via the give-and-take of motivated discussion. To demonstrate teaching methods appropriate to extension work, Allen assembled his staff at the Thessalonika Agricultural and Industrial Institute for a month's practice in farming. He wanted to be certain that his extension workers could *do* as well as *teach*.

Training a native counterpart who would be not Allen's assistant but his successor was fundamental to the design of the Macedonian experiment, for Allen's objective was to assist the Greeks to help themselves master better methods of agriculture. He had no intention of operating an extension service in Greece permanently. Before the exploratory period was over, Allen found a tentative counterpart, Basil Moussouros, a teacher

[7] Allen, *Macedonia*, 53–55.
[8] *Ibid.*, 66–80.
[9] *Ibid.*, 79–82.

of agronomy. Moussouros was offered a year of post-graduate work at Cornell University if he would agree to work for the Foundation for a minimum of two years upon his return to Greece.[10]

· II ·

While Harold Allen empirically worked out an agricultural extension program in Macedonia, the Near East Relief matured plans for an organization to support and continue the work. In February, 1930, it transmuted itself into the Near East Foundation. The Foundation was charged with liquidating the residual institutions of the Near East Relief and with administering the demonstration projects begun by the relief committee. Directors of the Foundation were drawn from the same group who had long been active in Near East philanthropy. Cleveland Earl Dodge, whose family for four generations had been active in missionary and educational work in the Near East, was elected president of the Foundation. James L. Barton, the missionary executive, became its vice-president. The directors chose Edwin M. Bulkley, a layman who had long been active in Presbyterian mission work and chairman of the executive committee of Near East Relief, to be treasurer. Other directors of the Foundation, Otis Caldwell, Thomas Jesse Jones, Paul Monroe, and Ora Morgan, were specialists whose professional advice had guided Near East Relief in the 1920's.[11]

The sponsorship of the Near East Foundation was decidedly more secular than that of its predecessor, Near East Relief. With the exception of Dr. Barton and his successor, Fred Field Goodsell, the clergy was not represented on the Foundation's Board of Directors. Nor were positions on the Foundation Board portioned out to representatives of missionary societies as had been the case with Near East Relief. Altogether lacking were the politicians and publicists who joined Near East Relief during World War I. Nor did the Foundation have any ties to American financial, commercial, or industrial interests in the Near East. Until the end of World War II the Foundation neither solicited nor received funds from any business house.

Within the Foundation's Board two permanent committees emerged. The first was the Program Committee consisting of Otis Caldwell, Thomas Jesse Jones, Paul Monroe, and Ora S. Morgan. Although not formally appointed until November, 1930, this committee began to function as the brain trust of the Foundation even before its formal incorporation. The committee was to designate those projects of the Near East Relief that had "permanent values"; subsequently its responsibility was to ex-

10 *Ibid.*, 71.
11 NEF, *Minutes*, Feb. 21, 1930.

pand or to liquidate existing projects and to recommend the initiation of new ones.

The other permanent committee was the Finance Committee. Set up in November, 1931, to "review budgets, compensations, and other related matters," the Committee was composed of the president, Cleveland Earl Dodge, the treasurer, Edwin Bulkley, and a third director, Harold Hatch. There were no changes in its personnel for over a decade.[12]

One of the most important organizational problems was the creation of a constituency to support the work. Unlike the great foundations, Rockefeller, Rosenwald, Jeanes and Slater, Commonwealth, or Phelps-Stokes, the Near East Foundation had no grand bequest. Nor did it have any related agency through which it might solicit funds as had the mission schools and hospitals. Further, it lacked the advantage accruing to domestic philanthropies of doing a job which its patrons could personally inspect. Finally, its program was relatively new to the field of philanthropy. Early reports indicated that of those persons contributing to the final fund drive of Near East Relief perhaps fifteen percent would contribute to the Foundation. When the Foundation began functioning in 1930, it had approximately a million dollars with which to complete the relief work. For its own program it was initially able to raise $292,000. These were depression years, however, and annual income fell steadily to a low of $140,000 in 1934–35. While such funds were not adequate to permit the Foundation to undertake new ventures tentatively projected for Iran and Transjordan, they were sufficient to support the maturing program in Macedonia.[13]

After years of planning, discussion, and experimentation, the Foundation formulated a coherent set of principles of "philanthropy for backward peoples." Rejecting the wholesale imposition of foreign cultures on an underdeveloped area, the Foundation operated on the assumption that there were some specific techniques or institutions familiar to Americans which, if introduced abroad, might raise the standards of living. At the same time there was recognition that there were "climates of culture" that produced institutions that could no more be transplanted to another climate than an oak might be removed to a semi-tropical oasis and be expected to thrive. The task of the Foundation in organizing its projects was to discriminate between what was useful and exportable and what was without value to the Near East. In this way it hoped to maximize cultural change while minimizing social disorganization. Extensive, highly technical projects and those requiring large capital investments were ruled out for financial reasons. The Foundation concentrated on "those projects

---

[12] *Ibid.*, May 15, 1930, 15; *ibid.*, Nov. 19, 1931, 109.

[13] Robert L. Daniel, "From Relief to Technical Assistance in the Near East," Ph.D. dissertation, University of Wisconsin, 1953, 180–188. E. Miller to E. Bulkley, June 18, 1934, in NEF, *Docket*, July 12, 1934, 20.

which can be promoted and carried through to completion merely by intelligent leadership plus the utilization, on a large scale, of local labor and local materials." [14] This is to say, the Foundation was prepared to provide technical assistance rather than economic aid.

The principles that the Foundation formulated complemented the methods that Harold Allen evolved abroad. Accordingly, the Foundation did not aim at creating a super service organization that would transform the Near East single-handedly. Rather it employed Allen's extension agents in pilot demonstrations that illustrated the worth of specific technical innovations and at the same time trained a cadre of native technicians who would be competent to expand the work over a whole region or nation. Aside from training the native technicians, the function of the American staff was to induce the native governments to assume responsibility for the demonstrations and to duplicate them on a nationwide basis. [15]

The Foundation also crystallized an attitude toward rural life. There was more than a suggestion that it considered rural life inherently more wholesome than urban life. It was certain that one problem of the Near East was an over-emphasis upon urban civilization. The idea was repeated in various forms. Thomas Jesse Jones was particularly concerned with an overemphasis upon the upper class, which he identified as urban, while Otis Caldwell drew a Jeffersonian distinction between agriculture that produced new wealth and commerce that traded existing wealth for profit. A corollary of this deprecation of urban life was a romantic interest in "growing things, in the miracle of fruition, and the ways of nature." This did not mean that the Foundation was carried away with romantic notions about the noble peasant. Harold Allen especially abhorred romanticizing agriculture. He was convinced that substantive reforms were necessary to make rural areas more attractive places in which to work and live. [16]

Allen's ideas about methods for rural reconstruction, which had been well formulated by 1930 or 1931, were given sharper focus in a book by Thomas Jesse Jones, *Essentials of Civilization*. Drawing on his experiences at Hampton Institute and with the Phelps-Stokes Fund, Jones tried to identify the necessary and sufficient ingredients of a tolerable civilization. "Permanent and effective civilizations," he wrote, "must be rooted in jus-

[14] Barclay Acheson, "Statement of Near East Relief Work, Mar., 1927," in William W. Rockwell Papers, Union Theological Seminary Library, New York; Harold Allen, in NEF, *Basic Project Reports*, 1932, 45.

[15] *Ibid.* Harold B. Allen, *Rural Reconstruction in Action: Experience in the Near and Middle East* (Ithaca: Cornell University Press, 1953) summarizes Allen's conclusions after a lifetime of work in the area of technical assistance.

[16] L. Archer, "Special Report of the Foreign Director," June 20, 1931, in NEF, *Docket*, June 24, 1931, 37; Allen, *Macedonia*, 224.

tice, in contentment, and in opportunities for all the people all the time." When all the camouflage of buildings, organization, and propaganda was cleared away, Jones found a residue of four essentials:

1. Physical welfare or health.
2. Technological mastery of the environment.
3. The home.
4. Recreation, physical and spiritual.[17]

This philosophy, which struck Allen as "a simple but all embracing concept of educational philosophy," seemed to apply "most forcefully" to the Macedonian problem.[18] In practice it led Allen to rely on his agricultural extension workers to gain entrée to a community through some simple or dramatic service that clearly and immediately brought rewards to the peasant. The prestige thus gained by the demonstration agents was then employed to encourage the peasant to take other steps in which the rewards were less readily apparent or in which they were non-economic, for example, a village recreation program, simple sanitary measures, or home-making and child care. Utilizing the four essentials framed by Jones as a guide, Allen structured a workable program in a relatively few months, a program that required few changes in the years that followed, and that was adapted to the dissemination of a wide variety of technical information.

By 1931, the experimental period behind him, Allen had outlined the proximate goals for the demonstration area. He hoped to inaugurate but one or two innovations per farm, innovations that however small in themselves would, in the aggregate, result in tangible progress. The case of John Kalaidjis is illustrative of the method. Kalaidjis had a farm of some forty-eight stremmas (about twelve acres), most of which he habitually planted to sesame seed. The Foundation's agent talked him into planting four stremmas in hemp, a crop Kalaidjis had never tried before. The net income from the hemp was 5,600 drachmas ($72.80), not a large sum, but almost twice the return the same area planted to sesame seed would have yielded. Nearby farmers were induced to experiment, sometimes with a special variety of wheat, sometimes with vetch, at other times to build a simple, neat poultry house, or again to breed their native livestock to blooded bulls. Within the demonstration area farmers copied each other.[19]

By 1935 Allen's big job was to interest the Greek government in supporting the project and in duplicating it elsewhere. The first step came in 1935 when the Verria-Edessa region, an area more accessible to Athens,

---

[17] Thomas Jesse Jones, *Essentials of Civilization: A Study in Social Values* (New York: H. Holt & Co., 1929), xxiv–xxv.
[18] Allen, *Macedonia*, 68.
[19] *Ibid.*, 250 ff.

was designated as a national demonstration area by the Greek Ministry of Agriculture. This was especially notable since it was the first official cognizance taken of the work. Because selection of the Verria-Edessa region resulted in a slight shift in the area of operations, demonstration work in several communities was abandoned; in other communities the work continued.[20]

The final step in the integration of the demonstration into the work of the Ministry of Agriculture came almost unsolicited. In January, 1937, the Ministry of Agriculture conferred civil service rank on the Greek staff of the Foundation, an act that enlarged their authority and prestige. It also precluded invidious comparisons between the Foundation and the Ministry as to the relative efficacy of their work.[21] In addition, the Greek agricultural extension service was revamped. New legislation provided both for regional agriculturists whose duties were supervisory and community agriculturists who worked directly with the peasants. At the time this service was created, the ministry had two hundred men who could be assigned to the work, and it hoped to add three hundred more within two years. Basil Moussouros, Dr. Allen's counterpart, was recalled from his assignment to the staff of the Near East Foundation to administer this new program of agricultural extension.[22] At this point the demonstration area was converted into a training school for extension workers and for use as a laboratory for testing new methods that might be utilized by the government's extension agents in other parts of Greece.

· III ·

In developing a home demonstration and public health program for rural areas the Foundation encountered many more problems than in modifying agricultural practices. The tradition-bound Greek peasants were still enmeshed in a subsistence economy and lacked ready cash to spend on items such as soap, screens, cod-liver oil, or recreation equipment. The patriarchal family structure, by subordinating women and children to a secondary role, limited what might be accomplished through them. As Harold Allen saw it, a primitive home life contributed to poverty and disease from which the only means of escape was enlightened training for the peasant woman. The Foundation empirically sought ways and means of transmitting the best knowledge of home management and child welfare to the peasant home.

[20] *Ibid.*, 272–275. See also "Report of the Executive Secretary," NEF, *Docket*, May 23, 1935, 21–23.
[21] Allen, *Macedonia*, 272–275.
[22] *Ibid.*, 277–279; NEF Program Committee, "Minutes," Oct. 28, 1938, in NEF, *Docket*, Jan. 5, 1939.

Martha Parrott, a former home demonstrator from New York and one-time teacher at the Thessalonika Agricultural and Industrial Institute, explored ways to correct the substandard diet of the peasant, the primitive care of babies, and the unnecessary exposure of rural folk to dysentery and typhoid. To do so, she adapted the home demonstration program used in the United States to the conditions of rural Greece. She began, as Allen had, by sending personnel into the field to make initial contacts in order to discover what might work and what to avoid. She employed rural teachers with experience in cooking or sewing to hold classes in the late afternoons and on Saturdays and Sundays. Also she organized day nurseries to care for small children while their mothers worked in the fields. A trained nurse examined the children and treated such minor ailments as skin rashes. The children were fed hot lunches and given afternoon naps. Capitalizing on the curiosity generated by the day nurseries, Miss Parrott organized classes in child care, cooking, and sewing for these same women during the winter months.[23]

Out of this preliminary activity emerged a plan that served as a model for the Foundation's rural work among women and children for the remainder of the 1930's. In the absence of a well-developed secondary school system in rural Greece, it was impossible to base the program on the public schools as in the United States. Nor in terms of Greek customs could a single woman be sent into rural villages by herself. Thus, Miss Parrott employed nurse-home economist teams, housing them in typical Macedonian dwellings that served both as model rural homes and as classrooms. The houses were equipped with sanitary latrines, screened doors and windows, and whitewashed walls. Furnished tastefully, they represented a standard within the reach of the average peasant family. As with the agricultural extension work, all the contacts with peasant women were through the medium of the native staff of the Foundation, Miss Parrott remaining in the background to supervise and counsel her staff.[24]

Five centers were organized initially. The first task invariably was that of breaking down the native's fear of the "evil eye" of strangers. This was usually accomplished by such service activities as day nurseries and well-baby clinics. Having established rapport by such means, the nurse and home economist secured an entrée to peasant homes where they might informally disseminate knowledge of improved techniques of homemaking. In turn the demonstrators received the village women at the center, where they answered questions and held formal demonstration classes.

The most striking results of this demonstration was in the reduction of infant mortality. When the Foundation began its home demonstration in 1932, one child in four or five died in infancy; by 1938 the rate had

---

[23] Allen, *Macedonia*, 153–160.
[24] *Ibid.*, 162; see also, NEF, *Basic Project Reports*, 1932, 40 ff.

dropped to one death in thirty-four. There was local recognition of the value of the day nurseries, and the communities undertook to support them. Other villages began to ask for the establishment of similar centers in their communities. Missions from Egypt, the Sudan, South Africa, India, Burma, and China visited the centers, while the governments of Cyprus and Albania sent young women to observe the work in the centers in order that they might absorb the spirit and bring the experience of the centers to their own countries.[25]

A second approach to home demonstration work was organized by Dr. Alice Carr in the Marathon district of Greece. This program reflected the medical training of its director, a veteran of Near East Relief and the Kaissariani clinics. She established a more elaborate home welfare center staffed by two nurses, two hygienists, a mosquito control worker, and a doctor. The opening of the center in October, 1934, was attended by the Prime Minister's wife. A major objective of Dr. Carr's program was to eradicate malaria from the Marathon plain, an area bordered by a thousand-acre swamp. Her methods were those of pre-DDT days: drain as much stagnant water as possible and cover the rest with oil. Within the first year, 1934–35, the incidence of disease as measured by infected spleens was reduced from forty-two percent to twenty percent, and chronic malaria was cut seventy percent. Half of the persons whom Dr. Carr treated for malaria during 1934 considered themselves cured a year later.[26]

While it was one thing for the Foundation to defeat the mosquito, it was quite another to enable the native to hold it in check. The oil and screens necessary for continuing malaria control cost money that the villagers could not easily raise. Accordingly Miss Carr sought innovations in the local economy by which the family income in Marathon might be increased. One proposal was to introduce the spinning wheel in place of spindles that were held in the hands and twirled with the fingers, a technique so slow that it took sixty days of spinning to produce enough yarn for one day's weaving. With a simple spinning wheel costing less than two dollars, a woman could produce the same quantity of yarn in two days. In one day's weaving a woman might earn fifty to sixty drachmas, as compared with perhaps twelve drachmas by working in the fields. Between the savings accrued from making clothes for her family and the cash profits from selling surplus cloth, a woman might add as much as a hundred dollars a year to family income.[27] Another proposal to increase peasant income was to undertake sericulture. Fifty women were taught to raise silk

[25] Allen, *Macedonia*, 212.
[26] L. Archer, "Annual Report of the Foreign Director," 1935, 15.
[27] B. Acheson, "Annual Report of the Executive Secretary," Feb. 6, 1936, 37–39; L. Archer, "Annual Report," 1936, 22–26.

worms, and school children were taught to feed them. The first year some of the women reported profits of twenty-five dollars for forty-five day's labor. The sum was small, but by Greek standards, substantial.[28]

At the end of four years, in 1938, Dr. Carr reported an eighty-two percent increase in family income for Marathon. Part of this accrued from new enterprises, but in large measure the peasant income increased because the natives were enjoying better health. No longer bed-ridden at critical moments in the growing season, the Marathon peasant did not have to divert his precious little cash to hire others to tend to his crops.

Independently of the home welfare demonstrations conducted by Miss Parrott and Dr. Carr, Harold Allen sought ways of improving the general health level of peasant families in his demonstration areas. The Ross-Fry-Sibley survey had indicated the widespread presence of endemic disorders, many of which could be controlled or eliminated by malaria control, sanitary latrines, and pure water supplies. Many of the public health measures that were indicated could be carried out by members of the community with materials at hand, if leadership could be provided to arouse interest in the problem and to organize the community in carrying out the required reforms. For this, Allen turned to his interpreter, Apostolos Koskinides.

Koskinides went to the village of Tourkohori, a community of not quite five hundred persons, to begin the experiment. The village was socially disorganized, for the twenty-five native born villagers resented the alleged encroachments of 450 newcomers, all refugees. The latter in turn were discouraged by the small allotment of land they had received from the Greek government and by the poor quality of the soil. Malaria was endemic. Enclosures about the two springs serving the town had fallen into disrepair, permitting mud and filth to seep into the water, while the free-flowing water turned the adjacent area into a small swamp. At another spot in the village there was an insanitary accumulation of garbage and dead animals. The task of rehabilitating the village was primarily one of community organization. Moving to the village, Koskinides enlisted local cooperation and in five months cleaned up the worst insanitary conditions.[29]

After this initial experience, Allen and Koskinides planned a general program to be directed by the latter. Simple projects in sanitation were designed to be directed by Allen's extension workers, while Koskinides directed more complex projects. As with the agricultural work, Allen selected one community in which to carry on a concentrated program to demonstrate what might be done. The village of Makriyalos was selected for a malaria control demonstration. In 1934 at the start of the project 44

[28] *Ibid.*, 1935, 18.
[29] Allen, *Macedonia*, 172–174.

percent of the children of the village were infected with the disease. A program of screening windows and doors, of draining small pools of standing water, and of oiling others or spraying with Paris green reduced the proportion of infected children to twenty-three percent at the end of the first year. In a nearby area used for control purposes malarial infection increased six percent in the same period. Among adults the lost time due to illness declined almost ninety percent during the first year. The results were incisive, but as at Marathon there was much work involved in draining standing water and in oiling ponds. Whether the native community would continue such a program under their own initiative was momentarily an unanswered question.[30]

Another project was to introduce sanitary latrines. Among the forty-eight villages in Allen's demonstration area, ninety-five percent either had no sanitation facilities at all or facilities dangerous to the public health. To provide an example of good practice, the Foundation built fly-proof latrines for the schools in twelve of the villages. In accordance with Near East Foundation principles, the village was asked to contribute labor and materials, while the Foundation supplied the supervision and supplementary funds amounting to about thirty-five dollars per latrine. Soon other villages requested Foundation help in building school latrines, and they offered to provide greater proportions of the materials.[31]

A third venture was to cap free-flowing artesian wells. Villages blessed with artesian wells had let the water flow uninterruptedly lest the water supply be "lost." Koskinides experimentally capped a well to establish the point that it was possible to have water when one needed it without having a mosquito-breeding swamp surrounding the well. As a result of this initial demonstration the provincial department of health in Macedonia promptly ordered all artesian wells capped, and within a month 126 wells were brought under control.[32]

In order to round out his program of rural reconstruction Allen undertook a recreation program. As with the sanitation program, he selected a native, Theodore Pays, to assume responsibility for planning, directing, and coordinating the work, much of which was carried out at the local level as an additional duty of the extension workers. Under Pays' direction several plans were developed. At Kyrghia he established a reading room on the first floor of the village hall in quarters previously housing the village coffee house. To make the room more attractive Pays hung homespun curtains and decorated the walls with scenic travel posters and pictures of Greek heroes. To give it an educational flavor he displayed agri-

[30] L. Archer, "Annual Report," 1935, 11–12.
[31] Ibid., 10.
[32] Allen, Macedonia, 199–201; L. Archer, "Annual Report of Foreign Director," 1936, 19.

cultural charts and stocked the room with magazines and some three hundred books. Within a year reading rooms were organized in five other communities.[33]

Pays also had Allen's agriculturists carry books to be lent to peasants living at a distance from his reading rooms. Late in 1932, while reading about the bookmobiles then being introduced in some rural counties of the United States, Pays hit on the idea of powering a mobile library with a donkey. Cabinets, similar to those used by itinerant dry goods merchants, holding 150 to 200 books were fitted to the donkey's back, and a boy was engaged to guide the donkey on his errand of culture. Working from a central reading room, each donkey library served five villages on a regular schedule.[34]

A venture that did not succeed was the use of educational films. Although the movies drew crowds because of their novelty, they proved expensive, while the themes of available films were often too far removed from the experience of the peasant to be useful. Stereopticon slides and film strips, on the other hand, for which it was easier to secure appropriate material, proved useful.[35]

To Pays was assigned the task of nurturing wholesome athletic programs in the rural areas. Children's play equipment that peasant villages could afford had to be designed. In collaboration with Lewis Reiss of the Greek YMCA Pays developed a set of equipment—see-saws, swings, parallel bars, rings, climbing poles and a sand box—that could be reproduced for about fifty dollars. In the evening hours, when chores were over, Pays had his extension workers coach the older youth who were ready for individual and team sports. He arranged district contests, the winners going to Salonika to compete in an annual field meet held on one of the holy days.[36]

In spite of the reading rooms, donkey libraries, and organized sports, the recreation program remained amorphous. Allen felt that youth between the age at which they completed elementary school and the age at which they entered the army needed group organizations. The Boy Scout movement seemed unsuitable, because in Greece it had become militarized to serve political ends. The American 4-H movement was also rejected, for Greek parents were not likely to take kindly to suggestions from their children on how to improve their agricultural techniques. A solution was found in the newly organized Future Farmers of America, which emphasized having the youth study the work of his father: the planting, harvesting, and marketing. The clubs were encouraged to organize and supervise the reading rooms and donkey libraries and to sponsor athletic contests.

[33] Allen, *Macedonia*, 122–128.
[34] *Ibid.*, 134.
[35] *Ibid.*, 130.
[36] *Ibid.*, 131–133; L. Archer, "Annual Report of Foreign Director," 1935, 12.

The ideal of community service was stressed, and the boys took it upon themselves to repair chuckholes in roads and to plant trees.[37]

To induce the Greek government to take over sponsorship and support of the home demonstrations, public health work, and recreation programs for rural areas was difficult. Several factors were responsible. The work cut across the fields of the ministries of Education, Health, and Agriculture, each of which zealously protected its fields from trespass. Bureaucratic rivalries, however, were a less serious deterrent than the prevailing attitude that education for women was of marginal value. Then, too, the home demonstration program was relatively expensive, for it entailed a capital investment in a model house in addition to the salaries for two women specialists for each demonstration area. Nevertheless, the home demonstration work proved its utility, and in the late 1930's Basil Moussouros, the Foundation-trained director of the Greek agricultural extension service, prepared legislation that would permit the Ministry of Agriculture to assume operation of the centers. World War II broke before a transfer could be accomplished.

The Foundation found less resistance to its sanitation work as undertaken by Koskinides, probably because its value was almost self-evident, but also because it raised no jurisdictional questions. The Ministry of Health in 1937 proposed to take over the program, and it acted with dispatch in doing so. It gave Apostolos Koskinides a civil service appointment and assigned him to continue working with the Foundation. Secondly, graduates of the School of Hygiene in Athens financed by the Rockefeller Foundation were sent to Macedonia to acquire firsthand experience in rural sanitation work. In effect the Foundation's demonstration area now became a training center for Greek sanitarians. The demonstration area was transformed quickly, as every school and home in the district acquired a sanitary latrine. Bedrooms were screened, standing water was drained, and manure was removed. On completion of their apprenticeship, the Ministry assigned these sanitarians to other Macedonian villages to work under Koskinides' supervision.[38]

The Ministry of Health additionally designated Makriyalos as the Macedonian Training Center in Malaria Control. Here the Foundation conducted an intensive program to maximize the reduction in malarial infection. By 1939 Koskinides was prepared to show the improvement that could be made by community cooperation in undertaking simple anti-malaria measures. His figures indicated that whereas 9,177 working days had been lost to malaria in 1932, only 127 days were lost in 1939. Reduced expenditures for medicine and higher levels of good health added to general prosperity of the community, which was reflected in the building of

[37] Allen, *Macedonia*, 223–231.
[38] *Ibid.*, 201, 284–290.

forty-five new houses, a new church, and a new school. At this point the sanitation work, like the home demonstration and extension programs, was interrupted by the coming of World War II.[39]

· IV ·

Despite the Near East Foundation's preference for extension education, it employed other techniques in responding to opportunities elsewhere in the Near East. One such example was the founding of the Rural Life Institute at Talabaya, Syria, in conjunction with the American University of Beirut. A combination of the agricultural experiment station and a secondary school for agricultural education, the Institute was decidedly more institutionalized than the Macedonian demonstration. It began in November, 1931, under the direction of J. Forrest Crawford, a young man who had grown up in the Near East. The school was open to boys in their late teens who had worked on a farm and who indicated an intention of returning to farm life. By this policy Crawford hoped to minimize the use of the school as a stepping-stone to a niche in the Syrian bureaucracy. Instructional methods were progressive. Such simple farm skills as poultry care were taught in courses lasting two to three weeks; more complicated skills were allotted six to eight weeks in the curriculum.[40]

Aside from its work with resident students, the Institute carried on experimental work, although it attempted little original research. It placed emphasis on the adaptation of what was known about plants, commercial fertilizers, and blooded livestock, for example, to the peculiar conditions of Syria. Talabaya also served as a center for producing and publishing bulletins on such topics as grafting, pest control, and plant diseases. In the summers the Institute offered refresher courses for rural teachers from the Lebanon and Transjordan and short courses for farm students.

The environment in which it worked limited the Institute's effectiveness. Most damaging was the political disorganization of Syria in which the Moslem majority sought independence from France, the Lebanese Christians demanded freedom from both Moslem and French control, and the Armenian refugees dreamed of an independent homeland. In such a milieu the local government was incapable of inaugurating energetic reform measures. Because of the financial crisis in America the Foundation was unable for a time to provide the Institute with a full-time American director. On the other hand, some positive gains were made. Officials of

[39] Apostolos Koskinides, "What Malaria Control Means to Makriyalos," in L. Archer, "Annual Report, Foreign Director," 1940, 17–18.

[40] J. Forrest Crawford, "Talabaya Experimental and Instructional Farm," in NEF, *Basic Project Reports*, 1932, 90–94; Allen, *Rural Reconstruction*, 142–156.

the American University gained experience in conducting agricultural education that proved useful after World War II. As Lebanon secured a greater measure of autonomy, the government reorganized its department of agriculture, choosing Halim Najjar, a project director of the Foundation, to head the department. This appointment strengthened the Foundation's work considerably, as Najjar lent his official support to the continuing work of the Foundation. In particular Najjar, who had organized the first farm marketing cooperative in the Lebanon in 1937, drafted legislation prescribing and improving the status of cooperatives in the Lebanon.[41]

The Foundation also undertook agricultural work in Albania and Bulgaria. In both countries the Foundation took over agricultural schools which their American founders could no longer support. The Foundation's objective in assuming these responsibilities was to salvage as much as possible of the enterprises by operating the schools until the local governments could be persuaded to assume their operation and in the meantime to broaden the influence of the schools.

In Albania, American philanthropy had supported four schools. At Korcha the Reverend Phineas Kennedy returned after World War I to operate an elementary school with the financial support of the American Board. The boarding school founded by Gerasim Kyrias reopened as the Kyrias Institute for Girls at Tirana. Operated by Sevasti and Christo Dako and Parashkevi Kyrias, the school was supported by the personal benefactions of Charles R. Crane. Also at Tirana was the American Technical School, founded in 1921 by the American Junior Red Cross and offering instruction in mechanics, elementary engineering, and agriculture. In the course of its operations the school built the first electric and ice plants in the capital. The fourth institution, the American-Albanian School of Agriculture, was located at Kavajë, a pleasant little town of eight thousand in the most fertile but least attractive part of Albania. Its guiding spirit was C. Telford Erickson who, after pleading Albania's case for national independence at the Versailles Conference, returned to Albania to organize a school.[42]

By 1930 the Erickson school, in financial difficulties, asked the Near East Foundation to help out. In accepting responsibility for the American-Albanian School, Dr. James Barton made clear that the Foundation was not abandoning its emphasis upon demonstrations. Rather the Foundation, he declared, would "loan its experience, and expert men and women to assist in the completion of the organization, and to help its work, until the

[41] Bayard Dodge, "Report," in NEF, *Minutes,* Jan. 24, 1935, 295 ff. E. Miller, "Report of the Executive Secretary," in NEF, *Docket,* Apr. 24, 1941, 5; L. Archer, "Annual Report of Foreign Director," in *ibid.,* Oct. 29, 1942, 20–21.

[42] Stavro Skendi, ed., *Albania* (New York: F. A. Praeger, 1956); Federal Writers' Project, *The Albanian Struggle in the Old World and New* (Boston: The Writer Inc., 1939), 83; Joseph Swire, *King Zog's Albania* (London: R. Hale & Co., 1937), 84.

Education Department of the Kingdom is ready to assume entire conduct of the school." [43] Before this came to pass the Foundation had to take over entire support of the school as Erickson, whose goodwill toward the Albanians surpassed his skill as a manager, lost the school's endowment.

A second crisis, political in nature, forced all the American schools in Albania except the American-Albanian School to close. Albania, which by 1933 was already experiencing menacing gestures from Mussolini, in an effort to protect itself rewrote its constitution so as to nationalize all schools. The American-Albanian School, alone, survived; the Foundation in undertaking to assist Erickson's institution had contracted with the Albanian government as well, giving the school a quasi-official status within the Albanian national school system. Depression economies, which forced Albania to close most of its secondary schools, served to magnify the importance of the Foundation-supervised school. [44]

Although the American-Albanian School was expensive to operate, the Foundation employed it to good use. The curriculum was revised to make it less academic. As housing facilities for the students had not been erected when the Foundation took control, a decision was made to quarter students in cottages rather than dormitories. This permitted the students of each cottage to be assigned a "farm" on which they worked as part of their schooling. These "farms" were small, akin in size to those of the average Albanian farmer, and were worked with the tools ordinarily available. Students were taught to adapt modern farm knowledge to the existing environment. The school also utilized part of its acreage as a modern experiment station, using Western techniques and machinery. Through this work two pests, the tent caterpillar and a grape parasite, were brought under control. The school bred superior chickens that it exchanged for the inferior birds raised by native farmers as a means of upgrading poultry flocks. The Albanian government also utilized the school, designating it as the agricultural machinery center for Albania and making it a government weather station.

While the school made an impact on the outside community, it succeeded in its educational mission as well. The best evidence of this was that an overwhelming majority of its graduates remained in agriculture. A check of the graduates made in 1935 revealed that one-half were farm operators, one-third were teachers—often of agriculture—and the remain-

[43] James L. Barton, "Albanian Address," in NEF, *Docket,* Nov. 24, 1930, 18; for difficulties of the founders of the Albanian-American Schools, Inc., see B. Acheson, "Report of the Executive Secretary," in *ibid.,* Oct. 13, 1932, 56–57 and *ibid.,* Mar. 8, 1934, 14. "Memorandum of Agreement on Cooperation Between the Albanian-American Schools, Inc. and Near East Foundation for Work in Albania," in *ibid.,* July 8, 1930, 48–51.

[44] Laird Archer, *Balkan Journal: An Unofficial Observer in Greece* (New York: W. W. Norton, 1944), 14.

ing one-sixth worked for the government. When in 1939 the Albanian government organized an agricultural extension service, the Foundation counted fifty-four of its nearly two hundred graduates among the ranks of the extension agents. Beginning in 1938 the Albanian government assumed major financial and complete administrative responsibility for the school preparatory to its complete integration into the Albanian national school system.[45]

But time had run out on the Foundation's work in Albania. In April, 1939, Italy occupied Albania, and in mid-July Italian authorities moved to take over the school from the Americans. Albanian students and teachers were bitterly divided in their reaction to the Italian take-over, some choosing an attitude of patriotic defiance, others the course of expediency and collaboration. There were knife fights at the Institute, and the Foundation resolved to get out as quickly as possible. Supported by Hugh Grant, the American minister to Albania, the Foundation secured ten thousand dollars for its movable property and turned over the school to Italian officials. Albania was closed as a field for American philanthropy.[46]

The Foundation enjoyed fewer opportunities to build a demonstration program about the Folk School at Pordim, Bulgaria. The founder, Edward Bell Haskell, who had participated in organizing the Thessalonika Agricultural and Industrial Institute, opened the school in 1929 only to discover that his sponsoring committee in America could not raise the necessary operating funds. The Ross-Sibley-Fry survey had indicated that Bulgaria, compared with other countries in the Near East and Balkans, was the most advanced. It already possessed an embryonic extension service, and in the opinion of both C. Luther Fry and Harold Allen more could be accomplished by working with existing agencies in Bulgaria than by founding new ones. Although the Foundation assumed operation of the school in 1934, it transferred the school as quickly as possible to the Bulgarian government.[47]

The salvage operation on behalf of the Folk School had worthwhile results. The Bulgarian government made good use of its properties, improving the existing plant and adding to it. Under the title "People's Rural University" the school was converted into the center for the Bulgarian continuation schools. This initial contact with the Bulgarian government led to a request by the Bulgarian Ministry of Agriculture for assistance in

[45] Allen, *Rural Reconstruction*, 128–139; Daniel, "From Relief to Technical Assistance," 191–195; see also L. Archer, "Annual Report, Foreign Director," 1935, 30; E. Miller, "Report of the Acting Executive Secretary," NEF, *Docket*, Feb. 10, 1938, 13; L. Archer to Abdurrahman Dibra, June 26, 1938, cited in *ibid.*, Apr. 13, 1939, 9–10.

[46] Archer, *Balkan Journal*, 95–101.

[47] E. B. Haskell to B. Acheson, Sept. 25, 1930, in NEF, *Docket*, Nov. 24, 1930, 31–33; "Agreement with NEF Regarding the Pordim Folk School Demonstration," in *ibid.*, Sept. 24, 1931, 29–35; NEF, *Basic Project Reports*, 1932, 104–115.

reorganizing and further developing its extension system. As Harold Allen believed that this was probably the greatest service the Foundation might perform in Bulgaria, the Foundation promptly compiled with the request and sent Clayton Whipple, Allen's assistant in the Macedonian demonstration, as an adviser.

Whipple's task was analogous to that which Allen had undertaken in the Verria-Edessa region. He was assigned to a reasonably typical area, Lovech County, some one hundred miles northeast of Sofia. His mission was to illustrate for the Ministry of Agriculture what might be accomplished by skilled extension agents. The techniques Whipple employed were similar to those Allen had employed. Because wheat was glutting the world market and depressing prices, Whipple advised farmers to shift to other crops and activities, such as dairying, fruit-growing, and poultry-raising. He showed peasants that improved livestock would yield over twice as much milk as their native stock and that selected seed and good methods of tending the soil would double the yield of grain. His duties also called for him to consult and advise officials in the Ministry of Agriculture, the extension service, and the schools.[48]

In Bulgaria, as in Albania, the achievements of American philanthropy were curtailed by the War. Early in World War II Bulgaria, too, succumbed to the Fascists, who in turn were overwhelmed by the Communists. Thus the area was closed to further efforts by American philanthropists.

The work of the Foundation in Greece, Syria, Albania, and Bulgaria was noticed elsewhere. British officials in Palestine and Cyprus invited the Foundation to conduct work in their jurisdictions. At Tulkarem, Palestine, the Foundation cooperated with British authorities in directing a training school for Arab village teachers. The Palestinian department of education sent trained teachers there to learn how to orient their teaching to the interests of rural students, how to plant school gardens, and how to stimulate improvements in village environments. Pleased with the work, the British High Commissioner adopted the Tulkarem program as a model for other training institutions in Palestine.[49]

In Cyprus British officials invited the Foundation to advise on the formulation of an agricultural program. The colonial government had already decided to organize a Macedonian-type demonstration and had secured tentative support for such work from a Carnegie grant. The Foundation's Program Committee recommended a four-point program. First, a Macedonian-type demonstration should be set up using an existing agricultural school as a base. Second, the Cyprus government should

[48] L. Archer, "Annual Report, Foreign Director," 1935, 19–22; *ibid.*, 1940, 39–45.

[49] Allen, *Rural Reconstruction*, 144–156; NEF, *Basic Project Reports*, 1932, 92–94; B. Acheson, "Report of the Executive Secretary," in NEF, *Docket*, Oct. 25, 1934, 6.

found a school for training rural leaders. Third, the Foundation proposed to lend two of its Greek agriculturists plus the advisory services of its staff. Finally, the Foundation offered to arrange the training of the Briton who would direct the project.

For its part the Carnegie organization pledged the necessary funds up to a maximum of fifteen thousand dollars. An agricultural instructor for the projected training school was engaged, while the project director was sent first to Macedonia to observe the work there and then to Cornell University for a year's training before beginning work. The Carnegie organization additionally provided equipment for visual education to be used in the school. Before the program could mature, World War II broke, and the project was abandoned.[50]

· V ·

Although agricultural extension, home demonstrations, public health work, and recreation programs claimed most of the Foundation's attention, it conducted sizable social welfare programs in Athens and Sofia. In Athens the Foundation's program represented an effort to salvage the Near East Relief's work among refugees. At the time the Foundation was organized there were some thirty thousand persons, a third of whom were refugees, living in makeshift barracks in the Kaissariani section of the city. Basic sanitary facilities were inadequate, while over-crowding and malnutrition contributed to respiratory diseases. Recreation facilities were non-existent. The Foundation followed three lines of work.

First, it established a clinic. One of its earliest activities was to identify active cases of tuberculosis and to treat pleurisy as well as mild cases of tuberculosis. A fresh air camp for persons with active tuberculosis was established on the slopes of nearby Mt. Penteli. The clinic's major purpose was to demonstrate methods of disseminating sound health practices. Since the general health level was so low, measures that in the United States would hardly form a major part of a public health program were capable of effecting significant changes. Thus the clinic promoted the use of soap, fluid milk, screens, and exposure to sunlight as a means of preventing illness. The degree of poverty and malnutrition was such that during the winter months the Foundation dispensed cod-liver oil and phosphate to undernourished children.[51]

This work with children was used also as an instrument to enroll the

[50] Ibid., Jan. 16, 1936, 6–7; H. Allen to Sir Herbert Richmond Palmer, May 8, 1936, in ibid., June 25, 1936, 26.

[51] Alice Carr, "T. B. Prevention Demonstrations," in NEF, Basic Project Reports, 1932, 6–8.

mothers and older sisters of these children in classes on good health practices. Two Greek public health nurses advised the women on the general subject of hygiene, the care of the sick, prenatal care, and first aid. Instruction was relatively formal; pamphlets published by the U. S. Public Health Service served as texts. To implement the formal instruction the two nurses and the clinic doctor visited homes to observe the extent to which their advice was followed. The clinic reported it reached nearly nine hundred children and over twelve hundred women.[52]

As important as the clinic was to the individuals it served, it was even more significant as a model center that could be observed by students of public health work. Twice a week teachers from the Maraslion Normal School came to observe the demonstrations. As these young people were preparing to teach in the villages of Greece, the Foundation hoped that they might absorb some of the principles of public health work and carry a favorable attitude toward such work into rural Greece. Still more important, men from the National School of Hygiene, nurses from the Greek Patriotic Foundation for the Child, and agricultural extension workers of the Foundation observed the clinic.[53]

A second facet of the Athens demonstration was the community recreation project employing the Kaissariani Playground. This playfield of four acres, the first of its kind in Greece, was laid out according to the recommendations of the National Playground Association of America. It had two sections, one for free play and one for organized sports. Along one side were concrete-surfaced bleachers seating three thousand persons. Controlling the entrance was a stone and concrete structure housing a staff room, showers, lavatories, lockers, and ping-pong rooms. The Foundation held the property from the Greek government on a ten-year lease, at the expiration of which the property was to revert to the government. Actually the Foundation hoped to induce the government to take over sponsorship of the programs in half that time.[54]

As the neighborhood was deficient in community organization, the development of a broad recreation program constituted a challenge. During school hours children from four nearby schools used the facilities for gymnastics and free play. At other times it served young workingmen for whom team competitions were scheduled in volleyball, football, and basketball. This phase of the program won enthusiastic support from the neighborhood, and the basketball team won the National Federation championship. Creative handicrafts such as sewing, embroidery, water coloring, and modeling were also taught, as were classes in playground lead-

[52] *Ibid.*, 11–14.
[53] *Ibid.*, 8–9.
[54] Andrew W. Asthalter, "Community Recreation Demonstrations," in *ibid.*, 1932, 27–30.

ership. The playground program, supplementing the clinic, scheduled short talks on the value of good health practices. Also the staff identified pre-tubercular youth who were provided with supplemental meals.[55]

A third aspect of the demonstration sought to better the social, physical, and moral environment of working-class youth through self-improvement programs analogous to those of the American YMCA-YWCA. Four centers were developed, two for young men and two for young women; some of these were located so as to serve youth living in or near the refugee camp, while others were adjacent to centers of employment. Altogether nearly a thousand youth enrolled in the program. The most formal part of the youth centers was the operation of accredited night school classes. At a more informal level the centers maintained carefully selected lending libraries to stimulate a taste for good reading. Staff members provided personal and vocational guidance.[56]

The task of inducing the Greek government to assume responsibility for these programs was compounded by the depression. The government had to be convinced that the work was worthwhile and then be persuaded to divert scarce funds to its support. The Kaissariani clinic early attracted attention, and the Ministry of Health participated in the project from 1930 by assigning selected public health nurses to serve an apprenticeship with it. In 1933 the Ministry began to share the support of the tuberculosis demonstration, and within its budgetary limitations duplicated the work elsewhere. By 1934 the government had assumed sufficient responsibility for the clinic in terms of money and personnel to enable the Foundation to transfer its program director elsewhere. The playground was less fortunate. While the government provided personnel to direct the playground, it could not—or would not—assume the full cost of its operation. Although the Foundation continued to subsidize the Kaissariani Playground, the Greek government used it as a training center for the National Physical Training School, and it served as a model for twenty-two other playgrounds founded by the government. The centers for working youth fared somewhat better. By January, 1933, the Greek government began its own program directed by personnel trained by the Foundation.[57] Under the sponsorship of the government the programs grew. Seven new centers for working girls were opened by the government between 1935 and 1940, and membership increased from 743 to over 4,400. The center

[55] *Ibid.*, 30.

[56] William M. Jessop, "Welfare Work for Working Boys and Girls," in *ibid.*, 16–22.

[57] "Report of the Executive Secretary," in NEF, *Docket*, Jan. 26, 1933, 15; L. Archer, "Annual Report, Foreign Director," 1940, 33. B. Acheson, "Report of the Executive Secretary," in NEF, *Docket*, Jan. 26, 1933, 14–15; *ibid.*, Oct. 25, 1934, 11; L. Archer, "Cross Sections of Significant Aspects of Principal Overseas Projects," Dec. 23, 1931, in *ibid.*, Jan. 28, 1932, 57.

for young men grew less spectacularly, but membership nevertheless tripled.

The experience that the Foundation gained in its public health and recreation programs in Athens was put to work in duplicating the demonstrations in Sofia, Bulgaria, where the Foundation followed up work that had been initiated by Near East Relief. Direction of the work in Sofia was entrusted to Leonty E. Feldmahn, a versatile Russian refugee. His competence lay in managerial rather than technical proficiency, and the program was modified to match the talents of its director. Feldmahn was sent to the United States for two months to observe American recreation programs and social welfare centers before assuming his duties in Sofia. His public health demonstration was less broad than the Kaissariani prototype. A child welfare clinic was organized, but it lacked facilities for X-ray diagnosis and ultra-violet ray treatment. The recreation program, however, was comparable to that at the Kaissariani Playground and was immediately successful. Less than two years after the beginning of the playground, the Sofia schoolboard organized twelve similar playfields. A third project undertaken in Sofia was the organization of a clothing reconditioning project much like one Near East Relief had operated in Athens to recondition second-hand clothing sent from America. Feldmahn's clothing project provided employment for some refugees and at the same time vastly increased the utility of the second-hand clothing. As a result of Feldmahn's success in Sofia, the Bulgarian government in 1935 invited the Foundation to advise it on the organization of health centers in rural communities.[58]

By 1940 the Near East Foundation had established itself. Administratively and financially it had weathered the break with its predecessor, the Near East Relief. It was a new kind of philanthropic agency. Where Samuel Gridley Howe was a "loner," the Foundation's technicians abroad were supported by expert advisers at home as well as by a modest bureaucracy to recruit personnel, order supplies, and raise funds. Where missionary benevolence experienced much difficulty in reaching beyond the Protestant minorities of the old Ottoman Empire, the Foundation reached peasant farmer and urban dweller without respect to religion. Where the independent colleges brought Western-style schools, to the Near East, the Foundation fashioned native institutions for the transmission of selected Western techniques and practices by natives to other natives. Where the prestigious, endowed foundations operated chiefly

[58] L. E. Feldmahn, "Child Health Station," *Basic Project Reports*, 1932, 135–138; L. E. Feldmahn, "Koniovitza Child Recreation Project," in *ibid.*, 129–131; L. E. Feldmahn, "Clothing Reconditioning Industries," in *ibid.*, 117–119. NEF, *Minutes*, May 23, 1935, 301; L. Archer, "Annual Report of Foreign Director," 1938, 21.

through grants-in-aid, the Foundation raised its own funds year-by-year and directed its own programs abroad. There were no miracles: half-literate peasants were not transformed Cinderella-like into sophisticated gentlemen farmers. Much of the success of the programs depended upon close attention to the multiplicity of individual innovations. The gains were real, enabling the peasant to live more comfortably than heretofore. These gains, achieved by the peasant himself, contributed to a frame of mind in which future innovations might be introduced with greater dispatch. While the Foundation worked quietly to help the peasant help himself, the independent colleges sought to train a wide variety of future leaders for the Near East.

Independent Colleges Since 1930

SINCE 1930 the independent colleges have weathered depression, war, and revolution. The last vestiges of provincialism disappeared. Led by the American University of Beirut, the colleges entered the mainstream of the intellectual life of the Near East and provided a cutting edge by which Western ideals and techniques were introduced to the rapidly changing cultures of the Near East. To a degree never before attained the colleges, while remaining American in character, accorded natives of the area they served major roles in teaching and administration.

· I ·

Overall the Great Depression of the 1930's did not paralyze the Levant, for a relative degree of political stability encouraged economic growth. Egypt and Iraq were quasi-independent kingdoms, while Lebanon and Syria were moving towards independence. Ibn Saud had opened northern Arabia to the economic and social influences of Western culture. Reza Khan continued his policy of reducing the power of "feudal" chieftains in Iran, opening the country to more rapid Westernization by linking the Persian Gulf with the Caspian Sea by railroad. British and French political influence brought much of the Near East into closer economic ties with the West. The development of commercial aviation reduced travel time between Baghdad and Beirut from a month (by camel) to a morning. The exploitation of oil in Iraq, Iran, eastern Arabia, and Bahrein provided a new base for the economy of the region. Natives founded firms in competition with Europeans. Shops were modernized with show windows and well-arranged counters. Newspaper advertising became popular. Inevitably traditional social patterns were undermined as the telephone, radio, and movie brought new alternatives to old customs. Paternalism in family life began yielding to a freedom of choice hitherto unknown for children and women. Moslem women began lifting their veils—or abandoning them—in the presence of males. Young husbands set up homes of their own rather than lingering in the patriarchal establishment. "Modern" girls smoked cigarettes, imitated Parisian fashions, and served cognac. The traditional defender of values, the Church, found itself on the defensive against the new idol of the age, science.[1]

This changing social milieu particularly affected the colleges. The growing sophistication of the Near East expanded the demand for college graduates. The political changes placed a premium on ability rather than birth, while the quickened economic life generated more and bigger enterprises with more managerial positions and greater executive responsibilities. Syrian Protestant College, which in the nineteenth century had served mainly a limited number of Protestant families living in towns along the Mediterranean, was called on to provide leadership to the whole community: Protestant, Orthodox, Catholic, and Moslem, from the Sudan to Iran.

Despite general growth, the depression affected the Near East at several specific points. The economies of Turkey, Syria, and Lebanon suffered from a contraction of tourist business, a decline in remittances from abroad, the cessation of emigration, and a decrease in exports. The direct impact of the depression on the colleges, however, was delayed until 1932–33, when income from endowment funds in America declined sharply. Savings were effected by President Dodge of the American University of Beirut by cutting salaries, withholding promotions, postponing furloughs, engaging fewer assistants, and increasing teaching loads. Programs in agricultural extension and dentistry were terminated. The continuing secularization of the Near East added to these financial problems, since more and more Catholic and Moslem families sent their children to the AUB, necessitating an expansion of the school plant to accommodate the increasing student body.[2]

In the long run the depression did not cripple the AUB. The shift of the International College to Beirut made available the assets of that institution for the support of the preparatory school at Beirut. Tuition income remained steady, since the University drew its students from economic

---

[1] AUB, *Report of the President,* 1938–39, 3–7; *ibid.,* 1929–30, *passim.* NECA Archives, New York.

[2] *Ibid.,* 1930–31, 1; *ibid.,* 1932–33, 7.

classes that could afford to send their sons to college regardless of economic conditions. The financial salvation of the University, however, lay in the continued generosity of the Rockefeller Foundation, the Laura Spelman Rockefeller Memorial, and the Rosenwald Fund. Although the Rockefeller Foundation's first interest was in the medical program of the school, it also gave large sums to construct new buildings and to add still further to the endowment. The Laura Spelman Rockefeller Memorial and the Rockefeller Foundation together provided modest but timely aid in the social sciences, while the Rosenwald Fund contributed $250,000 that the University was free to employ in meeting current expenses.[3]

The scholarly life of the University flourished as never before. As the trade and political center of the Levant, Beirut would have been a cultural center without the University, but the University enriched the intellectual life of the city. Visiting scholars often made the AUB their base of operations. In 1930–31, for example, Dr. C. U. Ariens-Kappers, Director of the Neurological Institute of Amsterdam, used the campus as a center for his anthropological studies. Another visitor, Sir Arthur Smith Woodward, carried on a research project making use of the University's collection of fossil fish. The University community gained more directly, perhaps, from the lectures of the Danish archaeologist, Dr. Harald Ingholt, who was then directing excavations at Hama. On one occasion the Egyptian Medical Society held its annual convention at the Beirut campus.[4]

During the 1930's the University began to assume a responsibility for promoting scholarship. Before World War I heavy teaching loads, combined with the physical isolation of Beirut from Europe and America, inhibited the senior faculty from making scholarly contributions to their fields. As late as 1928, the University took the stand that much as it was desirable to extend the opportunities for research, it must not lose sight of the fact that it was "primarily a teaching institution." [5] Nevertheless, President Dodge took steps which led toward an emphasis on research and the development of graduate studies.

It is significant that the school did not use the economic crisis as a rationalization for neglecting its library, described by the administration as "lamentably inadequate." [6] Annually the administration commented on its diminutive size and the need for funds to expand it. The Rockefeller Fund financed an expansion of the medical library in the late 1920's and in the

---

[3] *Ibid.*, 1933–34, 19, 28. Bayard Dodge, "The American University of Beirut; An Introduction to Beirut and the University," mimeographed, Princeton, 1952, 73. Terse reports of specific grants may be found in the *Annual Reports* of the Rockefeller Foundation and the Commonwealth Fund. See especially, Rockefeller Foundation, *Report*, 1938, 196–197.
[4] AUB, *Report of the President*, 1930–31, 12–14.
[5] AUB, *Report of the Acting President*, 1927–28, 16.
[6] AUB, *Report of the President*, 1928–29, 29.

1930's of the general library. The latter collection, which numbered but 31,720 volumes in 1929, grew to 67,704 volumes in 1938. The library was still scarcely adequate for general undergraduate use, but it more than doubled during the depression decade.

Encouraged and prodded by President Dodge, the faculty plunged into a variety of activities, most of which sought to apply textbook knowledge to workaday problems. Thus University staff members advised local firms on management problems, helped organize a building and loan society for Beirut, assisted in the Lebanese census, and prepared a civics course for use by Iraqi schools. Because President Dodge felt that Arabs ought to know more about the wealth of their romantic poetry, the University sponsored a jubilee in honor of the Arab poet al-Mutanabbi. Members of the faculty compiled a bibliography on the postwar Near East, studied the influence of Arab culture on French and English literature, and translated ancient manuscripts. Professor Costi Zurayk prepared a pioneer study of the Yazidi religion.[7]

Special efforts were made to employ the University facilities and staff in raising the level of rural society. An Institute of Rural Life was created in 1930 as a joint undertaking by the University and the Near East Foundation to induce landowners and tenants to cooperate in the application of scientific knowledge to solve rural problems. President Dodge hoped that by acquainting his faculty with the practical needs of the land, he might add to their usefulness as classroom teachers. Two centers developed, one at Tulkarem, a teacher-training institution in Palestine, and the other at Talabaya, Lebanon. In the former an AUB graduate was assigned to maintain contacts with graduates of the Tulkarem institution as they worked with school children and farmers. At Talabaya, the principal center, the University gave native farmers a five-month course in the care of livestock and poultry, and the cultivation of wheat, vegetables, and fruit. A teacher's institute was also conducted for teachers in rural Lebanon and Transjordan. The Talabaya Farm School closed in 1935 when the Near East Foundation shifted its approach to agricultural extension work. While the school had not revolutionized agricultural technology in the Levant, it introduced the University to the problems of the rural Near East and gave it experience that helped it develop an agricultural education program after World War II.[8]

Closely related to the Institute was the Village Welfare Service begun in the spring of 1933. Similar in organization to Quaker work camps in the United States, the Village Welfare Service sent groups of faculty and students to work in various villages. In northern Lebanon, for example, one

[7] *Ibid.*, 1934–35, 6–7; *ibid.*, 1932–33, 11.
[8] *Ibid.*, 1931–32, 13–14; *ibid.*, 1934–35, 5–6, 22–24; Dodge, "The American University of Beirut," 71–72.

summer work camp organized a general cleanup of neighboring villages, repaired the village fountain, conducted a recreation and handicraft program, and gave instruction in hygiene. Three or four work camps operated each summer, some of them serving several villages each. The government of Syria in 1936 and the government of Transjordan in 1939 asked the University to demonstrate work camp techniques.[9]

The University raised educational standards in spite of the depression. Lebanon and Syria, reflecting the influence of their French rulers in educational matters, required that persons licensed in law, engineering, medicine, or pharmacy possess the baccalaureate diploma or its equivalent. This in turn compelled the AUB to bolster its French preparatory program for students from Lebanon and Syria. Likewise when French authorities demanded well-trained pharmacists, the University found that swelling enrollments strained the facilities, and the school was able both to adopt a selective admissions policy and to lengthen its program. The medical school required students to complete the junior year of the arts and sciences college before entering medical training. The nurses' training program was bolstered by permitting a girl to work for both a B.S. degree and a registered nurse's certificate in a combined curriculum. On the other hand, the University found little support for its effort to raise the standards of dental education. Enrollments dwindled as potential students entered the less demanding dental schools operated by the Université Saint Joseph and the Syrian University at Damascus. Discouraged, the head of the University dental school resigned, and in 1937 the dental program was suspended altogether.[10]

The University's impact on the community was manifested in the varied activities and achievements of its alumni. Graduates were credited with introducing new techniques in preserving fruits and vegetables and in the manufacture of soap. Many graduates became teachers, but whereas prior to World War I they found employment chiefly in American mission schools, after the war they were widely dispersed in the public schools and colleges from Sudan to Iraq. Heads of the state school systems in Iraq and Transjordan were AUB alumni. Even Moslem and Druze societies recruited teachers from the AUB, while Greek Orthodox and Armenian church leaders sent selected youth to the University for training.[11]

Political and economic conditions in Turkey were such that the depression was felt more quickly and keenly than in Beirut. The Turkish goverment, hard pressed for funds, levied personal taxes that took from twenty to forty percent of the salaries of the American teachers. At the

[9] Stephen B. L. Penrose, Jr., *That They May Have Life: The Story of the American University of Beirut, 1866–1941* (New York: Trustees of the AUB, 1941), 271–278.
[10] AUB, *Report of the President,* 1934–35, 21; *ibid.,* 1932–33, 17; *ibid.,* 1936–37, 16.
[11] *Ibid.,* 1931–32, 6–8; *ibid.,* 1933–34, 5–7.

same time the government put pressure on the American schools to reduce their fees. Robert College trustees attempted to hold their staff by
cutting faculty salaries ten percent and paying the Turkish taxes for staff
members, a policy which added to net operating costs. Similar problems
confronted the Woman's College.[12]

Efforts to economize led the colleges at Istanbul (Constantinople) to
consolidate their administrations, a move made practicable by the fact that
the schools were within walking distance of each other. Some specialists
were given teaching appointments in both schools. A joint library board
was created that established a joint catalogue, arranged for the exchange of
books, and reduced the duplication of book orders. Cooperative purchasing of food and utilities was arranged, and standardized accounting procedures were adopted. By 1936 a common bursar had been appointed and
the calendars of the two schools made uniform. Finally, the retirement of
Caleb Gates as president of Robert College and the resignation of Kathryn
Newell Adams as president of the Woman's College brought the appointment of Paul Monroe as common president, although the two schools retained separate corporate identities. An internationally known specialist
in comparative education with experience in the Near East, Monroe was a
real "catch." The Turkish Ministry of Public Instruction was reported to
be delighted at having a man of so much distinction at hand.[13]

Faced with increasing financial difficulties, Monroe found his tenure as
president decidedly uncomfortable. Close on the heels of salary cuts ordered by President Gates, came the devaluation of the American dollar by
the Roosevelt administration, reducing further the real income of the
American staff. When Monroe adjusted salaries to offset the loss of purchasing power, the college budget was again unbalanced. Substantial savings were achieved by reducing the staff, especially in the preparatory
school, by about one-third below the level of 1928–29. Major differentials
in the salary schedules between Robert College and the Woman's College
became a source of dissatisfaction as soon as the schools began sharing
instructors. Some of the American staff remained unreconciled to the necessity of any salary cuts, while Turkish instructors insisted on being
compensated at the same rate as their American colleagues. Monroe, who
opposed discriminating in hiring and promotion policy, felt salary differentials between American and Turkish faculty were both inevitable and
just. The financial crisis was further magnified by a drop in enrollments,
largely in the preparatory school and the Industrial Department. Monroe
attributed part of this loss to the depression, but he warned that much of

[12] RC, Report, 1931–32, 1–3; "Report of the Dean, Eleanor Burns," in CWC, Annual
Report, 1931–32, 1.
[13] "Report of the Acting President, Marion Talbot," in ibid., 1–3; "Report of the
Dean, Eleanor Burns," in ibid., 5; ACG, Report of the President, 1935–36, 1; New York
Times, Apr. 13, 1930, May 21, 1932, and June 11, 1932.

it reflected the rise of adequate public schools in Turkey and the growth of hostile sentiment toward all foreign schools.[14]

This latter development raised a fundamental question: Was Robert College still necessary to Turkey? It was certain that under Ataturk the Turks had made rapid progress in creating a national school system. The Turkish Engineering School began to offer shop and laboratory work, making it more competitive with Robert College. The fact that the Turkish institution charged no tuition and that the government paid board and room for the students put Robert College at an obvious disadvantage. The Robert College Engineering School was also hampered because under Turkish law it was still classified as a secondary school. As Monroe reported the situation, the Turks had "no particular hostile attitude" toward the American colleges, yet they were "determined to complete their own educational system so that they need not have any dependence upon foreign educational institutions." [15] He detected a "rather indefinite and insidious propaganda against the College" which took the form of "throwing discredit upon the youth who attend a foreign institution as being unpatriotic," of regarding any exercise of discipline by a foreigner over a Turk as "an indefensible attack" upon their nationality, and finally that foreign institutions have "no right to attempt to formulate attitudes, mental, social or moral, of Turkish youth." [16]

At other levels Monroe found minor, but still irritating problems. He felt little of the charm and goodwill that his predecessor had experienced in relations with Turkish officials. Rulings on tax questions he regarded as capricious with ominous implications for the future. Frequent changes in the Ministry of Education were unsettling, as were rumors that the Turks were going to require teachers to wear uniforms, to prohibit the use of cosmetics by students, or to regulate haircuts. Still again, Monroe was troubled when the government expelled Dean Edgar J. Fisher, allegedly for publicly voicing hostility toward the Nationalists in offensive terms a decade earlier and subsequently providing materials to a journalist who published a "contentious criticism" of the Republic. Although Monroe suspected Fisher was being framed by some petty Turkish bureaucrats and fellow faculty, he declined to challenge the decision of the government and jeopardize his institution.[17]

Finally, the place of religion in the college was questioned. The original charter had created two mandates for Robert College, one to maintain a scientific and literary institution, the other to acknowledge and honor the word of God. In view of new modes of thought and feeling as well as the

[14] P. Monroe to A. Staub, Dec. 1932, in RC, *President's Report*, 1932–33, n.p.; *ibid.*, 2–6; *ibid.*, 1934, 24–25.
[15] *Ibid.*, 6.
[16] ACG, *Report of the President*, 1934, 2.
[17] RC, *President's Report*, 1934, 17–19; New York *Times*, Sept. 14, 1934.

requirements of the Turkish constitution and law, Monroe felt that it was no longer possible to fulfill both requirements, so he dropped courses in the Bible and compulsory religious assemblies in 1933. When some of his Board of Trustees demurred, Monroe reminded them that overt religious instruction had been a development of the Gates' regime, not of Hamlin's or Washburn's. The latter had, to be sure, read the scriptures, but always from the Psalms which were acceptable to Jews and Moslems alike. He concluded: "We should make it perfectly clear to the Turkish community and to the authorities that the institution is thoroughly committed to carry out a purely secular policy and that neither the administration nor the Trustees are any longer interested in the religious program." [18]

Monroe, who had been engaged on a three-year contract, left Turkey in 1935 with a feeling of defeat. He had gone abroad hoping to reshape the colleges academically so they could set a standard for excellence in teaching and undertake some experimental work in progressive education, but most of his energies had been absorbed in financial controversies and in adjusting relations with Turkish officials. At the end of his tenure he had to report that Turkey was not yet ready to allow this liberty to a foreign institution, and "the staff of the College is not sufficiently interested or adequately trained to serve as a model of efficiency in respect to teaching." [19] In many respects Monroe was a victim of circumstances, for his term of office coincided with the nadir of the depression and the zenith of Turkish nationalism.

His successor was Walter L. Wright, a youngish man, an historian, and a linguist. Of a sanguinary disposition, Wright saw no reason why the two colleges should not continue to grow and render service to Turkey. He did much to dispel the pessimism that permeated the staff, assisted by improving economic conditions in America and by the slow ebbing of militant Turkish nationalism. He was further able to reap the benefits of some of Monroe's economies without assuming the onus of having instituted them. Yet it must be said that there was still too little money. The colleges were understaffed; salary schedules remained low; buildings and grounds suffered continued neglect. [20]

When the financial situation eased in 1937, Wright had an opportunity to deal with the problem of faculty morale and low salaries. As he saw no chance of offering large salaries, Wright stressed fringe benefits which would hold senior faculty at Istanbul: reestablishment of sabbatical leaves with pay, provision for the education of faculty children, and a contribu-

---

[18] RC, *President's Report*, 1935, 28.

[19] *Ibid.*, 8; Lynn A. Scipio, *My Thirty Years in Turkey* (Rindge, N. H.: R. R. Smith, 1955), 258, says Monroe was "discouraged from the beginning."

[20] New York *Times*, June 3, 1935; *ibid.*, June 9, 1935; RC, *Report of the President*, 1938–39, 7–9.

tory pension plan. By insisting on a single salary schedule for faculty regardless of nationality, he hoped to reduce the attrition of faculty which had reached the level of twenty-seven percent per year. Wright's goal was to have a senior professor, preferably an American, in charge of each department, the remainder of the staff consisting of relatively low paid instructors and tutors.[21]

Relations with the Turkish government remained a matter of concern, and Wright was harassed at times by the ponderous bureaucracy with its "multitudinous regulations" and "inquisitional methods." The Turkish government often seemed more concerned with providing students with "a full panoply of official documents all duly signed, countersigned, numbered and sealed" than with educating the student. Turkish nationalism led to a deterioration of student discipline and the gravest crisis of Wright's presidency. In 1937 graduating seniors at Robert College expressed resentment toward the school at an annual alumni banquet, and individuals subsequently "exposed" the school in letters to local editors and in secret complaints to the Ministry of Education. Wright was charged with holding Communist views and with defaming the Republic. In the subsequent investigations he was cleared.[22]

In spite of the cloud under which Wright operated, there were perceptible indications of improved relations with the Turks. One sign was the action of the Turkish government in granting tax exemption to the colleges. Other evidences were seen as the Ministry of Public Works appointed graduates of the College to executive posts, and the Ministry of Education opened teaching appointments to those holding degrees from the American schools. Just prior to World War II the American colleges were the beneficiaries of a Turkish-British rapprochement that enhanced the value of an English-language education to Turkish nationals.[23]

The academic quality of the colleges in Istanbul, particularly Robert, suffered as a result of the depression. For financial reasons the school abandoned its selective admissions policy in 1932. Furthermore, to conserve the collegiate program, the preparatory school was left to shift for itself under inadequately supervised American tutors with little or no previous teaching experience. The younger boys were again housed with older youth with the renewal of the "boy problem." Although a study made at the Turkish University of Istanbul indicated that Robert College graduates still outperformed graduates of any other school in Turkey, complaints from American universities, to which approximately half the engi-

[21] *Ibid.*, 1935–36, 16; *ibid.*, 1936–37, 10; New York *Times*, June 3, 1935; June 9, 1935; and Mar. 31, 1935.

[22] RC, *Annual Report*, 1937–38, 6.

[23] *Ibid.*, 11; Lynn Scipio, "Annual Report of Robert College Engineering School," *ibid.*, 1938–39, 4.

neering students went for postgraduate study, indicated that the students were less well prepared than in former years. This was a problem that President Wright could not immediately solve.[24]

· II ·

In 1939 the American colleges in the Near East exchanged the problems of depression for those of war. Turkey maintained an uneasy neutrality until February, 1945, when she entered the war on the allied side, but Syria and Lebanon were overrun in a brief, bloody invasion by the British and Free French. Old problems of finance, recruitment of teaching staff, and maintenance of academic standards continued, while new problems emerged. During the war years the growth of Turkey, Syria, and Lebanon was tremendously accelerated, and the United States government began taking note of its cultural relations with other nations. The effect of the war years proved revolutionary.

The impact of the war was felt as the Turkish government enrolled 118 military personnel in the engineering school at Robert College. In 1941 the colleges at Istanbul closed a month early when German troops ominously poured into Greece. At Beirut, air raid shelters and slit trenches were dug on campus, and windows were equipped with blackout curtains. Commencement exercises were cancelled, and students from outside the French mandate were sent home. During the summer of 1941 British and Free French forces liberated Syria and Lebanon from control of Vichy France. For the rest of the war Turkey, Syria, and Lebanon were free from military action, but they were isolated from western Europe and America.[25]

One of the first of the wartime problems was securing an adequate teaching staff. Many of the American teachers returned to the United States in the summer of 1941 and either allowed their contracts to lapse or resigned; others were unable to secure transportation to return to the Near East. In the fall of 1941 the AUB resumed classes staffed largely by native alumni. The University was able to secure textbooks in adequate numbers, but it was cut off from sources of library books, medical supplies, and laboratory equipment. Robert College experienced graver difficulties, for its trustees took no steps to employ teachers for the fall of 1941. President Wright sought to convince the American State and War Departments

[24] "Report of the Turkish Vice-President, Huseyin Pektaş" in RC, *Annual Report*, 1938–39, 4; *ibid.*, 1938–39, 10.
[25] *Ibid.*, 1940–41, 1; *ibid.*, 1941–42, 2. New York *Times*, May 6, 1941; *ibid.*, May 10, 1941.

that the national interest would be served by assigning American personnel to keep Robert College open. As he was not immediately successful, the College resorted to makeshifts until the fall of 1942, when a contingent of U. S. Army reserve officers arrived to take teaching posts. American civilians were also secured, and they arrived in time for the second semester. By such expedients Robert College operated through the end of the war.[26]

The perennial issue concerning academic standards at Istanbul was revived during the war. The heart of the difficulty lay in the impossibility of the two colleges operating as lycées, the status of the American institutions in Turkish law, and at the same time as fully accredited American colleges. For financial reasons the colleges had to compete with Turkish lycées, yet in doing so they imposed an intolerable load of ten or more subjects on the student and necessitated class attendance for thirty-five hours a week. The students inevitably spread themselves too thin and were not prepared for American-style work. On the other hand military students sent to Robert College by the Turkish government were mature and well-prepared academically. By the fall of 1942 Robert College was again in a position to employ entrance examinations to screen out poorer students. By the end of the war the Engineering School felt strong enough to plan ahead for a selective admissions policy that would require prospective students to complete their sophomore year in the College before entering the engineering program.[27]

In the midst of wartime problems the colleges at Istanbul experienced a change in top administrators. In 1942 Lynn Scipio, who had provided professional direction to the Engineering School since 1912, retired, and after eight years of service President Wright resigned. He was succeeded by Dr. Floyd Black, a former teacher at Robert College and president of the American College at Sofia.

Far more significant was the appointment for the first time of a cultural affairs attaché to the American Embassy at Ankara. The first appointee, Donald E. Webster, was a specialist in Near Eastern affairs and used his influence to promote the American schools with both the American and Turkish governments. As the first concrete by-product of the American government's new concern over cultural relations, the State Department granted Robert College $73,000 to carry on several specific projects such as a study of the currents of the Bosporus, revision of a textbook in elementary Turkish, and the updating of the English-Turkish dictionary. New chairs were also established in the applied sciences and additions made to the library holdings. This financial aid providentially solved the

[26] RC, *Annual Report*, 1942–43, 6.
[27] *Ibid.*, 1943–44, 8–9; *ibid.*, 1941–42, 2; *ibid.*, 1944–45, 9.

budgetary problems of the American schools during the latter months of the war.[28]

War thrust the American University of Beirut into an even more active public role than in the past. Difficulties in securing wartime transportation and the isolation of Beirut from the West compelled the University to utilize its laboratories to supply the Near East with various serums such as insulin, vitamin K, and adrenaline, as well as vaccines for typhoid, bubonic plague, smallpox, cholera, and tetanus. Varied and expanded public health and relief programs were also undertaken, reviving work the University had done earlier in conjunction with the Near East Foundation. Special efforts were made at malaria control and in mass immunization. Since the war in the Near East produced nothing comparable to the individual suffering that accompanied the Armenian persecutions of World War I, there was no counterpart of the soup kitchens and orphanages of 1915–30 in the Levant. Native members of the University staff were drawn into important positions by the local regimes. Professor Zurayk became counsellor to the Syrian Legation at Washington, while his colleague, Professor Husni Sawwaf, was commercial attaché. Professor Charles Malik was appointed Lebanese Minister to the United States.[29] It was a mark of the University's stature that identification with the University did not preclude official appointments.

The Levant itself experienced a speeding up of the forces of Westernization that had been modifying its social and cultural life for a century. The Allies used the University campus as a hostel for men on leave. The presence of European troops brought large sums of money into the area and increased the amount of gambling, drinking, and commercialized vice. Greater contact with Europeans also speeded up the emancipation of women; for the first time social dancing was allowed on the main campus, and male and female students were cast together in college plays. By bits and pieces new values were shaped.

As at Istanbul, the American government began to take cognizance of the University. The Office of War Information arranged a visiting professorship for Nabih Faris of Princeton University to fill the vacancy left by Professor Zurayk. In the first months of American participation in World War II the State Department made grants for scholarships, equipment, and visiting professorships. While the amounts were small, they helped the University emerge from the war without a heavy indebtedness.[30]

[28] *Ibid.*, 1943–44, 2–3, 10–11.

[29] AUB, *Report of the President*, 1942–43, 5, 7; *ibid.*, 1944–45, 2; Dodge, "The American University of Beirut," 85 ff.

[30] AUB, *Report of the President*, 1945–46, 6.

· III ·

At the end of the war the American colleges in the Near East again faced major problems. Their faculties had been riddled by the retirement of senior professors and the resignations of others. College plants were run down from the lack of timely repair. Inflation in both the Near East and America had made the income from endowments inadequate to postwar needs. In 1945 political conditions were unpredictable, but it was certain that the era of European control was dead. Syria and Lebanon became independent nations in the spring of 1946, and the United States government began a modest program of subsidizing the colleges in peacetime.

The postwar era brought expanded opportunities for work and new sources of support. During a period of adjustment from 1945 to 1949, the colleges at Istanbul encountered annual deficits because of expenses entailed in rehabilitating class buildings and in raising faculty salaries to a level comparable to those paid in other local institutions. By 1950 the colleges at Istanbul were able to balance their operating budgets. Both colleges during the 1950's enjoyed peak enrollments. Student fees provided seventy percent of the operating costs, while the remainder was supplied by the income from endowment funds and from subsidies from the United States government. Also by 1950 inflation in the United States increased the income from endowment more rapidly than the cost of goods rose in the Near East. Lastly, the schools benefitted from the appointment of two or three Fulbright professors each year, adding to the strength of the teaching staff without expense to the colleges.[31]

The tension that had long existed between the colleges and Turkish nationalists subsided for a time, and relations with the bureaucracy ceased to be a major concern. The chief factor in this turn of events was undoubtedly the dependence of the Turkish government upon the American government for economic and military aid in resisting the pressure of the Soviet Union. But it was no less true that there were subtle changes in the colleges themselves that facilitated the changed mood. The Woman's College that had once attracted the daring daughters of the Turkish intelligentsia now was a comfortably respectable institution that combined the functions of a good liberal arts program and a finishing school. A degree from the College conveyed prestige to its holder.

At Robert College the bonds between the school and the Turkish people were strengthened. An alumni association was organized for the

[31] RC and ACG, *Annual Report*, 1954–55, 4.

first time. In addition, a native board of advisers was created. At a time when European control of institutions throughout Asia and Africa was slipping away, inevitably the question arose whether Robert College should become a native institution. An open debate was avoided by President Black. He recognized that the school would gain in prestige if it were accorded university rank on a par with the Turkish universities. Yet he envisaged Robert College as a spokesman for American values and educational practices, and it was apparent that he would be loath to let the College become an indigenous institution. The "true position and function" of the Engineering School are, he declared, "the training of a considerable number of able young men, citizens of Turkey and neighboring countries, in American methods of engineering studies and work through the medium of the English language and primarily under the direction of American professors." [32] The quality of the students and of instruction was more important to the realization of this goal than the number of students. One may even infer that Black regarded Robert's lack of university rank as a modest blessing, for it spurred the able and ambitious student to complete his training in the United States, thus adding to the ties between Turkey and the United States.

The policies of the American colleges at Istanbul took a new turn under President Duncan S. Ballantine (1955–61) who felt Robert College was slipping into a "static state" and that there was too little money to support adequately both Robert and the Woman's College. As one step to make more money available for the collegiate program, Robert Academy was converted from a four-year preparatory school into a three-year lycée. As a second step the two colleges were further integrated by initiating coeducational instruction. Under this plan the Woman's College continued to offer its regular curriculum, roughly equivalent to an American junior college program, while Robert College offered women a four-year degree program. Ten women were admitted on an experimental basis to Robert College in the fall of 1958, and full coeducational operation began the following year. To stimulate the academic life of Robert College, a graduate program was instituted. In 1957 the Turkish government granted Robert the right to offer graduate instruction leading to the Master's degree, the first time such a privilege had been conferred on a foreign institution. Simultaneously a Ford Foundation grant of $500,000 provided the necessary funds. As further evidence of its increased vitality, a School of Business Administration and Economics was established in 1960 supported by a $150,000 grant from the Rockefeller Brothers Fund. When Patrick Murphy Malin succeeded Dr. Ballantine as president in April, 1962, the combined colleges with a faculty numbering 150 and a student population

32 *Ibid.*, 2.

of a thousand men and six hundred women were better prepared than ever before to serve the needs of modern Turkey.[33]

After the war the American University of Beirut enjoyed a period of growth comparable to that of the 1920's. Newly independent governments looked to the AUB for sources of trained leaders, while United States government agencies, philanthropic foundations, and American business firms provided funds for the expansion of the University.

While French cultural influences remained dominant in Syria and Lebanon, the passing of formal French control increased the opportunities for an English language college. During the interim period in 1945–46 the Syrian government asked the AUB to assist it in establishing a college in Syria proper. Accordingly in November, 1945, Damascus College was established as an American school affiliated with the Near East College Association and headed by Archie S. Crawford of the International College. Damascus College began with 125 boys, some in special English language classes and others in the eighth and ninth grades. The Syrian government provided the physical facilities. In 1948 Syria organized a National University, and Professor Costi Zurayk was given leave from the AUB to become the first president of the University, a post he held for three years before returning to Beirut as vice-president of the American University.

Several governments called on the AUB to take bursary students in a teacher-training program. When the Iraqi government requested that the AUB take two hundred, the University, lacking facilities for so many students, agreed to take sixty in the first year and ninety thereafter, if the Iraqi government would provide funds for housing the students. Westernization of the region had proceeded so rapidly that the Imam of Yemen, leader of one of the most tradition-ridden areas of the Near East, asked the AUB to train students from his sheikhdom. By the summer of 1951 elementary and secondary teachers from Kuweit, Bahrein, and Saudi Arabia were also coming to Beirut for special summer school sessions in education.[34]

The medical program of the University was greatly expanded at the end of the war. Dr. Allen O. Whipple, a trustee of the University and emeritus professor at the College of Physicians and Surgeons of Columbia University, went to Beirut to advise on the reorganization of the medical curriculum. Shortly thereafter the Rockefeller Foundation made a grant of $100,000 to re-equip the medical school. The Commonwealth Fund also financed a survey for a projected public health program for Lebanon to be jointly directed by the Lebanese government, the Université St. Joseph,

---

[33] New York *Times*, Dec. 5, 1957; Aug. 10, 1958; Nov. 25, 1958; and Aug. 25, 1960, and July 31, 1961.

[34] AUB, *Report of the President*, 1946–47, 11–12; AUB, *Annual Report*, 1950–51, 6–7.

and the AUB. As its share, the AUB, with a $500,000 grant from the Rockefeller Brothers Fund, created a department of preventive medicine and public health. Within a year the program was broadened still further when the United States government, as part of its Point Four program that was just starting, made funds available for training sanitarians, medical technicians, and public health nurses. In 1953 the University organized a School of Public Health to direct and coordinate the various programs.[35]

Simultaneously with the growth of public health work the University opened a new five-story hospital in October, 1953. Costing approximately $300,000, the structure was the most modern facility in the Near East with 207 beds and twenty-three bassinets. The curriculum of the medical school was revised, the students were placed on an eleven-month school year, and the clinics of the University were put on a year-round basis.[36]

Expansion of American business interests in Near East oil led to the establishment of an engineering college by the AUB. It was based on the limited program that had been started before the war and had grown into a full-fledged degree in civil engineering during the war. Further steps were taken in 1948–49 after the Syrian and Lebanese governments granted transit rights to Trans-Arabian Pipe Line (TAPLine) to build a pipeline linking the Iraqi oil fields with Sidon on the Mediterranean coast. The University felt the time had come to develop a comprehensive engineering college, "providing basic training if not specialization in the various aspects of the engineering profession." [37] The oil companies agreed, and funds for construction of needed classrooms and laboratories were promptly forthcoming from Iraq Petroleum Company, Kuwait Oil Company, and Bechtel Corporation. Later the Arabian-American Oil Company (ARAMCO), Bahrein Petroleum Company, Gulf Oil Company, and the California-Texas Oil Company joined in sponsorship. Offering degrees in civil, mechanical, chemical, and electrical engineering with opportunities for graduate study, the new college hoped to produce fifty graduates a year. The necessary buildings were completed in 1952 and auxiliary shop and laboratory buildings a year later.

As the American firms aided the expansion of the University, the school in turn facilitated the work of the companies. AUB educators advised the oil firms on the problems of educating children of Arab employees at the American petroleum installation at Dhahran. Special summer school pro-

[35] AUB, *Report of the President*, 1946–47, 4; AUB and IC, *President's Report*, 1948–49, 5–6; AUB, *Annual Report*, 1949–50, 2–3; *ibid.*, 1950–51, 6. New York *Times*, Sept. 13, 1946; July 1, 1949, May 21, 1950, and June 3, 1952.
[36] AUB, *Annual Report*, 1951–52, 11; *ibid.*, 1953–54, 8; "Beirut University to Expand," *American Journal of Public Health*, XL (July, 1950), 820.
[37] AUB and IC, *President's Report*, 1948–49, 4; AUB, *Annual Report*, 1949–50, 2. E. S. Hope, "Engineering Education at the American University of Beirut," *Technology Review*, LVIII (Feb., 1956), 194–198.

grams were conducted at Beirut to train Saudi-Arabian teachers for ARAMCO as well as to train native employees in techniques of bookkeeping and office management. After holding the sessions at Beirut for two summers, AUB faculty went to Dhahran to direct the courses. As TAP-Line brought American personnel to the Levant, it contracted with the AUB to provide hospital care for them. Since this preempted a number of hospital beds otherwise allocated to the University's medical research and teaching program, TAPLine compensated the University by building a separate pediatrics unit. The University hospital reciprocated by admitting TAPLine doctors to its staff.[38]

As plans for the engineering college materialized, a College of Agriculture was projected on the basis of a $500,000 grant from the Ford Foundation. Dean of the new college was Samuel Edgecombe from the Utah State College of Agriculture, a school that had long specialized in the problems of agriculture in arid climates. The original Ford grant sufficed to construct two class buildings at Beirut. A second grant of $500,000 made possible the acquisition and equipping of a 250-acre experimental farm at the north end of the Bakka Valley. Students in the agricultural college took their freshman year with other students in International College. The next three years were spent in the College of Agriculture, two years in formal classes at Beirut and one year in residence on the experimental farm. The faculty—following the fashion of the better American colleges of agriculture—was assigned to half-time teaching and half-time research. The school solicited its student body from Lebanon, Syria, Jordan, Iraq, and Iran.[39]

The University administration was concerned that the development of technical education in medicine, engineering, and agriculture would overshadow the liberal arts. President Stephen B. L. Penrose, who succeeded Bayard Dodge in the fall of 1948, felt that the liberal arts college was "the hard core of the University" and that no program of technical education would amount to anything without a "solid foundation of liberal arts training."[40] A variety of steps were taken to strengthen the quality of the arts faculty and program. A basic concern was to attract and hold a strong staff. One step was to raise salaries, made possible by a grant from the Ford Foundation. Another was to increase faculty housing facilities. A third device was to expand opportunities for faculty research.

President Penrose felt that the AUB had nearly inexhaustible opportunities for research in Arabic studies. The Rockefeller Foundation made a grant in 1948 for a three-year period to release selected professors in the

---

[38] AUB and IC, *President's Report*, 1948–49, 6; AUB, *Annual Report*, 1950–51, 6–7; *ibid.*, 1953–54, 8; New York *Times*, July 4, 1949.

[39] AUB, *Annual Report*, 1951–52, 3–4; New York *Times*, Mar. 21, 1954.

[40] AUB, *Annual Report*, 1951–52, 7; see also, S. B. L. Penrose, Jr., "Beirut Plan for Higher Education," *Journal of Higher Education*, XIV (Mar., 1943), 126–128.

fields of Arabic language, history, sociology, political science, and economics from their normal teaching duties to undertake interpretative studies of the modern Arab world. As the researchers proceeded, the University sponsored a conference on Arabic Studies at the Beirut campus in 1950. An additional grant from the Rockefeller Foundation financed the translation of important Western works into Arabic, and the United States Department of the Interior commissioned the group to identify and transliterate the geographical place names of the Near East. By 1953 the first of the series of Arabic studies began to emerge, ranging in topics from Arabic folklore to the Moslem Brotherhood. At this point a Department of Arabic Studies, an interdisciplinary group, was formally organized, and graduate and post-doctoral students from Europe and America were enrolled.[41]

It was only a step from the Arabic Studies program to the development of a graduate school, for a faculty actively engaged in research could direct at least a limited doctoral program. In turn the presence of a doctoral program would enhance the attractiveness of a teaching appointment at Beirut. President Penrose felt that the whole university would benefit through instruction by better teachers and through the broader perspectives gained from the realization that all knowledge was not encompassed in the confines of a B.A. or M.A. program. By 1955 a Graduate School was instituted with Dr. Charles Malik as Dean. Doctoral programs were begun in Arabic history, Arabic literature, physics, chemistry, biochemistry, and agronomy.

The most specialized undertaking of the University was the formation of an Institute of Economic Research established in October, 1952, and supported by a Ford Foundation grant. The purpose was to accumulate and publish accurate, uniform statistics on the economic development of the Near East, including data on agricultural credit and national income that local governments might use in formulating public policy. The Institute staff consisted of six senior research professors supplemented by correspondents in Egypt, Iraq, Jordan, Saudi Arabia, Syria, and Turkey. Once the Institute was underway, the Ford Foundation made a second grant to enable it to train specialists in the collection and interpretation of statistics.[42]

Of prime importance in the development of the University's burgeoning program was the United States government. Grants for scholarships and equipment and the provision of visiting professorships by the Department of State helped the University through the transition between war

[41] AUB, *Annual Report*, 1951–52, 7; AUB and IC, *President's Report*, 1948–49, 3–4; AUB, *Annual Report*, 1952–53, 4; New York *Times*, Apr. 27, 1953.

[42] AUB, *Annual Report*, 1952–53, 4; *ibid.*, 1953–54, 3; P. Beckett, "Public Administration Training as Technical Assistance: Some Further Observations Based on Experience in Beirut," *Western Political Quarterly*, IX (Mar., 1956), 151–172.

and peace. It was the Point Four program that made large sums of money available, however. The initial grant in 1951, for example, provided $624,-000 over a two-year period to provide all-expense scholarships to 120 students from a half dozen countries who would participate in the public health program then underway. An additional grant of $62,000 by the State Department helped subsidize the public health program itself. At the same time $116,000 was provided to help start the agriculture college. In the 1952–53 school year American government aid was extended to programs in education, public administration, and engineering. The number of students to whom scholarships were granted steadily increased, until by 1954–55 the University held contracts providing for a minimum of 303 fellows and a maximum of 405, at a maximum cost of $4,029,780. Students were to be recruited from as far off as Egypt, Ethiopia, and Pakistan.[43]

The extension of American government aid to the American University seemed to occasion no loss of independence. The grants had no strings attached to them other than assurance that the services contracted for were provided. Most of the grants were in the form of scholarship aid which assured the University full classrooms of paying students. Funds the University might have otherwise diverted to scholarships were released to support other projects. On the whole the government scholarships complemented the grants of the private foundations and business firms which generally provided for construction and equipment costs of instructional facilities.

Inevitably the University became involved in the fringes of the Cold War. Both the United States Air Force and the Foreign Service Institute of the State Department sought help from the University. After the Air Force established a base at Dhahran, it detailed officers and enlisted men to special summer session courses at Beirut to receive orientation in Arabic culture and history. In addition both the Air Force and the Foreign Service Institute sent personnel from the United States to study at Beirut in special summer training programs in the early 1950's.[44]

The partitioning of Palestine in 1948, accompanied by war between Israel and the Arab states, became a source of continuing difficulties for the AUB. The sympathy of AUB students, most of whom were Arabs, was with the Arab refugees from Palestine. Students and faculty raised money to assist Palestinian students who were stranded at the University without funds to continue their education. Students also raised funds to provide a minimum of one hot meal per day during the winter of 1948–49 for the

[43] AUB, *Annual Report*, 1951–52, 2–3; *ibid.*, 1952–53, 11; *ibid.*, 1953–54, 16; New York *Times*, May 1, 1951; "American University of Beirut Undertakes Point Four Project," *U. S. Dept. of State Bulletin*, XXIV (May 21, 1951), 825; S. B. L. Penrose, Jr., "Point Four Program at the American University of Beirut," *Institute of International Education News Bulletin*, XXVIII (June, 1953), 9–11.

[44] AUB, *Annual Report*, 1951–52, 5; *ibid.*, 1952–53, 7; *ibid.*, 1949–50, 5.

residents of two refugee camps.[45] As the crisis stretched out, student attention was increasingly focused on American foreign policy.

Arab disapproval of American foreign policy, which they regarded as too pro-Israeli and too anti-Arab, produced some hostile reactions to American activities. The Syrian government became so offended by alleged American support of Israel that it declined to enter contractual relations with Point Four authorities, with the result that Syrian students were excluded from United States scholarship aid.[46] As students became incensed over real or imagined offenses against Arab peoples, academic life at the AUB was disrupted periodically during the 1950's. At the outset of the 1950–51 school year the University dismissed twelve students for distributing a pamphlet attacking the school as an agent of American imperialism and praising the Soviet Union as the leader of the peace-loving nations. Later in the year students demonstrated against repressive acts by the French in Morocco. Fearing that further demonstrations would disrupt the University, the administration forbade students to join in a demonstration of sympathy with Egypt at the time of the 1951 Suez crisis. A small group of students ignored the ban, scuffled with Lebanese police, and were expelled from the University. The student body, interpreting the expulsion as an expression of American hostility toward Arab aspirations, staged a general strike. A march on President Penrose's house which followed was broken up by Lebanese police, but at the request of the Lebanese government the University reinstated the students it had previously expelled.[47]

In January, 1952, following a demonstration aimed at the Syrian government, the University sought to curb future disorders by requiring students to sign a statement promising to "refrain from any individual or collective action which interferes with the academic function of the University." [48] Students were inhibited for a time, but in March, 1954, a demonstration against the formation of the Baghdad Pact led to a riot in which Lebanese police fired on students. Although Arab nationalism proved highly volatile in the 1950's, relations between the University administration and the Lebanese government remained cordial.[49]

After 1955 the emphasis of the University shifted from physical expansion to improvement of the existing programs. Essentially this reflected the completion of the building programs undertaken by the new schools of engineering and agriculture. Because of the untimely death of Presi-

---

[45] AUB and IC, *President's Report,* 1948–49, 1–2; New York *Times,* Sept. 5, 1949.

[46] Dodge, "American University of Beirut," 99–101, contends that U. S. prestige was "disastrously undermined."

[47] AUB, *Annual Report,* 1950–51, 11–12; *ibid.,* 1951–52, 16–18.

[48] *Ibid.,* 18.

[49] *Ibid.,* 1953–54, 13–14; New York *Times,* Mar. 28, 1954; Apr. 1, 1954; and Apr. 4, 1954.

dent Penrose, administrative responsibility for many of the measures fell to the Dean of Faculty, Costi Zurayk, who directed the course of the University until the inauguration in July, 1957, of J. Paul Leonard, former President of San Francisco State College. To raise academic performance, enrollments in beginning classes were limited to the most promising students. Simultaneously the faculty worked with preparatory schools to raise the level of students applying for admission. To assist in recruiting and retaining faculty, salaries were raised and paid sabbatical leaves resumed. To relieve over-crowding on the Beirut campus, the preparatory school was moved to a new site south of the city, thus providing the University with needed space for future growth and isolating the less mature secondary students from the influence of the college youth. Particularly important was a grant of $1,500,000 from the Ford Foundation to meet the general operating expenses of the University as President Leonard took over and a grant of five million dollars from the Rockefeller Foundation to be spent over a ten-year period to develop the arts and sciences.[50]

As the University entered the 1960's, it was completing a century of service. The University proper included eight schools: medicine, pharmacy, nursing, public health, arts and sciences, engineering, agriculture, and graduate studies. Because its students came from so diverse an area, it continued the operation of an elementary school (largely for the children of American faculty) and two preparatory schools: the Section Secondaire for Lebanese students and the English-language International College for others. Enrollment in the University proper passed the two thousand mark by 1954, a level which the University regarded as optimum, while the other schools enrolled an additional 1,500 students. A majority of the students came from Lebanon, but two hundred or more students each came from Jordan, Israel (Palestinian refugees), and Syria. The student body was diverse in religious background; Moslems constituted a plurality, but there were large minorities of Greek Orthodox and Protestant Christian with smaller minorities of Gregorian (Armenian), Greek Catholic, Maronite, Roman Catholic, and Druze. The number of women students, which had never exceeded thirty before 1930, climbed steadily. In 1945 their numbers passed a hundred and by 1962 approached four hundred. Although most of the women were from Christian families in Syria or Lebanon, Moslem families were increasingly appreciating the value of collegiate education for women.

The faculty was nearly as diverse as its students. It was a rough measure of the changes wrought by a century that of the thousand members of the University staff, but ten percent were Americans; Lebanese nationals con-

[50] AUB, *Annual Report,* 1956–57, 3; *ibid.,* 1955–56, 5, 9; *ibid.,* 1956–57, 4, 18; New York *Times,* May 1, 1957, and July 7, 1957.

stituted approximately two-thirds. Although the Americans controlled many of the key positions, they did not monopolize them. The President of the University was an American, but Lebanese and Syrian faculty members had attained positions of responsibility as departmental chairmen and deans.

The independent colleges as they approached the end of their first century of service could look back with satisfaction. First, they served as spokesmen for American ideals and values. Though the number of students and alumni could never be but a fraction of the total population of the Levant, the schools reached a highly influential group who provided leadership in the business, professional, political, and intellectual life of the Near East. Robert College influence was long felt in the Balkans as well as in Turkey, while the AUB had become a regional institution serving an area from Ethiopia and the Sudan to Saudi Arabia and Iran. No other agency conveyed American ideals so directly and persistently to the leaders of the Near East. Second, the schools had contributed significantly to the rise in the status of women. The Woman's College pioneered both secondary and collegiate education for women. The Syrian Protestant College, beginning as an all-male institution, eventually admitted women to such specialized programs as nursing and ended by becoming coeducational, demonstrating the equality between the sexes that its staff had long endorsed. Third, they introduced enlightened materialism. While the Americans believed in material progress, they stressed that material wealth, like knowledge, was to be emphasized for "life's sake." [51] More specifically this meant developing the material resources of the Near East in order to provide better health through improved medical services and to provide opportunities for all through universal education. Fourth, the colleges promoted moral training and conduct while disclaiming any interest in proselytism by emphasizing honesty and character and the use of knowledge for social betterment. Finally, the American colleges were leaders in higher education. While other institutions grew up along with them, or in their wake, the American schools remained a major intellectual force in the Near East.[52]

At the same time the prospects for the future were sometimes disquieting. Turkish nationalism, as the events of the early 1960's indicated, still had militant, xenophobic undercurrents that regarded the colleges at Istanbul as trespassing on areas that should be exclusively reserved to Turks.

[51] Paul Monroe, "America's Educational Institutions Abroad," *Essays in Comparative Education* (2 Vols., New York: Teachers College, Columbia University, 1927–32), II, 150–154.

[52] Stuart Carter Dodd, *Social Relations in the Near East* (2d ed., Beirut: American Press, 1940), 110 ff.; Dodge, "American University of Beirut," 115–116.

Also ominous were the emotional outbursts of Arab students in Lebanon, who exhibited their displeasure with the contemporary political scene by demonstrations that disrupted the University. Altogether the political environment of the early 1960's impaired rather than aided the effective operation of the American schools.

CHAPTER

XI

Near East Foundation Since 1940

WORLD WAR II brought great changes to the Near East and the role of American philanthropy. The war profoundly shook the power relationships of the great nations, Britain and France being shouldered aside as the major forces in the Near Eastern politics by the United States and the Soviet Union. At the same time Arab and Moslem leaders vacillated between aligning with one or another of the major powers or following an independent course. The sweep of the totalitarian states, first Italy and Germany and then the Soviet Union, into the Balkans placed some areas beyond the reach of American philanthropy. The Cold War brought some problems of such magnitude that private philanthropy could not solve them. The natives of the Near East displayed mixed attitudes toward the West, recognizing the efficiency and power of Western technology and industry, and at the same time resenting Western political domination. In this context American philanthropy terminated some activities, renewed others, and branched out in still new directions.

· I ·

The Balkans first felt the impact of the war. While this region had been on the periphery of the Near East Foundation's interests, what happened there was indicative of the shape of things to come. As Albania and Bulgaria succumbed to Axis control, Foundation financial support was terminated. The programs continued, however, at least for a time. In Albania the occupation government repaired the girl's school at Kavajë and re-christened it the Arnaldo Mussolini Institute.[1] In Bulgaria the Foundation recalled its technical advisor, Clayton Whipple, in the fall of 1940. When the Foundation terminated its support of Leonty Feldmahn's work in Sofia as a concession to anti-Bulgarian feeling in the United States, some Bulgars, led by Metropolitan Stephan, urged the Foundation to continue the work or at least to delay its liquidation until the Bulgarian government could formulate plans for financing it. The Bulgarian government subsequently invited Feldmahn to continue, and, when the Foundation posed no objection, he stayed on.[2]

In Greece the agricultural and home demonstration work was inter-rupted for the duration of the war, but relief work on a limited scale was undertaken once more. As Italian troops pushed into Greece in October, 1940, Laird Archer, the Foundation's Foreign Director, placed the facili-ties and personnel of the Foundation at the disposal of the Greek govern-ment. Amalia Lycourezou left her work at the Girls' Center in Athens to organize the first hospital train in Greece; Meverette Smith, a home welfare supervisor, prepared facilities for the wounded at Salonika; while in Athens Alice Carr, director of the Marathon project, organized the preparation of surgical dressings. Miss Carr and Priscilla Hill, head of Near East Industries, also supervised some two thousand women in the reconditioning of used clothing for use by refugees.[3]

German and Italian troops succeeded in overrunning Greece in April, 1941; the hard, bitter, winter campaign of 1940–41 left a residue of 2,500 Greek veterans crippled and disabled by frostbite and gangrene. Other victims of the war were orphaned children. Generally the conditions of life in occupied Greece were more austere than usual. As the Germans invaded Russia, they requisitioned food reserves, motor vehicles, raw ma-terials, and medical supplies in Greece. Steadily the level of living in Greece deteriorated. By July, 1941, Laird Archer estimated that there were two and a half million children under fifteen years of age in danger of succumbing to starvation or disease before the spring of 1942.[4]

Americans in Greece responded to these conditions by use of their own resources. Joan Vanderpool, the wife of an American archaeologist, opened a small soup kitchen for village children in her home in Amaroussi, a suburb of Athens. Initially Mrs. Vanderpool was supported by personal

[1] Program Committee, "Minutes," Apr. 5, 1940, in NEF, *Docket*, Apr. 11, 1940, NEF Archives, New York.

[2] Laird Archer, *Balkan Journal: An Unofficial Observer in Greece* (New York: W. W. Norton, 1944), 122; Metropolitan Stephan to NEF, Mar. 21, 1941, in NEF, *Docket*, Apr. 24, 1941, 11; *ibid.*, Mar. 25, 1941, 12; L. Feldmahn to NEF, Mar. 26, 1941, in *ibid.*, 13; L. Archer to NEF, Mar. 28, 1941, in *ibid.*, 14.

[3] Archer, *Balkan Journal*, 127–128; L. Archer, "Annual Report, Foreign Director," 1941, 17–18, in NEF Archives, New York.

[4] *Ibid.*

friends in the United States, but when communication with America was cut off, the Foundation assumed support of her project. In the United States Greek-Americans and native Americans organized the Greek War Relief Association. Cleveland E. Dodge, Mrs. John H. Finley, Albert Staub, and Edward C. Miller, all of the Near East Foundation, accepted membership on the Board of Sponsors of the new group, and Prime Minister Metaxas of Greece named Laird Archer, among others, to administer the funds collected in the United States. At about the same time the American Ambassador to Greece, Lincoln MacVeagh, urged the Foundation to take the lead in "humanitarian assistance which may be offered from the United States." [5]

Although MacVeagh felt the Foundation was "admirably fitted for expansion," the Foundation limited its commitment. Beginning in November, 1940, it appropriated five thousand dollars a month for relief activities. Occupation authorities in Greece were not enthusiastic about the presence of an American organization, and one Greek employee of the Foundation was warned that Americans were "damn bad." Although occupation officials asked the Foundation to cease functioning as an American organization, they posed no objection to the organization of a Greek corporation to carry on the Foundation's activities. Accordingly in June, 1941, Greek staff and friends of the Foundation organized the Hellenic Near East Foundation. Funds were borrowed locally by the new group at the rate of five thousand dollars a month subject to repayment at the end of the war by the Foundation in New York. [6]

The Hellenic Foundation carried on portions of the pre-war programs. In Athens four welfare centers provided clinic treatment to over four hundred children and supplemental food rations to 1,600. Physical therapy treatment was provided for crippled children. Outside Athens some six hundred children were sheltered, fed, and clothed. The agricultural program and home demonstrations were abandoned. In addition to its own projects, the Hellenic staff supervised relief work financed by others. Milk bought by the Greek government-in-exile and the Swiss Red Cross was distributed to forty thousand children. In conjunction with the Greek Orthodox Archbishop's Relief Committee some three thousand children were evacuated to rural areas where food was more plentiful. [7]

The Foundation's work in Syria and Lebanon, although checked momentarily, expanded through the vicissitudes of war. After the fall of France in June, 1940, Syria and Lebanon passed under the control of Vichy France, only to be liberated by the British and Free French a year

[5] Archer, *Balkan Journal*, 146; L. MacVeagh to C. E. Dodge, Nov. 8, 1940, in NEF, *Docket*, Apr. 24, 1941, 17.

[6] NEF, *Minutes*, Nov. 28, 1940, 3; *ibid.*, June 27, 1940, 3–5; Archer, *Balkan Journal*, 207.

[7] L. Archer, "Report," 1942, 4–6.

later. The fighting lasted but thirty-seven days, and battle damage was less serious than the destruction of foodstuffs. British and French authorities imported flour and other food supplies to meet the emergency. The American Red Cross also sent food and milk, while the Karagheusian Foundation, organized by a family of Armenian-American merchants of New York, sent seed corn and wheat as well as cows, sheep, and goats to aid the distressed Armenians living in central Lebanon.[8]

Free French control of Syria and Lebanon permitted a continuation of the Foundation's agricultural work. Halim Najjar, a project director for the Foundation, became Director of Agriculture for the new Lebanese government as well. In villages in the Damascus area he conducted a demonstration of fruit and vines; in the Bakka, bee-keeping, poultry-raising, and wheat-growing were promoted. Farmers' institutes were held at both Damascus and Beirut. As in other areas, progress depended upon the cumulative benefits of a wide variety of innovations.[9]

Rather than mark time until the end of the war permitted a full-scale resumption of its projects, Near East Foundation officials in America concentrated on plans for postwar reconstruction. It joined other American agencies in surveying conditions and needs of the Near East. A first step was the creation in June, 1942, of the Coordinating Committee of American Organizations Interested in the Reconstruction of Greece. Member organizations included the Rockefeller Foundation, the American Classical School, Athens College, and the Near East Foundation. The Coordinating Committee produced a five volume report on rural reconstruction, public health, communications, and relief that outlined the work that might be done, but it did not parcel out assignments to specific agencies. In fact the tasks outlined far exceeded the combined capacities of the member organizations. More important was the formation of the American Council of Private Agencies for Foreign Service. This committee combined some forty organizations, mostly temporary war relief committees of the "peace" churches, non-denominational groups like the YMCA and the YWCA, the Girl Scouts, the World Student Service Fund, and numerous Jewish groups. The American Field Service, American Women's Hospitals, Near East Foundation, and Rockefeller Foundation also joined. The American Council met bi-monthly, providing executives of member groups an opportunity to exchange information and to discuss mutual problems.[10]

For itself the Foundation wanted to resume its unfinished work in Albania and Greece, and it had in hand requests from the governments of

[8] L. Archer, "Report," in NEF, *Docket*, Oct. 29, 1942, 16–18.

[9] E. Miller, "Report of the Executive Secretary," in *ibid.*, Apr. 24, 1941, 5; L. Archer, "Report," in *ibid.*, Oct. 29, 1942, 20–21.

[10] NEF, *Minutes*, Jan. 11, 1940, 4; E. Krimpas to L. Archer, Dec. 18, 1940, in NEF, *Docket*, Apr. 24, 1941, 22.

Yugoslavia, Rumania, Iraq, and Iran to undertake new projects at the end of the war. As it studied the prospects, the Foundation became especially interested in the possibilities of working in new geographic areas of the Near East and of pushing further into the field of technical assistance through pilot demonstrations. In particular the need for physical therapy among the crippled in Greece and the potentialities of artificial insemination for quickly upgrading livestock caught the fancy of the Foundation. Unable to begin such work immediately, the Foundation consulted with technical experts over future plans and lined up personnel to be sent abroad at the war's end.[11]

The war years brought substantial changes in the organization of the Near East Foundation. Until 1942 the responsibility for program planning had lain with Thomas Jesse Jones, Ora S. Morgan, Otis Caldwell, and Paul Monroe, men who helped transform Near East Relief into Near East Foundation. Now old age, ill-health, and conflicting wartime assignments brought about their replacement by a younger generation of specialists, thus assuring the Foundation of continuing leadership.

Likewise the war altered the financing of the Foundation's programs. During the depression annual income had declined from $700,000 for 1932–33 to less than $132,000 for 1939–40. The war, by reviving prosperity within the United States and increasing interest in overseas areas, brought in new revenues. However, to avoid waste, duplication of services, and even fraud that might occur as a result of the more than six hundred relief committees organized between September, 1939, and January, 1942, President Roosevelt created a War Relief Control Board to license agencies sending funds and supplies abroad. As a next step the National War Fund was created in January, 1943, to appraise needs and apportion funds among the various organizations operating overseas. The Near East Foundation, while cooperating with the War Fund, found the relationship a restive one. War Fund policies that required member organizations not to solicit the public worked no hardship on the temporary relief committees, but they threatened to cut off the Foundation from contact with perennial contributors who had provided much of its income before the war. Because the Levant was outside the zone served by the War Fund, the Foundation secured permission to solicit funds for projects in that area.[12]

[11] L. Archer, "Report," Jan., 1943, 8–10; "Reports Prepared for the Coordinating Committee of American Agencies in Greece" (5 Vols., 1942), in NEF Archives.

[12] *Cong. Record*, 65 Cong., 2 Sess., 7914; Harold J. Seymour, *Design for Giving: The Story of the National War Fund, 1943–1947* (New York: Harper, 1947); Robert H. Bremner, *American Philanthropy* (Chicago: University of Chicago Press, 1960), 169–172; Dorothy Seelye Franck, "Cultural and Scientific Cooperation in the Near East," *The Record* (Apr. 2, 1946), 1 ff.

· II ·

At the end of the war the Near East Foundation returned to Greece to salvage what it could of its earlier work and to undertake new ventures. Conditions in Greece were as chaotic as they had been in Anatolia at the end of World War I. A short, bloody civil war in December, 1944, was, if anything, more destructive than either the initial invasion or the liberation. Albania, Yugoslavia, and Bulgaria, having been occupied by Soviet troops, established pro-communist regimes, and in short order communists from Yugoslavia and Bulgaria joined Greek communists in an effort to overthrow the Greek government. Before the communists succeeded, however, American military and economic aid under the Truman Doctrine permitted the Greek government to overcome its enemies and retain control.

At first the Foundation's energies were directed to limited relief work. Laird Archer, the Foundation's Foreign Director, had returned to Greece as head of the United Nations Relief and Rehabilitation Administration, and he was accompanied by other members of the Foundation's pre-war staff. Hostels for children, such as the Hellenic Foundation had conducted during the war, were expanded. Most of the operating funds for these came from UNRRA, although the Foundation provided supplemental rations in the form of fats, vegetables, fruits, and fresh meat. Swiss philanthropists supplied barracks and equipment to outfit two camps of seven hundred children each. During the winter of 1945–46, five thousand children were cared for.[13]

Although this venture aided but a small portion of the million children whom UNRRA estimated were subsisting on a substandard diet during the winter of 1945–46, it had some lasting impact. When UNRRA expired and the Foundation was unable financially to assume the full responsibility, the Greek Ministry of Welfare appropriated funds to keep a hostel at Distamo open. More important, the Queen's Fund, a social welfare organization led by Queen Frederika, assumed support of other hostels. Greek social workers trained by the foundation were retained as supervisors, and Amalia Lycourezou, by this time one of the most experienced social workers in Greece, became director of the Queen's Fund.[14]

Medical relief work was undertaken in the Aegean islands, financed first by UNRRA, then by Near East Foundation. The personnel included

[13] Bayard Dodge cited in NEF, *Docket,* Feb. 9, 1943, 4–6; NEF, *Minutes,* June 19, 1945, 3; George Woodbridge, *UNRRA: The History of the United Nations Relief and Rehabilitation Administration* (New York: Columbia University Press, 1950).

[14] L. Archer, "Report," Fall Summary, 1945, in NEF, *Docket,* Dec. 27, 1945, 67; L. Archer, "Report," Spring, 1946, 5–6, 17–18.

Ruth Parmelee and Emilie Willms, both of whom had seen extensive service in the Near East under the patronage of a variety of American agencies. During the latter years of the war, Dr. Parmelee and Miss Willms served in the refugee camps in Egypt. As the Aegean islands were liberated, they accompanied the Allied troops. A fifth of the pre-war population of the islands were dead; among the survivors intestinal diseases, trachoma, and tuberculosis were endemic. The two women organized a trachoma clinic and instituted malaria control measures. By way of making a permanent contribution, a nurses' training program was undertaken. The objectives were to train fifty-five practical nurses and eighty fully trained girls in a two-year period. By September, 1946, fifteen girls had been capped, at which point the training center was shifted to Evangelismos Hospital in Athens.[15]

In Athens the Foundation undertook to upgrade the quality of nurses' training and nursing efficiency. Miss Willms found conditions in the Athens Municipal Hospital "incredibly below par." The nurses' quarters lacked hot baths; bedrooms were damp. One nurse in ten had active tuberculosis. The Foundation installed bathing and sanitary facilities in the nurses' quarters and outfitted the girls with shoes and uniforms. Next, at Miss Willms behest, the Foundation undertook to conduct a demonstration of pediatric nursing which was novel in at least two respects, for at that time Greece had no training program for children's nurses nor had student nurses ordinarily been assigned to wards to gain experience. Under the guidance of Emilie Willms, student nurses from five Athens hospitals were sent to the children's hospital, St. Sophia, for twelve weeks' work and training.[16]

As conditions permitted, the Foundation revived its pre-war programs. Attention was given to work for the blind. Although Near East Relief had pioneered education of the blind and had trained several Greek girls to carry on this work, except among veterans such training had remained a function of private charities in Greece. The school needed repairs, the staff required training in newer techniques of teaching and vocational rehabilitation, and funds were needed to expand the scale of operation of the school. Eric Boulter, an English expert in vocational education of the blind, was engaged by the Foundation; he substantially revived the work during the course of a year. The Greek government gave financial assistance to send six teachers to England to observe current aspects of welfare work. The school at Kallithia was expanded, while funds were solicited in England to found a second school at Salonika. The Greek government was also induced to establish an employment service for the blind. The Ameri-

[15] L. Archer, "Report," 1947, 11.
[16] L. Archer, "Report," Spring, 1946, 35–37.

can Foundation for the Overseas Blind, which since 1915 had worked with the blind especially by operating a braille press, assisted financially in perfecting a braille code in Greek. By the time Boulter completed his assignment, there were new fields of employment open to the blind, increased opportunities for training, and a quickened interest in the welfare of the blind.[17]

Social welfare work among urban youth was given a boost. The Kaissariani Playground in Athens, which had been used by both German and British troops, was restored and reopened under its pre-war director, Demetrius Lezos. A variety of American, British, and Greek groups joined in financing the floodlighting of the fields; six acres of land were added for track and field sports. The Ministry of Education doubled the government subsidy for the operation of the field.[18] Centers for working youth in Athens were reopened and expanded under the pre-war directors. For the first time the Greek government took the initiative to open a center of its own at Patras in the raisin district of Greece. A member of the Greek Supreme Court, Justice Rangourisis, made available a site for another center. The Foundation restored the girls' summer camp and subsidized the supervisory staff, while the Ministry of Welfare met the other operating expenses.[19]

In the rural areas the Foundation turned to its unfinished business, its home welfare demonstration. The fundamental problems had been native indifference to the value of the project and the paucity of Greek funds with which to support it. By way of resuming the demonstration a new center was established at Aspropyrgus, fifteen miles from Athens, in order that officials of the Greek Ministry of Agriculture could observe the work more conveniently. The project got a substantial boost in 1948 when the American Military Aid to Greece contracted to have the Foundation train home welfare workers for the government service. A second development came when Helen McCune, the Foundation's new home welfare director, abandoned the home center for a less expensive technique. A year's experience indicated that the "centerless" demonstration was somewhat less efficient, yet Miss McCune reported, "a measure of success can be achieved with a good worker." By 1949 the Foundation was ready to make an all-out effort to sell home demonstration work to the Greek government. In this final phase the demonstration, now located at Ghida, was a joint undertaking of the Foundation, the Federation of Cooperatives, and the Ministry of Agriculture. The Foundation supplied technical supervision; the

[17] *Ibid.*, 9–10, 25; *ibid.*, 1947–48, 23–24; "Forty Years of Overseas Service," *New Outlook for the Blind*, XLIX (Nov., 1955), 325–328.
[18] L. Archer, "Report," 1946–47, 34–41; *ibid.*, 1947–48, 22.
[19] H. Allen, "Report," 1949, 35; "Greece, Playground Reports," Sept., 1949–June, 1950.

cooperatives raised most of the budget; and the government provided some financial aid and established standards of performance.[20]

The Ghida demonstration was considerably more ambitious than pre-war demonstrations. Farm wives, for example, were taught to combat Newcastle's disease, which afflicted their chickens. Most of the inoculating was done by Foundation demonstrators, but over three hundred men and women were taught to use the hypodermic needle. Canning was also stressed, especially of meat, for the natives lacked refrigeration facilities. To increase satisfaction with rural life, a club for girls following the general lines of the American 4-H club was organized. Called YEP, the organization stood for:

Ygheia—health of body and mind, the basis of human life.
Ergassia—work, resultful work which makes man useful to the community.
Proodos—progress, the ultimate aim of civilized human effort.[21]

Progress was made, but not without surmounting obstacles. Some of the home demonstrator trainees left the program to get married, others to teach school, and some because solicitous parents objected to their daughters remaining in peasant villages overnight. A few farmers, still feeling no need for the work, declined to contribute to it. In spite of these difficulties the idea took root. The Greek Ministry of Agriculture organized its own division of Home Economics, appointing as its director Sophia Kyriakou, a home welfare demonstrator for the Foundation. As the Ministry of Agriculture took over direction and sponsorship of the program, the Foundation's center at Ghida became a training station for government home economists. The Foundation retained its specialists at Ghida to experiment with new ideas and to operate a model program to be imitated elsewhere in Greece. By June, 1956, the Foundation, concluding that the Greeks had sufficient experience and expertise to carry on the work alone, withdrew.[22]

The Foundation's mission in agricultural extension work was to revive and nurture the program that the Greek government had adopted prior to the outbreak of World War II. Extension work was handicapped by shortage of native administrators possessing a knowledge of good practice and by the lack of a training center. To solve the problem the Foundation sent several Greek extension agents to the United States for postgraduate training. Through the Fulbright program American agricultural educators were sent to Greece to help Greek agricultural schools to broaden their programs. The efforts of one of these appointees, Dr. William A. Broyles, culminated in the establishment of a Department of Rural Education at

[20] L. Archer, "Report," Spring, 1946, 14, 30–31.
[21] "Home Demonstration Report," 1948–49, 15; Howard W. Beers, "Reports," Aug. 4, 1949; "Home Welfare Reports," Sept., 1949.
[22] L. Archer, "Greece, Area Reports," 1950–51, 4; "Home Welfare Reports," May 8, 1952, May 12, 1950, and Jan. 22, 1949.

the national Agricultural College. As Foundation-financed scholars returned from their studies in the United States, they were appointed to posts of responsibility in the Ministry of Agriculture.[23]

In conjunction with this invigoration of the pre-war program, the Foundation undertook to demonstrate the technique of artificial insemination. The project began in the summer of 1945 under the direction of Irvine Elliott, a Cornell University graduate, and his assistant, Mathias Dietrick. After selecting two Greek veterinarians to work with them, they commenced their breeding service in the fall of 1945, using the Superior School of Agriculture as a center of operations. A second center was organized and opened in the Salonika area in May, 1946.[24]

Early progress was striking. The Athens milkshed provided a ready market for fluid milk. Confidence of the peasant was quickly won, and nearly 2,300 cows were bred artificially in the Athens area during the first season. In the second year double this number, or approximately half the cow population of the Athens-Aspropyrgus district, were so bred. The offspring when a year old were as large as native cows eighteen to twenty-four months old. Such achievements were impossible of attainment in the Salonika area, where farmers had but one or two cows apiece. Nevertheless, nearly two thousand cows were bred during the first operational year at Salonika.[25]

The problems of convincing Greek farmers and officials that artificial insemination was the least expensive, most efficient way of upgrading native herds were varied. Fearing that the natives might have religious scruples at employing an "unnatural" technique, the project directors had a Greek Orthodox bishop give his blessing to the work by dedicating the Salonika center. The most serious obstacle was posed by the guerrilla war then going on. Roads near Salonika were mined, and some 700,000 peasants abandoned their fields for the protection of bigger cities. As the Greek army mobilized its reservists, Elliott and Dietrick lost irreplaceable inseminators. Still more difficulties arose when American Military Aid officials offered to finance a conventional stud farm. The prospect of administering the extensive tracts of land, the large herds, and the big staffs required by a stud farm was appealing to some Greek officials, but the efforts at empire-building by some Greek administrators led the Military Aid officials to withdraw their offer.[26]

Caught in the middle, the Foundation persuaded the cooperatives to exert political pressure on the Ministry of Agriculture in support of the

[23] L. Archer, "Annual Report, Education Director," Oct. 1945, in NEF, *Docket,* Oct. 4, 1945, 46–47; *ibid.,* Apr. 15, 1948, 11.

[24] L. Archer, "Report," Spring, 1946, 13; *ibid.,* 1947–48, 6.

[25] J. Halpin, "Greece, Livestock Reports," Aug. 8, 1947; M. Dietrick, "Livestock Improvement Program for Greece," Sept., 1947, *passim.*

[26] J. Halpin, "Final Report," 5; "Greece, Livestock Reports," Apr., 1949.

artificial insemination program. The Federation of Cooperatives in Salonika, indeed, began to subsidize the program in 1948, and two years later the Ministry of Agriculture reversed itself and assumed nominal direction of the project. In point of fact the cooperatives, at both Athens and Salonika, operated the service, hiring the inseminators and underwriting the losses up to $250 a month. At this point the Foundation ended its formal relationship to the project, but as in other instances it arranged for the appointment of a Fulbright professor to advise and counsel with the cooperatives.[27]

One of the most sophisticated undertakings of the Foundation was a physical therapy project. It began casually, just prior to the outbreak of World War II, as an effort to assist crippled children. As in other projects a native counterpart was secured who would replace the American supervisor once the local government took over the project. During the war the work was kept going by the Hellenic Foundation. The need for it increased greatly as the war swelled the numbers of disabled soldiers and civilians requiring assistance. The initial plan was to establish separate rehabilitation centers for children and adults and to develop a training school for physical therapists.[28]

These plans encountered numerous obstacles, many of which were insurmountable. Belle Greve, General Secretary of the International Society for the Welfare of Cripples, who was to inaugurate the project was unavailable by the time Greece was accessible to Americans. The Foundation found difficulty in competing with the United States Veterans Administration, the armed forces, and UNRRA for scarce therapists. Although the rehabilitation centers were organized in 1945 and a School for Physical Therapists was set up in April, 1946, local problems in Greece continued to harass the project. Scanty hospital facilities limited the number of corrective operations that could be performed, while the cost of custodial care for children undergoing treatment exceeded the means either of the Foundation or of the Greek government. Greek doctors feared competition from the therapists and exhibited hostility toward the School, resulting in its closing. Thus, the project limped along until United States foreign aid programs made sufficient funds available to underwrite the costs and to command the highly trained specialists required to direct the program.[29]

After 1949 the Foundation became the focal point for organizing and

27 *Ibid.*, May, 1948, Mar., 1949, and Apr., 1950; C. Richards, "Report," July 16, 1951.
28 "Current Items from the Foreign Field," in NEF, *Docket*, Feb. 10, 1938, 31; *ibid.*, Apr. 14, 1938, 14; E. C. Miller, "Report of the Executive Secretary," in *ibid.*, June 29, 1939, 2.
29 NEF Program Committee, "Minutes," Nov. 22, 1944, in *ibid.*, Jan. 18, 1945. H. Allen, "Report," in *ibid.*, Oct. 4, 1945, 4; L. Archer, "Report," Spring, 1946, n.p.; *ibid.*, Fall, 1946, 13; *ibid.*, 1947, 15-19; *ibid.*, 1947-48, 19.

coordinating the activities of a variety of groups, each with something to offer the demonstration. Fulbright appointees, drawn from the personnel of the Kessler Institute for Rehabilitation, provided competent, continuing leadership. By their persistent efforts fears were calmed and vested interests placated. Arthur T. Brown finally, in April, 1952, had the satisfaction of seeing the Greek parliament authorize a government-operated school of physical therapy. Marshall Plan funds made possible the conduct of a demonstration on a sufficiently large scale to serve significant numbers of the disabled. In particular these funds subsidized the cost of artificial limbs for civilians. The Foundation directed programs of vocational training in such fields as cobbling, tailoring, and dress-making.[30]

Throughout the period the most limiting factor in the demonstration was a lack of well-made artificial limbs. Greek civilians had long been dependent upon "ignorant and uneducated" artisans to modify semi-fabricated limbs to the personal requirements of the patient. The result was extreme disappointment, and amputees often abandoned ill-fitting or poorly constructed appliances to resume the use of crutches and canes or, in extreme cases, became bedridden from the devices. Not until the fall of 1950 did Greek craftsmen develop sufficient skill to produce an adequate supply of well-made limbs. Even then the Foundation experienced problems, as ECA seemed to insist on treating amputees too rapidly to provide adequate outpatient care. But more serious was the difficulty in convincing Greek officialdom that it was worthwhile to train the physically disabled to become self-supporting. When ECA ended its financial support in November, 1951, the Foundation continued the project on a smaller scale, at the same time working to induce the Greek government to assume financial responsibility for the work, which it did in 1952.[31]

By 1950 the Foundation's work in Greece had reached a degree of maturity. The demonstrations in agricultural extension and sanitation in rural areas and the recreation and social welfare programs in Athens had been revived after World War II, and increasing administrative and financial responsibility for them was being assumed by the Greek government. The home welfare work in rural Greece and the physical therapy projects, though recently established, had progressed from demonstrations to training centers operated and supported by the Greek government. The Foundation, feeling that its contribution to Greece had been made, began to withdraw. American specialists, often Fulbright professors, were recruited to counsel the Greek agencies during the final stage. At last in

30 S. Brunnstrom, "Greece, Physical Therapy Reports," Nov. 3, 1950; A. T. Brown, "Greece, Physical Therapy Report," Mar., 1952.
31 Signe Brunnstrom, "Amputee Rehabilitation in Greece," Comeback, II (May, 1951), 3–4; E. Willms, "Greece, Rehabilitation Report," July, 1950.

1955 the Foundation withdrew completely from Greece, turning its attention and resources toward Syria, Lebanon, and Iran.[32]

· III ·

The Foundation's experience in the Levant was very different from that in Greece. Internal disorders attendant to Syrian and Lebanese independence, friction between the Syrians and Lebanese on one side and the French and Israelis on the other, and hostility toward American foreign policy made the Syrian and Lebanese governments reluctant to assume responsibility for projects initiated by an American organization. At the same time the Foundation's work suffered from lack of financial support and continuous, able leadership. As in Greece, the Foundation increasingly acted as a catalyst in bringing together the resources of several groups to conduct a program.

In Lebanon the Foundation's influence radiated from its office on the campus of the American University at Beirut and from demonstration centers at Anjar on the Bakka plain and at Chatura. The Foundation's work in Lebanon and Syria was not integrated because of frequent government changes. The program was directed by a native, Halim Najjar, who held appointments, sometimes concurrently, from the Lebanese government, the Foundation, and the American University. Serving as instructor in farm management at the AUB, Najjar used the University as a base for Near East Foundation-supported extension programs. He was particularly active in writing and publishing agricultural bulletins in basic Arabic, which the American Office of War Information reprinted and distributed in quantity. Najjar also used campus facilities to hold farm institutes and short courses as well as to organize an agricultural fair.[33]

The demonstration center at Anjar at the south end of the Bakka plain primarily reached the Armenian population made famous by Franz Werfel's *Forty Days of Musa Dagh*. The project was designed to counteract, at least in part, the efforts of the Soviet Union to induce these Armenians to return "home." Having fled from Turkey to Alexandretta and subsequently to Anjar, the Anjar Armenians were poverty stricken, and many were susceptible to the appeals of Soviet propaganda. In this instance the Armenian General Benevolent Union, a worldwide organization for charitable projects among Armenians, and the Karagheusian Foundation, established in 1921 by an Armenian-American family, supplied the funds, while

---

[32] H. Allen, "Annual Report of the Director of Programs," 1955, 10–14.
[33] H. Allen, "Report," in NEF, *Docket*, Oct. 4, 1945, 49; H. Allen, "Report," 1946, 11–12.

the Near East Foundation assigned Leonty Feldmahn, formerly in charge of its projects in Sofia, to administer the work. Much of his task was organizational rather than technical. He induced existing community groups to modify the village water facilities so as to assure the purity of the water. He organized a program of mosquito control to check malaria. He induced the Lebanese Ministry of Supply to place an order for 100,000 sweaters to be produced by the Anjar Armenians. He systematized the work of some seventeen committees whose work had often overlapped and which had been marked by bickering and jealousy.[34]

At Chatura in Lebanon and in Syria the Foundation worked with Arab fellahin who technologically and culturally were behind the level of the Greek peasants among whom the Macedonian demonstration was conducted. The work went slowly. Agricultural work at Chatura was directed by American technicians assisted by students from the American University. The home demonstrations were the first conducted by the Foundation among Arab women. Considerable attention was devoted to developing native leaders. On the job training was directed by Foundation personnel, while an occasional native was given a fellowship to attend a college or a special institute in the United States for short periods to acquire new skills. For this the Foundation enjoyed some financial support from the Rockefeller Foundation.[35]

In Syria the Near East Foundation encountered considerable difficulties as a result of the political environment. Although Syrian officials, suspicious of the political intentions of the Western powers, were reluctant to identify themselves as pro-Western by signing agreements with Western governments, the Foundation negotiated a contract to conduct a full rural improvement program, several features of which differed from earlier programs in Greece. First, the Foundation started sanitation and home welfare demonstrations before initiating the agricultural program, a step which added greatly to the difficulties of the home economist in charge. Another significant variation in the program was the employment of a native, Amin Bey Nazif of the Syrian Ministry of National Economy, to initiate the agricultural work. Only belatedly was an American agricultural specialist, Clarence Eyer, sent abroad.[36]

The development of the Point Four program in the early 1950's permitted a sharp expansion in the Foundation's activities in Syria, as the Foundation contracted to direct rural improvement programs for the agency. The number of demonstration centers was increased from two to

[34] H. Allen, "Report," in NEF, *Docket*, Oct. 4, 1945, 54–55; H. Allen, "Report," 1948, 28.

[35] *Ibid.*, 1946, 16–17; L. Archer, "Report on the Holy Lands," 1946, 6; L. Archer, "Report," 1947–48, 7–8, 38.

[36] H. Allen, "Report," 1946, 9–10.

five, both in agriculture and home welfare. One of the home welfare centers became a training post to prepare home economics extension workers and nurse-midwives for use in other demonstration areas. Experiments were conducted to introduce such new crops as alfalfa, to test the yields of various strains of sugar beets, and to check insect damage to cotton crops through dusting operations.[37]

The rising popular resentment in both Lebanon and Syria against the United States for the role of American Zionists in financing the Israeli cause made the Foundation's position tenuous. The war between the Arab League and Israel in 1948 flooded Lebanon and Syria with thousands of Palestinian refugees. A special fund of $214,000 to purchase foodstuffs was raised from the oil companies operating in the Near East as well as from the American Red Cross. The World Health Organization assigned public health workers to work under the direction of the Foundation's Clarence Eyer. The Foundation's role was to supervise the distribution of foodstuffs and to organize the relief camps. Refugees were deloused, and their quarters were sprayed with DDT.[38]

In spite of this work with the refugees, the Foundation met mounting suspicion and resistance from Syrian officials. The American government insisted, as a condition of United Nations assistance, that the Arab governments must accept responsibility for the refugees within their boundaries. The Syrians, resenting the refugees and fearing their competition, declined to grant them asylum in Syria. The brooding refugees refused to consider any action other than returning to Palestine. Foundation representatives and Syrian officials occasionally exchanged recriminations. Whereas in August, 1951, Clarence Eyer felt pleased by the ascension of Hassam al Hakim to power, a month later he reported that the new government was backsliding "into the routine of do nothing," and "graft." In turn Syrian officials objected to labor policies of the Foundation. Increasingly, the Foundation served as a scapegoat for Arab hostility toward American government policies. Nevertheless, in March, 1952, when the Syrian government declined to sign a new Point Four contract, and foreign organizations generally were banned from operating in Syria, the Foundation was permitted to continue its operation. The loss of Point Four funds was offset by grants from the Ford Foundation that permitted continuation of the demonstrations on a reduced scale. In 1956 relations between Syria and the United States deteriorated further as the Suez crisis compounded the earlier Arab-Israeli conflict, and all Americans were or-

[37] Technical Cooperation Administration, "Point Four Agreements with Near East Foundation For Rural Programs in Iran and Syria," Press Release, May 3, 1951, in NEF, *Docket*, May 24, 1951, 25.
[38] H. Allen, "Report," 1949, 9–11.

dered to leave Syria. When the Foundation withdrew, it turned over its projects to the Syrian government. Although it had not succeeded in training a Syrian to direct the agricultural extension work, it had trained a native home welfare worker who might, with moderate support from the Syrian government, continue the demonstration at a high level of competence. As experience had indicated in the Ottoman Empire, in Albania, and in Bulgaria, a hostile political atmosphere soon spoiled prospects for fruitful work.[39]

· IV ·

In contrast to its difficulties in Syria and Lebanon, the Foundation made fine progress in establishing new pilot demonstrations in Iran. Notwithstanding interruptions occasioned by the temporary seizure of Tabriz in 1946 by the Soviet Union, an agreement was completed with the Iranian government in June, 1946, defining the conditions under which the Foundation would operate. A demonstration area was organized in the Veramin district, some twenty-five miles southwest of Tehran. Under the terms of the contract the Foundation was accorded a thirty-acre tract on which to conduct experiments, meeting rooms in three villages in the district, and office space. In return the Foundation agreed to provide agricultural instruction for village boys in the fifth and sixth grades, to organize schools in three villages, and to conduct experimental projects in raising sheep, poultry, and cattle and in the use of fertilizers and mechanized farm equipment.[40]

The district was neither more advanced nor more depressed than many other districts of Iran. Of the 116 people in Veramin, ninety-two had malaria and ten or twelve had trachoma. The community drank and bathed in the "jube," the ditch carrying water to the village. Only the village chief and three others could write their names. In good years the villagers raised a total of 1,200 bushels of wheat on 180 acres, half of which went to the landowner as rent; another third went for the hire of oxen. No one raised vegetables; only a few raised chickens.[41]

Dr. Lyle Hayden, the project director, while employing the general approach which Harold Allen had developed in Macedonia, made some distinctive modifications. As Iran was arid, Hayden experimented with drilled wells as a means of obtaining sufficient water to permit an expansion of tillable land. As the first wells produced enough water to double the

[39] "Syria, Eyer Reports," Sept. 13, 1951; *ibid.*, Mar., 1952.
[40] H. Allen, "Report," 1946, 1–4; L. Archer, "Report," 1947–48, Foreword, 4; also see J. B. Badeau, "Programmes of Rural Development in Iran," *Yearbook of Education*, 1954, 179–183.
[41] Morley Cassidy, in Newark (N.J.) *Evening News*, June 20, 1951.

area under cultivation, Hayden experimented with various types of ditches and techniques of irrigation to find the most efficient.[42]

Because of the nearly universal illiteracy, the Foundation, in cooperation with the Iranian Ministry of Education, for the first time undertook to organize an elementary school system in the villages it served. After a one-year experiment in operating schools, the Ministry of Education agreed to subsidize ten schools for the district, all to be supervised by the Foundation. Year-by-year the number of schools was increased until by 1949 the district had eighteen schools and thirty-one teachers. The schools taught not only the Iranian equivalent of the three R's, but they acquainted the children with new ideas about sanitation and agriculture. The Foundation sanitarian spoke to the children; their teachers guided them in planting a school garden. Playgrounds were provided for the schools, and Western-type recreation was introduced. Although Iranian schools had generally terminated with the fourth grade, the Foundation succeeded in introducing a fifth grade to some of its schools and a sixth grade in one. Women teachers were engaged as a means of attracting girl pupils, who traditionally were not educated in Iran. [43]

Since the educational base was fragile, the Foundation found it necessary to organize and operate a teacher-training school to produce adequate rural teachers. The initial program was undertaken with two dozen boys between the ages of eighteen and twenty who were given a one-year course. The student teachers spent part of their time in the fields under the direction of the Foundation's agriculturist and part of their time in practice-teaching in a three-room, six grade school of the Veramin district. Pleased with the first year's work, the Ministry of Education in 1950 authorized the expansion of the program.[44]

Until 1951 the Foundation was hard put to provide the funds required to operate its program on the scale the opportunities permitted. Point Four funds provided the means. An initial grant of fifty thousand dollars permitted the Foundation to employ a variety of American specialists— four agriculturists, two sanitarians, a teacher, and a home economist— whose major responsibility was to provide on-the-job training for the Iranian nationals who worked with them. A second Point Four contract in 1950 permitted expansion of the demonstration area from thirty-five to 135 villages.[45]

Point Four funds also permitted the Foundation to undertake an ever-widening variety of projects. As its experimental tracts provided data on the types of plants best suited to Iranian conditions, the Foundation began

---

[42] H. Allen, "Reports," 1947, 43.
[43] *Ibid.*, 45–46.
[44] "Annual Report, Iranian Area," in NEF, *Docket*, Oct. 20, 1949, 55.
[45] H. Allen, "Report," in *ibid.*, Apr. 13, 1950, 13.

to produce high test seeds for its own use and for the Iranian Ministry of Agriculture. In the course of its work it tested the efficacy of a variety of plows, finally settling on a moldboard plow suitable for use with ox teams. Much time was devoted to improving the quality of Iranian poultry flocks. The Foundation imported day-old chicks and raised them until they matured, whereupon the pullets and cockerels were exchanged for native birds. However, to assure that these birds would thrive under native management, the Foundation taught the Iranian peasant the importance of proper feeding, sanitation, and housing. Inexpensive feeding and watering equipment were demonstrated, as were model poultry houses. Much time was devoted to devising an adequate, inexpensive feed, for the carefully balanced mashes used in the United States were too expensive for the Iranian. Likewise Foundation agriculturists found it necessary to modify American-built incubators in order to provide proper moisture control.[46]

Much thought was given to the advantages and disadvantages of powered equipment. For the purpose of spraying crops against insect pests and fungus infections, ground powered equipment proved destructive to grain crops and was difficult to operate in irrigation-ditched fields. Although aerial spraying was effective and feasible, hand spraying was preferable. The hand sprayer entailed a smaller initial cost, required a minimum of maintenance, required the least training, and permitted the peasant to participate in saving his own crop. After testing both the gasoline tractor and combine, the Foundation recommended against their widespread adoption. The combine proved to be of limited utility, for it tore up irrigation ditches and could not chop up the straw that the natives used for brickmaking. Thus it proved to be a costly machine that, in terms of the Iranian economy, saved neither time nor labor. Instead the Foundation introduced a light-weight wire cradle for harvesting grain crops. To speed up the winnowing of the grain, Foundation personnel devised a fanning mill that could be fabricated by village craftsmen.[47]

Efforts to improve sanitary conditions in rural Iran were more ambitious than in Greece. Because drinking water used by Iranian villagers arrived via irrigation ditches in an uncertain state of purity, it was necessary to design an inexpensive filter to purify it. Eventually the Foundation encouraged villagers to band together and lay pipes to carry the purified water and to provide at least one water outlet for each block. As in Greece, a bored-hole latrine covered by a concrete slab was urged as a substitute for the omnipresent open-pit latrine. Because of its sluggish

[46] "Iran, Agricultural Reports," Feb., 1952; "Iran, Koch Reports," Apr. and May, 1951; "Iran, Spaulding, Agricultural Reports," Apr., 1952.
[47] "Iran, Spaulding, Special Reports, Sen Control," 1952; "Noe's Reports, Annual Report," July, 1950–June, 1951; "Iran Reports," July-Aug., 1950; ibid., Apr., 1950.

jubes and irrigation ditches, Iran had a high incidence of malaria. Foundation sanitarians organized inhabitants of thirty-one villages in 1951 and some three hundred villages a year later to straighten and clean the ditches as well as to assist in spraying with DDT. Finally, the Foundation organized a training program for sanitarians in its demonstration area. After its first year of operation, this program was taken over by the Iranian government.[48]

After Shah Mohammed Reza Pahlavi announced on January 27, 1951, his "heartfelt desire" that the arable lands which he had inherited from his father "should pass into the ownership of the farmers of each locality themselves," the Foundation became an important instrumentality for preparing the peasant to assume the responsibilities that land ownership would impose. The Shah, reputedly the largest landowner in Iran, possessed more than 2,100 villages with a population of 300,000. The plan as first announced called for the transfer of ownership of land to three thousand families per year over a twenty year period. As a means of facilitating the land transfers in September, 1952, the Iranian government and Point Four authorities organized an Agricultural Bank. With the special assistance of Ford Foundation representatives, a program for providing rural credit was established, and personnel were trained to direct the work. A Ford Foundation grant made available a credit fund of $100,000 which Iran's Agricultural Bank was required to match with $200,000. Next, the government arranged to provide agricultural extension workers supported out of tax income to work with the new land owners.[49]

The first land transfers occurred in the Veramin district where the Foundation conducted its demonstrations. A grant from the Ford Foundation permitted the Near East Foundation to employ the Veramin district as a training center for the extension workers who would go into other areas as more and more land was released to peasant operators. This training program itself was lengthened to two years, and the facilities were expanded to accommodate two hundred students. Inevitably, this rapid expansion was at the expense of selectivity in recruitment of Iranian personnel. Many of the newly trained teachers declined to live in the "sticks," while others disdained working with peasants or demonstrating manual skills.[50]

The Foundation also promoted the development of rural cooperatives. Although Point Four authorities established the first such cooperative in Iran, the responsibility for nurturing the cooperative movement was

48 H. Allen, "Annual Report," Dec., 1952, 24; "Iran, Health Reports: Jon Ali Returns to the Village," 1951; "Iran, Sanitation Reports," Mar., 1952.

49 Shah Mohammed Reza Pahlavi quoted in E. R. Fryer to E. C. Miller, July 2, 1952, in NEF, *Minutes*, July 10, 1952; "Point Four Aid to Iran," *U. S. Dept. of State Bulletin*, XXVII (Oct. 6, 1952), 535–537.

50 H. Allen, "Report," Oct., 1952, 4.

shortly assigned to the Foundation. From the start the cooperatives functioned at several levels simultaneously. Arrangements were made for the cooperative marketing of cotton and for merchandizing consumer goods. A farm machinery cooperative was organized to permit Iranian farmers to enjoy the use of laborsaving equipment where practicable. A final venture was a cooperative feed mill.[51]

Near East Foundation's work in Iran exhibited a sure skill, reflecting lessons learned in other areas in earlier years. The Foundation entered upon its work as a partner of the Iranian government, providing technical and administrative expertise not locally available. As in Greece it focused on pilot demonstrations that, in the first phase, experimented with ways of rousing a demoralized, apathetic peasantry. Having gained an entrée, Foundation agriculturists, home economists, and sanitarians sought to demonstrate within a limited area the transformations that were possible: better crop yields, improved health, and higher planes of living. Finally, it used the demonstration area as a training ground for native leaders who, sponsored by indigenous organizations, would spread the work to all areas of their nation.

The success of the Foundation rested on the soundness of its assumptions and the integrity with which it executed its work. Expert, outside advisors seemed essential. As experts they had a breadth of knowledge and skills; as outsiders they enjoyed a degree of prestige not shared by natives; above all, they were not trapped by the desperate apathy that forms an essential part of the world view of tradition-ridden societies. While confident that it knew better than the natives what must be done, the Foundation was wise enough to know that any changes, to be enduring, must be sustained by the local citizenry. It directed its energies through native technicians. The American personnel invariably were the resource men, the prompters, the expediters, but they stayed discreetly in the background. In many respects the Foundation's role required as much emphasis upon the mobilization of community energies as upon the dissemination of American concepts of agriculture, home management, public health, or recreation. Finally, the success of the program depended upon the willingness of the project leaders to "make haste slowly." The pressure for change was gentle, but persistent. This approach permitted the Americans to think out clearly their priorities and to ponder the consequences of the changes they espoused. In the end the Foundation achieved its goals, and the Iranians had a more abundant life, retaining their self-respect in the process. The work of the Foundation was not accompanied by a flight of natives from their homeland, the result of some of the educational work sponsored by the missionary societies in the late nineteenth century.

[51] William A. Fuller, Jr., "The Iran Program of Near East Foundation, As Presented by Excerpts From Overseas Reports," 1955–1956, 36–45.

· V ·

Financing the Foundation's programs proved to be a major problem in the postwar years. The National War Fund, from which the Foundation received a large part of its income during the war, conducted its last drive in the fall of 1945. Thrown back on its own resources, the Foundation watched its income drop from a wartime high of $400,000 to just under $250,000. Although this latter sum was double the income of the depression years, it was less than the organization needed to accept the challenges of the postwar Middle East. Relatively mild inflation in the United States and severe inflation abroad decreased the real value of the dollar income. An effort to offset these losses by trading in gold and profiting from the differences in exchange rates proved disappointing, as did the employment of a professional fund-raiser. In the mind of Foundation officials, the greatest difficulty came from a widely held view that private aid had become unnecessary because of the growing foreign aid programs underwritten by Congress. To contradict such impressions, the Foundation solicited statements by responsible American officials. Loy Henderson, then ambassador to Iran, decried the "unfortunate misconceptions" that private philanthropy was outmoded, and he publicly attested that the Foundation was an agency whose "experience and reputation . . . are priceless assets which, if lost, could not be replaced." The efficacy of such statements was limited, particularly as President Truman's "bold new program," Point Four, projected the Federal government into the financing and operation of technical assistance programs.[52]

During the 1950's the Foundation, like the independent colleges, found economic salvation in securing financial grants from one or another of the endowed foundations or from the Federal government. For the first time American firms operating in the Near East—Trans-Arabian Pipe Line and the Standard Oil Company of New Jersey—made modest gifts. In 1951 a series of contracts for work in Iran and Syria were signed with Point Four authorities. These contracts, ranging in size from fifty thousand dollars to $482,000, permitted the Foundation to expand its work ten-fold in Iran, while smaller contracts covering Syria permitted a three-fold expansion of activities there.[53]

[52] See Robert L. Daniel, "From Relief to Technical Assistance in the Near East," Ph.D. dissertation, University of Wisconsin, 1953, 268–271, 311–315; "Treasurer's Report," in NEF, *Docket*, Jan. 22, 1948, 7–8; NEF, *Minutes*, Apr. 15, 1948, 2; C. I. Crowther, "Memorandum Re: Overseas Area Expenditures," May 7, 1947, in NEF, *Docket*, June 12, 1947, 31–32; E. C. Miller, "Report," in *ibid.*, Oct. 9, 1947, 2; *ibid.*, June 12, 1947, 3; Loy Henderson quoted in *ibid.*, Jan. 22, 1948, 47.

[53] Trans-Arabian Pipeline Co. gave $10,000, "Treasurer's Report," in *ibid.*, Dec. 17,

The tie with the Federal government brought some limitations, but generally the relationship proved fruitful. First, and most obviously, Federal funds permitted the conduct of programs that could not otherwise have been undertaken. The Foundation lacked the requisite income; the government lacked the experienced staff. Subsidies from Point Four were large enough to inaugurate operational agricultural extension systems in Syria and Iran rather than limiting the Foundation to its pilot demonstrations. Negatively, dependence upon the Federal largess partially destroyed the political innocence of the Foundation. This was forcefully illustrated in Syria where the Syrian government, upon taking offense at United States foreign policy, declined any American government foreign aid. Ultimately Syrian objections to American policies led to the exclusion of all American organizations and the liquidation of the Foundation's projects there.[54]

Generally the Foundation preserved its independence in spite of its reliance on government and foundation funds. Whereas in the early 1930's the Foundation raised all of its funds from private contributors, during the 1950's only one-sixth of its income came from the general public. Edward Miller, the Executive Secretary of the Foundation, stated the problem: "We are still desperately in need of private support and we devote much energy and time to this very difficult effort. We cannot survive as a private agency without the voluntary gifts we receive. . . ."[55] In a sense the problem proved to be hypothetical. The record of the 1950's and 1960's indicated that the two could live side-by-side.

1951, 2; Standard Oil Co. gave £5,000 Syrian ($2,293.57), NEF, *Minutes,* May 24, 1951, 2; "Treasurer's Report," NEF, *Docket,* May 24, 1951, 3; NEF, *Minutes,* Mar. 17, 1952, 4; NEF Program Committee, "Minutes," Oct. 11, 1951.

[54] *Ibid.,* Mar. 5, 1952; NEF, *Minutes,* May 17, 1952, 3; "Treasurer's Report," in NEF, *Docket,* Oct. 16, 1952, 6.

[55] E. C. Miller, "Report," *ibid.,* 3.

CHAPTER

XII

Retrospect and Prospect

As AMERICAN philanthropy in the Near East approaches its sesquicentennial, it is in a state of tranformation. Improvement of the lot of the Near Easterner, which was an incidental activity of the early nineteenth-century mission, has become the explicit objective of the twentieth-century philanthropist. In this interval philanthropy has become systematized and its practitioners professionalized. Financial support, which initially came from innumerable anonymous donors to missionary societies, now derives from a variety of sources in which the handsome gifts of business firms, endowed foundations, and governmental agencies predominate. Much as the business world has been transformed from a private to a mixed economy, so philanthropy has acquired a mixed character in which private agencies often contract with the United States government to manage overseas projects on a scale which private philanthropy alone could never afford. Finally, overseas philanthropy has become an accepted instrument of foreign policy. Whether the opportunities for increased service will be nullified by the intrusion of domestic and cold-war politics into philanthropy remains to be seen. As philanthropy in the Near East continues to evolve, a retrospect of various aspects of private philanthropy overseas seems in order.

· I ·

A major characteristic of American philanthropy in the Near East has been the active role and continuing influence of religious societies. Prior to 1860 American philanthropy in the Near East was largely the prerogative of the missionary. While church groups and individual clergymen were leaders in domestic philanthropy before 1860, philanthropy at home had a secular aspect that was entirely lacking in the Near East. Businessmen like Stephen Girard, Arthur and Lewis Tappan, and Amos Lawrence who made notable benefactions in the United States made no move to challenge the missionary's role as philanthropist in the Near East.

The handful of such businessmen as Christopher Robert and the Dodges, who began to support philanthropies in the Near East in the 1860's, had been affiliated with mission boards working in the Near East. But no great fortunes such as those of George Peabody or John F. Slater were pledged to the support of American enterprise in the Levant before 1900. Although Andrew Carnegie wrote of the disgrace of dying rich and gave generously to the cause of philanthropy at home, no project in the Near East enjoyed a part in sparing him from disgrace. John D. Rockefeller, Sr., who gave some aid to the Woman's College before 1914, found his chief outlet in China. Largely by neglect or default, philanthropy in the Near East remained closely allied to the missionary movement until World War I. Indeed, Near East Foundation, an avowedly secular organization, had as its founding officers the Reverend James L. Barton and Cleveland Hoadley Dodge, men whose interest in the Near East derived from earlier church-related philanthropies.

Another characteristic of philanthropy in the Near East was that its range of activities was decidedly narrower than that of philanthropy in the United States. In large measure this may be attributed to the fact that the missionary movement itself was a manifestation of a brand of American philanthropy of the period 1810–50 which aimed at moral and social reform. The missionary as philanthropist was largely indifferent to the other brand of American philanthropy which was preoccupied with relieving human misery. As a result the missionary satisfied his philanthropic impulse in the sponsorship of schools, presses, and medical doctors. For the same reasons the missionary philanthropists during the nineteenth century eschewed the library, the savings bank, the life insurance society, the alms house, the children's aid society, and the asylum for the insane, although these were popular expressions of philanthropy at home.

This dichotomy between the kinds of American philanthropic projects at home and in the Near East continued unabated between 1860 and the end of World War I. Philanthropy in the United States became concerned with preventing social ills that arose from disease, pauperism, ignorance, and crime. Increasingly it developed a discipline and became professionalized. But transmission of these concerns and approaches to the Near East lagged behind. Missionaries operated orphanages temporarily in times of crises; their hospitals were modest compared to those founded by philanthropists in the United States. While training for the deaf and blind was attempted abroad, its start lagged behind the beginning made at home, and it was not a sustained effort. Although the Syrian Protestant College began in the 1870's to provide specialized training in medicine and related fields, not until the turn of the century were the first tentative efforts made to train engineers or businessmen.

To overemphasize the narrow range of the American philanthropic enterprises minimizes the most significant characteristic of the Near East philanthropic efforts, which was that of developing native leadership. While the Near East Relief in the late 1920's and the Near East Foundation thereafter deserve full credit for realizing the principle that philanthropy should help the recipient to help himself, the officers of the American Board and Samuel Gridley Howe anticipated this concept by a century. From the start of its overseas work the American Board made clear that its objective was to stimulate changes within the native society that would be carried on under native leaders. David Greene's "The Promotion of Intellectual Cultivation and the Arts of Civilized Life in Connection with Christian Missions," [1] written in 1842, warned that the casual contacts of economic intercourse between the cultivated nations and the unenlightened communities of the earth would not effectively elevate the intellectual and social condition of the latter. Not only was such a technique slow, but its tardiness brought a multitude of corrupting influences with it. The proper approach, Greene implied, was to deliberately teach natives how to care for themselves; the Christian philanthropist must help them learn to use agricultural tools, to construct comfortable dwellings, to make decent clothes, and to supply their own wants while living in permanent settlements. This position was reaffirmed forcefully and explicitly by the Prudential Committee and other spokesmen for the American Board in post Civil War years.[2]

Not only did the American Board talk about training leadership, but it had a good measure of success in implementing its ideas, as did the independent colleges. Although the missionaries failed in their effort to reform

[1] ABCFM, *Annual Report*, 1842, 69–75.
[2] Prudential Committee, "Memorandum: For the Missions in the Turkish Empire, and Recommendations, Apr. 1881," *ibid.*, 1882, lxv–lxxvi; A. L. Chapin and C. M. Mead, "Report of the Special Committee," *ibid.*, 1883, xxxii–xliii; N. G. Clark, "Higher Christian Education as Related to Foreign Missionary Work," *ibid.*, 1890, xxxii–xxxvi.

the Orthodox Church, the Protestant church they created was an indigenous institution, and most of the elementary schools that the missionaries founded were taught by native teachers in buildings provided by native congregations. Graduates of the independent colleges quickly took positions of responsibility in the economic, political, and intellectual life of the Near East.

The undertakings of the American philanthropists in the Near East were characteristically imitative. Certainly the Christian philanthropist sought only to introduce elements of American culture with which he was familiar. At the same time the missionary was often up-to-date in his selection of institutions and practices. Thus coeducation at the elementary level was employed in the Near East from the start, while the separate secondary schools for boys and girls had their counterparts in America. When the Lancastrian school was fashionable in America, it was employed in the Near East; when graded schools were introduced in America, they were tried out in Turkey, Syria, and Persia. The growing interest in scientific medicine that produced The Johns Hopkins Medical School, brought a quickening of medical work in the Near East. But to argue that the nineteenth-century philanthropist in the Near East was ever ready to adopt the newest innovation would be fallacious, as witness George Washburn's unwillingness to make use of the elective system or his fear of promoting programs in business education. Not until the 1920's were American philanthropists in the Near East committed to seeking out vigorously the latest practice and the most recent innovation for possible introduction into the Near East.

For the most part, the philanthropists in the Levant exhibited a fine sense of selectivity in the choice of projects. Because funds were in short supply, the course of wisdom dictated a concentration on activities that, if successful, would transform the character of the native community, enabling it to provide better for its own needs. The costly task of alleviating poverty was left to native communities except in cases of extraordinary disaster, when the Americans dispensed alms until the native society recovered from the first shock and could care for its own.

American philanthropy owed much of its success to the persistence of the philanthropists. The missionary experience indicated that significant cultural or technical changes occur over a time span measured in years and decades. When war and disease forced abandonment of mission posts, the faint-hearted, the ill, the aged, and the dead were replaced, and work resumed. Behind the tenaciousness of the missionary lay a sense of dedication arising from religious commitment. He willingly accepted a subsistence income, lived in isolation from fellow countrymen, risked violence at the hands of fanatics, and continued the good fight in the face of reverses, hostility, and indifference. This pattern, moreover, was duplicated simultaneously in a dozen centers from the Mediterranean to the Caspian Sea.

This capacity to remain at a task over an extended period of time continued to be an important factor in the conduct of the independent colleges and the Near East Foundation. The independent colleges relied heavily on a few career teachers supplemented by larger numbers of short-term appointees. Of even greater importance to the colleges was the stubborn stick-to-itiveness of the various presidents, whose personal commitment and drive enabled their schools to survive official indifference and opposition on one hand and inadequate funds on the other. Likewise the long tenure of overseas directors, as well as that of administrators at home, gave the Near East Foundation stability.

There were omissions as well as achievements. For all the gains resulting from technical assistance, there can be only limited or temporary improvement in the lot of rural peoples until land is redivided into units capable of providing far higher levels of income to the man who tills it. Philanthropic organizations long shied away from the promotion of land reform. And for good reasons. Easily as the outsider may diagnose the ills and prescribe the solutions to basic problems, he is impotent to act. Lacking the sovereign power, he cannot initiate land reform unilaterally. Such reform, threatening the vested interests of the native power elite, is revolutionary. Inevitably the philanthropist has had to be circumspect in suggesting it, lest by offending he lose his opportunity to do anything at all. At most he can urge reform privately and stand ready to help when the local government of its own accord agrees to undertake land reform. To this extent the success of the philanthropist rests on the willingness of the recipient to embrace change. Near East Foundation's greatest opportunity lies in its programs to make Iranian land reform successful.

Secondly, philanthropists have been slow to provide technical aid to business, industry, and government. The need for more efficient methods in record-keeping and personnel management, particularly among small businesses and local governments, has long been recognized. But one must confess that at home we have never developed a counterpart of the agricultural extension agent to convey new ideas and techniques to the main-street merchant, the factory manager, or the city hall. The entrepreneur or manager of a small establishment is very much the individualist, often with unique problems. His whole outlook regards his business as a personal affair and any suggestions are viewed as an invasion of privacy.

Finally, Americans in the Near East long experienced difficulty in working among the Jews. Missionaries had been unsuccessful in making lasting contacts either in Palestine or in the cities of Ottoman Turkey. The independent colleges proved most appealing to Christians. After Jews began pouring into Palestine following World War I, the hostility of

Arab populations made it virtually impossible for an agency to work amicably with both Arabs and Jews. American organizations, chiefly Jewish, ultimately undertook work among Jews. Such enterprises arose independently of the century of American philanthropy that preceded them, and at most they had tangential contacts with the American organizations working in nearby Syria and Lebanon. Their work was diverse in scope, conducted on broad lines, and was vital in its impact, but this is a story in itself. The goodwill of the philanthropist cannot invariably dissolve the racial, ethnic, and religious prejudices of others.[3]

· II ·

Inasmuch as American philanthropists were frequently concerned with changing the traditional culture, the degree to which American activities contributed to social readjustments or maladjustments warrants special attention. Change is usually disconcerting, for it alters the relationships within the existing order as benefits accrue unevenly to various groups and individuals. In one instance a hitherto unimportant group is catapulted to influence, while in the next the disparity between groups is accentuated. Inevitably, in a rapidly changing society some members become estranged from it.

In assessing the American performance one must keep in mind that a multiplicity of forces acted to alter the character of the Near East: reforming rulers from Selim III to Mustapha Kemal; army officers and literary men; officious English ambassadors and visiting technical advisers; the steamship and the telegraph. Some of these pressures began before the arrival of the Americans, and they continued independently alongside them. The American influence was one among many contributing to reform. The efforts of American philanthropists, then, are to be measured as they added to or reduced social tensions in the Near East.

As a philanthropist, Samuel Gridley Howe was surprisingly modern. Howe, as a perceptive outsider, identified changes in the native environment that, if realized, could contribute to a more productive life for members of the community. At Aegina, Megara, and Hexamilion he mobilized otherwise despairing, destitute refugees into an organized force for effecting specific reforms. Tied as he was to an *ad hoc* relief committee, Howe was unable to fashion a continuing organization.

The missionary was often compromised by the divergent requirements of his role as evangelist and as philanthropist. As evangelist, he sought to effect changes within the framework of the existing ecclesiastical bodies,

[3] Merle Curti, *American Philanthropy Abroad: A History* (New Brunswick: Rutgers University Press, 1963), 361–390.

but in practice the changes he championed provoked militant opposition from the leaders of the traditional churches. To become a Protestant, a native risked his livelihood, bodily harm, and imprisonment. As a result, during the heyday of missionary philanthropy, the missionaries were restricted in their contacts to members of the Protestant community.

In his philanthropic character the missionary was less disturbing. Cyrus Hamlin at Bebek stands out for his imaginative, energetic measures to enable his Protestant students to make the best of their limited prospects in Ottoman Turkey. But missionary educators were perennially concerned because many students who came from the provincial villages were reluctant to return home and provide enlightened leadership at the grass roots. The school often aroused aspirations and trained capabilities beyond the point that the student could find fulfillment in the Near East. Christians emigrated following the 1860 disturbances. Within a few years Syrian colonies existed in Argentina, Brazil, Mexico, the United States, Australia, and Egypt. The Lebanese also migrated; in time, as many lived outside the country as within it. Late in the nineteenth century the Armenians joined the exodus from Ottoman Turkey. Immediately prior to World War I the "American fever" became epidemic. William Shedd, commenting on the situation at Urumia, Persia, in 1902, illustrated the problem concretely. If a man were determined to migrate, he should go to the United States rather than to Russia, Shedd concluded. "Shall we educate young men to go to America? I say, yes, not meaning that we should educate them in order to create the desire, but that it is advantageous to us to have those who do go a longer or shorter time under our instruction." [4] Protestants participated in this migration, but the data does not establish whether they moved in larger or smaller proportions than other Christians.

As early as the 1840's, the Americans took note of the problem of denationalization, and they sought to minimize it. Rufus Anderson pressed hard on the mission schools to use the vernacular rather than English. John Van Ess took the same tack in his school in Iraq a century later. Their object was to avoid alienating students from their countrymen. But other educators—those who believed that the tide of Western ideas and practices was irresistible—were inclined to champion the use of English in order to enable their students to master a range of ideas that were unavailable in their native tongue and to enable them to compete successfully in a modern community. Americans did not control the pressures to which the native was subjected. So far as the missionary philanthropist is concerned, then, one may conclude that the advantages of Western-style education did not suffice to offset the disabilities that accrued from being a Protestant; that the mission school did more to shape the destination of the emigrant than it did to shape the decision to emigrate.

[4] BFMPC, *Annual Report*, 1902, 233.

Students who attended the independent colleges were generally successful in finding a place in the native society. Whether the greater adaptability of the college student reflected the student's store of talent or the results of exposure to a sophisticated curriculum is unmeasurable. Surely both factors operated. Bulgarian graduates of Robert College in the 1860's and the 1870's rose to positions of local and national leadership. In more recent times, as Robert served Turkish students, more than half of the graduates went to the United States for further professional training and then returned to Turkey. At the AUB, although the graduates did not always return to their native towns, they remained in the Near East. There was a strong, active market for AUB graduates.

As agents of reform the mission schools and the independent colleges had a non-directive quality. The schools and colleges exposed their students to a wide spectrum of Western ideas, values, and practices, but they left to the individual student the initiative for adapting the lessons of the classroom to his local environment. In this arrangement of things there might be little or no relationship between the innovations undertaken by graduates and those changes deemed most urgent by the American teachers. Change was haphazard. Certainly, the school left the alumnus as reformer in an exposed, isolated position.

Even though graduates of Robert College or the AUB moved into positions of responsibility, many were alienated men. One source of alienation lay within the structure of the existing system, which resisted assimilation of ideas that came from outside. An AUB graduate in Latakia spoke for many when he posed the dilemma: "How to adapt the environment to myself?" [5] Another source of alienation lay in the closed social structure that afforded minimal opportunities for talented, educated youth not born into the established families. But it is doubtful whether the graduates of the independent colleges were worse off than the graduates of the University of Istanbul, the Université St. Joseph, or the Syrian University.

The triumph of technical assistance work as demonstrated by the Near East Foundation has been its ability to introduce specific changes that the Foundation's studies indicated were desirable and its power to accomplish these changes without offending individual self-esteem. The situation required leaders with scientific knowledge—skilled people who commanded confidence—who were willing to go into the fields and to live in the villages. The Foundation sought the sanction of the church and of historical precedent in support of change. Recognizing that the family, the circle of family friends, and the village community were traditional social units, the NEF sought to win their respect and to employ them as agents of

---

[5] Roderic D. Matthews and Matta Akrawi, *Education in Arab Countries of the Near East* (Washington: American Council on Education, 1949), 559–576, discusses this problem at length.

modern change. It spent its funds not on labor to accomplish the reforms for the natives but on education until the villagers cooperated freely in undertaking reforms themselves. Observing the native doctrine of "slowly, slowly," the Foundation carefully tested its ideas before pressing them on the native community, abandoning some as unworkable and modifying others. The Americans remained in the background as organizers, consultants, and teachers. In a tradition-bound society that has made a virtue of patching up and making-do, the NEF succeeding in making a wide range of carefully selected changes possible and palatable.[6]

· III ·

When American philanthropy in the Near East is compared with philanthropy in other overseas areas, the Americans in the Near East were often in the lead. Although a few missionary schools and presses had been established abroad prior to those in the Near East, the effort in the Levant came early. From the 1820's the Near East was a major center of overseas philanthropy, ranking alongside similar efforts in India and China. Robert College and the Syrian Protestant College were the first American colleges organized abroad. The medical school at Beirut, while enjoying less prestige in the early twentieth century than the Peking Union Medical College, antedated the latter by a quarter century, and from the beginning it has ranked as the major medical school in the Arab world. Near East Relief, which arose alongside the American Relief Administration as an agency for overseas disaster relief, still ranks as a major undertaking in international relief in terms of the numbers served, the breadth of area covered, and its duration. Its successor, the Near East Foundation, by any standard remains the pioneer in the field of overseas technical assistance, antedating by more than a decade the Rockefeller-financed Institute for Inter-American Affairs and by two decades the work of Point Four and the United States technical assistance programs.

As national and international organizations began to sponsor technical assistance programs at the end of World War II, the techniques and principles of operation that they employed were ones that had been hammered out by the Near East Foundation. Among these were the emphasis upon introducing small, concrete, technical changes that would add to income or improve health without unduly disrupting the native economy or value system. Securing the blessing of an Orthodox bishop at the start of the cattle-breeding program has been especially singled out as a brilliant example of linking the traditional with the new. The pilot demonstration "in

[6] Margaret Mead, ed., *Cultural Patterns and Technical Change* (New York: New American Library, 1955), 57–95.

which seeing is believing" minimized the financial requirements, while it maximized the prospects of success, and has been widely imitated by other agencies, private, national, and international. Likewise, the use of native counterparts to create an indigenous institution to continue the work, a key feature of Foundation projects, has become standard procedure. The objective in technical assistance is not to do *for* people, but to work *with* people in helping themselves. The establishment of a contractual relationship with native governments proved a means of avoiding the appearance of competition with local officials and of paving the way for the gradual transference of demonstrations to local agencies and to their expansion to a nationwide operation. Also of importance was the employment of knowledgeable leaders, both American and native, who would share the experience of the villagers.[7]

· IV ·

Inevitably the experience of the private philanthropists invites comparison with that of government missions. As Merle Curti's study of official American technical missions abroad illustrates, the Near East was an early and frequent scene of semi-official and official efforts to introduce technical change.[8] Chief among these were the efforts in the 1830's of Henry Eckford and Foster Rhodes to improve the design of Ottoman ships; the agricultural misssions of James Bolton Davis in the 1840's; the geological survey of J. Lawrence Smith, also in the 1840's; the financial missions to Persia of Morgan Shuster just before World War I and of Arthur Millspaugh shortly afterwards; and the ambitious economic survey of Turkey directed by Major Brehon Somervell and Goldthwaite Dorr in the 1930's.

Despite the varied activities of these missions, certain themes recur. Most notable was an unwillingness on the part of the State Department to assume responsibility, lest the United States become involved in Near Eastern politics. Although Henry Eckford went abroad on his own initiative, asking only a letter of introduction, Secretary of State Van Buren cautioned the American *chargé d'affaires* at Constantinople against letting Eckford's activities compromise American neutrality "in the smallest degree." [9] Again in the case of Dr. J. Lawrence Smith, the Department of

---

[7] See for example, M. L. Wilson in Harold B. Allen, *Rural Reconstruction in Action: Experience in the Near and Middle East* (Ithaca: Cornell University Press, 1953), vii; Mead, *Cultural Patterns and Technical Change*, 183–189; Willard R. Espy, *Bold New Program* (New York: Bantam Books, 1950), 142–143, 193–194.

[8] Merle Curti and Kendall Birr, *Prelude to Point Four: American Technical Missions Overseas, 1838–1938* (Madison: University of Wisconsin Press, 1954), 22–24, 154–155.

[9] M. Van Buren to D. Porter, Apr. 22, 1831, in Instructions, Turkey, Vol. 1, General Records of the Dept. of State, Rec. Group 59, National Archives, Washington, D.C.

State rejected the suggestion of its minister to Turkey, Dabney Carr, that it supplement Davis' work by sending examples of American farm equipment. Rather it limited itself to locating the American technicians.[10] Even though American power had grown markedly by the start of the twentieth century, the Department dissociated itself from any responsibility for the financial missions to Persia other than protecting Shuster and Millspaugh in the rights accorded all American citizens abroad.[11]

A common feature of the government missions was opposition by significant elements within the native society, which generally led to the demise of the mission. Foster Rhodes, who succeeded Eckford, encountered so much jealousy on the part of Turkish officials that he quit his job in disgust to return to the United States.[12] J. Lawrence Smith complained bitterly that his work was hampered by Ottoman bureaucrats who unnecessarily detained him in Constantinople or else surrounded him with a "troop of lazy, ignorant scoundrels" when he traveled.[13] His efforts to open a new coal field were frustrated by the Sultan's mother and some of the great pashas who, as owners of existing mines, objected to competition.[14] The experiences of Morgan Shuster and Arthur Millspaugh provided variations on the theme, for both men encountered opposition from Persian landowners who resisted reforms that would require them to pay taxes and from Persian bureaucrats who took exception to the new standards of efficiency and honesty.[15]

There was substantial evidence in the late nineteenth and early twentieth centuries that official missions often had political overtones. It was apparent that the Persian government hoped to use the Shuster mission as a means of warding off both British and Russian intervention in her internal affairs.[16] There were indications that Persia hoped to use the Millspaugh mission as a lever to secure financial aid in the United States.[17] While not involving the United States government, the Dorr mission foundered when Italian militarism prevented Turkey from putting the recommendations into operation.[18]

Certainly the record of official or semi-official missions prior to 1941 revealed no inherent advantage in government sponsorship. On the other

[10] D. Carr to Sec. of State, June 6, 1847, in Despatches, Turkey, Vol. 10; Carr to J. Buchanan, Oct. 24, 1848, and Dec. 14, 1848, both in *ibid.*, Vol. 11.

[11] Curti and Birr, *Prelude to Point Four*, 76, 168.

[12] David D. Porter, *Memoir of Commodore David Porter of the United States Navy* (Albany: J. Munsell, 1875), 413, implies that Rhodes was sent home.

[13] P. Brown to J. Clayton, Jan. 14, 1850, in Despatches, Turkey, Vol. 11.

[14] Curti and Birr, *Prelude to Point Four*, 24.

[15] *Ibid.*, 77, 170; Arthur C. Millspaugh, *Americans in Persia* (Washington: Brookings Institution, 1946), 23.

[16] W. Morgan Shuster, *The Strangling of Persia* (New York: Century Co., 1912), 332; Curti and Birr, *Prelude to Point Four*, 74.

[17] *Ibid.*, 169.

[18] *Ibid.*, 186.

hand America's relation to the Near East has changed markedly since that date. Currently the United States government exhibits a willingness to make binding commitments in the Near East; likewise natives of the Near East display a new receptiveness to innovation. The experience of American organizations in the Near East has indicated that philanthropy can still become entangled in foreign policy. The American colleges at Istanbul and Beirut have been embarrassed by student demonstrations against the native governments.[19] The experience of the Near East Foundation suggests that the character of Near Eastern nationalism makes technical assistance directed by private organizations more acceptable than aid directly from the United States government.[20] The willingness of the United States Congress to appropriate funds for technical assistance has often been predicated on the argument that it is a device for waging the Cold War, a tactic that embarrasses the recipient.[21] The one clear advantage possessed by government-financed projects is the relatively large sums of money available.

· V ·

In spite of the proliferation after World War II of official United States and international agencies for relief, economic aid, technical assistance, and public health, privately supported American philanthropy in the Near East exhibited much vitality. While the independent colleges and the Near East Foundation remained the principal private agencies of American philanthropy in the Levant, a host of new organizations entered the field: church groups, endowed foundations, and a miscellany of special purpose organizations.

These new organizations, highly specialized and operating small projects in many parts of the world, represented a broadening of philanthropic work. Their specialized interests permitted them to attract a body of contributors and to develop technical competence in their operations. Their limited scope gave them a high degree of mobility, allowing them to initiate programs quickly in areas where need was matched by the receptivity of local authorities. The emphasis upon technical expertise offered on an international scale allowed self-conscious, nationalistic governments to accept their services without sacrificing self-respect. Individually the impact of these organizations was limited, but collectively, as the number of groups and the variety of services increased, their potential became

---

[19] New York *Times*, Mar. 28, 1954; May 11, 1955; May 24, 1960.

[20] *Supra*, p. 263.

[21] For example see, Harry S Truman, "Inaugural Address of the President," *U. S. Department of State Bulletin*, XX (1949), 123–126; "Point Four: An Investment in Peace," *ibid.*, xxiii (1950), 93.

significant. These organizations secured a foothold in the late 1940's and the 1950's. Beyond 1960 they were sufficiently numerous and well established to constitute a third force in American philanthropy in the Near East, ranking alongside the independent colleges and the Near East Foundation.

In the postwar years, 1945–60, missionary societies, although no longer the major agency of philanthropy, continued to function. The American Board, reorganized as the United Church Board for World Ministries, continued to operate four secondary schools and a single hospital in Turkey, the latter giving residency training to Turkish doctors and a training course for nurses' aides. The American mission press at Istanbul specialized in the publication of children's books and the production of reading materials for newly literate adults. With the support of a Ford Foundation grant, it revised the Redhouse English-Turkish Dictionary.[22]

Other church organizations entered the area, particularly in Israel, Jordan, and Lebanon, to undertake projects directed at the refugees created by the Israeli-Arab war. Catholic Relief Services, an agency of the National Catholic Welfare Conference, while organized primarily for the administration of relief, conducted educational and vocational training programs both for teachers and for handicapped and abandoned children. In the field of health it employed a mobile clinic in remote refugee camps of Jordan. Church World Service, an agency of the National Council of Churches of Christ, conducted relief work, but it also employed loan programs to assist refugees and non-refugees alike to develop small businesses and to promote resettlement in rural areas. Relief work by Protestant groups was coordinated by the Near East Christian Council's committee on relief, enabling smaller church bodies like the Mennonite Central Committee and the Unitarian-Universalist Association to contribute individual specialists or to sponsor single educational or medical projects that in the aggregate formed part of a balanced whole.

Another measure of the vitality of American philanthropy was the appearance of newly organized groups, conducting limited but widely differing programs. Emergency relief in Arab countries was provided by the American Middle East Relief. Organized in 1948 with Beirut as the principal distribution center, its energies were focused on the distribution of food, clothing, blankets, and medical supplies to refugees. Reflecting the current interest in technical assistance, the organization joined forces with the Universalist Service Committee in several projects in the field of vocational and medical training.

One of the largest of the new organizations that began work in the

[22] Wayland Zwayer, ed., *American Voluntary and Non-Profit Agencies in Technical Assistance Abroad: A Summary* (American Council of Voluntary Agencies For Foreign Service, Inc., Oct., 1961), *passim.*

Near East was CARE, now called Cooperative for American Relief Everywhere, organized in 1945 to undertake relief, rehabilitation, and economic assistance at the "grass roots." Rather than attempt mass feeding, CARE conducted pilot projects and secured equipment for the new training programs started by Near Eastern governments. In Iran it provided plows, physical education equipment, and sewing and knitting materials needed by Iran's agricultural extension and home demonstration personnel, as well as a wide variety of equipment needed for vocational and medical training programs being started by the Iranian government. In Turkey CARE's giving took the form of providing an incubator for a pediatric ward and boilers required in processing blood plasma.

Two organizations, the American Friends of the Middle East and the Institute of International Education, concentrated on student exchange programs. The American Friends of the Middle East, founded in 1951, worked exclusively in Arab countries, devoting most of its energies to programs for advising, placing, and assisting Near Easterners who sought academic or technical training in the United States. The Institute of International Education, which had long included the Near East in its worldwide program, not only assisted Near Easterners in arranging for study in the United States but arranged for visits by American students and specialists to the Near East.

Vocational training programs claimed much attention. The American Organization for Rehabilitation through Training worked with Jews in Iran and Israel, while the American Foundation for the Overseas Blind extended its operations to the Near East after World War II. The latter also trained teaching personnel for schools for the blind in Greece, and it undertook surveys preparatory to initiating training programs for the blind in other countries of the Near East.

Of all the new organizations the one most fully utilizing the principles of technical assistance was the Iran Foundation. Organized in 1948, the Iran Foundation was interested in medical education and research. Its center was Shiraz, where an Iranian philanthropist, Mohammed Namazee, had built a medical center in which Western-trained Iranian doctors and medical students could continue their research and studies. With help from the United States International Cooperation Administration and the Ford Foundation, the Iran Foundation recruited specialists for the Shiraz University Medical School as well as for its School of Nursing and Vocational School.

The organization which did the most to expand the amount and range of philanthropic activities in the Near East was the Ford Foundation. The giant of the endowed foundations, it supplanted the Rockefeller Foundation, which was no longer active in the Near East. Beginning in 1951, the Ford Foundation made available consultants, helped pilot projects that, if successful, could be reproduced with funds from other sources, and aided foreign governments in establishing and strengthening research and training institutions essential for their development. Geographically its programs by 1960 covered a wider area than those of any other private organization in the Near East. Furthermore, its role as a private grant-making agency permitted it to underwrite programs in both Israel and the Arab countries, a most uncommon feat. The Ford Foundation continued to be a major factor in supporting the expansion of the American University of Beirut and in subsidizing Near East Foundation programs. The Ford Foundation also undertook new types of activities. Grants were made to native institutions to promote faculty and curriculum development and, in some instances, to finance new construction and to purchase equipment. Thus in Iran, for example, the University of Shiraz received aid in developing a Faculty of Agriculture, while at the University of Istanbul an Institute of Business Administration was organized in cooperation with Harvard University. Attention was given to the production of reference and textbooks, to problems of currency control and central banking, to appraisals of manpower resources and requirements, and to investment planning. In Iran, Jordan, and Lebanon problems of public administration became subjects for investigation. Thus, aid was given to the Lebanese Association of Political Science for a conference on democracy. More than ever before, American philanthropy in the Near East was concerned with the problems of a modern business, financial, and political society.

Despite the proliferation of activities of other organizations, the range of activities of the independent colleges and of the Near East Foundation was never greater. Both the colleges and the Foundation exhibited an organizational capacity to adjust to new conditions. In particular they were able to recruit successive generations of sponsors and administrators. The prestige which they had acquired through the years stood them in good stead with the governments they sought to aid. The Near East Foundation, in fact, found itself responding to requests for its expertise in directing technical assistance programs by organizing similar work in Ghana and Korea. Some of its technicians assumed leadership roles in the newly organized technical assistance programs of the federal government.

Finally, American philanthropy had overcome the chief restriction of the nineteenth-century Christian philanthropist, the inability to reach the Moslem majority. The secularization of Moslem society reduced Moslem suspicion of the Americans; the Americans, too, scored breakthroughs. The independent colleges, having lost their character as Christian schools gained opportunities to provide a broad range of academic and technical training to Near Eastern students and to offer increasing teaching and research opportunities to native scholars, regardless of religious background. The Near East Foundation with its reliance on technical assistance could and did reach natives of all economic and social levels. Above all, the techniques of technical assistance that it had pioneered proved highly flexible, lending themselves to simple or to complex projects, to both small and large scale operations, and to private, public, or mixed support.

Although political affairs in the Near East, as elsewhere, remained tense in the 1960's, American philanthropy was not only more active than ever before, but it faced the greatest opportunities of its long history.

GLOSSARY OF PLACE NAMES

The transliteration of Near Eastern place names has changed considerably in the period covered by this study. Furthermore, nationalistic regimes have renamed some towns. In the text I have followed the usage of the times, and this table is intended for those who wish the current spelling or name.

Former Name	Present Name	Former Name	Present Name
Adabazar	Adapazari	Malatia	Malatya
Adrianople	Edirne	Marash	Maraş
Aintab	Gaziantep	Marmouret-ul-Aziz	Al 'Aziziya
Alexandretta	Iskenderun	Marsovan	Merzifon
Alexandropol	Leninakan	Mersin	Mersin, also
Angora	Ankara		Icel
Bahrayn	Bahrein	Monastir	Bitolj
Bakka	Bekaa, also Bika	Nicomedia	Izmit, also
Brousa,	Bursa		Izmid
Brusa		Philippopolis	Plovdiv
Caesarea	Kayseri	Salonika	Thessaloniki
Diarbekir	Diyarbekir,	Scutari, Turkey	Üsküdar
	Diarbekr	Sidon	Saida
Der-el-Zor	Deir-ez-Zor	Smyrna	Izmir
Erivan	Yerevan	Syra	Syros
Erzerum	Erzurum	Trebizond	Trabzon
Eski Zagra	Stara Zagora	Urumia	Urmia, also
Hadjin	Göksün		Rizaiyeh,
Harpoot	Harput		Rezaieh
Karahissar	Afyon	Verria	Veroia
Konia	Konya	Zeitoun,	Firnis
Korcha	Korçë	Zeytun	

BIBLIOGRAPHICAL NOTE

As the sources upon which this study of American philanthropy in the Near East is based have been acknowledged paragraph by paragraph, an alphabetized list of them would be of less value than a commentary on the nature and limitations of the records organization by organization.

The Grecian Adventure:

Because of the *ad hoc* nature of American aid to Greece, there is no one neatly organized repository of materials. Edward Mead Earle, "American Interest in the Greek Cause, 1821–1827," *American Historical Review*, XXXIII (Oct., 1927), 44–63, is still useful both for its insights and its bibliographical suggestions. Larger in magnitude and broader in scope is Stephen A. Larrabee, *Hellas Observed: The American Experience of Greece 1775–1865* (New York: New York University Press, 1957).

Of the primary materials relating to the domestic front, the starting point is Edward Everett, "Affairs of Greece," *North American Review*, XVII (Oct., 1823), 389–424, the article which brought the plight of the Greeks to the attention of the American public. The files of *Niles' Weekly Register* carry intermittent reports on the activities of various fund-raising committees. The *Annals of Congress*, particularly for the Seventeenth Congress, report efforts at a political solution to the Greek struggle, but the behind-the-scenes maneuvering is revealed in the papers of Daniel Webster, Henry Clay, John Quincy Adams, and Edward Everett. For this study Daniel Webster, *Writings and Speeches of Daniel Webster* (National Ed., 18 Vols., Boston: Little, Brown & Co., 1903), Henry Clay, *The Works of Henry Clay*, Calvin Colton, ed. (10 Vols., New York: G. P. Putnam's Sons, 1904), and John Quincy Adams, *Memoirs of John Quincy Adams*, Charles F. Adams, ed. (12 Vols., Philadelphia: J. B. Lippincott, 1874–77) proved useful. Paul Revere Frothingham, *Edward Everett: Orator and Statesman* (Boston: Houghton Mifflin, 1925) is shallow.

For the relief work abroad the most important single item is the first volume of Samuel Gridley Howe, *Letters and Journals of Samuel Gridley Howe*, Laura E. Richards, ed. (2 Vols., Boston: Dana Estes & Co., 1906–09), the work of his daughter. Jonathan P. Miller, *The Condition of Greece in 1827 and 1828* (New York: J. & J. Harper, 1828) is by a fellow relief worker. Other eyewitness accounts that are useful are Henry A. V. Post, *A Visit to Greece and Constantinople in the Year 1827-8* (New York: Sleight and Robinson, 1830); George Finlay, *History of the Greek Revolution* (2 Vols., Edinburgh: W. Blackwood & Sons, 1861). [James E. DeKay], *Sketches of Turkey in 1831 and 1832* (New York: J. & J. Harper, 1833) is by a layman well-acquainted with the educational work of William Goodell and H. G. O. Dwight.

Missionary Benevolence:

The basic materials for the entire Near East to 1870 and for Turkey to the present are the American Board Papers, Houghton Library, Cambridge, Massachusetts. These records, while voluminous, are manageable by reason of an index to the general contents of the various series of bound volumes.

ABC 16.7.1. Armenian Mission. 15 Vols. These volumes contain materials relating generally to Turkey prior to 1860 and particularly to work among the Armenians.

ABC 16.8.1. Syrian Mission. 6 Vols. This series is concerned with work in Syria and Lebanon to 1870. Volume 3 treats the Nestorians.

ABC 16.9. European Turkey Mission. 16 Vols. The early volumes contain materials for the first mission in Constantinople. Volume 1 has the letters and journals of William Goodell as well as the letters of H. G. O. Dwight and Eli Smith reporting their exploration of Armenia, Kurdistan, and Persia. The bulk of the series is devoted to materials bearing on activities in Bulgaria and Albania from the 1870's to World War I.

ABC 16.9.3. Western Turkey Mission. 38 Vols. Collected and bound decade by decade, the first volume in each decennial group usually contains annual reports of the mission and its several stations, while the subsequent volumes contain letters from mission personnel organized alphabetically by author.

Generous portions of this manuscript material are found in the *Annual Reports* of the American Board (1810-date). Typically these run to several hundred pages and contain extensive verbatim extracts of the correspondence as well as important policy statements by the Prudential Committee. Much of this material also appears in the monthly *Missionary Herald* which at its peak prior to 1860 was the most widely circulated missionary paper in either the United States or England.

The *Annual Reports* of the Board of Foreign Missions of the Presbyterian Church in the United States of America provided the most useful body of material on the growth of the philanthropic enterprises in Syria, Lebanon, and Persia after 1870. The *Annual Reports* issued in the twentieth century by the American and Presbyterian boards are of less value than those of the previous century. An apparent effort to shorten the reports and at the same time spice them up in the interest of readability has been at the expense of the hard facts upon which the historian must depend.

To the manuscript and printed records of the mission boards must be added a number of memoirs, reminiscences, autobiographies, and biographies of the participants. Much of this material is disappointing, for the questions of pre-eminent interest to the editors, compilers, or authors are not the primary concerns of the secular historian. The teachers and doctors tell precious little about their classrooms or their medical practice. Of greatest value are Henry Harris Jessup, *Fifty-three Years in Syria* (2 Vols., New York: Fleming H. Revell, 1910) based on diaries and thirty letter copy books. Jessup who went to Beirut in 1855 met most of the founders of the Syrian mission, Eli Smith, Simeon Calhoun, and William Goodell, and so reports on these personalities as well. His *The Women of the Arabs, with a Chapter for Children*, Charles S. Robinson and Isaac Riley, eds. (New York: Dodd and Mead, 1873) gives considerable details on early schools for girls. Thomas Laurie, *The Ely Volume; or, The Contributions of Our Foreign Missions to Science and Human Well-Being* (Boston: ABCFM, 1881) systematically surveys missionary contributions to travel literature, meteorology, natural science, archaeology, philology, the press, education, and medicine. Also invaluable is Joseph K. Greene, *Leavening the Levant* (Boston: The Pilgrim Press, 1916) which sketches the work of the mission in Turkey in the last quarter of the nineteenth century. As one-time editor of *Avedaper*, Greene gives valuable data on the operations of the mission press at Constantinople.

Although less revealing than the foregoing, the following can scarcely be ignored. Materials for Malta and Syria include Levi Parsons, *Memoir of Rev. Levi Parsons*, compiled by Daniel O. Morton (Poultney, Vt.: Smith & Shute, 1824); the more informative Pliny Fisk, *Memoir of the Rev. Pliny Fisk*, Alvan Bond, ed. (Boston: Crocker & Brewster, 1828) deals with Syria and Lebanon in the 1820's. Daniel H. Temple, *Life and Letters of Rev. Daniel Temple* (Boston: Congregational Board of Publications, 1855) is good for the mission post at Malta and for the pioneer efforts at printing. Edward W. Hooker, ed., *Memoir of Mrs. Sarah Lanman Smith* (Boston: Perkins & Marvin, 1839) treats a pioneer in the education of girls in Syria. There is no adequate biography of either Homan Hallock or Eli Smith.

For Turkey H. G. O. Dwight, *Christianity Revived in the East* (New York: Baker and Scribner, 1850) recounts the events leading to the creation of a separate Protestant community in Turkey. E. D. G. Prime, *Forty Years in the Turkish Empire; or, Memoirs of Rev. William Goodell* (New York: R. Carter & Bros., 1876) is by the son-in-law of this pioneer missionary educator. William G. Schauffler, *Autobiography of William G. Schauffler For Forty-nine Years a Missionary in the Orient*, ed. by his sons (New York: Anson D. F. Randolph & Co., 1887) relates work with Jews in Constantinople. Cyrus Hamlin, *Among the Turks* (New York: Carter & Bros., 1878) and *My Life and Times* (Boston: Congregational Sunday School and Publishing Society, 1893) recounts the operation of the boarding school at Bebek. George E. White, *Adventuring with Anatolia College* (Grinnell, Iowa: Herald-Register Publishing Co., 1940) is by the president of the school who led it through the painful experiences of World War I and the Turkish War for Independence and relocated it in Greece.

For the Nestorians the most useful accounts are Justin Perkins, *A Residence of Eight Years in Persia Among the Nestorian Christians* (New York: M. W. Dodd, 1843) by the founder of the mission. D[aniel] T. Fiske, *The Cross and the Crown, or Faith Working by Love as Exemplified in the Life of Fidelia Fiske* (Boston: Congregational Sabbath School & Publishing Society, 1868) which details early efforts to operate a girls' boarding school.

Supplementing the correspondence and reports produced by the medical missionaries are a variety of biographies and autobiographies. Brief but informed are two sketches by Lutfi M. Sa'di, "Al-Hakim Cornelius Van Alen Van Dyck (1815–1895)," *Isis*, XXVII (1937), 20–45, and "The Life and Works of George Edward Post (1838–1909)," *Isis*, XXVIII (1938), 385–417. Thomas Laurie, *Dr. Grant and the Mountain Nestorians* (3d ed. revised, Boston: Gould & Lincoln, 1856) tells more of the distractions than of the professional life of this pioneer doctor. Henry Lobdell, *Memoir of Rev. Henry Lobdell, M. D.*, W. S. Tyler, ed. (Boston: American Tract Society, 1859) and George F. Herrick, *An Intense Life: A Sketch of the Life and Work of Andrew T. Pratt, M. D., 1852–1872* (New York: Fleming H. Revell, [1890]) are marginal. Mary Lewis Shedd, *The Measure of a Man: The Life of William Ambrose Shedd: Missionary to Persia* (New York: George H. Doran, 1922) and Clarence D. Ussher, *An American Physician in Turkey* (Boston: Houghton Mifflin, 1917) treat two doctors active in eastern Turkey in the early years of the present century. John G. Wishard, *Reminiscences of a Doctor: A Personal Narrative* (Wooster, Ohio: Collier Publishing Co., 1935) recalls life in Tehran. The most useful study of the professional life of a missionary doctor is Robert Speer, *"The Hakim Sahib" The Foreign Doctor, A Biography of Joseph Plumb Cochran, M. D., of Persia* (New York: Fleming H. Revell, 1911). Also useful is Paul W. Harrison, *Doctor in Arabia* (New York: John Day, 1940).

Charles T. Riggs, "Near East Missionary Biographies," typescript, Istanbul, July 9, 1953, in the Archives of the United Church Board for World Ministries, Boston, an invaluable who's who among missionaries, is compiled by a son of the missionary movement. The library of the United Church Board (successor to the American Board), Boston, Massachusetts, contains items not found in either the Library of Congress or the British Museum. And the latter, incidentally, contains many items by American Board personnel that never found their way into the collections of the Library of Congress. The Presbyterian Mission Library, New York City, likewise has many books and pamphlets not otherwise available.

There are official histories of both the American Board and the Presbyterian Board. William E. Strong, *The Story of the American Board: An Account of the First Hundred Years of the American Board of Commissioners for Foreign Missions* (Boston: The Pilgrim Press, 1910) is satisfactory for the period it covers. Arthur Judson Brown, *One Hundred Years: A History of the Foreign Missionary Work of the Presbyterian Church in the U.S.A.* (New York: Fleming H. Revell, 1936) covers a longer time span; both place the mission work in the Near East in the perspective of denominational efforts in other parts of the world. Rufus Anderson, *History of the Missions of the American Board of Commissioners for Foreign Missions to Oriental Churches* (Boston: Congregational Publishing Society, 1873) is a summary by one of the great mission board executives of the middle nineteenth century. His *Memorial Volume of the First Fifty Years of the ABCFM* (Boston: The Board, 1861) is unexcelled for its account of the evolving administrative structure of the American Board. Julius Richter, *A History of Protestant Missions in the Near East* (New York: Fleming H. Revell, 1910), though not an official account, is particularly sensitive to the political implications of missionary education.

Two particularly fruitful sources of primary materials relating to the missionary enterprises are the Despatches and Instructions of the American State Department, Record Group 59, National Archives, Washington, and the analogous British materials in the archives of the Foreign Office, File 78, Public Record Office, London. These contain comments on the mission enterprises *per se*, accounts of efforts by successive diplomats to promote or protect the mission institutions and personnel, and some correspondence with mission officials. These materials are indispensable for assessing the impact of the philanthropic enterprises on native culture and institutions and the contributions to emerging nationalism.

Independent Colleges:

The official records of Robert College, the Syrian Protestant College (now the American University of Beirut), and the American College for Girls are to be found at the offices of the Near East College Association, New York City. These consist of *Annual Reports* which in the first few years were in manuscript but in later years were generally printed, if not published. For Robert College the reports for 1867, 1868, 1869, and 1871 were drafted by Christopher Robert alone or with William Booth. In most cases the *Reports* were drafted by the college president, or, in his absence, by the acting president or dean. For all the colleges the *Reports* were likely to contain reports by the college deans and treasurers as well.

Most of the early college presidents have left reminiscences or autobiographies. For Robert College these include Cyrus Hamlin, *My Life and Times* (Boston: Congregational Sunday School and Publishing Society, 1893) which tells more of missionary life and Hamlin than of the College, though chapters 13 and 14 contain details not available elsewhere. Most helpful for the years 1875 to 1903 is George Washburn, *Fifty Years in Constantinople and Recollections of Robert College* (Boston: Houghton Mifflin Co., 1909). Caleb Frank Gates, *Not to Me Only* (Princeton: Princeton University Press, 1940) covers the period from 1903 to 1932. Lynn A. Scipio, *My Thirty Years in Turkey* (Rindge, N.H.; Richard R. Smith, 1955) focuses on the Robert College School of Engineering, of which Scipio was dean from 1912 to 1942.

For the nineteenth century history of the Syrian Protestant College there is much material in F. J. Bliss, ed., *The Reminiscences of Daniel Bliss* (New York: Fleming H. Revell, 1920). The editor was the eldest son of the subject. By far the best account of any of the colleges is Stephen B. L. Penrose, Jr., *That They May Have Life: The Story of the American University of Beirut, 1866-1941* (New York: Trustees of the AUB, 1941). Bayard Dodge, "The American University of Beirut; An Introduction to Beirut and the University," mimeographed, Princeton, 1952, is brief and often anecdotal, but it is informed and particularly useful for the period since 1940. For earlier periods it relates the University to the leading social, economic, and political changes of the Levant. A. L. Tibawi, "The Genesis and Early History of the Syrian Protestant College," *Middle East Journal*, XXI (1967–68), 1–15 has details not found in earlier published accounts.

Mary Mills Patrick, *A Bosporus Adventure: Istanbul (Constantinople) Woman's College, 1871–1924* (London: Oxford University Press, 1934) is somewhat more useful than her *Under Five Sultans* (New York: Century Co., 1929), although the latter cannot be ignored. Hester Donaldson Jenkins, *An Educational Ambassador to the Near East: The Story of Mary Mills Patrick and an American College in the Orient* (New York: Fleming H. Revell, 1925) is by a colleague of Miss Patrick. There is still room for a full-length history of the Woman's College.

A variety of other sources make occasional reference to the colleges. Most valuable of these are the Despatches and Instructions in the General Records of the State Department, Record Group 59, in the National Archives which illumine the relations between the colleges and the Turkish government especially relating to property rights and the licensing of doctors. Materials relating to the establishment of the Syrian Protestant College are to be found in the American Board Papers, ABC 16.8.1, Vol. 6. The *Annual Reports* of the American Board and the Presbyterian Board carried reports on the colleges during the 1860's and 1870's. After 1920 developments in these colleges were periodically reported in journals on higher education and international education. The New York *Times* has given spotty, but sympathetic, coverage of the growth and problems of the colleges. Fund-raising drives, grants by the endowed foundations, and changes in administrations have received notice.

Balkan Ventures:

The basic source is the American Board Papers, ABC 16.9, in the Houghton Library, Cambridge, Massachusetts, but as in other areas of the Near East, American activities must be examined in the light of the European power struggle. William Webster Hall, Jr., *Puritans in the Balkans: The American Board Mission in Bulgaria, 1878–1918* (Sofia, 1938) offers a decade by decade account of the mission. Floyd Black, *The American College of Sofia: A Chapter in American-Bulgarian Relations* (Trustees of Sofia-American Schools, Inc., 1958) is by the president of the school, 1926–1942. Chapter 1 is an account of the Samokov Schools in the late nineteenth century; the rest of the work treats Black's administration.

Christo A. Dako, *Albania, The Master Key to the Near East* (Boston: E. L. Grimes, 1919) is particularly useful in relating the role of his in-laws, the Kyriases, in promoting Western education and in stimulating Albanian nationalism. Dako, it should be remembered, was politically ambitious. The role of the controversial C. Telford Erickson is documented in the State Department Numerical File 367.112 Er4, National Archives, Washington. Erickson and his colleagues, P. B. Kennedy and J. H. House, sought to keep Americans abreast of conditions in the Balkans via the columns of the *Missionary Review of the World*, Vol. XXXI–XXXVII (1908–1914).

Development of the Thessaloniki Agricultural and Industrial Institute can be followed in its *Annual Reports*, starting 1907. Earlier contemporary reports are in the American Board Papers, ABC 16.9, Vols. 15 and 16. *A Life for the Balkans: The Story of John Henry House of the American Farm School, Thessaloniki, Greece* (New York: Fleming H. Revell, 1939) fills many voids but it slights the early contributions of E. B. Haskell.

Relief Organizations:

Records of missionary relief work in Syria, Bulgaria, and Turkey are scattered and often incomplete. As the burden of administering relief in Syria in the early 1860's fell on American Board personnel, the most complete accounts are to be found in the American Board Papers, ABC 16.8.1, Vol. 6. But as funds for relief came from England and as that government was concerned with restoring public order in Syria, British diplomatic correspondence in FO 78, Vol. 1513, Public Record Office, London, is indispensable.

The Bulgarian relief efforts of 1876 produced an international response. The scanty reports of the Reverend James Clarke, in whose hands most of the relief work was centered, are in the American Board Papers, ABC 16.9, Vols. 5 and 6. The official English report on the extent of the massacre is in FO 78, Vol. 2463, #964, Public Record Office, London. An American view is in Despatches, Turkey, Vol. 30, #106, in the General Records of the Department of State, Record Group 59, National Archives, Washington. A missionary view, H. O. Dwight and J. F. Clarke, "The Suffering in Bulgaria," Oct. 17, 1876, is in the American Board Papers, ABC 16.9, Vol. 5, #36. Edwin Pears, *Forty Years in Constantinople: The Recollections of Sir Edwin Pears, 1873–1915* (New York: D. Appleton, 1916) is by the resident correspondent of the *Daily News* who passed the first accounts of the massacre on to the British press.

Materials relating to the relief of survivors of the Armenian massacres of the mid-1890's are found in British diplomatic correspondence, FO 78, Vols. 4693 and 4792–4794, Public Record Office, London. These bear chiefly on fund-raising activities, the monies thus collected being disbursed through American Board personnel in Turkey. American Board Papers, ABC 16.9.3, Vols. 18–26 should be consulted, particularly the correspondence of W. W. Peet. Because of the role of Louis Klopsch in raising funds, the files of the *Christian Herald* are useful as are the files of *Outlook* and *Lend a Hand*. A broad view of Klopsch as a philanthropist is in Charles M. Pepper, *Life-Work of Louis Klopsch: Romance of a Modern Knight of Mercy* (New York: The Christian Herald, 1910). Clara Barton's role is recorded in Clara Barton, *The Red Cross* (Washington: American National Red Cross, 1898). J. Rendel Harris and Helen B. Harris, *Letters from the Scenes of the Recent Massacres in Armenia* (New York: Fleming H. Revell, [1897]) is an eye-witness account of the massacres as well as of the relief work. The *Congressional Record*, 54 Cong., 1 Sess., XXVIII, Pt. 1, 108, 959–995, 1000–1016, contains the debate on proposed official American aid. The correspondence of the American Minister to Turkey, Judge Terrell, is vital, especially Despatches, Turkey, Vols. 58–64, in the General Records of the Department of State, Record Group 59, National Archives, Washington.

American missionaries and their friends were often critical of the State Department for the latter's alleged refusal to defend American interests and personnel in Turkey. Everett P. Wheeler, *The Duty of the United States to American Citizens in Turkey* (New York: Fleming H. Revell, 1896); Frederick D. Greene, *The Rule of the Turk, and the Armenian Crisis* (New York: G. P. Putnam's Sons, 1897); Edwin M. Bliss, *Turkey and the Armenian Atrocities* (Philadelphia: Hubbard Pub. Co., 1896); and Cyrus Hamlin, "America's Duty to Americans in Turkey: an Open Letter to the Hon. John Sherman," *North American Review*, CLXIII (Sept., 1896) were all part of a concerted effort to secure a more aggressive American posture in Turkish affairs. The campaign also had the effect of defaming the Turks.

Office records of the various relief organizations of World War I have been destroyed, but copies of many of these records are still extant in scattered places. *Minutes* of the boards of trustees of both the Persian War Relief and the Syria-Palestine Relief Committee are to be found in the files of the Presbyterian Mission Library, 156 Fifth Avenue, New York City. These are supplemented by correspondence between the missionaries abroad and mission executives in New York which is also to be found in the Presbyterian Mission Library. Correspondence relating to the formation and business of the Armenian Atrocities Committee, the American Committee for Armenian and Syrian Relief, and Near East Relief are to be found in the American Board Papers, Houghton Library, Cambridge, Massachusetts. These materials are voluminous, consisting of separate series of numbered volumes of incoming and outgoing correspondence, both foreign and domestic:

ABC 1.1. Letters Domestic. Vols. 315–319. These volumes contain correspondence between James L. Barton and others in the United States relating to the Armenian atrocities for the years 1915 and 1916.

ABC 3.2. Foreign Department, General. Vols. 320–388. These were the most useful materials with respect to relief activities of the American Committee for Armenian and Syrian Relief and the Near East Relief.

ABC 3.3. Foreign Department. General Letters: Supplementary. Vol. 3 of this series contains correspondence with the State Department for the years 1912–1918. Vols. 5–14 contain letters filed alphabetically by correspondent.

ABC 16.9.1. Turkey Mission. New Series. Vols. 1, 2, 4, 12, 13. This series consists of incoming correspondence from the Turkey Mission which geographically included the western portions of Anatolia and the Balkans. It contains material relating to the Smyrna fire of 1922 and subsequent relief efforts.

ABC 16.9.7. Eastern Turkey Mission, 1910–1919. Vol. 5 contains incoming correspondence from the Caucasus area.

The William Walker Rockwell Papers at the Union Theological Seminary Library, New York City, contain correspondence, *Minutes,* and publicity releases relating to the relief work particularly in 1915 and 1916, during part of which time Rockwell was in charge of publicity for the Armenian Atrocities Committee and the American Committee for Armenian and Syrian Relief. Near East Relief, *Dockets,* which brought together relevant reports from the

Executive Secretary, Treasurer, and Program Committee as well as important correspondence for the use of the Board of Trustees, can be found for the years 1923 through 1927 in the Talcott Williams Papers at Union Theological Seminary Library.

The *Annual Reports* of the Near East Relief were published privately and/or as *Senate Documents:*

1920 67 Cong., 1 Sess., *Senate Document* 5.
1921 67 Cong., 2 Sess., *Senate Document* 192.
1922 67 Cong., 4 Sess., *Senate Document* 343.
1923 68 Cong., 1 Sess., *Senate Document* 111.
1924 National Headquarters, New York, 1925.
1925 National Headquarters, New York, 1926.
1926 69 Cong., 2 Sess., *Senate Document* 229.
1927 70 Cong., 1 Sess., *Senate Document* 70.
1928 70 Cong., 2 Sess., *Senate Document* 257.

In addition to these reports there are the mimeographed *Bulletins* (1915–1916) of the Persian War Relief Fund and the *News Bulletin* (1917–1919) of the American Committee for Armenian and Syrian Relief which became the *New Near East* (1920–1927), the magazine of the Near East Relief.

Aside from the official materials relating to the relief organizations that are found in the American Board Papers, there is much personal correspondence of James Levi Barton, particularly in ABC 3.2, that is of major value. The Papers of Henry Morgenthau, Sr., contain important materials on the founding of the relief committees in 1915. The Woodrow Wilson Papers, particularly his correspondence with Cleveland Hoadley Dodge, is indispensable for the years 1915 to 1920. Both the Morgenthau and Wilson Papers are in the Division of Manuscripts, Library of Congress, Washington, D.C.

Another major source of manuscript material is the State Department Decimal Files, National Archives. It provides information on the relationships between the Department of State and the relief committees from 1914 to 1930. As much of the relief committee's correspondence was transmitted through State Department channels, this collection duplicates much that is also to be found in either the American Board Papers or the Henry Morgenthau Papers.

There is a considerable volume of printed material relating to the atrocities which has the character of primary sources. Most important is Arnold J. Toynbee, ed., *The Treatment of Armenians in the Ottoman Empire, 1915–1916, Documents Presented to Viscount Grey of Fallodon* (London: H. M. Stationery Office, 1916), the contents of which were supplied chiefly by missionaries of the American Board and the Presbyterian Board, and copies of which were distributed to influential citizens, including Congressmen, by the ACASR. Aurora Mardiganian, *Ravished Armenia, the Story of Aurora Mardiganian,* interpreted by H. L. Gates (New York: Kingfield Press, 1918) provided the story line for the propaganda movie made and circulated in behalf of the ACASR. Grace H. Knapp, *The Tragedy of Bitlis* (New York: Fleming H. Revell, 1919), Mary Lewis Shedd, *The Measure of a Man: The Life of William Ambrose Shedd, Missionary to Persia* (New York: George H. Doran, 1922), and Clarence D. Ussher, *An American Physician in Turkey* (Boston:

Houghton Mifflin, 1917) give first-hand reports by missionaries of the Armenian "deportations." Also important are Mary Edna Lewis, *The War Journal of a Missionary in Persia*, Mary Schauffler Platt, ed. (BFMPC, 1915) and Francis B. Packard, *The Story of Our Missions in Persia* (BFMPC, 1920).

Of the books relating to the conduct of relief clearly James L. Barton, *Story of Near East Relief (1915–1930) An Interpretation* (New York: Macmillan, 1930) is the most important, but it tells little of the work in Syria. Barton, a leading figure in the relief work, visited the Near East many times. Margaret McGilvary, *The Dawn of a New Era in Syria* (New York: Fleming H. Revell, 1920) is the best first-hand account of the relief operation in Syria during the war years. The author was secretary to Charles A. Dana, Manager of the American Mission Press at Beirut and a key figure in the distribution of remittances from Syrian-Americans. Mabel Evelyn Elliott, *Beginning Again at Ararat* (New York: Fleming H. Revell, 1924) is by a medical director of NER who went abroad in 1919; Esther Pohl Lovejoy, *Certain Samaritans* (New York: Macmillan, 1927) worked with NER and American Women's Hospitals in the Greek islands following the Smyrna fire.

The effort of the American Committee for Armenian and Syrian Relief to prescribe a postwar settlement for the Near East is contained in William H. Hall, ed., *Reconstruction in Turkey* (ACASR, 1918) and Harold A. Hatch and William H. Hall, *Recommendations for Political Reconstruction in the Turkish Empire* (ACASR, 1918). The careful student will examine the James L. Barton correspondence in the American Board Papers as well as the letters of Cleveland H. Dodge to Woodrow Wilson in the Wilson Papers.

The newspaper press reported the atrocities in 1915, the more spectacular fund-raising campaigns of 1917–1919, and the Smyrna fire in considerable detail. It provided little day-to-day coverage of relief activities. Because their editors were on the boards of directors of the relief committees, the *Literary Digest*, *Christian Herald*, and the *American Review of Reviews* accorded the ACASR and NER somewhat more attention than other journals.

For the transition from relief to technical assistance work Paul Monroe, R. R. Reeder, and James I. Vance, *Reconstruction in the Near East* (New York, 1924) and General Committee of the Near East Survey, *The Near East and American Philanthropy* by Frank A. Ross, C. Luther Fry and Elbridge Sibley (New York: Columbia University Press, 1929) are official reports. Both are the products of field studies, while the latter is a compendium of factual data on social and economic conditions in the Balkans, Greece, Syria, Iraq, Turkey, and Armenia.

Near East Foundation:

The records of the Near East Foundation are located at its offices, 54 East 64th Street, New York City. These consist primarily of the *Minutes* and *Dockets* of the trustees. The *Dockets*, which are usually the more informative, contain "Reports of the Executive Secretary," the "Treasurer's Report," the "Minutes," of both the Program Committee and Finance Committee, and

"Reports" of the Educational Director and Foreign Director as well as special reports and copies of important correspondence. In 1932 NEF produced *Basic Project Reports*, a compendium of reports by the directors of the various projects then directed by NEF, many of which it had inherited from NER. From 1934 until his retirement in 1948, Laird Archer produced an "Annual Report of the Foreign Director," which was bound separately. He also made "Reports" which were included in the *Dockets*. Beginning in 1947 Harold Allen produced a series of "Annual Reports of the Educational Director" which were bound separately. For the period after 1947 the organization had the monthly reports of its overseas personnel which are cited here by the titles on their respective file folders.

There is relatively little other material relating to Near East Foundation of an official or semi-official character. Laird Archer, *Balkan Journal: An Unofficial Observer in Greece* (New York: W. W. Norton, 1944) is primarily an account of Archer's reactions to the approach of World War II from June, 1934, to July, 1941. Harold B. Allen, *Come Over Into Macedonia: The Ten-year Adventure in Uplifting a War-torn People* (New Brunswick: Rutgers University Press, 1943) contains material found nowhere else in relation to the Macedonian demonstration. His *Rural Reconstruction in Action: Experience in the Near and Middle East* (Ithaca: Cornell University Press, 1953) is indispensable for a study of the development of Allen's principles of philanthropy. Thomas Jesse Jones, *Essentials of Civilization: A Study in Social Values* (New York: H. Holt, 1929) is indispensable for understanding the evolution of philanthropy in the 1920's. Laymen's Foreign Missions Inquiry, *Re-Thinking Missions: A Laymen's Inquiry After One Hundred Years* (New York: Harper & Bros., 1932) emphasizes the need for an irenic approach by Americans in their relations with other peoples.

General Works:

A number of general works, all of a secondary character, have proved useful. Among these, four bear primarily on the theories and practices of philanthropy: Robert H. Bremner, *American Philanthropy* (Chicago: University of Chicago Press, 1960) is a brief overview of the subject. Merle Curti, *American Philanthropy Abroad: A History* (New Brunswick: Rutgers University Press, 1963) is a solid review of private philanthropy overseas with a judicious mixture of narrative and interpretation. Merle Curti and Kendall Birr, *Prelude to Point Four: American Technical Missions Overseas, 1838–1938* (Madison: University of Wisconsin Press, 1954) focuses on official efforts to introduce change in overseas societies. Oliver Wendell Elsbree, *The Rise of the Missionary Spirit in America, 1790–1815* (Williamsport: Williamsport Printing and Binding Co., 1928) is essential to understanding the missionary's interest in secular good works.

Among the general works that proved particularly useful, the following deserve special mention. David H. Finnie, *Pioneers East: The Early American Experience in the Middle East* (Cambridge: Harvard University Press, 1967), while highly readable, tells more about the personalities and impressions of the first Americans than of their activities. A. L. Tibawi, *American Interests in Syria 1800–1901* (Oxford: Clarendon Press, 1966) treats missionary activities exclusively. George Antonius, *The Arab Awakening: The Story of the Arab National Movement* (Philadelphia: J. B. Lippincott, 1939) overstates the case for the existence of Arab national feeling in the 1880's and should be read along with Zeine N. Zeine, *Arab-Turkish Relations and the Emergence of Arab Nationalism* (Beirut: Khayat's, 1958) and Albert Hourani, *Arabic Thought in the Liberal Age, 1798–1939* (London: Oxford University Press, 1962). Hans Kohn, *Western Civilization in the Near East* (London: George Routledge & Sons, 1936) is a sensitive interpretive essay on the forces of Westernization and nationalism in Turkey. Carl Brockelmann, *History of the Islamic Peoples*, Joel Carmichael and Moshe Perlmann, translators (London: George Routledge & Kegan Paul, 1949) relates political developments to social and cultural changes in the Near East. William R. Polk, *The Opening of South Lebanon, 1788–1840: A Study of the Impact of the West on the Middle East* (Cambridge: Harvard University Press, 1965); Frank Edgar Bailey, *British Policy and the Turkish Reform Movement: A Study in Anglo-Turkish Relations, 1826–1853* (Cambridge: Harvard University Press, 1942); and Roderic H. Davison, *Reform in the Ottoman Empire 1856–1876* (Princeton: Princeton University Press, 1963) provide details of crises that the broader surveys necessarily omit. Henry Elisha Allen, *The Turkish Transformation: A Study in Social and Religious Development* (Chicago: University of Chicago Press, 1935) interprets the changes wrought by Ataturk.

Constantine Stephanove, *The Bulgarians and Anglo-Saxondom* (Berne: Paul Haupt, 1919) is useful as a Bulgarian view of American activities, but it is patently designed to flatter the Americans. L. S. Stavrianos, "The Influence of the West on the Balkans," in Charles and Barbara Jelavich, eds., *The Balkans in Transition: Essays on the Development of Balkan Life and Politics Since the Eighteenth Century* (Berkeley: University of California Press, 1963), 184–226 is a sound scholarly interpretation.

An overview of the American role in Turkey is provided by Leland J. Gordon, *American Relations with Turkey, 1830–1930: An Economic Interpretation* (Philadelphia: University of Pennsylvania Press, 1932). The work focuses narrowly on political and trade issues in the late nineteenth and twentieth centuries. John A. DeNovo, *American Interests and Policies in the Middle East, 1900–1939* (Minneapolis: University of Minnesota Press, 1963) is a model of its genre.

The following theses and dissertations proved useful in checking my evaluation of source materials: Alford Carleton, "The Development of Missionary Policy in Turkey," Thesis, Hartford Theological Seminary, 1930; Robert Carlton Delk, "The History and Influence of American Education in the Near East, 1823–1914," Typescript, 1949, in Archives of the UCBWM, Boston. William Webster Hall, Jr., *Puritans in the Balkans: The American Board Mission in Bulgaria, 1878–1918* (Sofia, 1938) was prepared as a dissertation at Yale University in 1937; Bernhard Frederick Nordmann, "American Missionary Work Among the Armenians in Turkey (1830–1923)," Ph.D. dissertation, University of Illinois, 1927; and Walter Livingston Wright, Jr., "American Relations with Turkey to 1831," Ph.D. dissertation, Princeton, 1928. Robert L. Daniel, "From Relief to Technical Assistance in the Near East," Ph.D dissertation, University of Wisconsin, 1953, confines itself to the Near East Relief and the Near East Foundation.

INDEX